Minds and Mechanisms:
*Philosophical Psychology
and Computational Models*

Minds and Mechanisms:
Philosophical Psychology and Computational Models

MARGARET A. BODEN
Professor of Philosophy and Psychology
University of Sussex

CORNELL UNIVERSITY PRESS
Ithaca, New York

First published 1981 by Cornell University Press.
International Standard Book Number 0-8014-1431-8
Library of Congress Catalog Card Number 81-66652
Printed in Great Britain

Let one try as one will to represent the cerebral activity in exclusively mechanical terms, I, for one, find it quite impossible to enumerate what seem to be the facts and yet to make no mention of the psychic side which they possess. . . . The psychic side . . . seems, somewhat like the applause or hissing at a spectacle, to be an encouraging or adverse *comment* on what the machinery brings forth. The soul *presents* nothing herself, *creates* nothing, is at the mercy of the material forces for all *possibilities*, but amongst these possibilities she *selects*, and by reinforcing one and checking others, she figures not as an 'epiphenomenon', but as something from which the play gets moral support.

William James, *Principles of Psychology*

For Aaron Sloman

Contents

Acknowledgements

I am grateful to Roy Edgley for his help in making this selection from my papers. In addition, I should like to thank the following publishers for their permission to reproduce the essays listed:

Methuen & Co. Ltd., for chapter 1 'The computational metaphor in psychology', reprinted from *Philosophical Problems in Psychology*, ed. Neil Bolton, pp.112-32; Philosophy of Science Association for chapter 2 'Intentionality and physical systems' reprinted from *Philosophy of Science*, 37 (1970), 200-14; The British Psychological Society for chapter 3 'Artificial intelligence and intellectual imperialism' reprinted from *Models of Man* eds. A.J. Chapman and D.M. Jones; chapter 4 'The case for a cognitive biology' is a slightly extended version of a paper originally published in *Proceedings of the Aristotelian Society, Supp. Vol. LIV* (1980), 25-49, reprinted by permission of the Aristotelian Society; chapter 5 'The paradox of explanation' is reprinted from *Proceedings of the Aristotelian Society N.S., Vol. LXII* (1962), 159-78, by permission of the Aristotelian Society; Basil Blackwell for chapter 6 'The structure of intentions' reprinted from *Journal for the Theory of Social Behaviour*, 3, (1973), 23-46; Oxford University Press for chapter 7 'Real-world reasoning' reprinted from *Applications of Inductive Logic* eds. L.J. Cohen and M.B. Hesse (1980) pp.359-75; Lawrence Erlbaum Associates Inc. for chapter 8 'Implications of language studies for human nature' reprinted from *Language, Mind and Brain: Interdisciplinary Perspectives* eds. R.J. Scholes and T.W. Simon (in press); Duke University Press for chapter 9 'McDougall revisited' reprinted from *Journal of Personality 33* (1965), 1-19, copyright © 1965 by Duke University; Doubleday & Company Inc. for chapter 10 'Freudian mechanisms of defence' reprinted from *FREUD: A Collection of Critical Essays* ed. R. Wollheim, copyright © 1974 by Richard Wollheim; D. Reidel Publishing Company for chapter 11 'Artificial intelligence and Piagetian theory' reprinted from *Synthese*, 38 (1978), 389-414; Harvester Press Ltd. and Humanities Press Inc. for chapter 12 'Human values in a mechanistic universe' reprinted from *Human Values: Royal Institute of Philosophy Lectures Vol. 11* ed. G. Vesey copyright © 1978 by the Royal Institute of Philosophy pp.135-71; Royal Institute of Philosophy for chapter 13 'Optimism' reprinted from *Philosophy XLI* (1966), 291-303 published by the Royal Institute of Philosophy.

Introduction

These essays are concerned with four closely related questions at the heart of philosophical psychology, or the philosophy of mind. Firstly, what is the nature of the mind, and of specific mental phenomena (such as intentions, reasoning, choice, or repression)? Second, what sorts of concepts are required for an adequate theoretical psychology? Third, how is it possible for the mind to be embodied, and what is the relation between psychology on the one hand and physiology or biology on the other? And last, what implications (if any) do theories in the life sciences have for moral thinking about individuals and society?

These questions similarly unite my three books — *Purposive Explanation in Psychology* (1972), *Artificial Intelligence and Natural Man* (1977), and *Piaget* (1979) — and a few essays discuss issues explored at greater length therein. Most, however, give extended attention to matters only briefly mentioned in the books, and so are complementary to them.

A further reason for gathering them here is that they first appeared in widely disparate publications, whose readers are primarily concerned with one specialism only — whether philosophy, psychology, or computer science. It is increasingly recognized that an interdisciplinary approach may be helpful in thinking about the mind, and the label 'cognitive science' has recently been coined to cover all the relevant fields of study, from physiology and comparative biology at one pole to semiology and pedagogy at the other. My own work is intended as a philosophical contribution to cognitive science, rather than as 'pure' philosophy conceived in abstraction from empirical studies.

As well as their commitment to interdisciplinarity, many cognitive scientists share a particular approach to the mind which leads them to give broadly similar answers to the first three questions listed above. They see their common endeavour, whatever their preferred area of emphasis, as the study of the mental representations that mediate a person's (or animal's) thinking, action and experience. Thus they explore the meanings, or symbol-systems, that generate psychological phenomena of diverse kinds — not only thoughts and beliefs, but also actions, intentions, decisions, values, and emotions. Specifically, they enquire into the content, structure, transformation, function, and development of these meanings, or representational systems. And they aim to formulate theories of the mind that take account of its structural and procedural complexities.

1

In general, cognitive scientists believe that a computational approach, based on the information-processing concepts developed within computer science and artificial intelligence, may be helpful or even necessary in articulating these multifarious complexities. These concepts were specially developed to express qualitative distinctions between representations, and between symbol-manipulating procedures for effecting transformations of representations, which is why they are potentially so useful to cognitive science. In all essays but two, I take an explicitly computational approach to the problems of philosophical psychology.

The essays in Part I (chapters 1 – 5) deal with the general issues of computation and explanation, asking how concepts drawn from computer science can contribute to explanations in the life sciences. I explain what is meant by a 'computational' approach in chapter 1 ('The computational metaphor in psychology'). I also sketch there why it is that this approach is not dehumanizing, nor antithetical to humanistic or hermeneutic approaches to the mind. Basically, the reason is that the intentional categories of subjectivity are central to computational accounts just as they are to humanistic psychologies. What a computational system — whether program or person — does, and how it does it, depends upon its stock of representations of the world (including itself and its abilities) and the way in which distinct representations are compared with or transformed into each other. It is precisely when behaviour (or experience) is mediated by representations that intentional categories are attributable to it. Intentional categories include all the common psychological terms, such as knowledge, belief, mistake, perception, purpose, intention, and emotion, as well as the less familiar technical concepts used in artificial intelligence.

The concept of intentionality, with various philosophical accounts of it, is discussed at length in chapter 2 ('Intentionality and physical systems'). It is there related to a striking 'psychosomatic' phenomenon, hysterical paralysis. In this pathological condition, the patient's paralysis can be shown not to depend on any injury to, or even temporary inhibition of, gross anatomical features such as nerve-muscle groups. Rather, the nature and boundaries of the paralysis (as also of 'glove-' or 'sleeve-anaesthesias') is determined by the person's *idea* of what an 'arm' or 'hand' is. By way of a *Gedankenexperiment* involving an imaginary robot with a functional paralysis, I argue that a computational account can enable us to understand both how psychosomatic phenomena such as hysterical paralysis are possible, and why irreducibly psychological language is needed to describe and explain the intentional phenomena involved.

This essay, like many of the others, thus implies that from a computational viewpoint we may entirely accept William James' claim that it is 'quite impossible to enumerate what seem to be the facts and yet to make no mention of the psychic side which they possess'. We may agree, too, that 'The soul . . . is at the mercy of the material forces for all *possibilities*, but amongst these possibilities she *selects*,' so cannot be regarded as an idle 'epiphenomenon' of the brain, compared by T.H. Huxley to the smoke emitted by a steam-engine.

The most powerful technological analogy available to James and Huxley was the steam-engine, whose powers can be adequately described without ascribing representations or interpretative processes to the engine (still less, the smoke) itself. Only in relation to the self-regulatory *governor* is one tempted to use intentional terminology, and here the 'information' involved in the feedback circuit is quantitative only and relates to only one feature, namely the steam-pressure. But in the case of a modern computer running a complex program, there is no alternative to adopting what D.C. Dennett has called 'the intentional stance' toward the machine and its program, if we are to understand and explain what is going on.[1] It is not merely that (as in the case of the steam-engine) functions are being performed, of which some are hierarchically subordinate to others. Rather, we have to think of the programmed machine as embodying many qualitatively distinct symbolic representations of the goals of, constraints on, and intermediate stages in these functionings, where the descriptions concerned play a crucial role in guiding, selecting, and monitoring the details of what is going on.

This intentional terminology is of course borrowed from everyday psychological language. As I shall argue presently, it cannot be assumed to carry all its familiar connotations when used (analogically) in a computer context. Still less can one assume that every use of an intentional term to describe some aspect of a particular program is a felicitous one: important psychological issues may be obscured rather than clarified by the appropriation of a term whose everyday implications mislead one's intuitions about the specific computational potential of the program. But it remains true that intentional terminology, borrowed though it may be, is inescapable if we are to express what the program is doing and how it is doing it.

Computers, then, are more closely analogous to embodied minds than steam-engines are. In addition, a programmer may choose to write a program with the declared intention of modelling a psychological process, or of expressing a verbal or mathematical psychological theory in precise computational terms. The question then arises whether, from a computationalist's viewpoint, other approaches to theoretical psychology are redundant. And, if not, just what is the relation between computational models and more familiar psychological theories, or between program-performance and empirical data? Should one ask for a program to be psychologically validated by being matched against experimental tests, and if so how is this matching to be effected?

These questions are considered in chapter 3 ('Artificial intelligence and intellectual imperialism'), where I argue that there really is no such thing as 'the' computational viewpoint, if by this is meant a monolithic position on the relation between artificial intelligence and empirical psychology. Some people impressed by the precision of computer science, and by its origination of many new concepts with which to distinguish various computational processes, draw the aggressively imperialist moral that non-computational psychological enquiries (including experiments) are now redundant, and will remain so until computer scientists are in a position to tell psychologists what questions need to be asked. Others draw the milder moral that psychologists should plan their experiments, and formulate their theories, with computational questions in mind. But just how this is to be done, and how a distinctly computational methodology is to be formulated for the practising psychologist, is still controversial.

One grave difficulty is that not all aspects of a functioning program will be believed by the programmer to have psychological significance, even when the program as a whole is intended as a psychological model — but which aspects are, and which are not, intended to be psychologically significant may not be clear even to the programmer concerned. For instance, we may be convinced that an important feature of some human problem-solving is the articulation of the problem into distinct goal-subgoal hierarchies, and write a comparable problem-solving program accordingly. Some specific features of the program will then be plausibly — though perhaps not truly — regarded as analogous to what goes on in the human case. But there will inevitably be others (among those defined during the construction of the program rather than those initially hypothesized) about whose plausibility we cannot be so sure, so that it is not clear whether they are even *candidates* for empirical validation. So, even if one knew how to match a program-feature against experimental human or animal data, *which* features should be thus matched are arguable. In other words, even those cognitive scientists who accept the explanatory analogy between computation and psychology are unsure about how far it can plausibly be regarded as empirically extensible in detail.

But it does not follow, as is often claimed by critics of the computational approach, that programmed models are unconstrained by reference to human psychology and are therefore uninteresting. Sometimes this complaint is expressed in general terms, and sometimes it is directed against specific programs or programming methodologies.

In its general form, it is argued for instance that this approach relies on a sort of 'Turing test' for its validation and so is essentially behaviourist in nature. That is, the comparison of a given program with human psychology can only be done via the matching of input-output relations, so that the more similar the behaviour of the program to the behaviour of the human, the better the program is assumed to be. This, say the critics, is to ignore the internal processes concerned, and so to repeat the mistake of behaviourism. But this criticism is not appropriate in general, however apposite it may be with respect to some individual programs, for it ignores both the fact that every psychological theory must rely on observable behaviour (including verbal reports of introspection) for its validation, and the fact that the strength of the computational approach is precisely that it offers specific hypotheses about what the inner processes of thought may be.

As remarked above, and also in chapter 3, there are indeed methodological difficulties in devizing experiments to test the degree of match between the detailed internal processes of program and person. There is no *a priori* rule for devizing ingenious experiments, whether we are concerned with the interior of the atom, the cell, or the mind. Much as Piaget or Freud tried to devize experimental or clinical situations that would provide externalized pointers to hidden psychological transformations, so the cognitive psychologist has to do likewise in order to test a programmed theory of the mind. To avoid the charge of 'behaviourism' the experimental research has to concentrate not only on the grossly defined overall characteristics of performance, but on the detailed sub-processes that generate it. Any interesting program is rich in computational detail, and since many of its processes are interactively mediated by others according to context and circumstance, there is little likelihood that the functioning of each process will always (or ever) be reliably signposted in observable behaviour. Where programs are concerned, the programmer can provide for a 'print-out' to be available if we wish to trace the precise functioning of the program at any point. But evolution has not provided the mind with an analogous print-out function, and we have to rely as best we can on the clues offered in observable behaviour and introspection. Despite the most ingenious efforts of the experimentalists, then, it may be that the human mind is so exceptionally complex that we will never be in a position to say with any confidence that *this* and *that* are the processes going on within it (though we might nevertheless be able to say something useful about the *sorts* of symbolic transformations possibly involved). But if so, the difficulty faces all types of theoretical psychology, not just the computational form.

A second general argument objects that artificial intelligence cannot model human thought, since thinking deals with indeterminate information and does not proceed as a series of discrete steps such as might be modelled in a (serial) program for a digital machine.[2]

This argument can be faulted on several grounds. It confuses the information code with the information coded: Shakespeare expressed the sort of information these critics have in mind by way of a digital code, the Roman alphabet. It assumes too quickly (what may of course be true) that thought is indeterminate, or unformalizable, without giving any clear alternative account. For instance, Merleau-Ponty and Wittgenstein are sometimes cited as authorities for the belief that bodily skills can be developed without any representation at all, and learnt by practice. However, practice is not a magical power, and the question remains as to *how* 'practice' helps development of skills. These critics typically assume that the answer will be found in physiology, not in psychology, but they rarely go to physiology to see what answers are offered there. Many physiologists (Lashley was a prime example) theorize about bodily skills in ways that have strong parallels to computational notions of hierarchically ordered schemata, of compiled *vs*. interpreted programs, and the like. Last, the critiques of serial (as opposed to parallel) processing, and digital (as opposed to analog) machines, imply that computationally inclined psychologists are committed to the view that current hardware and programming techniques will prove adequate to unravel all the complexities of human thinking. Even the most confident devotee of the computational approach would unhesitatingly reject such an idea.

A third general argument against the computational approach to psychology is based on the computational notion of a Turing machine. Thus it is said that because a Turing machine can in principle model an enormous array of possible mental events or knowledge it is uninteresting to those whose concern is specifically with human psychology. One might as well argue that because numerals can be used to express a wide range of sums, they are no use to people concerned only with doing calculations in greengrocers' shops. Having the abstract computational concept of an 'effective procedure' that is intrinsic to the general notion of a Turing machine is not the same as being able to write a specific effective procedure for computing a particular problem. Although in principle all programs are equivalent to a Turing machine, actual programs are expressed — and distinguished one from another — in terms of high-level computational structures and processes not specified within the abstract concept of a Turing machine. Substantive questions then arise as to whether *this* particular program, or *that* one, or neither, function by way of computational principles significantly analogous to those used by human minds.

At this point, the complaint against computational models may be couched in its more specific form, it being argued that actual programs (as opposed to an abstractly defined Turing machine) are unconstrained by considerations about the likely nature of human thought. The critics here are not (or should not be) directing their ire at self-confessed 'kluges'. These are programming tricks which avoid a problem rather than solving it, by providing a quick way of getting an answer at a certain point in the functioning of the program, because without some answer or other — howsoever provisional or superficial — the computation simply cannot proceed. Certainly, kluges should be confessed, and if they are slyly passed over in the verbal description of the program so as to suggest an achievement that has not been attained then criticism is indeed merited. (One of my personal bugbears is the common use by programmers of the verb 'to finesse' a problem, which sounds as though it denotes a subtle and delicate solution but in fact refers to a deliberate ignoring of the difficulty in question.) But an acknowledged kluge can do little harm, and may be essential so as to allow one to get on with the main job at hand. More to the point are criticisms of deliberately chosen programming methodologies, methods that are not regarded by their authors as fit topics for the computational confessional, but which seemingly conflict with the nature of human thought.

Admittedly, some people who try to write programs they describe as concerned with language, vision, reasoning, or knowledge are interested less (if at all) in the human mind than in producing some computational system (whatever its particular characteristics) which effectively does the job they want done.

Their interest is technological rather than psychological, and their approach is sometimes called 'artificial intelligence' as opposed to 'computer simulation' (which aims to model the internal processes and structures of natural intelligence). Programs written with primarily technological aims often employ computational procedures which there is no reason to believe are paralleled in living organisms. However, it is frequently the case that the best way of solving a technologically conceived problem within artificial intelligence is to try to mimic the way the human mind solves similar problems, so the distinction between 'artificial intelligence' and 'computer simulation' is by no means clearcut.

Admittedly, too (and already remarked above), even workers in computer simulation are forced to employ some computational procedures having no obvious human analogue. It is reasonable to insist that programmers should always be on their guard, so as to recognize the points at which they may be doing this. But to claim that the computational approach itself is unconstrained by the difference between artificial and humanly natural cognition is to ignore the attempts that are constantly made to identify and draw attention to these very differences. Above all, the assumption that these differences are evident beforehand, independently of any attempts to specify them in precise computational terms, is itself over-sanguine. Until we know what human thought processes are like, we must be very careful in declaring dogmatically what they are not like.

Chapter 4 ('The case for a cognitive biology') argues that there may be a place for computational explanations not only in human and animal psychology, but in biology also. Some recent work in theoretical biology — specifically, in embryology and comparative morphology — employs concepts that are independent of detailed physiological embodiments, or molecular biology, and that are drawn from cognitive or computational contexts. The processes of embryological development and regeneration (and, according to some theorists, evolution) may fruitfully be described in terms of the interpretation of symbolic descriptions embodying knowledge of the environment, which interpretation may be more or less intelligent depending on the adaptability of the processes concerned.

Experimental data show that the functional or developmental significance of a given metabolite may vary widely across species — and even within a given individual at different stages of the life-cycle. In other words, the significance of the substance is arbitrary with respect to its molecular biology, much as the significance of 'chair' is arbitrary with respect to its phonetic character. So the most appropriate experimental question for the biologist may be not 'what is the molecular biology of this substance, and how does it combine with other molecules?', but rather 'what computation is this substance performing for the organism: what information is it passing, what question is it asking, what instruction is it embodying — and what interpretative processes are required to make sensible use of it?'

Although many biological processes are thus arbitrary with respect to molecular biology, their actual interpretation or significance within any given organism at a given stage of its life-history is not 'arbitrary' in the sense that it might be changed overnight. We could, if we wanted to very strongly, decide to use 'chair' henceforth to mean table, or gratitude. Once Humpty-Dumpty had told Alice what he meant by 'glory', she was able to remember that he meant a nice knock-down argument; and we can take conscious decisions about what name to give a newly discovered phenomenon, as physicists did for the neo-Carrollian quark. But no comparable change in the meaning of one's basic physiological processes could happen, for their significance has been determined by evolution. For instance, a cell of the occipital cortex that is innately programmed to respond to a line-orientation of a certain angle, or a cell of the auditory cortex that responds to a rising tone, cannot be reprogrammed to embody another (still less, any arbitrarily other) meaning.

This is not to say that no reprogramming of physiological processes can ever occur, or that a process's significance must always be fixed. For I noted above that a substance may change its meaning for the organism at different developmental stages (examples are given in chapter 4). And some learning may involve the assignment of new significances to previously existing neurological circuits, as well as the building of new circuits with fresh significance. An example might be the sort of unthinking reorientation of the visual field which occurs in human beings, though not in all animals, after prolonged wearing of visually-displacing lenses. But the basic significances of our sensory and motivational apparatus are based in our evolutionary history, and are not amenable to non-evolutionary change.

This feature of human embodiment, and of all living things, is of course lacking in computers. For the meaning of a given instruction or piece of programmed code is arbitrary in just the sense that that of 'chair' is: the programmer, or the designer of the high-level programming language used, could always have chosen different symbols to designate the computational operations performed by the machine. It is partly because a programmer can irresponsibly or over-enthusiastically define a basically trivial computational process under a superficially impressive label like 'FINDANALOG' or 'AESTHETICSENSE', that one may be sceptical of a programmer's claims to have modelled analogical or aesthetic thinking within a program intended to do just this.

Even the most basic instructions of the machine code (such as *add* for instance), which have their effects not because of any further translation but because they are correlated with specific processes in the hardware which are determined by the engineering of the computer, have no meaning in themselves — they do not wear their interpretation on their face. And, crucially, it is we — not the computer — who give their interpretation to them. It is because we have realized that a given formal system (the machine code) can be reliably and usefully mapped onto what we know as addition, provided that specific correlations are built into the hardware, that we build the machines in just that way and that we use them for performing operations of addition. And someone who is unsatisfied with a given machine code, because it cannot be mapped onto a sufficiently powerful range of computational processes, will be motivated to compose an alternative formal system or machine code to be used instead, and/or to choose different hardware-effects as the engineered correlates of identical sets of formal symbols.

Evolution did not thus *choose* to make a certain nucleotide-triplet signify 'make *this* amino-acid' throughout terrestrial biology, and nor did it *choose* to alter the significance of one of the gill-slits so that in mammals it developed into a thyroid gland. Moreover, the fact that these meanings (rather than others) evolved depends crucially on other systematic facts about biological organisms. Only a certain type of creature is capable of having a thyroid gland (and identifying *which* type that is, is a theoretical problem for comparative morphology). One might even say that only a certain type of creature would be interested in having one.

This way of putting it reminds us that human beings and animals have intrinsic interests, and an intrinsic range of significances, which comprise the inescapable bedrock of their intentionality. No human significance, however bizarre, can arise except in the context of these underlying interests — which is why personality theorists such as Freud or McDougall have tried in differing ways to relate 'unnatural' motives or sentiments, such as religious asceticism or scholarship, to the basic biological givens of humanity. (Ethical and political theories, too, must somehow take account of the basic facts of human nature, as I argue in my discussion of optimism in chapter 13.) Because computers are deliberately engineered to function as artificial embodiments of computational or representational systems (programs) whose significance is assigned *by human beings*, any 'interests' we may choose (sic) to ascribe to them are not intrinsic to their nature, but parasitic on our own. It is this which leads me to say in several essays that psychological predicates could not be ascribed in a literal sense to any imaginable computer, even if its program were so rich in computational power as to be a much closer analogue of human motivation and thought than any existing program is.

To put the same point differently, one might say that computer programs are not really intentional systems. Some philosophers (particularly those of a phenomenological cast of mind) do say this, and conclude that artificial intelligence can teach us nothing about what intentionality really is, which they regard as the basic problem of philosophical psychology.[3] There are two reasonable rebuttals of this dismissive conclusion. First, one can point out that computational models of psychological processes might help to illuminate the structural and procedural characteristics of human intentionality, even if they have nothing to say about what the ultimate nature of this intentionality *is*. (I make this point in relation to my discussion of computational insights into consciousness, in chapter 3.) Second, one can remark that there are close analogies between 'intentional' or 'computational' processes in computers (or biological systems) and truly intentional processes in psychology, and that exploring these analogies may help toward the scientific understanding of all three domains.

This latter position, which is argued for in specifically computational terms in each of the first four papers, draws on a general claim about explanation that is outlined in chapter 5 ('The paradox of explanation'). Explanation in general involves the 'paradoxical' assimilation of unfamiliar to familiar that serves creatively to extend our understanding in various ways.

Where *scientific* explanation is concerned, the posited analogies between unfamiliar and familiar must be somehow related to observable phenomena, and the positing of one feature should be systematically dependent on others in some theoretically specifiable fashion. For instance, Harvey's hydraulic analogy for the blood-system involved the analogical matching of blood-vessels with fluid-carrying tubes, and also enabled him to explain the observable distinction between the aortic and pulmonary circulations (the blood in the pulmonary artery being darker in colour than other arterial blood, and that in the pulmonary vein being brighter than other venous blood). Moreover, the analogy should be empirically extensible, in the sense that it guides the active search for *new* observations — as Harvey predicted the constancy of blood-volume and performed novel types of experiment accordingly. Sometimes the analogy seems so close (and explanatorily useful) that a lack of validatory observation is ignored; thus Harvey postulated the existence of capillaries, but only with the later invention of the microscope were the capillaries observable.

In the terms of chapter 5, this is how one explains X in terms of Y, how the scientist assimilates X to Y in an empirically fruitful fashion. But since X is not Y, one must always expect the analogy to break down at some point. The hydraulic analogy, for example, is unable to explain the passage of the blood from arterial to venous capillaries, because it applies only to a closed, continuous system; but at the submicroscopic level the capillaries are open-ended, and the blood escapes into the body-tissues and has to be somehow reabsorbed into the venous capillaries. This reabsorption clearly has to be explained in *non*-hydraulic terms (and is in fact understood as an example of osmosis).

Sometimes, the breakdown of an explanatory analogy is conceptually evident long before it can be tested in practice. For instance, the kinetic theory of gases was used to predict that the gas laws would break down under conditions of very high pressure: for then the 'billiard balls' can no longer move freely, but are pushed against one another so that one may expect interactions between them to be important that under 'Ideal Gas' conditions may be ignored. But which molecular interactive effects are in fact present, and which range of pressures allows one to ignore them, are questions which have to be settled by actual experiments rather than by merely conceptual consideration of the analogy. In other cases, the points of breakdown may not be so clear ahead of time. It is understandable, for example, that Harvey assumed the capillaries to be closed channels — but it turned out, very much later, that they are not. In such cases, the prediction of the points of potential breakdown (never mind their empirical validation) may itself be a contribution to scientific knowledge.

The points at which artificial intelligence will fail to provide scientifically useful analogies to the mind are unclear in this way, which is why (as I noted earlier) it may be a difficult methodological problem to decide which aspects of a program should be matched against empirical data in its psychological validation. Undoubtedly, many computations which could be programmed as a series of steps are in fact 'hardwired' into our bodies as a result of evolution. Some of the most interesting work in artificial intelligence can be seen as an attempt to distinguish the visual computations automatically embodied in the retinal physiology from the more complex computations carried out at higher levels of the visual system.[4] And some important psychological phenomena may be influenced by physiological processes that are not intelligible in computational terms at all. It is sometimes suggested, for example, that creativity is in large part caused by non-representational physiological processes which cannot be understood computationally.[5] These issues are still so unclear that no confident definition of the likely scope and limits of the computational analogy can be given.

But this unclarity should deter no-one who shares Popper's view that scientific advance involves bold conjecture allowing of subsequent refutation. The best way to find out which mental phenomena cannot be explained in computational terms, and why, is to conjecture that some — or even all — are intelligible in these terms, and to push this conjecture as far as possible until a better theory becomes available. If Harvey had abandoned his hydraulic analogy because of the apparent (and, at the sub-microscopic level, actual) fact that the blood-carrying tubes do not form a closed, continuous system, then physiological science would have been the worse off. The refusal to abandon an explanatory analogy prematurely in no way implies the denial that some differences between the two sides of the analogy must inevitably exist, and that some of these may turn out to be scientifically significant.

The explanatory analogies offered by a computational approach encourage us to view the mind as a system of dynamic interacting processes whose complexity is (at best) only hinted at in previous psychological theory and philosophy of mind. This theme underlies Part II (chapters 6 – 8) and Part III (chapters 9 – 11), where I focus respectively on specific psychological phenomena (intentions, reasoning and language) and theoretical psychologists (McDougall, Freud and Piaget). My main aim in these essays is to highlight the computational complexities of familiar mental processes — complexities which any adequate philosophical psychology will have to reflect. In addition, I seek to relate these computational issues to the facts of human embodiment: our material being and our evolutionary origins.

So in chapter 6 ('The structure of intentions') I try to show that any specific instance of intention is a richly structured psychological phenomenon generated within a richly structured system. One cannot appreciate the nature of intention as a psychological reality unless one takes into account its aspect as a (more or less clearly articulated and articulable) action-plan, its relation to the biologically basic and personally central interests of the individual, and its effective control over (more or less basic) bodily operations of motor or intellectual activity. Identification of an intention by way of its goal — as in the general schema 'the intention to X' — masks the fact that there are important psychological distinctions between the many cases that could fall under one instance of this schema.

'The intention to buy bread', for example, covers a wide range of phenomena that are generated in different ways within the mind and function differently accordingly. Someone who seeks to purchase bread may be engaged in hunger-appeasing, sexual, competitive, avaricious, or even religious activities. And theoretical psychologists differ in the range of accounts they are able to offer of such differences. To exhibit the intention as fundamentally religious, for example, requires a specific account of the motivational or instinctual base of religious sentiments, about which theorists disagree; it requires also an account of the religious beliefs concerned that is able to show the significance of the bread in religious terms. Freud's theory of the Eucharist is just one example of a theory which attempts to do this. (And, as I argue more fully in chapter 10, Freudian psychology is in many ways close to a computational account.)

Much as the grammatical structure of a sentence influences its meaning and its relation to other sentences within the context (including what other sentences can sensibly occur in context), so the psychological structure or generative history of an intention determine its role within the economy of the mind. A psychological theory of intention that does not attempt to exhibit this inner structure (that conceptualizes intentions as vector-forces, for instance) is almost as unsatisfactory as one which refuses to admit intentions into the scientific domain at all. By the same token, philosophical accounts of intention and action should suggest the structural relations between different instances if they are to illuminate what intentions are and how they are possible.

Philosophical accounts of reasoning are criticized for their failure to do this in chapter 7 ('Real-world reasoning'), as also are some overly rationalistic psychological treatments. Traditional logic has not taken account of the computational constraints on finite systems engaged in processes of reasoning, but has considered instead the idealized justification of the results of idealized reasoning. But rationality cannot in practice do without the processes of natural reasoning, to which deductive and inductive logic are approximations. Charges of 'psychologism' should not blind us to the epistemological interest of these processes, to whose richness a computational vocabulary is more adequate than is familiar logic.

Real-world reasoning often makes intelligent use of specific content, of examples taken to be representative of a class, and of errors intelligently arrived at in the first place. The way in which Harvey articulated and explored his hydraulic analogy is a case in point, and current work in artificial intelligence dealing with the matching of 'frames' promises to deepen our insight into how such reasoning is possible. Computational analyses (and computer implementations) of inductive learning support the anti-empiricist epistemological view that learning requires prior knowledge and inferential competence, and would not be possible if the mind were a *tabula rasa*. This approach also highlights the computational inevitability of error in intelligent reasoning, while suggesting ways in which some errors can reasonably be said to be more intelligent than others. A rationalistic horror of error has led many philosophers (though not the fallibilist Popper) to ignore false or ill-founded beliefs as epistemologically uninteresting, and even Popper claims that the psychology of discovery — unlike the logic of refutation and confirmation — is no part of the philosophy of mind. But this is overly restrictive: the philosopher should seek to show not only how knowledge might in principle be best grounded but also how it can in fact be intelligently, if fallibly, approached.

The facts of human embodiment and psychological complexity are stressed from a different viewpoint in chapter 8 ('Implications of language studies for human nature'). Many disciplines within cognitive science suggest that basic features of natural language are as they are because we are bodily creatures situated in and acting upon a material world. In relation to various examples of such research, I suggest that had the angel Gabriel indeed visited Mary he could not have conversed with her in Aramaic, or any other natural language. For it is doubtful whether an essentially spiritual being would, or even could, share our capacity to ground countless ('localist') features of language in the biologically given human condition. Localist notions and distinctions (which according to some linguists and psycholinguists even include syntactic distinctions) are those which we first learn to apply with respect to our own orientation and the location or locomotion of other objects in the material world. But since angels can hardly be represented as having any orientation or location (facing due West on top of a pinhead?), it is difficult to see what they could make of such notions.

As for complexity, I discuss further examples of work which points to the subtlety and richness of the cognitive processes underlying everyday language use, including conversations between speakers of different status on topics of emotional import. For instance, a computational model of neurotic thought processes aims to simulate the effect of neurotic concerns on speech; it involves continual monitoring of sentence-generation that results in pauses, restarts, rephrasings, and evasive changes-of-subject more reminiscent of the Watergate tapes than of the grammatically perfect propositions beloved in academia. Bearing in mind the subject-matter of the Annunciation, one may well wonder at the perfection and economy of the reported exchange. And in view of the theologian's theoretical preference for simplicity over complexity in spiritual beings, one may be thankful: for how could Gabriel, lacking complex cognitive resources, have interpreted an anxiously stammering Mary?

I have included three papers on psychologists whose theories are not generally regarded as being amenable to, or perhaps even consistent with, a computational approach. The first, William McDougall, may indeed be turning in his grave at this moment. For he had scant patience with 'mechanistic' psychologies, by which he meant theories that denied purposiveness, eschewed purposive (or, generally, intentionalistic) explanation, and/or assumed our physiological embodiment to involve no cerebral mechanisms or energies at variance with contemporary physics. As an alternative he offered his own so-called 'hormic' psychology, in which purpose and other intentional categories were theoretically central. Largely because of his medical and psychiatric background, McDougall took pains to relate psychology to its evolutionary base and tried to develop a theory of personality within which the generation of normal and abnormal behaviour and experience would be mutually intelligible. His system was more comprehensive, if less detailed, than that of Freud: but despite their many similarities, McDougall did not share Freud's reductionist philosophy.

McDougall is a useful case-study for my purposes partly because of the generous range of his theorizing, and partly because of his antimechanist bias.[6] If the insights of such a *prima facie* unpromising theorist can fruitfully be interpreted in computational terms, the computationalist's case will be more strengthened than if a more sympathetic example had been chosen. The programming analogy explored throughout chapter 9 ('McDougall revisited') is instantiated in terms of early computational models such as TOTE-units and the General Problem Solver: it should be abundantly evident from other chapters that more recent computational work could be cited with reference to the general points made in this early paper.

A similar remark applies to my discussion of Freud's work in chapter 10 ('Freudian mechanisms of defence: a programming perspective'). The programmed model of neurotic thought processes mentioned above, for instance, is in some ways significantly more subtle than the early simulation of defence mechanisms briefly described in this chapter.[7]

Freud's concern with anxiety and conflict leads many people to doubt whether his theory could reasonably be assimilated to a computational model, it being often assumed that such a model could at most account for the cognitive aspects of the mind, being helpless to illuminate either affect or motivation. But Freud's discussions of emotional cathexis and psychodynamic conflict were largely concerned with their instantiations or effects at the symbolic level. His account of the repressive mechanisms of defence for instance, as of the dream-work, concentrates on the expression of one semantic content by way of thought or behaviour normally taken to signify some other content. Defence in general involves the total repression — or, more usually, the transformation — of representations symbolizing threatening issues. Symbolic transformations of various kinds were postulated by Freud, which can not only be modelled computationally but which may be clarified by so doing. Various subtly different types of 'denial', for example, which are generated by and result in rather different psychological conditions, can be clearly distinguished with the help of computational concepts and models.

Similarly, Freud's account (in *The Psychopathology of Everyday Life*) of searching one's memory for 'Signorelli' and producing instead 'Botticelli' raises crucial questions about the storage, indexing, accessing and creative transformation of memory, questions which arise in a more rigorously specifiable manner during attempts to develop computational procedures for using large knowledge-bases. This is not to say that we are yet in a position to answer these questions: the intelligent use of large amounts of data is one of the most important unsolved problems within artificial intelligence. But the point of general philosophical interest is that Freud's questions here were quite clearly in the computational domain.

Whereas neither Freud nor McDougall (both of whom died just before the outbreak of World War II) were in a position to have any opinion on computational psychology, Piaget has recently expressed sympathy for it on several occasions. Since he has a marked tendency to assimilate all intellectual currents to his own theoretical synthesis, one might be tempted to discount the significance of these occasional remarks. And to be sure, Piaget himself does not use a programming approach. Some Piagetians do, however, and their work is discussed in chapter 11 ('Artificial intelligence and Piagetian theory') where I try to show that Piagetian theory might be clarified, extended, and fruitfully criticized in computational terms.

Moreover, Piaget's commendation of computer simulations is not a mere all-embracing eclecticism. For there are several important ways in which his philosophical psychology (and biology) is resonant with this recent trend in cognitive science. For instance, Piaget's logicist bias has led him to try to express his psychological theory in formal terms, and to praise those theoretical biologists who try to do likewise. His strong approval for 'cybernetic' explanations (which he sees as crucial to the understanding of equilibratory processes in biological and psychological systems) is based partly in his insight that machines built by engineers (such as Grey Walter's electronic tortoises) provide a practical test of the effective realization and coherent operation of the underlying theory. Thirdly, Piaget's structuralist philosophy of science is one that eschews the traditional positivist model of explanation in terms of correlations between dependent and independent variables, arguing instead that one may give a scientific explanation of a phenomenon by 'interpreting the actual as an instance of the possible'. Similarly, a program intended as a psychological simulation need not (though it may) reflect statistical correlations between independently identified performance-features; rather, its explanatory power is that it shows how a wide range of superficially different phenomena can all be generated by the same underlying computational mechanism.

Fourth and last, Piaget's conception of the subject-matter of psychology is basically the same as that of those cognitive scientists who espouse the computational approach. For he sees psychology as the science of 'mind' rather than 'behaviour', and psychological (as opposed to physiological) explanations as concerned with 'systems of signification' inter-related by 'implication'. This view of psychology as basically semantic or intentional is closer to hermeneutics than to behaviourism, and parallels the computationalist's distinction between the software (representations and inferences) and the hardware (physical causes). In like manner, Piaget's wish to see a *cognitive* biology, and his praise of Waddington's work accordingly, suggests that he would be highly sympathetic to the theoretical developments in morphology that were the topic of chapter 4.[8]

The essays in Part IV (chapters 12 – 13) take up an issue touched on in many previous chapters — namely, the relation of psychological theory to human values and sociopolitical matters. Even biology, as I argue in the final section of chapter 4, has evaluative overtones, in the sense that one form of biological theory may encourage attitudes to the natural world, and to our place in it, that seems quite inappropriate against the background of a different sort of biology. And psychological theories are constantly supported or attacked because of their presumed implications for moral and political debate. Indeed, McDougall expressly stated that it was his interest in the theory of morals that led him to psychology in the first place. He believed that only purposive explanations can allow for the reality of moral choice, and that any non-purposive theoretical psychology risks throwing us into moral chaos because of its denial of the efficacy of moral effort.

Many recent writers have criticized Skinnerian theory on similar grounds. And the Third Force psychologists generally criticize not only behaviourists but Freudians also, for what they see as an overly pessimistic and determinist emphasis on past causes and unconscious mechanisms at the expense of present conscious choice. Computational psychology has not escaped criticism on such grounds, having been called 'obscene' and 'deeply humiliating', as well as being dismissed with Hobbes' scathing apophthegm, 'When men write whole volumes of such stuff, are they not mad, or intend to make others so?' Psychologists who do not join Skinner in denying, and perhaps even deriding, the concept of freedom should try to show how their theory allows some place for it and for human values in general. That is, unless they are to take refuge in an ultimately mystical or religious conception of values and choice, they must make an attempt to engage morals with the theoretical specifics of deliberation and bodily action.

In chapter 12 ('Human values in a mechanistic universe') I ask whether a computational account really is incompatible with concepts such as purpose, free choice, moral responsibility, and human dignity. It is in these concepts, according to humanist philosophers and psychologists, that the notion of human values is grounded. As regards the first three, I argue not only that this apparently mechanistic approach can allow for them, but that it can even illuminate them by showing how the psychological phenomena we mark with these terms are possible.

For example, thinking about deliberation in computational terms emphasizes the fact that only a creature with cognitive resources competent to make certain specific computational distinctions would be able to act in such a way as to incur blame for carelessness. Only a creature with a certain type of computational competence could reasonably change its mind at a certain point and (just as reasonably) change it back again later, making due allowance for the apparent difficulty that had made it change course in the first place. Only someone able to reason on the basis of universal quantification could act on or think in terms of moral rules understood as applying without prejudice to *any* person in the given circumstances. And only a mind enjoying the computational ability to draw and assess the strength of analogies would be able to draw a moral from a New Testament parable or cautionary tale.

This helps one to understand what lies behind the common definition of freedom as the ability to do something where one *could* have done differently. Provided that the computational resources (concepts, beliefs, preferences, values, inferential powers) of the person's mind are such that other relevant features of the choice-situation could have been hypothesized, recognized, weighed up, and taken into account during decision-making, then there is a real (and computationally characterizable) sense in which — had these features entered into the deliberations, or entered into them in a different way — the person could have chosen differently. And if the reason why these features were not considered itself depends on prior computations (such as decisions to ignore certain questions because of time constraints, or the promise of financial gain), then again there is a clear sense in which the person could have considered them and may therefore be held responsible for not having done so. Unconscious thoughts, such as the defensive computations typical of neurosis, threaten our freedom because they are less amenable to monitoring, evaluation, and correction by the higher-level deliberations of the mind (as remarked above, chapter 10 shows that high-level computations can be systematically biassed by certain assumptions or inhibitions, without their existence being reflexively recognized by the higher levels of the system.)

The paradigm case of free choice or moral deliberation is thus quite different from cases where a cause external to the mind prevents appropriate consideration of the relevant feature, irrespective of the computations autonomously carried out by the person. Such 'external' causes certainly include examples like gunmen and blindness, and possibly (though this is an empirical question) certain sorts of genetic make-up: if a certain sort of chromosomal constitution, such as the Z-Y syndrome, causes a man sometimes to behave violently *no matter what* the conscious efforts made and the moral values theoretically accepted by him, then his freedom (and blameworthiness) are lessened accordingly.

In general, freedom is a matter of degree rather than an all-or-none phenomenon. This may be especially clear in pathological cases, where the normal relations between physiology and computation are disturbed. For instance, patients with Tourette's disease (which is due to an excess of neurotransmitter chemicals in the brain) are subject to irrepressible tics, but at least one such was a superb drummer, turning these involuntary and unpredictable spasms to his advantage by making them the seed of musical improvisations of an exceptionally interesting character. It is not mechanism as such that is the enemy of freedom, but mechanism of a sort where the autonomous self-monitoring computations carried out by the system have no power (or a reduced power) to influence its actions. Thinking of the mind as a computational system, then, by no means prevents our giving a place to purpose, freedom, and moral responsibility.

With respect to the concept of human dignity, which implies that the interests of human beings ought *prima facie* to be respected simply because they are our interests, the point about explanation discussed above is relevant: *explanans* and *explanandum* are never identical, and at some point the explanatory analogy between them will break down. It is true that human beings (and animals) have interests in a sense in which computers do not, and that concepts of intrinsic 'dignity' or 'being worthy of respectful consideration' do not apply to programmed artefacts. This has nothing to do, however, with the fact that computers are mechanisms. So if one's biological and psychological theories suggest that all living organisms, including *homo sapiens*, are likewise mechanisms, it does not follow from this that the concept of dignity cannot be ascribed to them. It is primarily because a 'cognitive' biology of the type discussed in chapter 4 ascribes interests of a sort to all living things that it is believed by its proponents to entail a more respectful, less exploitative, attitude towards nature than theoretical biologies employing no quasi-psychological terms.

Whether a scientific theory can in principle allow for certain values is one thing, and whether its widespread acceptance by and use in society will encourage them in practice is quite another. Sociobiology, for instance, allows that even if a long-established and widespread social institution (such as monogamy or patriarchy) evolved because of its survival value for the societies concerned, it may now be maladaptive because the ecological constraints on the human species have changed. In addition, sociobiology allows that we might choose to modify certain institutions because of our extra-scientific values. Only if it could be clearly shown that any attempt at such a choice must necessarily lead to the extinction of the group could the sociobiologist defensibly present the decision as scientifically outlawed. Even in this case, we could consistently make the suicidal moral-political decision that life on certain terms is not *worth* living: 'Better dead than Red!' is not a logically incoherent sentiment.

Admittedly, a general commitment to sociobiology would tend to give traditional practices the benefit of the doubt, or *prima facie* acceptability, because of the theoretical possibility that they are essential factors in our communal equilibrium. Indeed, a distinguished social psychologist has argued precisely this point, correlatively remarking that the liberal penchant for questioning all traditions that has been shared by social psychologists as a profession may run the risk of disturbing the evolutionarily achieved *status quo* without any clear idea of which sociopolitical institutions might function as equally stable alternatives.[9] And individuals wishing to give a scientific legitimation to specific current practices, such as intelligence-testing or educational segregation for example, may of course claim to find support in sociobiological principles. This is why many people have tried to find flaws in the arguments concerned, and/or in sociobiology in general, believing that this theoretical approach must necessarily have unacceptably conservative implications.

The fact that some moral theorists have argued (in my view, rightly) that there must be some biologically given 'human nature' determining our basic interests and needs if there is to be any possibility of free moral choice at all is beside the point here.[10] For it might turn out, as a matter of historical fact, that the general public were more easily swayed by the apparently conservative (some would say, 'pessimistic') implications of sociobiology than by the more optimistically presented connotations.

The question of the likely sociopolitical effects of a widespread commitment to computational models in psychological theory is complicated by the inevitable presence of numerous technological applications grounded in the same scientific source. People who never have, and never will, read a word of theoretical psychology will nevertheless encounter increasingly many products of technology based on artificial intelligence and computer science in general. They will therefore come up against the computational model of the mind, in howsoever attenuated a form, in their daily life. Some sociopolitical dimensions of computer technology have long been recognized, including such important issues as privacy, unemployment, leisure, centralization of political power, and the military misuse of technology. These issues, clearly, are raised by work in artificial intelligence no less than by applications exploiting the mere 'brute force' of computers. But the specific interest here is in other matters, namely, the likely effects of the social use of *intelligent* machines in particular.

The commercial applications of artificial intelligence that have been professionally forecast for the next thirty years are extremely varied. They run from robot housecleaners, chauffeurs, and industrial workers, through programmed gameplayers and story-tellers, to automatic teachers, physicians, legal justices, marriage counsellors, and literary critics. In all these cases, the emphasis is on reasoned and flexible judgment on the program's part, as opposed to the storage and regurgitation of isolated facts, or the repetitive performance of a fixed sequence of discriminations and movements. For instance, a computer physician in experimental use in a large teaching-hospital gives the same advice as do human specialists in over 80% of cases.[11] This program engages in extended question-and-answer conversations with doctors need-ing specialist help in the identification of micro-organisms and the prescription of antibiotics. The human physician (or medical student) can ask it for explanations of its advice, expressed at the appropriate level of detail. This makes the program appear less godlike than one which prints out its conclusions and leaves it at that, so the human user is in a position to realize that it can in principle be questioned, that one can reject its advice if one is suspicious as to the plausibility of its reasoning.

Quasi-intelligent programs will be used in increasing numbers by the general public as individuals and by political and administrative institutions, and the limits on their powers must be recognized by those concerned if the risk of over-enthusiastic trust in their pronouncements is to be avoided. That is, the prefix 'quasi' qualifying the word 'intelligent' in the previous sentence is not intended to call to mind some abstract philosophical scruple about ascribing psychological predicates literally to machines. Rather, it is meant to remind one that there are *specific* limitations of individual programs, not all of which are shared by every other program, and that these particular bounds on the program's computational powers must be taken into account when it is being used. What specific sorts of weakness should constrain our confidence in a given program for medical diagnosis, for example? And is this other diagnostic program subject to identical limitations?

Much as in the case of sociobiology discussed above, the likely social effects of computational theory and its technological applications are problematic. A great deal depends on the background human context, not least the general public's implicit philosophical assumptions or 'image of man'. If they assume that science offers an image of man that is irreconcilable with humanism, they must either deny their humanity — with socially pernicious results — or else forfeit a scientific understanding of mankind. People who share the computational approach to psychology (and, of course, computer professionals in general) have a special responsibility to concern themselves with these questions while there is still time.

Clinical psychologists have long reported a tendency for mechanistic models of the mind (drawn from behaviourism, and encouraged by the success of the natural sciences) to undermine their patients' sense of autonomy. People who believe they are unable to make free choices are unlikely to devote much effort to making them, and those seeking a rationalization for the continuation of undesirable attitudes or behaviour patterns can find one all too easily in inhuman models of humanity. To the extent that people share the view criticized in chapter 12, namely, that mechanism in general and computer-based psychological analogies in particular are essentially incompatible with freedom, the increased public visibility of apparently intelligent programs might subtly undermine their view of themselves as morally responsible beings.

This dehumanizing effect would be even greater if programs were used in contexts previously thought of as human *par excellence*, and it is not surprising that the well-intentioned suggestion that computer programs be introduced into psychiatric diagnosis and therapy has been bitterly denounced as 'obscene'. Quite apart from these philosophical considerations, one should be wary of the dehumanizing effects of people's becoming decreasingly dependent on human contact for satisfaction of their needs. The social isolation commonly attributed to television is but a pale shadow of the alienation and loneliness that could follow on excessive reliance on home-based computing facilities fulfilling functions such as those listed earlier. There is reason enough, then, for deep pessimism about the computerized society of the future, should one care to indulge in it.

But there is room also for a reasonable hope that the quality of life, and even the publicly accepted image of man's nature and individual potential, may be significantly improved by the proper understanding of computational mechanisms. I have argued this already, with respect to freedom and responsibility. Here I will add only one example, the potential effects of the new type of computer-assisted instruction based on computational models of psychology.

Whereas traditional approaches concentrate on teaching specific subject-matter, this approach is focussed rather on helping people to think constructively about their own thinking activities. Educational methods based on this pedagogical philosophy might change our ways of thinking about 'failure', a change which would be very much for the better. Instead of the passively defeatist 'I'm no good at this', the child would say 'How can I make myself better at it?' This attitude is encouraged by the computational way of thinking about thinking, with its emphasis on the creative interrelation of many different procedures, and on the unintended effects of specifiable mistakes in basically well-conceived attempts to achieve one's goal. By contrast, constructive self-criticism is not encouraged by a conception of intelligence that views it as the product of a number of mysterious monolithic 'talents' or abilities, which one either has or lacks, willy-nilly. (The common emphasis on self-directed and self-corrective learning is a further feature uniting the psychological views of Piaget with computationalists.[12])

That the evaluative implications of sociobiology and computational psychology are problematic should come as no surprise, for this is a general feature of theories in the life sciences. Such theories are either so vaguely expressed as to permit many alternative interpretations differing in evaluative tone, and/or they are sufficiently complex that selective attention to their parts can imply widely varying moral-political evaluations. In addition, one's values are not determined, even if they are to some degree constrained, by scientific evidence, so that one and the same corpus of knowledge about human beings could coherently be assigned distinct and opposing evaluations. So it is not a simple matter to decide what general image of man is implied by a theory of biology, psychology, or sociobiology, and nor is it unproblematic to evaluate a particular image of man in seeking a general statement of the human condition. Skinner's behaviourist assault on the social value (quite independent of the truth) of the commonly admired concepts of freedom and dignity is a well-known contemporary example illustrating this ambiguity of psychological theory.

These general points are illustrated with reference to a wide range of historical examples in chapter 13 ('Optimism'). I ask there whether there could be a systematic, philosophical form of optimism (or pessimism), in contrast with a purely personal, psychological form. Any such optimism would have to evaluate facts about one's own society, or human society at large, with respect to a specific set of values, concluding that they are of positive rather than negative worth. This general schema allows for many subtly different cases, but it requires that any systematic optimist take the trouble to examine what appear to be the facts in question. That is, it requires some attention to scientific evidence and theory concerning life in general and humanity in particular. It follows that there can be no such thing as a wholly *a priori* optimism; this has the perhaps surprising consequence that Leibniz' notorious claim which so shocked Voltaire — that this is the best of all possible worlds — is not a genuine case of optimism. Philosophies of mind or psychology — computational, Freudian, behaviourist, phenomenological, existentialist or whatever — will form an essential part of any world-view properly described as either optimistic or pessimistic.

It is arguable that there could be no such world-view, that the schema outlined above cannot be coherently instantiated in either optimistic or pessimistic modes. Even if this is so, one is not precluded from taking up a general attitude toward the world and one's place in it that is positive or negative in evaluative tone. But any such attitude will be either a purely personal, psychological matter (which does not mean it is negligible: optimistic attitudes may be conducive to the enduring of suffering or the overcoming of difficulties), or it will be grounded in extra-scientific sources such as religious systems claiming to be logically independent of any actual facts about life on earth.

With this discussion of the role of philosophical psychology in one's overall world-view we come full circle, for a main theme of the opening chapter was that the computational metaphor is not intrinsically dehumanizing, as is so commonly feared by people who value human subjectivity and responsible deliberation. On the contrary, in committing us to the intentional stance in our theorizing, it offers us for the first time a theoretical account of these human characteristics which highlights instead of obscuring their awesome subtlety and complexity, and which is demonstrably consonant with the empirical sciences in general. William James distinguished between the tough-minded and the tender-minded in philosophy and psychology, and admitted to a sympathy for both sides. It is often implicitly assumed that to try to have a foot in both these camps is to be guilty of a mere sentimental eclecticism, if not of actual incoherence. In my view, one of the main strengths of the computational approach in philosophical psychology is that it gives us a reasoned philosophical rationale for combining the insights of the hermeneutic humanists with the findings of the sterner sciences. It pleases me to think that William James would have approved.

NOTES

1   D. C. Dennett, 'Intentional systems' in *Brainstorms: Philosophical Essays on Mind and Psychology* (Hassocks, Sussex: Harvester Press, 1979), pp. 3–22.

2   See H. L. Dreyfus, *What Computers Can't Do: A Critique of Artificial Reason* (New York: Harper & Row, 1972). I have discussed Dreyfus' objections at greater length on pp. 434–444 of my *Artificial Intelligence and Natural Man* (Hassocks, Sussex: Harvester Press, 1977).

3   See the claims and counterclaims in J. R. Searle *et al.*, 'Minds, brains, and programs (with peer commentaries)', *The Behavioral and Brain Sciences*, 3 (1980), 417–457.

4   The work of David Marr and his colleagues at MIT is paramount here. A statement of their general position is: D. Marr, 'Early processing of visual information', *Phil. Trans. Royal Society*, 275/942 (1976), 483–524. For a recent example of this approach, see S. Ullman, *The Interpretation of Visual Motion* (Cambridge, Mass.: MIT Press, 1979).

5   E.g., J. A. Fodor, *The Language of Thought* (Hassocks, Sussex: Harvester Press, 1976), pp. 200–203.

6   This computational interpretation of a purposive theoretical psychology is developed more fully in my *Purposive Explanation in Psychology* (Harvard, USA: University Press, 1972 and Hassocks, Sussex: Harvester Press, 1978).

7   In chapters 2 and 3 of my *Artificial Intelligence and Natural Man*, I have discussed these examples of neurotic programs in much greater detail.

8   A fuller discussion of Piaget's views on psychology, philosophy, and biology is in my *Piaget* (Brighton, Sussex: Harvester Press, 1979).

9   D. T. Campbell, 'On the conflicts between biological and social evolution and between psychological and moral tradition', *American Psychologist*, 30 (1975), 1103–1126. See also comments and reply in *American Psychologist*, 31 (May 1976).

10   M. Midgley, *Beast and Man: The Roots of Human Nature* (Hassocks, Sussex: Harvester Press, 1979). See also M. Midgley, *Man and Morality: The Varieties of Moral Experience* (Harvester Press, forthcoming).

11   This and other examples of commercial applications are discussed in chapter 15 of my *Artificial Intelligence and Natural Man*.

12   S. Papert, *Mindstorms: Children, Computers, and Powerful Ideas* (Brighton, Sussex: Harvester Press, 1980).

PART I

EXPLANATION AND COMPUTATION

1
The computational metaphor in psychology

INTRODUCTION

The past twenty years have seen an increasing use of computational concepts in theoretical psychology, and of computer programs as models of psychological processes. This has happened most noticeably within cognitive psychology, but social, dynamic and psychopathological issues have been addressed in these terms also. The seminal book *Plans and the Structure of Behavior*[1] introduced programming analogies into discussion of a wide range of psychological topics, and professionals within psychology and artificial intelligence (AI) have since then explored such analogies in increasing detail.[2] The philosophy of mind, too, has seen growing use[3] — and concomitant criticism[4] — of the computational metaphor.

The computational metaphor can aid in the generation and the rigorous formulation and testing of psychological hypotheses about the mind's contents and functions. These hypotheses form part of a distinctive theoretical approach that takes account of the complex structures and interacting processes that make thought and action possible. From the philosophical point of view, computational insights enable us to understand how it is possible for the immaterial mind and the material body to be closely related, and in particular how it is possible for the mind to act on the body during purposive action and voluntary choice. The nature of human subjectivity (the idiosyncratic interpretation of the individual's experiential world) also is illuminated by this approach.

Clearly, then, it is a mistake to regard the computational metaphor as essentially 'dehumanizing'. A psychology that looks to machines for some of its central concepts need not be crudely mechanistic in character, nor inhumanly reductionist in type. On the contrary, the computational approach to psychology stresses (and helps explain) important features of the human mind, such as purpose and subjectivity, which many psychological theories have ignored — or even denied.

THE COMPUTATIONAL METAPHOR AND SCIENTIFIC EXPLANATION

Someone employing the computational metaphor for the mind

uses the concepts and insights of computer science and artificial intelligence in describing and explaining psychological phenomena. The mind is seen as an information-processing or symbol-manipulating system, and the psychologist's task is to clarify the content, structure, transformation and use of the person's (or the animal's) mental representations of the world. In general, the theoretical emphasis is on mental *processes*; this of course does not exclude reference to mental structures (such as conceptual systems, for example), but the theorist tries to specify what processes build or transform a given structure, and what (inferential) processes can have access to the structure so making use of the knowledge stored in it. The concepts of artificial intelligence (the science of making machines do things that would require intelligence if done by people) are helpful in this regard since they are concerned with these very questions. Within artificial intelligence, such questions are asked in relation to a programmed system (a computer program) wherein every item of information and every process for manipulating that information can be rigorously specified.

The many computational concepts that may usefully be applied to natural psychological phenomena as well as to artificial information-processing systems include the following: subroutine; bug; recursive procedure; hierarchical organization; heterarchical control; compiler and interpreter programs; top-down and bottom-up processing; depth-first and breadth-first search; locally and globally bound variables; cue and schema; demon; antecedent and consequent theorems; iteration; mini-mixing; plan; linear and parallel processing; procedural v. declarative representation of knowledge; content-addressable memory.

A proponent of the computational metaphor need not claim (though many would) that *all* psychological phenomena can in principle be fruitfully discussed in such terms as these. Nor need such a person believe (though many do) that actually writing computer programs to simulate psychological processes — or, better, to model psychological theories — is the best way of employing the computational metaphor in psychology. Least of all need such a person assert that complete simulation of all human knowledge and abilities will ever in practice be achieved. This would be equivalent to saying that one day some psychological theory will exist that accounts for every least detail of someone's knowledge, action and experience. (One might well doubt whether biochemistry will ever be able to explain *all* the metabolic processes occurring within the human body — but it does not follow that biochemistry has nothing of significance to say about these processes.)

The use of metaphors is widespread in scientific theorizing. Examples include Harvey's hydraulic metaphor for the circulation of the blood, Rutherford's planetary metaphor for the atom, and the Sherringtonian 'telephone exchange' metaphor for the central nervous system. In all such cases, the metaphor provides an interlinked set of familiar concepts that bear some analogy to the phenomena requiring explanation. In exploring this analogy, the theorist is led to discover new phenomena, or newly noticed features of known phenomena, which are intelligible in so far as they can be assimilated to the more familiar pole of the analogy.

Every metaphor or analogy has its limits, and the scientist should ideally know what these are. But it is not always possible to predict — or even sensible to ask — what these limits are at the early stages of employment of a theoretical metaphor in science. The planetary and telephone exchange metaphors just mentioned, for instance, are now known to be misleading in important ways: but this knowledge has been gained only by way of the physical and neurophysiological investigations guided by these seminal metaphors. To have hoped to show their limitations before extensive exploration of their implications would not have been sensible. At most, various possible limitations might have been suggested (Sherrington himself suggested some) which later studies might confirm as significant.

In this chapter, then, I shall not discuss the question of what (if anything) no computer, in principle, could ever do. It will be enough for my purposes that they can already do some things that are sufficiently similar to human mental processes to make them useful as theoretical analogies of the mind. Doubtless they will be able to do more such things in future: *how many* more is uncertain, and both the theoretical psychologist and the 'pure' philosopher would be wise to leave this question open pending fuller experience with AI systems than anyone has at present. Suffice it to say that programs already exist that can do things — or, at the very least, appear to be beginning to do things — which ill-informed critics have asserted *a priori* to be impossible. Examples include: perceiving in a holistic as opposed to an atomistic manner; using language creatively; translating sensibly from one language to another by way of a language-neutral semantic representation; planning action in a broad and sketchy fashion, the details being decided only in execution; distinguishing between different species of emotional reaction according to the psychological context of the subject.

Nor does use of the computational metaphor commit one to saying (though some proponents would be happy to do so) that psychological terms may in principle be applied *literally* to any current or future AI program. You probably noticed that the list of 'computational' concepts given earlier included seemingly psychological items such as *control*, *search*, *cue*, *plan* and *memory*; and many other everyday psychological words are commonly used in describing programs. There are two reasons why one might feel bound to admit that all psychological terms applied to programs are being used in an analogical rather than a literal sense. First (and incontrovertible), the computational abilities of existing programs are puny as compared with those of the human mind, so that even words like 'deduce' and 'infer' — never mind 'know' and 'want' — are not used with the full range of implications implicit in their ordinary meaning. Second (and philosophically more controversial), it is often claimed that the possession of intrinsic interests — that is, interests whose existence cannot be explained by reference to the purposes of some other individual or agent — is essential to any creature that can merit the literal application of psychological terms, and that no imaginable computer program could possibly possess such interests. On such a view, terms like 'intelligent' (or even 'stupid') could never be applied in their full sense to any program, no matter how impressive its 'thinking' abilities.

But from the theoretical psychologist's point of view, the important point is that one may reasonably make use of words like 'plan', 'goal', 'represent', 'reason', 'deduce', 'ask', 'infer', 'choose', . . . and so on, in describing what programs do and how they manage to do it. Provided that these words are selected carefully, bearing in mind the precise functional details of the program concerned, their use is justified in that it leads to fruitful theoretical insights into and questions about how analogous processes might be carried out in the human case.

The use of psychological words in computational contexts even aids development of the programs themselves, for it highlights not only similarities but also differences between program and person that suggest dimensions along which the program's thinking could be improved. In other words, the psychological metaphor is useful to the study of computation much as the computational metaphor is helpful in the study of psychology. For instance, use of the word 'belief' for data-items in a program's data-base readily suggests — which the more technical 'data-item' does not — that one consider how one might provide the program with various degrees, or strengths, of belief; how one might allow for the program to recognize and correct its false beliefs; how the program should be enabled to generalize and make use of its beliefs; how it might suit the program, for certain purposes, to hold specific (perhaps erroneous) beliefs; and how one could represent the evidential relations between this and other items that might be thought to be relevant to the item in question. It is no accident that to label a sentence a 'data-item' makes it sound less interesting than if one were to label it a 'belief'. In general, sterile technical terms synthesized in the laboratory may be less heuristically useful to the scientist than a borrowed vocabulary that is already richly infected with implicit logical relations.

The technical vocabulary, however, has its own advantages, of which the chief are non-ambiguity and precision. In addition, if computational concepts can be embodied in a functioning computer program that can be run on a machine, then one *knows* that the programmed theory in question is sufficiently powerful to generate the performance evinced by the machine. Since the meaning of ordinary language terms — and also the technical terms of 'verbal' psychologies — is largely implicit rather than fully explicit, it is not usually clear just which phenomena they cover and which they do not. (What *is* cognitive dissonance, or denial, or frustration, or aggression, or . . . ?) The explanatory power of verbally expressed theories is thus intuitively sensed rather than rigorously articulated, and there is considerable room for disagreement over whether or not a given theory explains a certain phenomenon, let alone whether some other theory might not explain it better.

The comparative assessment or validation of psychological theories, as of any scientific theory, requires more than clear expression of the theories: it requires their testing by being matched against empirical facts. Since most of what goes on during thinking is neither introspected nor even introspectible, this matching necessarily has to be indirect. Rather than thinking of it as a testing of the *predictions* made by a programmed theory, one should think of this matching as a testing of the range of observed phenomena against the range of phenomena whose descriptions can be generated by the theory. The theory expresses and integrates a range of possibilities, and makes them intelligible in so far as it explains how they may be generated within the mind. To the extent that observed phenomena fall within that range, they are explicable in terms of the theory. But it does not follow that the theory can (or should attempt to) predict precisely *which* possibilities will be realized on a particular occasion. Analogously, one might say of Freudian interpretative theory that it shows how it is possible for someone to dream of a crumpled giraffe as a symbolic representation of the person's mother, even if it can neither predict that a specific child will experience this manifest dream-content next Saturday night nor prove (when he does) that the relevant latent dream-content is in fact 'mother'. In short, testing the explanatory power of a theory is not the same thing as testing its predictive power, positivist philosophies of science to the contrary. (Even non-psychological sciences may employ non-predictive explanatory theories, as the example of evolutionary theory in biology shows.)

The question whether one or another putative explanation is *the* (or *the best*) explanation of something is even more difficult than the question whether it *might* be the explanation. With respect to theories expressed as programs, it boils down to the question whether a human performance that is simulated by a program is carried out in our minds *in the same way*. This is not an all-or-none question, since two systems may think in the same way when their thought is represented at one level of detail, but in different ways when it is described at another level. Some of the functional levels involved in playing chess, for instance, may be common to all players of good chess (whether programs or people), whereas others may differ as between people and programs or even between one program and another. One must specify the aspect of thought concerned before one can ask whether the thinking is done in the same way; and for this specification one will require computational concepts that distinguish carefully between different aspects of the use, content and organization of thought.

Some workers have tried to write programs simulating human behaviour to a fair degree of detail. For example, their programs simulating cryptarithmetic problem-solving,[5] or young children's seriation behaviour,[6] predict the order of steps (and the nature of mistakes) taken by the human subject in the situation concerned. Such workers typically pay attention to detailed experimental evidence, and often generate more such evidence themselves. Assessing the importance of a match or mismatch between program and human performance, however, is not a straightforward matter. For instance, the programmer may attempt to incorporate processes modelling the person's 'protocols', or thinking aloud, while doing the task assigned. Suppose a certain program-process has no equivalent protocol: given that not all the significant thinking processes going on in the human mind are going to be introspected — or introspectible — one cannot hastily assume that the process is a mere programming artefact. Conversely, suppose the human's protocol differs radically from the program-process (the person might even say 'I didn't do it *like that*!'): since these protocols themselves (which are not normally produced outside the experimental situation) may involve a large element of rationalization, of unwittingly but misleadingly saying what the person's implicit theory of mind suggests *must* have been happening, they cannot be accepted at face value. There is long-standing evidence within cognitive psychology showing that people do not necessarily know how it is that they are managing to think (perceive, reason, remember . . .) on any given occasion.

Other workers regard it as premature to attempt a detailed matching with human performance, and unnecessary to generate new programmes of experimental investigation. For many visual, reasoning or language-understanding programs, for example, quite clearly cannot do many things which people can do; no further experimentation is needed to show this. Such experimentation will only be needed when the programs concerned are powerful enough to give a close approximation to human behaviour, so close as to make discriminatory experimental tests appropriate. As has been pointed out with respect to the experimental psychology of vision,[7] psychologists as yet have no clear idea of how most of the things we do (or the things that animals do) might or could be done, so there is no question of picking and choosing between different programs all capable of doing them. Rather, computational concepts and programmed models should be used to highlight the lacunae in current theories, and help formulate others more nearly adequate to the task of explaining mental processes.

Largely because of the non-introspectible nature of many thought-processes, methodological problems of validation will of course remain. But these plague the 'verbal' psychologist no less than his computational colleague — and some of them are common to the scientific enterprise in general, not just to psychological enquiries. Critics of the computational approach should take care to distinguish methodological difficulties specifically associated with computational theorizing from difficulties inherent in any psychological, or even scientific, investigation.

PEOPLE, PROGRAMS AND POSITIVISM

The positivist approach to psychology, characterized by stimulus-response and physiological theories of animal and human behaviour, is criticized elsewhere in this book. I shall not repeat those criticisms, but shall show that, contrary to common belief, the computational approach is itself radically antipositivist in nature.

A central characteristic of positivism is its incapability of expressing subjectivity, its avoidance of concepts incorporating the distinction between the psychological subject and the object of thought. These concepts are termed 'intentional' concepts, and only they can express the meaning attributed to the world by a mind, as opposed to the intrinsic features of the world considered independently of any interpretation or representation of it. All the psychological terms of ordinary language — and of non-positivist psychologies — are intentional (as is the concept of *representation* itself). Antipositivists regard such concepts as indispensable in any adequate psychology, and as irreducible to behaviourist or physiological terms.

Psychologists who employ intentional concepts in their theories include many groups, from the cognitive psychologists (who in general have some sympathy with the computational approach), through ethogenic and ethnomethodological groups within social psychology (who tend to ignore computational methodologies), to self-styled 'humanists' within clinical and personality theory (who often criticize 'mechanistic' models of man in general, and have no patience for the AI context of theorizing in particular). Despite their many differences, these psychologists agree that thought and behaviour must be conceptualized as meaningful action on the part of a subjective agent rather than as causal process in the natural world.

This concern with semantic rather than causal issues, with hermeneutic interpretation rather than objective process and prediction, is shared by workers in AI and by psychologists making use of the computational metaphor. To study representations (whether in natural or artificial systems) is to concern oneself with intentional matters, with the way in which meanings are constructed, organized, transformed and utilized by the system in question. And to explain the performance of their machines, AI workers need to specify the information-processing or symbol-manipulating properties of the program (which might have been very different in an alternative program running on the same physical machine).

For example, many scene analysis programs exist[8] which can interpret Figure 1.1 as a picture of a scene containing a cube — and some programs[9] can similarly interpret Figure 1.2. But there is an important sense in which these programs see different things in the pictures or, in other words, *see different pictures*. For some, these pictures contain lines and regions, for others lines and vertices; some see Figure 1.2 as consisting of a greater number of lines than do others; while only some programs are capable of seeing Figure 1.2 'meaningfully' as a solid object at all, instead of regarding it as an insignificant muddle of lines. These differences arise because the details of the interpretative process differ from one program to another, so that one and the same picture is 'experienced' in different ways.

In general, the interpretative process relates picture and scene (the representational and the target domains) by way of a conceptual schema embodying the system's knowledge of the 'mapping' relation between them. This procedure requires an analysis or structural description of the picture in terms that are relevant to the particular representational system, or theory of mapping, concerned. That is, the 'parts' of the picture must be *cues* that relate to the target domain in ways defined by the inner conceptual scheme. It follows that 'parts' (like 'cues') is a subjective, or intentional, notion and is not equivalent to purely physical features of the picture. (A microscopic examination of these two pictures would not show the straight lines we see, but much more complex and messy structures: even the lines are not objectively there *as lines*, and have to be interpreted by the observer.) From a strictly objective point of view, a picture just *is* marks on paper — and wholly meaningless, or uninformative, to boot. From a subjective (interpretative) point of view, however, it may or may not contain lines, or coloured regions, or angles of various sorts.

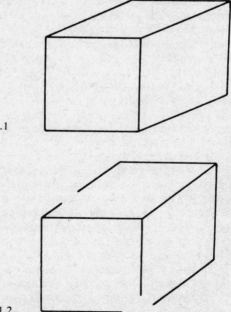

Figure 1.1

Figure 1.2

If the conceptual models of solid objects that are used by a visual system (whether program or person) in recognizing objects include no reference to colour, no way of mapping colour onto the objects concerned, then a colour photograph of them has *no* coloured parts *from the point of view of the object-recognizing section of the system*, even though other subsections may already have seen it as coloured. Similarly, sentences contain *no* grammatical parts, such as noun phrases, for systems (programs, babies or chimps) having no knowledge of syntax. Again, the behaviour of people in an alien culture will appear meaning*less* to an observer in so far as he does not share their implicit and explicit knowledge of the rules structuring the behaviour; and a neurotic's obsessional actions may equally seem meaningless to someone unable — or unwilling — to posit a set of mental schemata that could generate and so account for the neurotic 'symptoms'.

There are indefinitely many representational schemata one might employ in making sense, of one sort or another, out of a phenomenon. But any such interpretative schema requires an analysis of the phenomenon into the parts that it takes to be significant, and different questions may require reference to different parts, or cues. Whatever the specific details the parts of a picture — as of a sentence, or of any human action — are subjectively projected onto the picture (taking due account of the physical input provided to the eyes, or to the TV camera used by a program) rather than found objectively in it. Cues thus have to be defined intentionally, by reference to the method of representation assumed in the interpretative schema. It follows that *cue* is a concept that cannot occur within a strictly positivist psychology, and that cannot be straightforwardly identified with the behaviourist's *stimulus*.

Psychologists investigating animal and human, individual and social, or normal and pathological psychology have discovered many of the cues we take to be salient, many of the concepts we use in interpreting our world and acting accordingly. But they have in general been less successful in specifying how these cues are used, how these concepts are accessed and employed in everyday thinking. Even theorists who make some attempt to ask about the function of memory as well as its structure (for instance, Bartlett, Freud and Piaget) leave most of these questions unasked, and still more unanswered. They rely on intuitive inferences suggesting that such and such a thought process is possible (taking a policeman to be an analogue of one's father, for example), while saying very little, if anything, about just how this process is effected.

By contrast, theorizing in a programming mode forces the theorist to specify, not merely that a particular cue–schema pair is activated in a given psychological context, but how the cue is identified as such, how the potentially relevant schemata are accessed by it, how the most appropriate of these is identified in face of the essential ambiguity of the cue, and how the conceptual schema is used to mediate 'appropriate' thought and action. Many of the admittedly vague Gestalt notions, for example (such as the whole's being greater than the sum of its parts) can be more clearly (and more richly) formulated in computational terms. Programs already exist with an ability to pass from bottom-up to top-down processing and back again in the interpretation of highly ambiguous material, which are well suited to illuminating the sort of epistemological 'chicken or egg?' phenomena highlighted by the Gestalt psychologists.

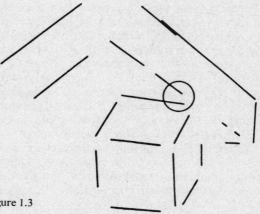

Figure 1.3

For example, a program which uses light-intensity gradients to construct line drawings on the basis of its input grey-scale TV picture may construct the lines shown in Figure 1.3. In trying to interpret this line drawing, it may first come across the two lines circled in Figure 1.3, and, quite reasonably, provisionally decide that they represent part of a corner of a wedge. On following these lines leftwards through the picture, it will even find some confirmatory evidence for this hypothesis. However, on consideration of the group of nine lines at the bottom-right of Figure 1.3 it will decide (as you doubtless do also) that these represent the sides of a cube. It follows that the two circled lines do not

constitute a genuine vertex (or corner-image) at all — a conclusion
that can be confirmed by noticing the two tiny little marks
representing the continuation of the upper circled line. Further
confirmation can be attained if the program accordingly directs its
line-finder to look again at the original TV input, adjusting the
physical parameters of its light-intensity measures so that the
expected lines and corners are 'filled in' by faint evidence that was
previously not noticed. This resolution of ambiguity is effected by
the program's sensible alternation between examination of
low-level details and interpretation by way of higher-level
schemata: cube and wedge are high-level with respect to line and
vertex, which are each high-level with respect to the grey-scale
image that is actually input to the program's visual sensors. In
much the same way, one and the same curve may 'be' a nose or a
chin in an ambiguous (old-young woman) picture of the type
studied by the Gestalt psychologists.[10]

It should be clear from these examples that a computational
model of man is radically antipositivist, in that it not only has a
place for subjectivity but gives intentional concepts pride of place
in its theoretical lexicon. Explaining why one program sees Figure
1.2 as a cube, whereas another (untroubled by Figure 1.1) does not,
necessitates appeal to the representations and interpretative
processes specified by the programs involved. To be sure, in order
to function at all the program has to be run on (embodied in) a
physical machine. But the important point is that the electronic
'physiology' of the computer is not a prime concern of the AI
worker who wishes to design or understand programs capable of
seeing Figures 1.1 and 1.2 as pictures of cubes. Computational
accounts cannot be replaced by electronic accounts without losing
sight of the intentional powers and properties of the system.

THE IRREDUCIBILITY OF PSYCHOLOGY

It is often assumed, by positivists and antipositivists alike, that any
basically mechanistic account of psychology must be inhumanly
reductionist in character. On this view, neurophysiology is
interpreted as implying that psychological phenomena are nothing
but brain processes, and the computational metaphor as implying
that people are nothing but machines — albeit machines fashioned
out of flesh and blood instead of tin-cannery. Supposedly, both
these approaches involve a commitment to the notion that
psychological explanations are in principle dispensable, that
everything that can be said in the 'human' vocabulary of values,
purposes, beliefs, actions and perceptions could in principle be

less misleadingly stated in terms of bodily mechanisms. Psychological language and theory, apparently, is at best a useful shorthand for neurophysiological matters (of which we are still largely ignorant, and which would take too long to state fully even if we had the knowledge) and at worst a mystifying illusion. Mechanism and reductionism are assumed to go hand-in-hand: and what could be more 'mechanistic' than an approach seeking to compare psychological phenomena to the computations carried out by electronic machines?

Despite the prevalence of these views, the previous section should have suggested that the computational metaphor does not view psychological terminology as dispensable. On the contrary, psychological vocabulary is deliberately imported into computational contexts to describe and explain what computer programs do. (Analogously, computational concepts are imported into neurophysiology in order to specify the functions which the brain is effecting, so that the physiologist may be in a position to ask how it is that the cerebral mechanism effects them.)[11] Philosophical justification of this *anti*-reductionist interpretation of the computational approach requires discussion of the concepts of reduction and mechanism, and of the relation between psychology and physiology.

The crucial point is that each of the key terms 'reduction' and 'mechanism' has two different senses. Given these distinctions, it is possible wholeheartedly to endorse the humanist stress on subjectivity in psychology without thereby jeopardizing the mechanist's firm insistence that psychological phenomena depend ultimately on causal processes within the brain.

One of the important senses of 'reductionism' in psychology is the (mistaken) view that psychological descriptions and explanations are mere shorthand for complicated sets of non-psychological statements about the brain, so that psychological statements could be translated into physiological ones without loss of meaning. This view is mistaken because intentional sentences, whose meaning involves the notion of subjectivity, have a very different pattern of logical implications from sentences that do not involve these notions. In technical terms, the logical peculiarities of intentional sentences include indeterminacy, referential opacity, failure of existential generalization, no implication of any embedded clause (or its negation), and non-extensional occurrence of embedded clauses.[12] More plainly, the intentional object (the object of thought that is mentioned in the sentence) can be described only by reference to the subject's thoughts (purposes, beliefs, expectations, desires). There may be no actual thing with which the object of thought can be sensibly identified; and even if there is, the identification will seem sensible on the basis of only *some* descriptions of the real thing, and the intentional object may be indeterminate in a way that no actual object can be.

For example, it does not follow from 'Hamlet intended to stab the man behind the arras' that 'Hamlet intended to stab Polonius', even though Polonius and the man behind the arras were one and the same, for Hamlet *did not know* that Polonius was behind the arras. Similarly, from the fact that someone sees pink elephants it

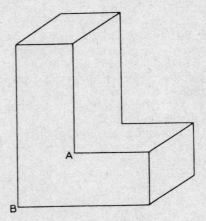

Figure 1.4

does not follow that there are any actual pink elephants (or even grey ones) to be seen. These all-too-human examples may be compared with the scene analysis programs mentioned in the section 'People, programs and positivism'. The more 'intelligent' visual programs can see an arrow-shaped vertex at the lower right-hand corner of both diagrams: but only in Figure 1.1 is there actually a vertex there. And even an intelligent scene analysis program may jump to mistaken conclusions, for instance in hallucinating a line joining points A and B in the L-beam of Figure 1.4.[13] Since intelligence is largely a matter of jumping sensibly to conclusions on the basis of the incomplete evidence which is all we ever have in a complex and rapidly changing world, making programs more intelligent will never exclude the possibility of their making mistakes.[14] Simply, like human beings, they may be expected to avoid the really stupid mistakes. But, stupid or not, illusory or veridical, the beliefs of programs must be described in basically intentional terms that share the range of logical peculiarities attributed to psychological vocabulary used in describing people.

Another reason why psychological language cannot be reduced to physiological terms (in the sense of *translation* into such terms) is that this language is basically computational in character.[15] It ascribes computational or symbol-manipulating processes (which are not so closely or rigorously specified as in the case of programs, but which are computational processes none the less) to the psychological system, saying nothing whatever about their physiological embodiment. It may not even be the case that computational processes falling clearly into one and the same class are all embodied by way of one and the same bodily mechanism (or electronic hardware): in fact, there are various reasons why this one-to-one correspondence between a class of computational processes and some unitary class of physiological events is highly unlikely to be the case. Each individual instance of computation, however, will of course be carried out by some particular series of cerebral events.

This raises the second sense of 'reductionism' to be distinguished: the view that subjective psychological phenomena are totally dependent on cerebral mechanisms, much as the information-processing functions of a program are grounded in the engineering details of the computer on which it happens to be being run. One can be a reductionist in this (second) sense without being a reductionist in the first sense. As the third section showed, proponents of the computational approach — whether in 'straight' psychology or in AI — in fact espouse this combination of views, which might be called an 'anti-reductionist reductionism'. (Essentially comparable views characterize philosophical debate concerning the relation between other pairs of sciences, such as molecular biology and quantum mechanics.)[16]

Passing from reductionism to mechanism, a 'mechanistic' psychology is sometimes defined as one that abandons conceptual schemes employing the subject-object distinction, and that refuses to interpret (or explain) behaviour in terms of meaning, phenomenology or purposive action. Psychologists who are 'mechanists' in this sense avoid subjective concepts if they can, and if they cannot they at least insist on their dispensability in principle: according to them, subjective or intentional concepts are mere convenient shorthand and could be replaced by a purely objective (non-intentional) vocabulary. It will already be apparent that computational theorists in general are not mechanists in this sense.

The second sense of 'mechanism' covers any psychology which

allows that subjective psychological phenomena can be generated
— and in a manner explained — by bodily processes. This is not to
say that psychological processes are identical with neural
processes (so this type of mechanism is not 'nothing-buttery'), nor
even that they are the effects of bodily causes. Rather, the crucial
notion in understanding how subjectivity can be grounded in
objective causal mechanism is the concept of an internal model or
representation; a concept which we have seen to be central to the
computational approach. It is possible for the categories of
subjectivity to be properly attributed to human beings because
bodily processes in our brains function as models, or representations, of the world — and of hypothetical worlds — for the
individual concerned. Since the 1940s, these cerebral models have
featured in neurophysiological theory, and much brain research
has focussed on asking how they are built up (or built in) in the
nervous system and how they are organized so as to influence
bodily action.[17] (The way in which programs influence computers,
by contrast, is already understood.)

To identify or describe the neural processes concerned *as*
models is itself to ascribe meaning, or intentionality, to them. They
could alternatively be described, at least in principle, at the level of
'objective' physiological events occurring at particular
neuroanatomical locations (such as the 'edge-finders' or 'bug-
detectors' within the visual systems of animals that have been
discovered by single-cell neurophysiology). At this level, however, their meaning cannot be expressed and so their (psychological) function in the life of the individual is lost to view. Even
so simple a neurophysiological concept as a 'bug-detector', for
example, is implicitly psychological in so far as it identifies a
functional relation within the animal's intentional world. Consequently, the categories of meaning, subjectivity and purpose
would still be required to describe a person as a psychological
being even if full neurophysiological knowledge were available.
Indeed, a large part of 'physiological' data would be expressed in
intentional terms. To forbid the use of such intentional language
would be to omit all mention of mental phenomena, since there is
no possibility of saying anything about the mind using only the
language of the body.

Correlatively, there is no possibility of specifying a computation, or of explaining it in terms of other computational
processes, if one limits oneself to electronic descriptions of the
engineering of the computer. The explanation of a program's
seeing Figure 1.2 *as* a cube, if it does, would require reference to
the program's inner model of, or expectations about, cubes —

including the ways in which cubes can appear to the eyes, considered as mere physical transducers. The knowledge that a (real) line can appear as an (actual) gap is a *computational* insight, having nothing essentially to do with either electronics or biochemistry.

It follows from all this that reductionism and mechanism do not necessarily go hand-in-hand. It is characteristic of the computational approach that it is reductionist only in the second sense defined above, and mechanistic only in the second sense also. Moreover, the complexity of the 'machines' (digital computers running complex AI programs) used as its tools and metaphorical exemplars is vastly greater — and significantly richer — than that of any previous machine. Likening a man to a machine was indeed insulting and basically dehumanizing in previous centuries, when this metaphor had to rely on relatively simple and inflexible (and non-representational) mechanisms such as the clock or the steam-engine. Even the cybernetic metaphor of the guided missile is not adequate to guide theoretical exploration of the computational nature of thinking, although it is closer to genuinely purposive behaviour than were the earlier mechanistic metaphors. With the advent of machines that store, transform and use complex and subtly structured inner models of their world, however, the psychologist has a metaphor for the mind that can do it considerably more justice than could any heretofore. Whether or not this metaphor will eventually elucidate *all* aspects of the human mind, it offers the psychologist an anti-reductionist version of mechanism that avoids the dehumanizing implications often mistakenly attributed to it.

In sum, the image of 'machine' provided by current computer science renders it intuitively less inconceivable that mental phenomena may be grounded in a mechanistic physiological base while also having a characteristically psychological guiding influence on bodily behaviour. The computational metaphor therefore contributes not only to theoretical psychology but to the philosophy of mind also, in that it illuminates the mind–body problem by suggesting *how it is possible* for an immaterial, computational process to direct bodily events. Associated problems concerning human purpose, self, consciousness, freedom and moral choice can each be clarified by this metaphor.[18] By this I do not mean that terms like 'free', for instance, can plausibly be applied to any computer example. But the computational distinctions that can be clearly made as between particular programs help one to suggest what may be the complex functional bases of the contrast between 'free' and 'involuntary' behaviour that each of us makes in daily life. Similarly, computation insights can make sense of some of the strange dissociations and the non-reciprocal coconsciousness between the different 'selves' that are observed in clinical cases of so-called split personality. For example, the well-known case[19] of Eve White and Eve Black involved two alternating personalities — demure and vulgar respectively — in the same body, such that Eve White had no knowledge of the experience or even the existence of Eve Black, but Eve Black knew everything that Eve White thought and experienced while the latter was temporarily in control of the shared body, and gleefully reported on it later to the psychiatrist. These phenomena are much less perplexing if we think of the two 'personalities' as different subroutines or modules of the same overall computational system, alternately using the same motor facilities and sensory apparatus, and having different degrees of access to each other's information or data-store. Not least, such insights can help clarify the way in which a person's aspirations and self-image can play a central role in the determination of action: persons and programs are not so different as they may seem.

CONCLUSION
The computational metaphor can help psychologists seeking a scientific understanding of the mind. Science can delight and fascinate because scientific metaphors and theories have their own kind of beauty. But, as Spinoza remarked three centuries ago, 'everything which is beautiful is as difficult as it is rare'.

   Some of the difficulties facing proponents of the computational approach have already been mentioned. The difficulties of validation include some that are general to all scientific enquiry, some that bedevil all psychological theories, and some that are specific to theories based on a programming methodology. The difficulties of implementing powerful computational theories lie less in the limitations of current hardware (though advances in hardware availability will undoubtedly contribute to theoretical progress), than in still unsolved theoretical problems concerning the expression and efficient use of large amounts of heterogeneous knowledge. The intuitive knowledge continually accessed by human minds must first be made explicit, and then — what is even more taxing — it must be organized and indexed in such a way (or multiplicity of ways) that the inferential processes of thinking can recognize when a particular aspect of the total knowledge is relevant, can find it when it is needed, and can use it sensibly, given the constraints of the situation in mind.[20] In addition, the computational approach has to face a political difficulty or philosophical prejudice, based on the popular view that to use machines of any sort as metaphors for the mind must be essentially dehumanizing. This difficulty can only be overcome to the extent that people can be made aware of the antipositivist and antireductionist features of the computational metaphor.

However, one often-cited 'difficulty' is not a difficulty at all. It is commonly claimed that no sense whatever can be made of talk about computers 'seeing', 'wanting', 'feeling', or even 'knowing'. The conclusion is drawn that computers are therefore useless as tools in the psychologist's search for scientific insight into *real* seeing, wanting, feeling and knowing. But this conclusion does not follow, even if one grants the truth of the premise (which in any event is philosophically controversial). Computational theories of the mind are no more than that: theories. One would not ask of a chemical theory that it fizz if put into a test-tube. Why, then, should one demand of a psychological theory that it see, or feel, if put into a computer? Psychologists try to understand human action and experience, not to mimic it; accordingly, their 'failure' to mimic it is irrelevant to their aims. In short, psychologists who espouse the computational metaphor are engaged not in science fiction, but in science.

NOTES

1   G. A. Miller, Eugene Galanter and K. H. Pribram (1960) *Plans and the Structure of Behavior*, New York: Holt.

2   A comprehensive discussion of recent work in this field is in M. A. Boden (1977) *Artificial Intelligence and Natural Man*, Hassocks, Sussex: Harvester Press. The early history of AI is described in a forthcoming book by Pamela McCorduck, to be published by Freeman Inc. Representative discussions by AI workers include: M. L. Minsky and Seymour Papert (1973) *Artificial Intelligence*, Eugene, Oregon: Condon Lecture Publications; Bertram Raphael (1976) *The Thinking Computer: Mind Inside Matter*, San Francisco: Freeman; P. H. Winston (1977) *Artificial Intelligence*, London: Addison-Wesley. Collections of relevant papers are in: R. C. Schank and K. M. Colby (eds) (1973) *Computer Models of Thought and Language*, San Francisco: Freeman; D. G. Bobrow and Allan Collins (eds) (1975) *Representation and Understanding: Studies in Cognitive Science*, New York: Academic Press. Many references to relevant psychological work are given in the notes to chapter 13 of my *Artificial Intelligence and Natural Man*.

3   M. A. Boden (1972) *Purposive Explanation in Psychology*, Cambridge, Mass.: Harvard University Press (to be published in paperback by Harvester Press); J. A. Fodor (1968) *Psychological Explanation: An Introduction to the Philosophy of Psychology*, New York: Random House; J.A. Fodor (1976) *The Language of Thought*, Hassocks, Sussex: Harvester Press; D. C. Dennett (1969) *Content and Consciousness*, London: Routledge and Kegan Paul; Aaron Sloman (1978) *The Computer Revolution in Philosophy: Philosophy,Science, and Models of Mind*, Hassocks, Sussex: Harvester Press; Allen Newell (1973) Artificial intelligence and the concept of mind, in R. C. Schank and K. M. Colby (eds) *Computer Models of Thought and Language*, San Francisco: Freeman, p. 160.

4   H. L. Dreyfus (1972) *What Computers Can't Do: A Critique of Artificial Reason*, New York: Harper and Row; Joseph Weizenbaum (1976) *Computer Power and Human Reason: From Judgement to Calculation*, San Francisco: Freeman; Alan Gauld and John Shotter (1977) *Human Action and its Psychological Investigation*, London: Routledge and Kegan Paul.

5   Allen Newell and H. A. Simon (1972) *Human Problem Solving*, Englewood Cliffs, N.J.: Prentice-Hall; Allen Newell (1973) You can't play 20 questions with nature and win, in W. G. Chase (ed.) *Visual Information Processing*, New York: Academic Press; pp. 283–310.

6   R. M. Young (1976) *Seriation by Children: An Artificial Intelligence Analysis of a Piagetian Task*. Basel: Birkhauser.

7   N. S. Sutherland (in press) Intelligent picture processing. In N. S. Sutherland (ed.) *Tutorial Essays in Psychology*, Vol 2. Hillsdale, N.J.: Erlbaum.

8   M. B. Clowes (1971) On seeing things, *Artificial Intelligence 2*: 79–116; M. B. Clowes (1973) Man the creative machine: a perspective from artificial intelligence research, in Jonathan Benthall (ed.) *The Limits of Human Nature*, London: Allen Lane pp. 192–207; Yoshiaki Shirai (1973) A context sensitive line finder for recognition of polyhedra. *Artificial Intelligence 4*: 95–120 (also available as pp. 93–114 of P. H. Winston (ed.) (1975) *The Psychology of Computer Vision*, New York: McGraw-Hill); L. G. Roberts (1965) Machine perception of three-dimensional solids. In J. T. Tippett et al. (eds) *Optical and Electro-Optical Information Processing*, Cambridge, Mass.: MIT Press, pp. 159–98.

9   Gilbert Falk (1972) Interpretation of imperfect line data as a three-dimensional scene. *Artificial Intelligence 3*: 101–44.

10   G. R. Grape (1969) *Computer Vision Through Sequential Abstractions*. Stanford University AI Department.

11   David Marr (1976) Early processing of visual information. *Phil. Trans. Royal Society B 275*: 483–524.

12   R. M. Chisholm (1967) Intentionality. In Paul Edwards (ed.) *The Encyclopedia of Philosophy*, Vol. 4. New York: Macmillan, pp.

201–4. Cf. M. A. Boden (1970) Intentionality and physical systems. *Philosophy of Science 37*: 200–14.

13   G. Falk. Interpretation of imperfect line data. Cf. A. K. Mackworth (1977) How to see a simple world: An exegesis of some computer programs for scene analysis. In E. W. Elcock and Donald Michie (eds) *Machine Intelligence 8*, esp. p. 524. Chichester: Ellis Horwood.

14   R. L. Gregory (1977) *Eye and Brain*, 3rd revised edn, London: Weidenfeld and Nicolson; R. L. Gregory (1967) Will seeing machines have illusions? In N. L. Collins and Donald Michie (eds) *Machine Intelligence 1*, Edinburgh: Edinburgh University Press, pp. 169–80.

15   J. A. Fodor (1976) *The Language of Thought*, esp. introductory section.

16   H. C. Longuet-Higgins (1970) The seat of the soul. In C. H. Waddington (ed.) *Towards a Theoretical Biology: 3. Drafts*. Edinburgh: Edinburgh University Press, pp. 236–41.

17   K. J. W. Craik (1943) *The Nature of Explanation*. Cambridge: Cambridge University Press.

18   M. A. Boden (1978) Human values in a mechanistic universe. In G. A. Vesey (ed.) *Human Values (Royal Institute of Philosophy Lectures, 1976–7)*, Hassocks, Sussex: Harvester Press.

19   C. H. Thigpen and H. M. Cleckley (1957) *The Three Faces of Eve*. London: Secker and Warburg. An even more complex case is described in Morton Prince (1905) *The Dissociation of a Personality: A Biographical Study in Abnormal Psychology*. New York: Longman.

20   M. L. Minsky (1975) A framework for representing knowledge. In Winston (ed.), *The Psychology of Computer Vision*, pp. 211–77.

2
Intentionality and physical systems

Intentionality is characteristic of many psychological phenomena. It is commonly held by philosophers that intentionality cannot be ascribed to purely physical systems. This view does not merely deny that psychological language can be reduced to physiological language. It also claims that the appropriateness of some psychological explanation *excludes* the possibility of any underlying physiological or causal account adequate to explain intentional behavior. This is a thesis which I do not accept. I shall argue that physical systems of a specific sort will show the characteristic features of intentionality. Psychological subjects *are*, under an alternative description, purely physical systems of a certain sort. The intentional description and the physical description are logically distinct, and are not intertranslatable. Nevertheless, the features of intentionality may be explained by a purely causal account, in the sense that they may be shown to be totally dependent upon physical processes.

I
The terms 'intentional' and 'intentionality' have been used in differing ways by different writers. Contemporary discussions of intentionality often draw heavily upon Brentano's account.[1] Brentano used these terms primarily in speaking of objects of thought, or mental events, such as a man's thought of a horse or a unicorn, or his belief that the earth is round or that it is flat. But in contemporary usage 'intentionality' is commonly given a somewhat wider sense, such that *intentional* sentences or verbs are identified as sentences or verbs whose meaning involves the notion of the direction of the mind upon an object. Accordingly, intentional verbs include not only 'believe', 'wish', and 'wonder', which have often been said to signify mental events — but also such items as 'ridicule', 'worship', and 'hunt', which signify pieces of overt behavior guided by thought.[2] I shall be using the words in this sense, so that I shall regard as 'intentional' all behavior which is guided by thought, or which requires for its explanation the notion of the direction of the mind upon some object. Any behavior which is guided by the purposes, desires, beliefs, concepts, or ideas of a psychological subject will therefore qualify as intentional behavior.

Brentano believed that intentionality is peculiar to psychological phenomena alone, and that it thus provides a criterion by means of which the mental may be distinguished from the non-mental. According to Brentano, intentionality is both a necessary and a sufficient criterion of the psychological. I shall not discuss the view that *all* psychological phenomena (including bare sentience and pain) are intentional. Rather, I shall be concerned with the view that intentionality cannot be based in a purely physical system, that there is some sharp logical *and* ontological distinction between intentional and physical phenomena. Chisholm has tried to express the difference between the mental and the physical in terms of purely logical distinctions. He hopes to find some list of logical properties which characterizes all and only intentional sentences, and which could therefore be used as a clear criterion of the psychological. One of his motives is that of supporting Brentano's thesis that no physical phenomena can be intentional. For Chisholm says that , if it can be shown that the sentences we use in describing intentional psychological phenomena have logical properties which are not shared by sentences describing physical phenomena, then 'the basic thesis of physicalism and the unity of science is false'.[3] I shall return to this claim shortly, but shall first say a little about Chisholm's suggested list of logical criteria.

Chisholm's original list was put forward in 1957, in his book on *Perceiving*,[4] but it has been amended by him more recently.[5] [6] Four of the criteria he has suggested are: failure of existential generalization; nonextensional occurrence; no implication of embedded clause or its negation; and referential opacity. It is clear that many intentional sentences *do* satisfy one of these four criteria. For instance, the first picks out the sentence 'John is thinking about a horse', for from the truth of this sentence we cannot derive the truth of 'There exists some horse which John is thinking about'. By contrast, the nonintentional sentence 'John is riding a horse' does imply the existence of some horse. Secondly, nonextensional occurrence picks out the sentence 'Plato believed that Socrates was a philosopher'; for from it we cannot infer 'Plato believed the world was round'. It thus differs from a nonintentional sentence like 'Either Socrates was a god, or Socrates was a philosopher'. Thirdly, from 'Plato believed that Socrates was snub-nosed', we can infer neither that Socrates was, nor that he was not, snub-nosed. But from nonintentional sentences such as 'It is true that Socrates was snub-nosed' or 'Socrates' difficulties in breathing were due to the fact that he was snub-nosed', we can derive the truth of the embedded clause. Finally, the criterion of referential opacity picks out the sentence 'Joe Martin believed that Dewey would be Truman's successor', for we cannot derive the sentence 'Joe Martin believed that Dewey would be Eisenhower'. By contrast, the sentence 'Joe Martin had lunch with Truman's successor' *does* imply 'Joe Martin had lunch with Eisenhower', simply because Truman's successor and Eisenhower were one and the same person.

However, these four criteria fail to characterize intentional sentences exclusively. For, while many intentional sentences satisfy one of them, so also do some clearly nonintentional sentences. For instance, failure of existential generalization applies to 'The dam is high enough to prevent any further floods'. Nonextensional occurrence covers 'It is necessarily true that if Socrates was a member of the class of philosophers, then Socrates was a philosopher'. No implication of the embedded clause or its negation is involved in the sentences 'It is contingent that Socrates was snub-nosed', and 'Possibly what caused the power-cut was that a swan flew into the wires'. And referential opacity characterizes 'It is necessarily true that if Dewey was Truman's successor, then Dewey was Truman's successor'. None of these sentences is intentional, in the sense of involving the direction of the mind upon some object; indeed, none of these sentences is psychological in any sense.

Chisholm has suggested that nonextensional occurrence and referential opacity can be saved as criteria by a modal condition which specifically excludes noncontingent sentences such as those used in the examples above. And he has offered two further criteria which purport to identify intentional prefixes (such as 'John believes . . .'), in terms of the logical properties of the sentences into which these prefixes are inserted, and of closely related sentences such as the universally or existentially quantified forms. But, as Cohen has recently shown,[7] these criteria also fail to provide necessary and sufficient conditions for the psychological. To be sure, each criterion clearly characterizes many intentional sentences, and clearly does not characterize most nonintentional sentences. They may therefore be useful in comparing intentional with nonintentional phenomena, and I shall refer to them again later on. But, as a purely logical criterion of the psychological, Chisholm's list fails. Cohen has remarked that:

The situation seems a characteristically philosophical one. Only by question-begging definitions of intensionality [*sic*] and/or psycho-logicalness shall we ever demonstrate, it seems, that the logical property of intensionality affords a sufficient and/or necessary condition of a proposition's constituting a psychological description. (*ibid*., p. 142)

That is, if we were to formulate necessary or sufficient logical conditions of intentionality, the universal coincidence of intentionality and the psychological would be merely trivially true. I therefore shall not attempt to draw up a list of such conditions, but shall rely rather on the more familiar (though less clearly analyzed) notion that many psychological phenomena involve the direction of the mind upon an object. These are the phenomena which I shall classify as 'intentional.'

I quoted earlier Chisholm's claim that if intentional sentences are logically unique, then the basic thesis of physicalism and the unity of science is false. This claim is a very strong one. It does not merely deny that intentional statements can be translated into or replaced by nonintentional ones without loss of meaning. Nor is it merely the claim that, once having identified a (behavioral) phenomenon in intentional terms, we cannot properly go on in the same breath to explain it by laws expressed in nonpsychological categories. It is the claim that there can be no necessary and sufficient causal explanation of any behavioral phenomenon as described in nonpsychological terms, if that phenomenon can also be correctly described as 'intentional'. The unity of science is indeed threatened, since this view implies that no neurophysiological explanation of psychological phenomena is in principle possible: if the body is a purely mechanistic system, then our intentional behavior cannot be completely determined by bodily causes.

Clearly, a type of example which would strongly support this view would be a case where a bodily event, even when initially described in nonpsychological language, required a psychological explanation. For, if the behavior had been initially identified and described as intentional, the necessity of an intentional explanation might be said to be due merely to a difference between causal and psychological *language*. From this it would not follow that there was any *ontological* distinction (threatening 'the unity of science') such that the phenomenon could not properly be alternatively described in purely causal terms. To take an analogy: it would seem at least logically *odd*, and perhaps *improper*, to say: 'That dog, Fido, is the father of that organization of carbon, nitrogen, phosphorus and water'; but, nevertheless, a puppy could be appropriately so described in a different context. From the category-difference between 'father' and 'phosphorus' it does not follow that biology and chemistry cannot be parts of a unified science. So, in rebutting Chisholm's view, I shall first discuss an example of behavior which seems to require a psychological explanation *even* when it is initially described in the language of muscle-movements, and which has often been regarded as a relatively clear case of the mind controlling the body. I shall try to show how a physical or physiological explanation could, in principle, account for this case; and how such an explanation could underlie the intentional characteristics of behavior.

II

My example is a type of pathological behavior which is commonly regarded as clearly psychosomatic in origin. When the physician Charcot was in charge of the *Salpêtrière* hospital in the late nineteenth century, his attention was drawn to certain strange cases of paralysis and anaesthesia — 'strange' in three ways. Firstly, there was no apparent physical injury or record of physical accident which could account for the paralysis or for the anaesthesia. Secondly, under hypnosis the 'paralysed' limb would move, and the 'anaesthetized' skin would be sensitive to stimuli which had no comparable effect before the hypnotic state was induced. This certainly suggested that there was no *simple* bodily explanation in terms of an injured sensory or motor nerve (or group of nerves) supplying the region in question. Moreover, the methods used to hypnotize the patients were such as to encourage the opinion that the phenomena required psychological explanation, explanation in terms of the mind rather than of the body. Charcot, and his associates and pupils (one of whom was the young Freud) did indeed explain these strange paralyses and anaesthesias in psychological terms, and so did many other workers who later discussed these cases. The precise theoretical terms they appealed to differed, as a few examples will show. The temporary paralysis of the limb was variously attributed to sexually based 'hysteria';[8] to 'suggestion';[9] to a 'secondary consciousness';[10] to 'dissociation of the personality';[11,12] and even to the workings of a separate, and subordinate, personality partially free from control by the dominant personality or self.[13]

We may feel that such 'explanations' in terms of 'the mind', 'suggestion', or 'subordinate personalities' are merely evasive labels for the problem, pseudo-explanations which have no place in a rational science and which should be replaced by neurophysiological explanations of proven respectability. Moreover, while a *simple* bodily explanation of the type I have mentioned is obviously excluded, since the muscle-movements which never occur in the unhypnotized state *do* occur under hypnosis, we may feel able to suggest in general terms how such phenomena may be satisfactorily explained. For the higher centres of the nervous system may be assumed to be capable of controlling the peripheral nerves so as sometimes to put them temporarily out of action, perhaps by blocking their normal paths of communication with other nerves. Consequently, the brain may function as a switching mechanism such that a given muscular movement is sometimes possible, and sometimes not. In this way, we may feel, all mention of the mind and all psychological terms can be avoided — and so much the better for that.

But then we shall be brought up against the third way in which these 'hysterical' phenomena are *strange*, and this is not so easily dealt with. The third feature itself has two aspects. Firstly, it is found that the extent, or boundaries, of the paralysis or anaesthesia is often of such a nature that it cannot be explained by any purely anatomical account, that is, one referring to a specific nerve or nerves being put out of action, whether because of lasting injury or because of temporary inhibitory control by the higher centres of the brain. The embryo grows on a segmental plan, with one pair of sensory and motor nerves supplying each segment; as a result, each nerve in the adult is distributed over a specific and clearly demarcated area, whether a particular group of muscles or a particular patch of skin. In these strange cases of hysterical paralysis, the muscles affected may not correspond to any group of muscles supplied by one or more nerves; and, similarly, the anaesthetic area of the skin may have limits which do not coincide with any anatomical boundaries corresponding to nervous distribution.

So far, then, we have a puzzle. But the second aspect of this feature of strangeness suggests to us a solution which may seem even more bizarre: the boundaries of the malfunction, whether paralysis or anaesthesia, may not correspond with real anatomical boundaries but they do correspond with something else — to wit, the layman's *idea* of anatomical boundaries. For instance, in everyday life an arm is conceived as a total unit which starts at the shoulder and extends down to the fingertips; its upper boundary is somewhat vague, but is roughly equivalent to the line of the arm-hole in a sleeveless shirt. Similarly, a hand is conceived as a unit bounded roughly by a line around the wrist, and so on. And the anaesthesia, in the cases we are considering, extends over *all* and *only* the skin covering the hand, or the arm, *as so defined*; likewise, the paralysis covers all and only the movements of *what the patient thinks of as* his hand, or his arm. Anatomically, the nerves supplying these areas also supply other (unaffected) areas. But the patient, we may assume, is like most of us unaware of these anatomical niceties. He has probably never even noticed that when part of his hand 'goes to sleep' after leaning heavily on his elbow, the side of his ring-finger next to his little finger will have lost its feeling, as will the little finger also, but the other side of the ring-finger will not. To him, a finger is a finger, and unless such facts are pointed out to him he just does not think of it as in any way naturally divided down the middle.

It seems, then, that we have found an explanation for at least one strange aspect of the hysterical paralysis or anaesthesia: its precise boundaries on the skin. But this explanation refers to a specific aspect of the patient's mind, i.e. his concept of, or thoughts and beliefs about, his 'arm' or his 'hand' and so on. It seems that we are forced to mention those psychological phenomena in explaining the particular motor or sensory malfunction concerned, and it is not at all clear that we could reasonably hope to give a neurophysiological account without mentioning these beliefs, or concepts, of the patient. The strange hypothesis of a subordinate personality being responsible for the paralysis or anaesthesia at least looks more respectable now that we see that explanation must be in terms of beliefs; for beliefs can be attributed to persons and cannot be predicated of brains. But how can this be? How *can* a person's concept of an arm affect his bodily reaction in such a manner? And does such psychosomatic control disprove the basic thesis of physicalism?

III

Can we postulate any physiological mechanism corresponding to the concept in a person's mind which would result in the behavior I have described? Or could we simulate a hysterical paralysis in some artificial physical system? And, if so, could a causal description of the physical mechanism make any intentional or functional explanations redundant? In this section I shall approach these questions in a general form; in the following section I shall develop an example in clarification.

The crucial step is for us to postulate that the brain somehow builds up *representations* or *models* reflecting various features of the environment; and that these models mediate between stimulus and response in determining the behavior of the organism as a whole. Being partly determined by them, behavior will naturally reflect their features. It may be clear from the structure of behavior that some representation of the world is available to the organism. For example, a passerine chick will crouch the first time it sees a hawk flying, and a female stickleback will respond in a species-characteristic fashion to her mate's 'dance'; these responses require the discrimination of one particular stimulus-class from others, and so we postulate some (innate) mechanism which is sensitive to this stimulus-class and which thus functions as a 'model' in the relevant sense. Similarly, in the pathological case I have described we are justified, on behavioral grounds, in saying that the patient has a certain representation or 'idea' of *a hand*. As we shall see, we may think of this 'idea' either in psychological (functional) terms, or in physiological (physical) terms. In postulating cerebral models underlying behavior we must initially identify them *via* behavioral features, but we may then enquire as to their neurophysiology.

A major source of the concept of cerebral models as controlling behavior is Craik's theoretical discussion, in which he said:

By a model we thus mean any physical or chemical system which has a similar relation-structure to that of the process it imitates. By 'relation-structure' I do not mean some obscure nonphysical entity which attends the model, but the fact that it is a physical working model which works in the same way as the process it parallels in the aspects under consideration at any moment.[14]

Craik discussed these models in very general terms, but his main point was that the brain may model environmental or abstract features that cannot properly be predicated of the models themselves. A cerebral model of a hand is not to be thought of as a little hand, but as something which *in certain respects* resembles a hand. As we shall see in the next section, a model of a hand might or might not be analyzable into independent models of parts of the hand (such as five fingers and a palm). And the relevant 'relation-structure' might involve not only features such as colors and shapes, but also the linguistic system learnt by the subject. In many cases of human behavior, the representation required to generate them may be nothing short of an internalized language. It may be objected here that this notion of 'modelling' is too wide to be useful, since language can express 'certain respects' in which *any* object resembles *any* other. But the basic sensory discriminations which enable us to 'fit' our language to the world must rely on some parallelism of physical relation-structures in the nervous system and the environment respectively; it is for the psychologist and the neurophysiologist to discover exactly which these parallels are. If any environmental property A is to be represented in the nervous system, there must be some neural property a which can have a range of values dependent on some different values of A. (A creature with no light-sensitive cells will not be able to see.) The range of possible values of a may parallel the range of A more or less closely. (A seeing creature may be colour-blind or not.) If different values of a are to be reflected in the behavior of the organism as a whole, then they must differentially influence the (typically cerebral) nervous parameters controlling overall behavior. (The retinae of cats and some fish are capable of color-discrimination; but the animals themselves are color-blind, since their central nervous systems are not of sufficient complexity to store this information picked up at the periphery, and so it is lost.) The values of a, b, and c must sometimes be directly determined by environmental features A, B, C, if the organism is to acquire any information about the external world in its interactions with the environment. But the values of a, b, and c may also be determinable relatively indirectly, so that representations or models of (actual or hypothetical) environmental features may be generated independently of experience of those features. Given appropriate values of the relevant parameters we could say that an organism had a model of *a purple cat*, even though no such animal exists.

As yet we are not able to attribute any particular cerebral representation to any living organism merely by identifying specific values of certain neural parameters. For very little is known about the detailed nature of the parameters crucial to complex brain-function, nor about the way in which cerebral models of the environment may be built up.[15] We can, to be sure, record the response of a single cortical cell which (earlier in the particular experimental session concerned) has been found to correlate with the presentation of a specific stimulus-class — e.g. *straight lines lying in a particular orientation*, or *frequency of auditory tone rising*.[16-19] But we cannot give a neurophysiological identification or description of the cerebral cells characteristically active (or the neural parameters involved) when someone sees, thinks of, fears or searches for *a purple cat*. We cannot specify the cerebral model of *a purple cat*, nor that of *a hand*. We can only postulate such models on behavioral grounds, and hypothesize that they correspond to actual neurophysiological mechanisms. It may, then, be asked whether such a hypothesis irresponsibly begs the question at issue: namely, whether any causal mechanism *can* be found underlying the 'concepts' and 'ideas' we attribute to persons, and accounting for their influence on behavior. But the actual example of computers which parallel logical or mathematical thought-processes to some extent, shows that it is not impossible for mechanistic systems to represent even highly abstract features of this sort. If information about external features (ranging from the finger-prints of some man to abstract logical relationships) can be somehow stored or represented in the machine, this representation may be referred to in any information-processing carried out by the machine which relates to the features in question. And the machine's overall performance will reflect the nature of its internal representations to some extent — as we shall see in more detail shortly. Psychologists are currently finding the concepts of information-theory and of cerebral modelling very useful in illuminating the control of behavior — for example, in discussing the visual constancies and visual illusions which have so far eluded explanation.[20] [21] Physiologists also use these concepts, in formulating questions about *what tasks* the nerve-cells are performing: though not much is known about which cells perform which task, and still less about how the cells are doing it. The precise details of how the information is stored in any particular physical system are crucial questions for the cybernetics engineer, and also for the neurophysiologist insofar as he seeks to regard the brain as an information-processing system. But they are not crucial questions for the philosopher. Nor, importantly, are they crucial for the psychologist either. His prime concern is with the overall structure and control-features of behavior, not with its physiological details. But it makes sense for him to suggest that the brain is an information-processing system which somehow models the environment (though we do not yet know exactly how), since physical systems — namely, computers — are already known which model or represent environmental features in a way which we fully understand.

IV

These concepts of internal modelling and information-processing can help in explaining the pathological behavior which I described earlier, and are also relevant to intentional behavior in general. To see how this is so, let us ask how we might attempt to simulate the motor aspects of a hysterical paralysis in a machine.

Suppose a computer built like a robot, with fingers and toes, upper and lower limbs, which can be flexed or extended just as human limbs can. The various wires carrying the electric currents responsible for these movements are distributed on a plan paralleling that in human beings. For instance, the wires leading to the little finger and the outside half of the ring-finger are encased together within the same insulating tube; only when they reach the base of these fingers do they separate to go to their final destinations. With this robot we could simulate what I have called 'simple' nervous injury, merely by cutting some wires. If we also provided a high-level switching mechanism in the head, we could simulate the temporary inhibition of particular nerve-groups which I mentioned before. But with the robot so far described we could *not* simulate the motor aspects of a hysterical paralysis.

Next we supply the robot's head with photo-electric cells, and attach variously coloured lights to the different parts of its body; it will now be able to discriminate its own bodily movements at an elementary level. Finally, we add some negative feedback mechanism such that an incipient movement may be immediately inhibited by a message from the central core of the robot. This feedback mechanism can be 'set' in different ways, so as to be activated for all and only those movements fulfilling certain criteria. How must this mechanism be set so as to generate performance simulating a hysterical paralysis? By means of the system of colored lights we can supply the robot with functional internal models, or simple 'concepts',[22] of the parts of its body, which will correspond to the human layman's ideas rather than to those of the anatomist. For the layman, five of the fingers and one palm together form the unit 'left hand', which is bounded by the wrist-joint. So all the colored lights which are positioned on those parts we list under one heading in the robot's memory-store; and the instruction 'Stop movement' is associated with that list-heading in the master-program. Clearly, if the negative feedback mechanism is thus connected to the heading 'left hand', the machine will show only incipient movements of any part of that hand; but it will be able to carry out other movements in a complete fashion.

If someone were to conclude from watching the behavior that the wire, or wires, supplying electric pulses to the hand were damaged — or even temporarily switched off at some higher level — he would be wrong. We could not explain the robot's performance merely by talking about the distribution of wires to the hand, but should have to mention the *model* or *concept* of the 'hand', instantiated in the core and connected to the negative feedback mechanism. Of course, there must be some very complex causal (electronic) account underlying the account using the terminology of information-processing. (Likewise, there is, presumably, some complicated physiological mechanism deter- mining the behavior in the human case.) But we do not need to know exactly what this is, since for our purposes the most illuminating account is the one which stresses the (representative) *functions* of the physical processes concerned. Since the high-level control directing the performance is primarily directed to the list-heading 'hand' (defined by the layman's 'visual' criteria) rather than to the hand's mechanical components, it would be unhelpful merely to list the components affected. Similarly, it would be unhelpful merely to list the affected muscles in a true case of hysterical paralysis. To understand *why* the structure of the behavior is as it is, we must refer to the concept of 'hand' involved, *even if* we know every mechanical detail. These details could be changed by engineers or surgeons, but the overall structure of behavior would remain the same: the hand would still be paralysed. This is why the purely causal account is insufficient to explain behavior even though it accurately lists all the physical factors determining the behavior in a given case. Such an account fails to point out that many different cases of behavior are all being directed by the same general model; the features of this model are reflected in the structure of behavior, and explain its overall pattern.

Were we to build a group of robots, we could build into them (or program them so as to build up for themselves) somewhat different concepts, or models. Any robot which was not provided with an appropriate concept of 'hand' just *could not* show the 'paralytic' behavior so far described, for no simple cutting or switching-off of any group of wires could effect such a result. The varying 'paralyses' shown by different robots could only be alleviated by cancelling the instruction in the master-program (perhaps tem- porarily, as in hypnosis), not by tinkering with the limbs themselves. If the robots had different internal models, their behavior could not be explained purely in terms of laws about robots (or even *these* robots) *in general* — for instance, in terms of the generic blueprints of their electrical circuitry or the principles of electronics. On the contrary, their behavior could only be fully explained (and successfully predicted) by referring to the details of information-storage within each individual robot. This is a first step to regarding each individual robot as a different psychological *subject*, its behavior varying from that of the other robots because of its *ideas* or particular *objects*; it is a first step to regarding the robot's behavior as *intentional*. (Of course it is only a first step: this robot simulates only *some* of the features of a true hysterical paralysis,[23] and only a very much more complex behavioral system could merit the use of psychological predicates without scare-quotes.)

V

How does our imaginary robot relate to the logical criteria of intentionallity suggested by Chisholm and others? It is charac- teristic of intentional propositions that their truth depends on psychological truths about the *subject*. It does not depend upon nonpsychological facts about the object, even assuming that there *is* something[24] in the material world which can be sensibly identified as the object of thought in the particular case. In particular, the description under which the object is thought of by the subject is crucial. It is this which suggests the application of intentional psychological predicates to the robots I have described, although such predicates can only be understood in an analogical sense when applied to robots as simple as these. For their behavior is idea-dependent, being governed by the concepts or models embodied in each individual robot rather than by the environmental input directly. And the intentional features remarked upon by Chisholm are present in sentences describing the performance of these machines.

For example, consider the criterion of referential opacity. We can say of our robot that it is avoiding moving its left hand (inhibiting movement of the left hand), and that it is avoiding moving the fingers of that hand; but we cannot truly say that it is avoiding moving that part of its body which is made up of such-and-such metals in such-and-such a combination. For this information is nowhere stored (represented) inside the robot. And, even if it were, we still could not say such a thing if this feature were not specifically connected to the negative feedback mechanism by the program, so that it acted as one of the criteria governing inhibition of movement. To say that the robot is avoiding moving these metallic components would be *untrue*, for it implies that the high-level control of its performance is directed to these components directly; whereas the control is in fact directed by more general ('visual') criteria defining *hand*. Thus the same performance would result if the components were rearranged, or replaced by others made of different metals.

Similarly, the indeterminacy of intentional statements remarked upon by Kneale (see ref. 2) could be exemplified if we gave the robot the instruction to raise a hand every ten minutes. Sometimes the left hand and sometimes the right hand would be raised, and either would fulfill the instruction. Whether the choice of hand were determined by some factor such as the current position of the limbs, or by regular alternation, or merely by a random operator, is irrelevant. Likewise, *any* cup of tea — weak or strong, Chinese or Indian — would satisfy the wish or demand for 'a cup of tea'.

Nonextensional occurrence would characterize phrases used in some sentences about our robot. For example, consider: 'The robot at time t_1 had the information that its foot was moving upwards'. Granted that its foot was so moving at that time, we could not substitute any true expression in the above sentence *salve veritate*: we could not derive the truth of: 'The robot at time t_1 had the information that Socrates was a philosopher'. Conversely, since in this sense the term 'information' (like 'opinion' and 'belief') does not imply truth, we could sometimes say truly: 'The robot at time t_2 had the information that its foot was not moving', even though this item of information was false. This state-of-affairs would occur, for instance, if the colored lights failed. But we could not derive: 'The robot at time t_2 had the information that Socrates was a greengrocer'.

Again, from 'The robot at time t had the information that its foot was moving', we can infer neither the truth nor the falsehood of the embedded clause, since we have no guarantee that the robot's mechanism was working properly at the time.

In general, any item of information stored in some system may be true or false. Its truth-value may depend primarily on some structural or mechanical feature of the system itself; or it may reflect the reliability of some other information-processing system (man or machine) which was the source of the item in question. Thus it follows that the simple sentence prefixes defined as intentional by Chisholm's two additional criteria include not only 'John believes' and 'John desires', but also 'The robot has in memory-store the information that'. Firstly, *every* sentence, whether it is itself contingent or not, is such that the result of prefixing it by this phrase is contingent (ref. 3, p. 203). And secondly, Chisholm's more complex criterion (ref. 3, pp. 203–4; cf. ref. 7, pp. 138–9) could also be satisfied by our imaginary case. This criterion deals with the logical relations between the universally and existentially quantified forms of sentences into which intentional prefixes have been inserted. For instance, the sentence: 'John believes that, for every x, x is material', does not imply: 'John believes that there exists an x such that x is material'. But these relations could also hold of the equivalent sentences about the robot's information-store.

Of course, they need not hold — for we could construct the

program such that the one sentence was always true, given the truth of the other. In those cases where these relations did hold, it would be irrelevant whether the set of sentences in question was specifically written into the basic program, or specifically provided as later input, or partially generated by the robot after a particular input-history. In like case, a man may be *told* that all unicorns are white, and that there are no unicorns; or he may *conclude* from illustrations that all unicorns are white, while keeping an open mind as to their existence. But these facts about the genesis of his beliefs are irrelevant to Chisholm's logical point, which is that a man might believe that all unicorns are white without believing that there are unicorns. Our robot might be programmed so as not to draw any existential inference from universally quantified propositions; in which case it could have the information that all unicorns are white, and yet not have the information that unicorns do exist.

Finally, consider the criterion of failure of existential generalization. Since a man may think of unicorns or search the skies for the planet Vulcan, neither of which exist, sentences containing the verbs *think of* and *search for* are intentional. So, too, are sentences stating some agent's purpose; for the end-state aimed at is always nonexistent insofar as it lies in the future, and is sometimes impossible of achievement (like squaring the circle). But our robot might be set to aim at a certain goal, which goal could direct its activity in various ways; and the goal might never be reached, for one of any number of reasons. For instance, we might give the instruction: 'Touch left elbow with fingers of left hand'. This would result in some movements for the robot could move its fingers *nearer* to its left elbow than they were before. But let us hope that it has been provided with some automatic stop-rule, so that it does not go on aiming at this unattainable goal for the rest of its days.

This latter example would probably not convince Richard Taylor who, in his discussion of mechanism and purpose, has derided 'the folly of speaking of machines as purposeful or goal-directed beings'.[25] He says:

An astronomer might search with his glass for the planet Vulcan, but no sense can be made of the idea of an automatic, self-guiding and self-adjusting telescope, of whatever complexity or elaborate design, undertaking a search of the skies for that planet; for no such planet exists. . . . There is no difference between two self-operating telescopes, one of which is designed to 'search' the skies endlessly, stopping at nothing, and the other of which is designed to 'search' the skies, stopping only if it chances upon the planet Vulcan. (*ibid.*, pp. 238–239)

It is true that there might be no difference in overt performance between these two telescopes, despite the difference in the minds of the designers. Similarly, our robot 'trying' to touch its elbow would perform the very same movements as one 'set' merely to flex the relevant joints maximally. And a quality-control machine in a canning factory would show the same performance if it was set only to reject overweight cans, as if it were set to reject underweight cans also but there happened to be no underweight cans on the conveyor belt. In all these cases the overt performance could be generated in the absence of any internal models, and might not seem to require explanation in terms of anything analogous to a 'purpose'.

But this is not the case if we consider a slightly more complex example. Suppose a robot built for manual library-retrieval: it can move along the lanes between the shelves, read the titles on the spines, pick out a book from its place on the shelf, and deposit it in the operator's briefcase. We give it the instruction: 'Find *The Spy Who Came In From The Cold*, by Ian Fleming'. Accordingly it looks for this item in the author-catalog, to find its detailed shelf-mark. Not surprisingly, it does not find it — for there is no such book. However, it allows for the contingency that the catalog-entry may be missing, and commences a physical search for the book. It sets its search-mechanism to '*F*', and moves along the lanes until it comes to the *F* section. Now it sets the mechanism to '*Fleming*' and moves accordingly; it ignores *George Fleming*, moving on to *Ian Fleming*; it moves up and down the *Ian Fleming* section (perhaps pausing awhile in front of *The Spy Who Worried*, if we allow ourselves to posit this hypothetical Fleming work); after ten minutes with no success it returns to the catalog room. At this point it may give up. Or, like some human beings in a comparable situation, it might allow for the possibility of faulty instruction: thus it may now search the title-catalogue, and find the entry for *The Spy Who Came In From The Cold* by John Le Carré. Accordingly it goes to the relevant shelf-mark, takes the book, and delivers it to the operator with the typed-out message: 'Was instruction faulty?' This performance is very different indeed from that of a robot designed 'to search [the library] endlessly, stopping at nothing'. Moreover, it could only be made fully intelligible (and capable of reliable prediction) by mentioning the instructions and search-rules controlling the performance, including the criteria for recognition of the book and the subroutines to be brought into play given certain kinds of failure. A purely causal account could in principle be given by an all-seeing engineer, but this would not be sufficient to describe or explain what was *really* going on. (This remains true even though in this case we could probably explain the whole episode in terms of the *operator's* predilections for bedtime reading. Whether the robot accepts a goal from this Svengali-figure, or generates it itself in the course of its operations, is irrelevant to the main point.)

VI

In sum: Those philosophers who have claimed that irreducibly intentional accounts are necessary to the explanation of behavior are correct. But this fact does not constitute a threat to 'the unity of science' in any way. We must suppose that behavior is largely mediated and controlled by means of internal — and often idiosyncratic — representations of the environment, rather than by the environment directly. Being mediated by them, behavior will naturally reflect their features as well as environmental conditions. It is this which accounts for the intentional characteristics of behavior, and which underlies the logical features remarked upon by Chisholm and others. Those who have stressed the close relationship between intentionality and intensionality (see ref. 2) are concerned to emphasize those cases where the 'representation' involved is a *verbal* form of thought. Explanation of behavior must include reference to these internal models, and to the general structure of the information-processing going on within the system, whether organism or computer. Description of the control functions of the system will include reference to its perceptual classifications (which may sometimes be faulty); to its hypotheses and beliefs (which may sometimes be false); to the tricks and heuristics it relies on in situations of difficulty (which may mislead it); and to its goals and purposes (which may be unachievable). This is why the use of one intentional term involves us in the use of others (see ref. 4, chapter 11). A causal account, although in a sense fully *complete*, cannot be fully *adequate*, for it cannot exhibit these structural features.[26] In spite of behavior which we most naturally explain in terms of 'the mind controlling the body', we need not abandon hope of a purely physicalist neurophysiology accounting for behavior at the causal level. It is not a special type of cause (nor any type of causelessness), but a particular type of physical *organization*, which allows us to speak of behavior as being directed by thoughts of non-existent objects and by purposes impossible of achievement.

NOTES

1   F. Brentano, *Psychologie vom Empirischen Standpunkt*, 1874. Partial translation in R. M. Chisholm (ed.), *Realism and the Background of Phenomenology*, Free Press, Glencoe, Illinois, 1960, pp. 39–61.

2   W. Kneale, 'Intentionality and intensionality', *Proceedings of the Aristotelian Society, Supplement*, 42, 73–90, 1968.

3   R. M. Chisholm, 'Intentionality', in *The Encyclopedia of Philosophy* (ed. P. Edwards) Vol. 4, 1967, pp. 201–204.

4   R. M. Chisholm, *Perceiving: A Philosophical Study*, Cornell University Press, New York.

5   R. M. Chisholm, 'Notes on the logic of believing', *Philosophical and Phenomenological Research*, 24, 195–201, 1963.

6   W. Sellars and R. M. Chisholm, 'Intentionality and the mental', in *Minnesota Studies in the Philosophy of Science*, 2, 507–539, 1958.

7   L. J. Cohen, 'Criteria of intensionality', *Proceedings of the Aristotelian Society*, 42, 123–142, 1968.

8   J. Charcot, *Oeuvres Complètes*, Vol. 9, 1890.

9   By the Nancy School, led by Liébault and Bernheim. Cf. H. Bernheim, *De la Suggestion et ses Applications à Therapeutique*, 1886.

10 W. James, *Principles of Psychology*, 1890.

11 P. Janet, *The Major Systems of Hysteria*, 1906.

12 M. Prince, *The Dissociation of Personality*, 1906.

13 W. McDougall, *Outline of Abnormal Psychology*, 1926.

14 K. Craik, *The Nature of Explanation*, University Press, Cambridge, 1943.

15 For relevant discussions of the neurophysiology of vision, see refs. 18 and 19 see also J. Y. Lettvin et al., 'Two remarks on the visual system of the frog', in *Sensory Communication* (ed. W. A. Rosenbluth), Wiley, New York, pp. 757–776, 1961 and J. Z. Young, *A Model of the Brain*, Clarendon Press, Oxford, 1964. For a general discussion of the neural parameters involved in cerebral information-processing, see B. D. Burns, *The Uncertain Nervous System*, Arnold, London, 1968.

16 E. F. Evans and I. C. Whitfield, 'Classification of unit response in the auditory cortex of the unanaesthetized and unrestrained cat', *Journal of Physiology*, 171, 1964.

17 E. F. Evans et al., 'The spatial distribution of unit characteristic frequency in the primary auditory cortex of the cat', *Journal of Physiology*, 179, 238–247, 1965.

18 D. H. Hubel and T.N. Wiesel, 'Receptive fields, binocular interaction and functional architecture in the cat's visual cortex', *Journal of Physiology*, 160, 106–154, 1962.

19 D. H. Hubel and T.N. Wiesel, 'Receptive fields of single neurones in the cat's striate cortex', *Journal of Physiology*, 148, 579–591, 1959.

20 R. L. Gregory, *Eye and Brain*, Weidenfeld, London, 1966.

21 R. L. Gregory, 'On how so little information controls so much

behaviour', *Bionics Research Reports*, Department of Machine
Intelligence and Perception, University of Edinburgh, 1968.

22   I have argued elsewhere (see M. Boden, 'Machine perception',
      Philosophical Quarterly, 19, 33–45, 1969) that complex machines
      could, in principle, possess concepts. I should not wish to claim that
      the 'concept' of *hand* possessed by the simple machine described in
      the present paper is a strong candidate as an example of a
      machine-concept. But this does not matter for my present purpose:
      it is enough that the 'concept' here described could contribute to the
      fuller concept of a more complex machine.

23   For example, the paralytic performance as described is arbitrary
      with respect to any of the machine's overall goals; but the clinical
      syndrome usually serves some purpose, such as defending the
      patient from certain traumatic situations. Charcot remarked that the
      aetiology of such cases was always sexual; but the Great War saw
      similar cases of 'shell-shock' paralyses which clearly functioned as
      a protection from the front-line. Such alternative defensive
      purposes are not represented in the simple robots I have described.
      Nor have I represented the unconscious, and seemingly involun-
      tary, nature of the clinical cases; this could be approached by
      varying the degree of interdependence and the availability of
      information-exchanges between the master-program and the
      various sub-programs. Again, the patient does not normally have to
      look at his limbs in order for the paralysis to occur — he presumably
      relies upon kinaesthetic information; this could be easily rep-
      resented in a robot where information as to the start of any
      limb-movement was relayed to the master-program as a matter of
      course, and then monitored by it.

24   What Elizabeth Anscombe refers to as the 'material object' in G. E.
      M. Anscombe 'The intentionality of sensation', in *Analytic
      Philosophy II* (ed. R. J. Butler), Blackwell, Oxgord, 1965, pp.
      158–180.

25   R. Taylor, *Action and Purpose*, Prentice-Hall, New Jersey, 1966.

26   See *ibid.*, p. 229: 'An engineer of suitable training can describe and
      explain the mechanics of [guided missiles and all 'goal-directed'
      machines] without needing any concepts whatever except those of
      physical science, and in particular, he can give a *complete* and
      adequate explanation without once introducing the idea of a
      purpose or goal.' (Italics in original.)

3
Artificial intelligence and intellectual imperialism

I: INTRODUCTION

Intellectual imperialism, like the political variety, comes in aggressive and in paternalist modes. The aggressive mode is based in the belief that no approach to a particular area of debate is worth pursuing unless it is governed by a specific principle, or guiding idea, which alone has any intellectual authority. The paternalist mode tolerates, even appreciates, differently principled approaches. But it sees its own authority as relevant to *all* points within the given area, no distinctions being drawn between those things that are God's and those that are Caesar's. The arrogance and insensitivity of the aggressive imperialist are missing. But the paternalist shares the common imperialist belief that, within the area concerned, all enquiries could benefit from some allegiance to the preferred intellectual regime. Both types of imperialism may be manifest in crusades, and both foster resistance movements — but crusade and resistance alike are fiercer in the aggressive than in the paternalist case.

Crusades, and their respective oppositions, are hardly uncommon in psychology. If one thinks of Kuhn's account of scientific paradigms as a description of the rise and fall of intellectual empires, then psychology is all imperialism but no empire. For there is no normal science, in Kuhn's sense, no universally accepted way of conceptualizing theory and experiment in psychology. It is as though opposing armies were fighting battles in order to win the right to define the nature of the war. Humanists, phenomenologists, behaviourists, sociobiologists . . . the armies are legion indeed. And the prize will be a power to influence basic presuppositions about human beings and society that are held by civilians no less than the militia. It is largely because the non-combatant population will be so intimately affected by the 'model of man' heralded by the victor that it is important enough to be a cause for battle.

Recently, a new intellectual force has entered the field. Its members see artificial intelligence (AI) as relevant to psychology, insofar as they take a computational approach to psychological phenomena. The essence of the computational viewpoint is that at least some, and perhaps all, aspects of the mind can be fruitfully described for theoretical purposes by using computational concepts. These concern rule-governed symbol-manipulations within information-processing systems in general, whether living or not. Computational processes, that is, are processes of symbolic transformation whereby information is stored, classified, and indexed: plans are formed, executed, and monitored; concepts are formed, extended, and linked; inferences are made and hypotheses tested; decisions are taken and later evaluated; memory is searched; problems are formulated and solved; interpretations are constructed; symbol-structures are compared . . . and so on. Their clearest embodiment is in computer science and AI, wherein rigorously defined computational concepts can be used to specify qualitatively distinct types of data-representation and transformation. This is why, although the computational approach in psychology is primarily concerned with these abstractly defined information-processes, writing and running computer programs is an important methodological weapon in the computationalist's armoury.

This new force has been called 'the artificial intelligentsia', a contemptous term used by its opponents not merely to mark the influence of AI research on its members' thinking, but also to suggest something unnatural or inhuman (not to say anti-human) about their position. Specifically, the suggestion is that the model of man that is implicit in psychologies influenced by AI is inadequate to allow for — still less to explain — phenomena such as subjectivity, purpose, emotion, creativity, and consciousness. Even intelligence itself, or so the suggestion goes, cannot really be illuminated by such an approach, which must necessarily ignore what is most distinctive and valuable in natural intelligence. The AI approach, it is said, involves an intellectual imperialism that rejects all other approaches to psychology as a waste of time, being based on sentimental and irrelevant models of man. On the contrary, say its critics, the computational viewpoint accepts a deeply misleading model of humanity that reduces us to the level of unthinking, unfeeling tincans.

Do psychologists who are convinced of the relevance of AI necessarily believe that it is germane to all areas of psychology, and that no other approach is useful? And is their psychology implicitly dehumanizing in its implications? I shall address these questions by way of asking whether and in what sense AI leads to imperialism in psychology.

II: AI AND AGGRESSIVE IMPERIALISM
Let us admit it: there are people within AI, as in other

psychological camps, who are imperialists of the most aggressive sort. Such people think, and sometimes tactlessly say, that traditional approaches to scientific problem-solving in psychology are essentially a waste of time. Behaviourists, Piagetians, Freudians, phenomenologists . . . all are misguided in their different ways. The only way forward is a computational one. This imperialism is focussed on the 'core' questions of consciousness, subjectivity, creativity, and emotion no less than on the more bread-and-butter issues of memory storage and motor skills. Far from being irrelevant to consciousness, AI is thought by proponents of this extreme imperialism to be the only approach that can throw light on the riddle of consciousness.

Insofar as such attitudes are expressions of eccentric personalities or the arrogance (and ignorance) of enthusiastic youth, they bear no relation to the intellectual essence of the computational approach. They may harm the computational cause in practice, because of the irritation and hostility they arouse in psychologists generally, but do not show it to be absurd in principle.

However, there is a more reasoned, and reasonable, version of aggressive imperialism which it is important to understand. This version typically gives credit to other psychological methods for the wide range of phenomena they have uncovered. But they see most psychologists as doing 'natural history' or fact-gathering rather than respectable theorizing:

Computer science has brought a flood of ideas, well defined and experimentally implemented, for thinking about thinking: only a fraction of them have distinguishable representations in traditional psychology . . . . But just as astronomy succeeded astrology, following Kepler's discovery of planetary regularities, the discovery of these many principles in empirical explorations of intellectual processes in machines should lead to a science eventually.

The reference to astrology should not lead one to think that these imperialists regard the traditional psychology of the past as a waste of time. For much of interest has been found out. With respect to the problem of consciousness, for example, many psychologists have contributed useful descriptions of conscious phenomena that will have to be borne in mind by anyone theorizing about it.

To mention just a few examples, work as diverse as Freud's and the experimental studies of subliminal perception sketch the range of influence on consciousness of unconscious processes of a kind significantly similar to those that we can introspect. Penfield's studies of the temporal cortex provide phenomenological support for the notion that a conscious memory of one and the same event may differ in nature according to whether it does or does not arise from (computationalists would say 'is or is not generated by') a complex system of associations in the mind, as opposed to an arbitrarily introduced physiological stimulus. And the many studies of perceptual masking and meta-contrast provide persuasive evidence that percepts are constructed within the mind, that the construction takes an appreciable time, and that certain processes within the overall constructive activity can be interfered with by others in various ways. Finally, the reports of clinicians dealing with cases of so-called 'multiple personality' have highlighted the strange fact that two or more apparently distinct minds can co-exist within the same body; even stranger, these may be non-reciprocally co-conscious, in the sense that personality A may have direct access to the thoughts and experiences of personality B, being able to remember and report them later and sometimes to influence B's actions accordingly, whereas personality B has no knowledge of the existence of personality A except as hearsay.

Many other examples could be given, but the general point here is that the AI-theorist may feel that we no longer have need of further facts such as these. Rather, we need to concentrate on seeking explanations that really are adequate to account for such phenomena, as the current 'theories' are not. Experiments in psychology thus tend to be regarded unfavourably by such people, who say either that they merely add more (unexplained) data or that they are theoretically uninteresting because of the conceptual vagueness and structural and procedural poverty of the theories they are supposed to be testing. In general, empirical studies based on the positivist *dependent–independent variable* model are not well-suited to capture the underlying generative structures and computational processes by which alone psychological phenomena can be theoretically understood. Even those studies that are aimed at underlying psychological processes typically fail to realize the existence of huge theoretical lacunae in their 'explanations' — lacunae which a computational viewpoint would at least have recognized, if not filled.

For instance, in commenting on the recent and admittedly 'fascinating' studies of symbol-using in chimps, a computational theorist has complained:

In the long run we shall all learn more if we spend a little less time collecting new curiosities and a little more time pondering the deeper questions. The best method I know of is to explore attempts to design *working* systems that display the abilities we are trying to understand. Later, when we have a better idea of what the important theoretical problems are, we'll need to supplement this kind of research with more empirical studies.[2]

As an example of the 'new curiosities' referred to here, we may take the symbolically-mediated co-operative problem-solving shown by chimps in Rumbaugh's experiments.[3] Using arbitrary symbols that it punched on a teletype, and which are automatically displayed in the adjoining room of a second animal, one chimp was able to ask another for a specific tool required to reach some food hidden by the experimenter in the first chimp's room. Only this chimp knew where the food was, and whether a long pole, or a key, or a spanner . . . was required to reach it, because while it was being hidden the window between the two rooms was covered. But only the other chimp had access to a toolbox. Both chimps shared the food once it was found. Both animals had initially been individually trained to associate a given symbol with a given tool, as well as learning which tools were effective for which hiding-places. If the teletype was put out of action, so that the first chimp was reduced to mere gesturing within view of the second chimp, the communicative success dropped drastically. Moreover, the nature of the first chimp's reaction to a 'typing error' (noticed by it when the second chimp picked up the unwanted tool which had been asked for in error) made it quite clear that something of the symbolic function of the teletype was somehow understood by the animal.

Examples of the 'deeper questions' involved here include these: How is it possible for a creature (of whatever species) to form means-end plans for reaching a desired object, plans within which other objects are represented as instruments to the overall end? How is it possible for an external symbol, as well as one in the internal representational medium of the creature's mind, to be employed by one animal and recognized by another as a request for a specific tool? How is it possible for an animal (or a human being) to realize that the tool being selected is not the one that was intended, and that the way to overcome this obstacle is immediately to change the symbol displayed while gesturing to draw one's colleague's attention to *the new symbol*, rather than to the desired tool? How is it possible for someone to represent to themselves that a long pole can be used in such-and-such a way to push a banana out of a tube, whereas a key used thus-and-so is required to get it out of a padlocked box? And so on, and on . . . .

These questions were not treated *as questions* by the experimenters concerned, so much as *as answers*. That is, these capacities were cited by them as 'explaining' the observed co-operation between the chimps, as though these capacities were themselves psychologically unproblematic. But the attempts to design working systems with comparable abilities show, to the contrary, how little is yet understood about their underlying psychological structure. Psychological theories of a non-computational type characteristically take such human and animal competences for granted, whereas the basic psychological problem is to explain them.

For instance, Rumbaugh's experiments may surprise us by showing an unexpected degree of co-operation between chimps able to use external symbols. But they afford no hint of how such co-operation can possibly occur, in whatever species, because they do not illuminate the nature of the organism's *internal* 'language' or representational medium, within which computational processes of inference and symbolic transformation take place to mediate complex experience and behaviour.

The aggressive imperialist insists that the only way of approaching such questions is to attempt to express our psychological theories as computer programs. A program (or subroutine) which could offer appropriate instrumental advice to another program (or subroutine) encountering a specific type of difficulty in achieving its current goal would suggest *how it is possible* for such co-operation to occur. Some relevant programs have already been written, which indicate the dimensions of the questions that need to be asked though they provide only the sketchiest of initial answers. One of these embodies problem-solving procedures for classifying the nature of the problem, selecting a potentially fruitful method of approach, monitoring and evaluating execution of that method, changing tack to a preferable method, and even changing back again (with appropriate suggestions as to how to fix the hitch that initially led to abandonment of this method) in certain circumstances.[4] Another incorporates a simple theory of how one goal-seeking system can co-operate with another only if each has some representation of the other's goal and current beliefs, as well as its own.[5] The AI-theorist would expect many of the representational and procedural constraints on problem-solving within co-operative programs such as these to be relevant also to the problem-solving that is going on in Rumbaugh's chimps. *That* it goes on in chimps is surprising, but *how* it goes on is mysterious. The aggressive imperialist regards the production of surprises as no substitute for the illumination of mysteries.

Aggressive imperialism shades into the paternalist variety, and might even be dubbed a 'paternalism of the past', insofar as it pays tribute to past discoveries in the 'natural history' of psychology. But what is important and worthwhile *now*, according to this view, is to define the problems and outline possible answers in computational terms. For only these are sufficiently rigorous to promise real theoretical advance. The notion that new evidence might alert us to computational possibilities that otherwise we might have missed is assumed to be very improbable. In sum, the best methodology is first to express psychological theories as computer programs, before seeking evidence of an experimental kind. The truly aggressive imperialist believes that the second methodological stage will not be reached for many years: meanwhile we will, and should, have our hands full trying to cope with the first.

III: AI AND PATERNALIST IMPERIALISM

Paternalist intellectual imperialism appreciates the contribution of different approaches, but like the more aggressive variety holds that there is *no* topic within the intellectual area concerned that cannot be illuminated to some degree by its own methods. Applying this to what is commonly seen as the most intransigent topic for the AI-theorist, namely consciousness, paternalists will of course admit that various psychological approaches (some of which were mentioned in Section II) have contributed to our knowledge of consciousness. And they will typically encourage further study along these various lines. But they will insist that a scientific understanding of consciousness can be advanced by taking a computational perspective. How could this possibly be, given the apparent gulf between conscious living creatures and mere tin cans?

Let us take as an example the phenomenon mentioned in the previous section, of non-reciprocal co-consciousness between the different 'personalities' within a case of 'multiple personality'. This phenomenon is strange not only in the sense that it is very unusual (as would be a purple-spotted cow). More interestingly, it is strange because our usual ways of thinking about consciousness give us no clue as to how it might be *possible*. Still stranger, we are used to thinking about the mind and consciousness in a way that suggests such phenomena must be downright *impossible*. The many claims within philosophical writings about the unity and indivisibility of consciousness, not to mention those which regard the higher mental processes as always open to introspection, bear witness to this. If we saw a purple-spotted cow, we would hypothesize some genetic mutation, environmental pollutant, or practical joker with a paintbrush. We would not regard the surprising creature as an existent impossibility, as a contradiction of the most basic principles of our thoughts about cows. But this is precisely how the phenomena of multiple personality may strike us.

However, thinking of the mind on the analogy of a complex computer program may help to make these phenomena intelligible. The various subroutines within a complex program may have differential access to each other's operations, both in terms of information about the actions and effects of each other's operations (mere monitoring) and in terms of possible interference with the actions of other subroutines, whether to help or to hinder. Similarly, the data-base or information-store accessed by one subroutine may or may not be the same as that accessed by another, and changes in one may or may not be automatically copied into the other. Moreover, such structural features of the program can readily be varied at different times (and for different reasons) within the running of the program. So two subroutines that 'normally' have access to the same memory-store and/or to each other's activities may 'abnormally' be dissociated from each other to some degree. Moreover, the AI-theorist would expect that at least some of the functional reasons that a programmer might have for building or for avoiding such a system might throw some light on the functional significance of dissociated personality in the human case. (Whether or not such clinical cases are the effect of experimenter bias, as has been claimed, is irrelevant: we are here concerned with the *possibility* of the phenomenon, not with its specific aetiology in actual cases.)

Similarly, the apparently paradoxical cases of aphasia, apraxia, and agnosia that are reported in the clinical literature, and that undermine our usual assumptions about the nature of consciousness, are more readily intelligible with the help of the computational metaphor. For example, programs that solve problems have to be provided with distinct procedures for distinguishing means-end hierarchies, for planning an overall sketch of the solution whose details must be filled in later, for translating such a plan into detailed execution, for monitoring the results of the action taken so far, for anticipating the effects of actions yet to be done . . . and so on. Workers concerned with clinical agnosias are currently looking to these specific computational concepts to aid in the detailed structural description (and perhaps eventually the explanation and cure) of their patients' anomalous behaviour in situations of practical problem-solving.[6] And theories of conscious and unconscious processes within the mind are commonly stated today with computational concepts to the fore.[7]

Someone might object that none of this even touches on, still less solves, *the* philosophical problem of consciousness. For computational theories, just like other psychological theories, 'bracket out' such philosophical questions, being content to take the existence of consciously experienced qualities as given. But the important point is that, even if one merely accepts experience as a given fact, the essential nature of such experience can to some extent be illuminated by a computational approach — as the example of dissociated personalities shows. And any adequate philosophical account of consciousness would have to be able to embrace and account for these clinical and everyday phenomena, which the Cartesian tradition (whether the Continental phenomenologist or the British Empiricist branch) strictly cannot.

Another example of a phenomenon that has seemed troublingly paradoxical to many psychologists and clinicians is the case of hysterical paralysis. As Charcot (watched by the young Freud) showed a century ago at the Salpetriere hospital, there is no neurological injury causing such paralyses. Even stranger, the limits of the paralysis correspond quite clearly to the patient's everyday concept of bodyparts, such as an arm, leg, or hand. The neuromuscular distributions discovered by anatomists do not support the idea, for example, that an arm is an anatomical unit bounded by the line of the armhole of a sleeveless shirt. But this is how we usually think of an arm, and this idea evidently constructs the limits of the malfunction observed in the hysterical patient.

There could be no clearer example of the influence of mind on body, but such influence is inexplicable if not impossible for most psychological theories. Empiricists (whether introspectionist or behaviourist) cannot explain it, and though phenomenologists — who make much of the close mutual relations between mind and body — are happy to cite such cases, they cannot give any well-understood non-psychological analogy in terms of which to make them more clearly intelligible.

The computational approach, however, can. Suppose a robot were to be anatomically constructed with joints, wires, and levers parallelling the human pattern of nerve-muscle connections, and suppose that it were given the programmed capability of monitoring its own actions (for example by visually inspecting the position of its bodyparts). It could be told to inhibit any incipient movement of its right arm, provided that the concept of its 'right arm' were defined for it (represented internally by it) in some way. Supposing that its inner representation, accessed by the inhibitory program, defined its arm as 'that part of my body distal to the sleevehole line', then it would exhibit behaviour comparable to that generated by the patient with a hysterical paralysis. Yet all its wires and levers would be physically intact. In short, the robot's internal representation of its arm, rather than any genuine anatomical feature of the arm itself, would be guiding its behaviour and inducing the functional paralysis.

It follows that some descriptions and explanations of the robot's behaviour (namely, those that are not purely mechanical and electronic, or 'physiological'), would have to involve an irreducible reference to this inner representation. As I have shown in detail elsewhere, such descriptions and explanations would share the various logical features characteristic of *intentionality*, which is so stressed by those theoretical psychologists who favour a subjective or hermeneutic account of the mind.[8] What the robot believes to be (or represents to itself as being) the case may be more important in explaining its behaviour than what actually is the case. The robot's arm *is not* an anatomical unit bounded by the sleevehole-line, any more than is a person's, for as in the human case the wires and levers which move the robot's arm also move other parts of its body which are not affected by the functional paralysis. But the robot's representation of its arm as such a unit is crucial in mediating the paralysis.

In this, paralytic programs resemble Polish peasants: Thomas and Znaniecki's seminal concept of the 'definition of the situation' similarly stressed the theoretical importance for social psychology of what is believed to be the case rather than what actually is the case. Hermeneutic psychologies in general take as theoretically basic the inner models of one's world and wants that make possible the subjectivity of experience and behaviour. The concept of *representation* (and its close cognates, *meaning*, *interpretation*, *construction* . . .) being central to AI also, the AI-paternalist has a specific philosophical justification for accepting the relevance of hermeneutic approaches to psychological problems, and cannot be accused of a woolly minded eclecticism that tolerates all views while basically respecting none. Hermeneutic, as opposed to behaviourist, views in psychology have in common with the computational approach that they emphasize the mental representations and transformational processes that guide intelligent, purposive action, and give to experience and behaviour their irreducibly intentional character.

For instance, surprising as it may be to people of a 'humanist' or 'anti-mechanistic' cast of mind, psychoanalytic and Gestalt writings are both closer to the computational viewpoint than are behaviourist theories, because they try to articulate some of the psychological processes and representational structures that underlie behaviour and consciousness. They encourage one to ask such questions as how it is possible for one and the same area of ink to be interpreted now as a young woman's chin, now as an old hag's nose; or how it is possible for a person to say 'Botticelli' when what they wanted to say was 'Signorelli'. The Freudian and Gestalt answers to these questions employ concepts of a broadly computational character, though they lack the rigour and specificity of symbol-manipulation concepts that are definable in programmed terms. Similarly, ethogenic and ethnomethodological approaches are basically compatible with AI insofar as they stress the underlying rules and representational metaphors (such as dramatic metaphors) that inform human behaviour. Social psychological concepts such as *role*, *attribution*, and *dissonance* similarly focus on the use and construction of representations of social behaviour that are stored in the mind of members of a given society, some of which are of course more culture-bound than others. Even Laingian psychology stresses the guiding role of internal representations of Self and Other, and their reciprocal perceptions, in a way that one might express in computational terms, so that Laing's view of schizophrenia as an intentional construction rather than a physiological symptom is compatible with an AI approach.

This is not to say that anyone interested in schizophrenia should rush to the computer terminal, eschewing all personal interaction with schizophrenics, and spending no time on statistically informed studies of possible hereditary and biochemical factors. The difference between proponents of the aggressive and paternalist modes of AI-imperialism is precisely that the latter expect some useful insights (theoretical as well as practical) still to be found by such methods whereas the former do not.

In general, AI-paternalists (unlike their aggressive fellows) are concerned to develop methodological principles of validation whereby psychological findings of a more traditional or experimental kind may be matched against the performance of complex programs. In a recent discussion of the computational approach to cognitive psychology, Pylyshyn has detailed a number of methods whereby strictly psychological data can be used in the validation of programmed models. But even he, paternalist (and professional psychologist) as he is, expresses sympathy for the more aggressive view that 'these experimentally based methods are relatively weak and may be most useful after some top-down progress is made in the understanding of methods sufficient for relevant tasks — such as may be forthcoming from artificial intelligence research'.[9]

(It is relevant to our example of consciousness to note that in an earlier paper Pylyshyn showed that the AI-approach is helpful even in the study of mental imagery — hardly a topic beloved of the behaviourist.[10] The recent upsurge of interest in imagery arose from 'traditional' areas of psychology, but is increasingly being pursued with computational concepts in mind. Some AI-paternalist groups, such as Marr's at MIT, are specifically trying to integrate AI-insights with psychological and neurophysiological evidence about vision, and are writing their programs and formulating their theories accordingly.)[11]

Pylyshyn reminds us that it is even difficult to know where attempts at validation should start, quite apart from the difficulties inherent in interpreting the result of a 'validatory' test. The reason for this is that a complex computer program, even one written with the specific aim of simulating psychological reality, will have many features that have no theoretical significance for the psychologist — and it may be a 'formidable' task to decide which these are. Some will be so obviously tied to the constraints of a particular programming language or machine architecture that no-one would be misled into assuming that they were psychologically relevant (though even here, 'obviously' is a relative term: *vide* the common confusions over whether the serial nature of current computers does or does not make them essentially inappropriate for psychological simulations).[12] But others may be more questionable.

For instance, work on problem-solving and programming languages (including that involved in Winograd's well-known language-using program) has shown the computational value of carrying a continually up-dated 'context' through the task and of storing it if and when backtracking is needed so that it can be used to guide future choices in a task-appropriate way.[13] This suggests that equivalent types of question might be fruitful in the psychological study of the role of memory in problem-solving, but does not settle the question of just how close to the original computational example (for example, the specific programming languages) the empirical psychologist should stay. Similarly, computational considerations can show the advantages of first creating a *copy* of a mixed-item list before trying to count the items of a given type on the list. This clearly expressible computational notion can support and illuminate psychological insights such as Piaget's when, in explaining the young child's inability fully to understand class inclusion, he remarked 'If he thinks of the part A, the whole B ceases to be conserved as a unit, and the part A is henceforth comparable only to its complementary A''.[14] But whether one should expect the way in which this copy is made, stored, and accessed to be precisely the same in the human and any given computerized case is another matter.

While we are still unsure about how to decide such issues of validatory relevance, the practice of writing complex programs will carry the risk of leading one into psychological irrelevancies which cannot even be clearly recognized as such. Also, of course, much time will be spent on programming details which the empirical psychologist may feel would be better spent (at least by all except programming geniuses) in activities of a more familiar kind.

Largely because of these difficulties, some AI-paternalists require merely that computational factors be kept in mind while theorizing and planning or interpreting experiments, the writing of programmed simulations being unnecessary or even counterproductive. But even these people insist that the psychologist should at some point undergo the intellectual discipline of learning to program, for the awareness this will bring of the clarity required to express matters as programs and the correlative unclarity of other forms of psychological theory. There is more difference between an inexpert programmer and someone who has never attempted this exercise than between the expert programmer and the tyro, and this difference is enormously helpful to any psychologist who wants to develop a feeling for clarity in psychological theorizing. Assuming that one does decide to sit down to write a program, the AI-paternalist is more likely than the aggressive imperialist to insist that psychological knowledge should be taken into account at every point, so far as is possible. Admittedly, *ad hoc* assumptions will have to be made, but the more the assumptions and constraints written into the program can be based on empirical psychological data, the better.

In sum, the AI-paternalist, who typically wishes to match programs against psychological data of more familiar kinds, admits that this validatory matching is not a straightforward affair. To some degree this difficulty is shared by any psychological, or even scientific, theory since the methodology of confirmation is a controversial area within the philosophy of science. But it is highlighted in the AI-context because the program itself, entire, is not a psychological theory and it may not be simple to distil out of it those features which do contribute to the theoretical position concerned. To insist that every aspect of a language-using program, for example, must be parallelled in the human case would be as blindly imperialist as to insist, not only that a postal system would be a Good Thing for a new colonized society, but also that all its pillar-boxes must necessarily be red. But this cuts both ways: an opponent of AI cannot justifiably object that their system is a Bad Thing because its pillarboxes are green, whereas ours are not.

IV: CONCLUSION

It is important to realize that one may be convinced of the usefulness of the AI approach in psychology without being an intellectual imperialist of either type I have described. In other words, one might be content to admit that there are some psychological phenomena that (certainly, probably, possibly) cannot be understood computationally. As Haugeland has pointed out in a recent critique of 'Cognitivism', such a position would be very tame unless at least some *prima facie* unsuitable phenomena were said to be intelligible in computational terms.[15]

Psychological phenomena very commonly said to be unsuited to computational concepts, so lying outside any area open to AI-colonization, include consciousness, creativity, emotion, moods and motor skills. Suggestions were made in the previous section as to how consciousness might be illuminated to some degree, if not completely demystified, by thinking about the relevant data as being generated by computational processes. And elsewhere I have defended the relevance of the computational viewpoint in each of the other cases also.[16]

But even were such a defence to fail, it would remain an open question whether AI-resistant phenomena were intelligible in any *other* terms of theoretical psychology. By this I mean two things, first that the appropriate theory or explanation might be non-psychological (non-intentional). For instance, Fodor has argued that certain aspects of creativity and emotions might not be open to a computational explanation, being explained rather in physiological terms.[17] But (admittedly because he defines 'psychological' in terms of 'computational' processes, and both in terms of intentional concepts), the upshot would be — surprisingly, perhaps — that these matters were not within the purview of theoretical *psychology* at all. Second, there might be no appropriate theory, whether psychological or not. If it were the case that some aspects of the human mind are not intelligible in general theoretical terms at all, but can only be intuited by some sort of insight (a position seemingly held by some proponents of 'clinical prediction' and idiographic explanation in psychology),[18] then no theory whatever could be adequate to characterize them. The most we could hope for is that our individual human 'intuition' could be prompted and deepened by literary and dramatic insights, while scientific approaches of any sort would be hopelessly out of place. This view is popular in some circles, and it is difficult not to feel some sympathy with it, but we should recognize its consequences. If the human mind is untheorizable, then AI is out — but so too are all other theoretical psychologies.

Finally, and in connection with the charges of dehumanization that are often levelled at the artificial intelligentsia, we must recognize that to see AI as relevant to psychology is not to assume that people are really computers.

It is even misleading to say that it is to regard people as very like computers, because the basic metaphysical 'model of man' that is suggested in many people's minds by this comparison is a thoroughly inhuman one. Computers are metallic machines, not living creatures; and they owe their existence entirely to their being fashioned by human beings for our own, human, purposes. As such, it is said, they can be attributed none of the purposes or properties that concern psychologists. Even a rat, a pigeon, or a lowly flatworm can prompt some degree of fellow-feeling, some hope that their antics might be interestingly like our own and so worthy of the psychologist's consideration. But utterly different attitudes and attributions, it seems, are appropriate to computers on the one hand and living beings on the other.

Tweedledum and Tweedledee made a similar point in relation to models made of wax, not metal.

'If you think we're wax-works', said the one marked 'DUM', 'you ought to pay, you know. Wax-works weren't made to be looked at for nothing. Nohow!'

'Contrariwise', added the one marked 'DEE', 'if you think we're alive, you ought to speak'.

But speaking to one another, if we are indeed essentially no different from computers, must surely be a radically illusory enterprise. Instead of effecting sympathetic communication between living minds, it can only mediate basically mechanistic and essentially meaningless responses, such as those elicited when the teletypes of two 'language'-programs are interconnected. There could hardly be a more dehumanizing implication than this.

However, this depressing conclusion does not in fact follow from the AI approach to psychology, not even from the most aggressively imperialist form. And this for two reasons, one 'positive' and one 'negative'.

The positive reason is that AI concentrates on the internal representations and symbolic transformations that underlie various and changing interpretations of the world (including the system itself). Intentionality is thus a core concept for AI, as for humanist, hermeneutic, and cognitive psychologies in general. What is more, far from forcing us to undervalue the mind, AI leads us to acknowledge its staggering power and representational potential.[19] It points to the awe-inspiring subtlety and richness of the human mind, a psychological complexity that has been intuitively appreciated by many (though by no means all) psychological theories, but which no other approach has illuminated in such explicit detail as the AI approach promises to do.

The negative reason is that the attempt to produce a theory to explain some phenomenon is not the same as the attempt to build some simulacrum of the phenomenon: a theory of the mind models but does not mimic it. Admittedly, if one were interested in building a simulacrum of something, then one would expect the theoretical representation of it to be highly relevant (so science is needed for science-fiction). And some aggressive imperialists do believe that some imaginable computer program could in principle merit the literal ascription of the entire range of our vocabulary of consciousness.[20] But then, though indeed like Alice we 'ought to speak', we would in fact be speaking to beings no less conscious than Tweedledum and Tweedledee.[21] The AI-imperialist need claim no more, however, than that computational theories, like the solar-system theory of the atom, are analogies, which break down at a certain point.

I have argued elsewhere that one important point where the computer analogy breaks down (and will always break down) is the artificiality of computers.[22] Because computers can have no purposes of their own *in the same sense* in which human beings (and animals) have purposes of their own, psychological terms — such as purpose, knowledge, intelligence, speak, communicate . . . . — cannot be literally applied to any conceivable computer. This is of course not to deny that a computer could generate a 'purpose' that had not been foreseen by its programmer, or that went against the programmer's purposes. Nor is it to deny that many generations of self-modifying programs might separate the program in question from the original human programmers — who might even be dead, along with all their conspecifics. But, in the last analysis, computers are man-made as babies are not, and have no *intrinsic* purposes at all.

So there is a very basic human sense in which it would be as inappropriate to speak to a computer program, no matter how sophisticated, as to speak to a waxwork. But even if we cannot really speak to programs, but only 'speak' to them, as psychologists we can nevertheless learn from them.

NOTES

1   M. Minsky and S. Papert, *Artificial Intelligence* (Eugene, Oregon, Condon Lectures, 1974), p. 25.

2   A. Sloman, 'What about their internal languages', *Behavioral and Brain Sciences*, 1979 (in press).

3   D. M. Rumbaugh *et al.*, 'Linguistically-mediated tool use and exchange by chimpanzees', *Behavioral and Brain Sciences*, 1979 (in press).

4   S. E. Fahlmann, 'A planning system for robot construction tasks', *Artificial Intelligence*, 5 (1974), 1–50. See also M. A. Boden, *Artificial Intelligence and Natural Man* (Hassocks, Sussex: Harvester Press, 1977), pp. 363–370.

5   R. Power, 'A model of conversation', unpublished working paper, University of Sussex, Dept. Experimental Psychology, 1976.

6   T. Shallice, personal communication.

7   T. Shallice, 'The dominant action system: an information-processing approach to consciousness', in K. S. Pope and J. L. Singer (eds.), *The Stream of Consciousness: Scientific Investigations into the Flow of Human Experience* (New York, Plenum Press, 1978).

8   M. A. Boden, 'Intentionality and physical systems', *Philosophy of Science*, 37 (1970), 200–214.

9   Z. W. Pylyshyn, 'Computational models and empirical constraints', *Behavioral and Brain Sciences*, 1 (1978), p. 93.

10   Z. W. Pylyshyn, 'What the mind's eye tells the mind's brain: a critique of mental imagery', *Psychological Bulletin*, 80 (1973), 1–24.

11   D. Marr, 'Early processing of visual information', *Phil. Trans, Royal Society* 275 (942), 1976, pp. 483–524.

12   H. L. Dreyfus, *What Computers Can't Do: A Critique of Artificial Reason* (New York, Harper & Row, 1972).

13   T. Winograd, *Understanding Natural Language* (Edinburgh, University Press, 1972). G. J. Sussman and D. V. McDermott, 'Why conniving is better than planning', AI Memo 255a,

(Cambridge, Mass., MIT AI Lab., 1972).

14   D. Klahr and J. G. Wallace, 'Class inclusion processes', in S. Farnham-Diggory (ed.), *Information Processing in Children* (New York, Academic Press, 1972), esp. pp. 165–168. See also M. A. Boden, *Piaget* (Fontana Modern Masters, 1979), ch. 7.

15   J. Haugeland, 'The nature and plausibility of cognitivism', *Behavioral and Brain Sciences*, 1 (1978), 215–226.

16   See my *Artificial Intelligence and Natural Man*, esp. chs. 11 and 14. Also M. A. Boden, *Purposive Explanation in Psychology* (Cambridge, Mass., Harvard Univ. Press 1972, and Harvester Press, Sussex), ch. 6.

17   J. A. Fodor, *The Language of Thought* (Hassocks, Sussex, Harvester Press, 1976), pp. 201ff.

18   P. E. Meehl, *Clinical Versus Statistical Prediction: A Theoretical Analysis and A Review of the Evidence* (Minneapolis, Univ. Minnesota Press, 1954).

19   D. Hofstadter, *Godel, Escher, Bach: An Eternal Golden Braid* (Hassocks, Sussex, Harvester Press, 1979).

20   A. Sloman, *The Computer Revolution in Philosophy: Philosophy, Science, and Models of Mind* (Hassocks, Sussex, Harvester Press, 1978).

21   D. C. Dennett, 'Why you can't make a computer that feels pain', in *Brainstorms: Philosophical Essays on Mind and Psychology* (Hassocks, Sussex, Harvester Press, 1979), pp. 190–229.

22   See my *Artificial Intelligence and Natural Man*, pp. 419–426; and *Purposive Explanation in Psychology*, pp. 43–45, 118–122, 158–198.

4
The case for a cognitive biology

I: INTRODUCTION
A cognitive biology would be one in which biological phenomena were conceptualized for theoretical purposes in terms of categories whose primary application is in the domain of knowledge. The focal example of such categories is knowledge itself, but related examples include hypothesis, test, description, interpretation, language, creativity, and intelligence.

The notion that there might be a place for cognitive concepts in describing and explaining biological phenomena is hardly new. On the contrary, pre-twentieth-century writings on animate nature abound with terms such as creativity, intelligence, idea, expression, language, guidance, and organizer. Henri Bergson's philosophy of creative evolution is but one example in this category. And even the physiologist Claude Bernard, who first outlined the self-equilibrating mechanistic basis of the organism's 'internal environment', spoke of the phenomena of embryology and regeneration in this way:

When a chicken develops in an egg, the formation of the animal body as a grouping of chemical elements is not what essentially distinguishes the vital force. This grouping takes place only according to laws which govern the chemico-physical properties of matter: but the guiding idea of the vital evolution is essentially of the domain of life and belongs neither to chemistry nor to physics nor to anything else. In every living germ is a creative idea which develops and exhibits itself through organization. As long as a living being persists, it remains under the influence of this same creative vital force, and death comes when it can no longer express itself; here as everywhere, everything is derived from the idea alone which creates and guides; physico-chemical means of expression are common to all natural phenomena and remain mingled, pell-mell, like the letters of the alphabet in a box, till a force goes to fetch them, to express the most varied thoughts and mechanisms. This same vital idea preserves beings, by reconstructing the living parts disorganized by accidents or diseases.[1]

Far from being novel, indeed, such a view of biological processes may seem embarrassingly outdated. Nor does its absurdity have the merit of being amusing, as is Lewis Carroll's cognitive-biological fantasy that Tiger-lilies can talk, provided that there is someone worth talking to. Yet a number of respected theoretical biologists are currently recommending the use of cognitive concepts in biology. They see significant parallels between biological processes and cognitive phenomena such as language and knowledge, parallels which often lead them to describe the development of the chicken in the egg in terms remarkably similar to Bernard's. A few examples drawn from different writers are as follows:

Language . . . I suggest may become a paradigm for the theory of General Biology.[2]

The view of the organism as an hypothesis-generating and testing system . . . could transform biology by placing model construction and observation at the centre of the biological process, not at the evolutionary periphery, the phenomenon of Mind.[3]

Embryogenesis may then be seen as the progressive, orderly manifestation of the knowledge which is latent in the egg.[4]

The problems of biology are all to do with *programs*. A program is a list of things to be done, with due regard to circumstances.[5]

Dependence on symbol structures and language constraints is the essence of life . . . . it is not the structure of molecules themselves, but the internal, *self-interpretation* of their structure as symbols that is the basis of life . . . . It is only the integrated set of rules of grammar and interpretation that gives these particular physical structures their symbolic attributes.[6]

A striking aspect of physiological systems is that cognitive processes occur inside the system . . . . Cognition, or the recognition of form, always comes down to the calculation of correlations . . . . From the physiology of synapses we suspect that the CNS has the capacity of adding and dividing, and it must find a special way to obtain subtraction and multiplication if it is to calculate any correlations.[7]

The classical cases of pattern regulation whether in development or in regeneration, . . . are largely dependent on the ability of the cells to change their positional information in an appropriate manner and to be able to interpret this change.[8]

There are two general claims involved here: first, that biological phenomena are not explicable in the terms of molecular biology alone, and second that the higher-level explanatory concepts needed in biology include many drawn from the domain of human cognition. In addition, it is sometimes suggested that theorizing in cognitive terms about biological matters would tend to improve our approach to animate nature in general. I shall discuss these three claims in turn.

II: ANTI-REDUCTIONISM IN BIOLOGY

Believing, like Bernard, that all vital processes take place 'according to' the laws of physics and chemistry but that in many cases their explanation 'belongs neither to chemistry nor to physics', some biologists today criticize what they see as excessive reliance on molecular biology as the explanatory mode characteristic of biological science. Even processes whose underlying biochemical details are relatively clear may not be intelligible in terms of molecular biology alone. As an example of such a process, let us consider the 'lac operon' system.[9]

The lac operon system controls adaptive changes in the activities of bacterial genes (without affecting the nature of the genes themselves). The changes in gene-activity enable the organism to survive in a sub-optimal environment, and subtle controls ensure that the changes do not take place until they are necessary. Overall, what happens is that a bacterium which normally can metabolize only glucose adaptively manufactures the (three) enzymes necessary for metabolizing lactose, given that the glucose-supply in the environment is exhausted and only lactose remains. But in a mixture of the two sugars, these enzymes are not produced and the bacterium uses only the glucose. This is adaptive behaviour, because when lactose is metabolized it is turned into glucose (which is then dealt with in the normal way). Consequently, if glucose is already present, it is a waste of energy for the cell to metabolize lactose. Lactose metabolism is needed for survival only when glucose is absent.

The core of the lac operon is a genetic control system triggered by lactose, and effecting the co-ordinated manufacture of the three new enzymes. But the fact that this happens only when it is strictly needed shows that there must also be some mechanism which either prevents the triggering in the presence of glucose or prompts it only in the absence of glucose. It turns out that a specific metabolite (cAMP) which is present only in small amounts when glucose is plentiful, but is abundant when glucose is scarce, induces the lac operon to synthesize enzymes. So cAMP functions as a necessary part of the activity of the lac operon (as also of many other metabolic systems which supply energy to the cell by breaking down sugars and other substances).

What I have referred to as the triggering effect of lactose on the core system, which initiates production of the three new enzymes, is in fact a double inhibition: inhibition of the resting-state repression of the three genes which directly effect enzyme-synthesis. The relevant chromosome has a 'regulator gene' and an 'operator gene' in addition to the three enzyme-synthesizing genes. The regulator gene initiates a process that builds a 'repressor' protein, and this combines with the operator gene thus repressing the activity of the three enzyme-producing genes. Lactose (or possibly one of the substances produced when it is broken down within the cell) can inactivate the repressor by combining with it so that it is unable to combine with the operator gene.

One might ask how the lactose is ever in a position to trigger the lac operon. For the repressor gene of the lac operon system is inside the cell; but two of the three enzymes needed for dealing with lactose are 'transport' enzymes which bring lactose into the cell from outside. If this system were perfect, it would never be able to get started. But — probably because of random variations in the 'steady-state' link between the repressor and the operator gene — a minuscule amount of the various enzymes is always present (less than one molecule per cell). The traces of transport enzyme on the cell membrane can thus bring small amounts of lactose into the cell from outside. Once the production of enzymes is started, it can increase due to a positive feedback mechanism, since the more lactose is carried into the cell, the more is available to trigger enzyme-production.

In order to understand the subtly adaptive control functions of the lac operon system — which give it its distinctively biological significance — we need concepts that are not drawn from molecular biology and which can be understood (and used in formulating experimental hypotheses) independently of specification of the actual biochemical substances involved. The concepts of negative and positive feedback, for example, which are crucial to the understanding of this system, are abstract terms drawn from cybernetics. They can be used in a wide variety of contexts, biological and otherwise, and the details of the physical mechanisms that embody them in each particular case differ widely. Indeed, other micro-organisms are known in which quite different substances are responsible for the (adaptively controlled) metabolism of lactose when glucose is scarce.

The logical inter-relations of the various control functions, too, are independent of any particular embodiment in one chemical (or organism) or another. And because of the reciprocal effects of positive and negative controls, the inner structure of a control defined as 'positive' at a given level of analysis may involve a 'negative' when considered at a lower analytical level. For instance, we have seen that the triggering of the core of the lac operon is in fact a double negative: an inhibition of an inhibition. Similarly, the wait-until-the-glucose-is-finished function could be fulfilled either by switching-on the core of the lac operon when glucose is low or by switching it off when glucose is high. And in other biological examples essentially similar in kind, it has indeed been found that regulation is achieved by a substance that actively inhibits the production of new enzymes when glucose (or some other crucial metabolite) is present instead of positively initiating it when it is absent. In short, essentially similar functions (such as the metabolism of lactose under conditions of glucose scarcity) can be fulfilled by systems comprised of different biochemical substances and/or of different internal control-structure. It follows that the lac operon is a system that exists and is defined at a higher level than molecular biology. Even though the low-level biochemical processes are largely understood, they do not express (but merely make possible) the characteristic properties and functions of the lac operon itself. (Biologists who favour a cognitive biology interpret the great degree of freedom between biological and physical levels as providing a realm of evolutionarily created 'rules' over and above that of physical 'laws'.)[10]

The biological phenomena described by Bernard as being guided by the 'vital force' or 'vital idea' were embryological development (including tissue differentiation and overall morphogenesis) and the regeneration of adult organs. Recent research has identified a few of the substances that apparently act as biochemical 'organizers' for these processes. But the main theoretical aim in developmental biology is to find ways of expressing the overall integration that characterizes developmental processes. How is it possible for the different organs to arise from a single cell or homogeneous mass of cells?; how can they be placed in the correct positions relative to one another?; and how can they be induced to develop in parallel so that they do not get out of step with each other? How is it that dividing cells can usually split themselves into two halves of similar size?; how can even very small fragments of a regenerative organism grow into a new adult of normal size?; how can parts (such as linear segments or radial tentacles) be repeated, and how can some of them be specialized?; and how can such repeated parts be counted, so that their number is constant to the genus or species concerned?

In order to answer questions such as these, both spatial and temporal dimensions will have to be represented within morphogenetic theory. Space features in molecular biology only when stereochemical factors are cited to explain why a substance will combine with one protein (or site on a protein) but not with another, and time features not at all. If and when a general theory of morphogenesis is achieved, it will be independent of molecular biology — although molecular biology will be needed to answer the question of how the morphogenetic functions are embodied in any given organism.

Some developmental biologists are therefore asking what general types of control are in principle possible, given what we know about the embodiment of organisms, and how these abstractly defined controls could give rise to the spatio-temporal integration so characteristic of biological phenomena. One of the first people to attempt an abstract analytical account of morphogenesis was the mathematician A. M. Turing, who in 1952 suggested that spatial repetitions (such as segmentation) might be generated by periodic waves of concentration of diffusible substances (or organizers).[11] He formulated equations showing that two substances diffusing throughout a given region would normally develop a wave-like distribution, and since then a number of comparable analytical results have been established. A comprehensive morphology would add to and integrate such results, and morphologists such as L. Wolpert and B. C. Goodwin are attempting to do this.[12]

For example, cybernetic considerations show that a negative feedback system that is not perfectly damped (which is to say, any actual example of a negative feedback system) will give rise to oscillations in the behaviour of the system. There will always be a delay in recognizing an excess of a key substance (which functions as a feedback signal), as also in reinstating the required level of that substance; and the more signal-substances are involved in a given system, the more such delays there will be.

The resulting oscillations, when they occur within a biological system, are a form of biological clock, whose time-phase will depend on the rate at which the signalling processes involved take place. Since different biological processes take place at different rates, there may be a hierarchy of biological clocks in which signals and responses at one level typically occur less rapidly than at the level below. For example, temporal cycles of different phase are found at the molecular, intracellular, intercellular, organic, and organismic levels. In such a hierarchy, the various levels are relatively independent of one another because of their different rates of change. But processes at one level can both constrain and be responsive to the (overall) nature of what is going on at the level below, even though its own slower time-phase prevents it from being able to influence the lower-level processes in detail. And it is possible for two time-cycles of similar phase to interact with one another, giving rise to a new temporal pattern of a distinctive nature.

Biological clocks can function not only as the basis of temporal organization at various levels, but of spatial organization also — provided that they can influence cell movement, division, and differentiation. Mathematical arguments show that they are in principle capable of giving rise to 'pacemakers' initiating waves of activity within cells and populations of cells. If these waves were to be actively propagated by successive cells, they would be able to travel over much greater distances than can substances which establish gradient fields by way of simple diffusion. This means that they might be able to influence the organism as a whole, rather than just that extent of tissue which is within a diffusible distance. And abstract consideration of the property of excitability in biological membranes (such as the cell-membrane) suggests how excitable membranes could contribute to the stabilization of biological clocks, and to the effective separation of distinct metabolic cycles occurring simultaneously within the organism.

Some such organizational uses of biological oscillations have already been identified in experiments on the processes of cell division and differentiation, as well as in the regeneration of simple adult organisms. For example, they are involved in the generation of polarity in some cells and simple organisms. Polarity is the differentiation of 'head' end from 'tail' end, on which are based the common biological phenomena of axial organization and cephalization. And in one simple organism (a form of slime-mould), pacemakers of varying kinds have been identified that co-ordinate the development of a disorderly mass of cells (which are neither spatially organized nor temporally synchronized) into a multicellular organism with a distinctive anatomical structure.

In the latter case, as in some others, some of the substances fulfilling specific functional roles have been identified (which is not to say that the way in which they are able to do so is understood). But the anti-reductionist point is that those biologists who are aiming at a general theory of morphogenetic processes express their hypotheses in mathematical terms dealing with such matters as periodicities, field gradients, and universal properties of excitable membrances. Factors like these are apparently responsible for the spatio-temporal integration in development that so puzzled Bernard, and this theorizing is on a level quite distinct from molecular biology.

III: COGNITIVE CONCEPTS IN BIOLOGICAL THEORY
The second claim is more specifically concerned with cognitive concepts, and it occurs in different forms. C. H. Waddington, for example, sees language as a general paradigm for biology. The biologist, he says, regards language as:

a set of symbols, organized by some sort of generative grammar, which makes possible the conveyance of (more or less) precise commands for action to produce effects on the surroundings of the emitting and the recipient entities.[13]

Waddington's work has been primarily concerned with the problems of embryological morphogenesis that were mentioned in Part II of this chapter, and with the implications of morphology for evolutionary theory. The aim of morphology is to discover the sets of generative rules whereby a single cell can be successively transformed into embryo and adult (or, more generally, how a part of an organism can give rise to a whole).

Waddington's use of the term 'generative grammar' in the above passage suggests that one might think of developmental changes in the embryo as analogous to the grammatical transformations posited by Chomsky. If this is so, one should be able to distinguish morphogenetic anomalies (corresponding to 'Colourless green ideas sleep furiously'), biological impossibilities ('Ate dog bone juicy the'), and superficially similar phenomena that are radically distinct ('John is easy/eager to please').

One could define teratology (the biological study of embryological monsters) as the study of morphogenetic anomalies. A human foetus in which instead of two legs there is one tapering mass, no external genitalia, and corresponding (sic) transformations in the associated internal organs, is — unfortunately — a biological possibility. Such creatures develop in a way which is creatively guided by many of the usual embryological constraints (for example, limb-budding should occur at the end opposite the head, skin should cover muscle, which should be attached to bone, and so on). But some of the constraints which normally ensure that the developing organism will be able to function correctly (to 'make sense' in its environmental context) are bypassed. The 'syntactic' rules of physico-chemical process have been strictly followed, but the 'semantic' rules of biological function have not.

By contrast, a mermaid (literally half-fish, half-human) is a biological impossibility, as is a cell that is simultaneously muscle and bone. Developmental choices guiding cell-differentiation and organ-growth have to be made continually, and while each of these leaves some options open for later decisions within the develop-mental process, other potential options are progressively out-lawed. Analogously, if one starts a sentence in a certain way then some syntactic forms which might otherwise have been produced cannot be generated. And at a deeper level, if a language has 'chosen' to follow certain rules of inflection, then other rules of inflection (or none at all) cannot be incorporated into it, even though they occur in other languages. A mermaid would be analogous to Latin with Anglo-Saxon inflections, whereas a cell that was both muscle and bone would be comparable to an ungrammatical string like 'If you don't leave or else I'll scream' (cf. 'If you don't leave I'll scream' and 'You'd better leave or else I'll scream').

In the case of the mermaid, the relevant choices have occurred at the evolutionary level, and are encoded within the genes. That is to say, the genetic endowment of a fish makes possible certain choice-sets and developmental constraints, which are so different from that of a human being that the one cannot in any circumstances give rise to the other or to half and half. (A humanoid mammal adapted to swim with the seals could, presumably, evolve: but that is not what I mean by a mermaid.) In the case of the single cell, the choices occur at the epigenetic or embryological level. So a cell that at an early stage has the potential of forming ectoderm or mesoderm will later be confined to one of these only; once within the mesodermal tissue-type, it still retains the potential of forming muscle or bone or cartilage; later still, developmental choices are made which further constrain its future development, until finally it is committed to one cell-form or another. (Regeneration involves the re-excitement of the initial developmental potential that was and is still present within the genes of the adult organism.)

Examples of superficially similar but radically different biological phenomena include cases where two organs look alike, and may even fulfil similar functions, but whose evolutionary and embryological histories differ. Cases of mimicry often involve strikingly similar appearance and different function, and can cross the plant–animal boundary so an insect may look like a dead leaf. (A linguistic analogy to mimicry might be the sort of phonetic pun exemplified by the French phrases 'assis sans maître' and 'à six cents mètres', by virtue of which a dog left at the base of the Eiffel tower may appear to be higher than his master, 300 metres up). Organs with similar functions may be biologically homologous or

non-homologous. The bat's wing and the bird's wing are
homologous, for each is a variant of the vertebrate pentadactyl
limb. Their differences are relatively superficial, and could
presumably be coded by relatively few genetic changes, as
compared with the difference between a bat's and a butterfly's
wing. Much more complex — and indeed biologically unin-
telligible — underlying transformations would be required to
change bat-wing into butterfly-wing, for (like 'equivalent' sentences in English and Latin) they are deeply dissimilar even in the
abstract terms of comparative anatomy. Even in the case of the
bird and the bat, the structural relationships are deeper than those
between chaffinch and bullfinch: to think that evolution could
transform a bat's wing into a bird's by changing just one or two
genes governing the wing's surface anatomy would be comparable
to imagining that the only difference between 'John is easy/eager to
please' is a single word. The requisite genetic changes would have
to alter high-level and inter-correlated morphological constraints
(of the general type discussed in Part II of this chapter), which
would not only change the wing ('sentence') itself but the animal's
body ('paragraph') also.

Waddington's view of morphology and evolutionary theory as
the search for generative grammars is reminiscent of Chomsky's
characterization of the 'creativity' of language. A generative
grammar allows for a distinctive set of possibilities, which are
infinite in number and indefinitely complicated in their inner
structure while also being constrained by the rules and their
potential interactions. Creativity in general is not mere novelty,
but novelty that follows previous constraints even if in some cases
it also goes beyond them. An artist may deliberately develop new
forms which have an intelligible connection with previous ones —
as in the move from tonal to atonal music.[14] Sometimes the new
creation arises due in part to random processes occurring within
the existing context of constraints, and the artist continually
selects (rejects, accepts, or develops) the intermediate forms of
novelty that arise.[15] In this sort of case, post hoc evaluations are
important in distinguishing creation from mere change.

It is random processes and post hoc evaluations which are
credited by orthodox neo-Darwinian evolutionary theory with the
formative power of evolution. Genetic mutation and natural
selection are said to suffice for the appearance of new forms. The
developmental relation between genotype and phenotype is
thought of as a more or less automatic 'translation' of the
information coded in the genes into its phenotypical form (the body
and behaviour of the mature organism).

But this theory ignores (though of course does not deny) the continuous influence of contextual factors on the 'translation' that is going on. Even in a genetic system so simple as the lac operon, what the structural or enzyme-manufacturing genes do (how they are translated) does not depend on their intrinsic nature alone. It depends also on the way in which environmental factors affect other (regulatory) genes, and it presupposes specific phenotypic features such as a cell-membrane in association with which the enzymes produced by the structural genes can function.

Neo-Darwinism thus has little or nothing to say about the hierarchically structured internal developmental constraints which contribute to the organism's self-regulation, or self-creation. These interacting constraints, as well as random mutations and environmental pressures, influence the formation of new creatures. To be sure, they are somehow coded in the genes and can be altered by mutations. But we saw in the previous section that they can be theoretically represented at a level quite distinct from the molecular biological level at which one expresses the mechanisms of genetic mutation. And any mutations which occur can have effects only within the context of these morphogenetic dimensions. It is largely for these reasons that Waddington has repeatedly criticized the account of development and evolution favoured by orthodox neo-Darwinism, and that he and his followers attribute a more genuinely creative power to the evolutionary process than most biologists do.[16]

One of Waddington's followers is the biologist Goodwin, who refers to evolution not only as 'creative' but as 'intelligent' also. Both Waddington and Goodwin welcome recent attempts within theoretical biology to draw on the (typically cognitive) concepts of artificial intelligence, and Goodwin is even more liberal than Waddington in his use of cognitive terminology. Goodwin's experimental and theoretical research is concerned with the spatio-temporal organization of developmental processes at various hierarchical levels. Examples include cell-division and differentiation in adult tissues, as well as the embryological and regenerative processes singled out by Bernard. Goodwin believes that 'embryos are essentially like minds',[17] and is explicit about his commitment to cognitive categories within biology:

In my approach the organism is regarded as a cognitive system, adapting and evolving on the basis of knowledge about itself and its environment. The dynamical modes of an organism's behaviour are represented as manifestations of co-operative or collective activity among cognitive units, development being seen as the orderly unfolding of these modes within a structurally stable, knowledge-using system.[18]

What Goodwin means by 'co-operative' activity is that observable features of biological systems such as growth, differentiation, and regeneration are to be understood in terms of the interaction of a number of smaller-scale processes. His mathematical theory of such interactions is a leading example of the type of theory referred to earlier, in the discussion of morphogenesis and biological clocks. While biologists differ about the precise nature of the interactive processes concerned, there is no dispute that collective activities of some sort underlie observable biological phenomena. What is less common is the choice of 'co-operation' as a descriptive category here, and the even more unusual characterization of the processes concerned as 'cognitive' units.

Goodwin speaks of co-operation because he sees the flexible interaction of the (largely autonomous) small-scale processes as a form of heterarchical functioning. 'Heterarchy' was originally used by W. McCulloch to describe neurophysiological activity,[19] and is now used also in artificial intelligence to characterize the flexibility of some types of complex program. In a heterarchical system, behavioural units or subroutines at a given level function to a large extent independently of levels that are above them in the hierarchy of the system as a whole. They interact with each other in a number of different ways, passing various types of message between them which affect decisions about what they will do and when. Knowledge that is available directly to one subroutine can on occasion be shared with (all or some of) the others, and a subroutine with access to a specific datum of information can either act on it itself or instruct some other subroutine to do so. As this cognitive language may suggest, heterarchical systems are commonly conceptualized in terms of co-operation, and even explicitly compared to a human 'committee of experts'.[20]

For Goodwin, then, biological structures and structural transformations should be conceptualized in terms of cognitive notions such as message-passing, pattern-recognition, description, and knowledge. The structural transformations are controlled by specific physiological processes which act as context-sensitive coded messages interpreted by the biological system at the level concerned. Even at the relatively low level of the biochemistry of enzyme action, Goodwin uses the cognitive concept of pattern-recognition to express what is going on.

Early theories of enzyme inhibition assumed (with experimental support) that the inhibitor has a molecular structure and stereochemistry closely similar to that of the normal substrate of the enzyme, and so can take the place of the substrate in interaction with the enzyme. If one were to use the term 'pattern-recognition' at all in describing such phenomena, one would do so only loosely. For the relation between inhibitor and enzyme in this case is no more cognitive than that between a square peg and a square hole of matching size.

But in the late 1950s new cases of enzyme inhibition were observed wherein the inhibitor and substrate have no such stereochemical similarity. In these cases, providing the enzyme with its normal end-product inhibited the earliest steps in the chain of enzyme-activity, steps involving substances quite different from the end-product itself. Further investigation showed that the action of specific recognition (sic) sites on the enzyme molecule depends on what is happening at other sites on the same molecule — whether they are bound to metabolic substances, and if so which substances they are bound to. So the overall configuration of the whole subtly determines the properties of the parts at a given instant, and the recognition of a metabolite by a particular site may occur or not, according to context. It is as though the metabolite has no significance (sic) for that site except in certain overall contexts.

Clearly, there is more scope in this type of enzyme-inhibition for using the concept of recognition than there is in the previous type. For it is characteristic of human perception that we recognize patterns by relying as much, or more, on their context as on their intrinsic properties.

However, if one is to use the term 'recognition' in describing a system, one should be prepared to use other cognitive terms also. For the concept of recognition is implicitly linked to concepts such as knowledge, description, meaning, significance, and interests. So to be able to see an ink-patch as either an old woman's nose or a young girl's chin (or, by means of a Gestalt-switch, as each of these alternately) one needs knowledge of the different contexts to which these distinct descriptions are intelligible.[21] Its significance is not inherent in it but varies with the context, and to say something is significant for a given system is to say both that it has some specific meaning for the system and that it has a potential for contributing to the system's goals or interests.

This is why the term 'significance' appeared so naturally in the description of enzyme-inhibition that was given above. Enzyme-inhibition in conditions of excess of the end-product clearly contributes to the organism's survival. The meaning of the metabolite in this sort of case is that the intermediate steps in enzyme-activity should be omitted. There is no non-arbitrary connection between the metabolite concerned and the substances produced in these intermediate stages (as there is in cases of stereochemical inhibition). The end-product is able to embody the meaning 'omit intermediate steps' only because of (as yet unknown) physico-chemical properties of the long, three-dimensional, protein molecule that is the enzyme in question. The nature of the intermediate steps does not uniquely determine the nature of the inhibitory substance. In this sense, the latter functions as an arbitrary 'code' or 'symbol', which in other (biological) contexts might differ radically in meaning.

Examples in which a substance has been shown to have different meanings according to context include the metabolite (cAMP) that was mentioned in Part II as triggering the lac operon when glucose is scarce. Among its many other meanings are the senses it carries during three distinct phases of the development of slime moulds. When there is food available, the slime mould is a disorganized mass of single amoebic cells; in this condition, there is no cAMP present. But after several hours without food, a few cells start rhythmically secreting cAMP. This substance diffuses out to other cells and instructs them both to start secreting cAMP themselves and also to move toward each other and to stick together. So at the end of the first (aggregation) phase, there is a mass of cells which stay together in space and show some degree of synchronization. This cell-mass is called a 'slug', and during the second stage the slug moves along the ground by means of contractions passing rhythmically from one end to the other. The synchronized waves of cAMP now act as a pacemaker controlling the contractions, and the cell-mass shows polarization in that a front and a back end are distinguishable by the direction of movement. In the final stage the slug stops moving about and the homogeneous cell-mass differentiates into a base, a stalk, and a spore-containing head. This differentiation is guided by the cAMP that is still being produced by the cells, but which has quite a different meaning in this stage. These three developmental contexts, then, result in differing interpretations of the cAMP messages.

One could, of course, describe this biological phenomenon without using the terms 'meaning', 'sense', or 'interpretation' (though one would be hard put to avoid using the term 'control', which originates in the cognitive domain), and most biologists would do so. The idea of context-dependent function is a classic concern of theoretical biology, but function is not (or not seriously) identified with meaning. Even those biologists who speak of 'recognition' sites on proteins — that is, the majority — would say that they use it merely as a convenient metaphor, having no desire to introduce cognitive terms en masse into biology. On the contrary, they would avoid such terms, feeling that they might encourage unscientific notions such as teleology to pervert biologists' thinking. They would not wish to describe the evolutionary process as 'intelligent', for instance, lest this suggest either direction within the evolutionary process or a guiding mind or purpose behind it.

Goodwin, by contrast, welcomes a host of cognitive terms into his conception of biology, and sees the natural world as being full of meaning and the recognition of meaning. He characterizes evolution as an intelligent system, saying that it shows learning through continual trial-and-error testing of hypotheses generated by the system, and that it is directed to the creation of new forms that embody increasingly adequate knowledge of themselves and their environment. The intelligence is immanent in the evolutionary process rather than external to it, but the progressive nature of evolution — difficult as it may be to define in precise biological terms — is to be conceptualized as a central feature rather than a by-product of it. According to Goodwin, all biological phenomena embody knowledge:

A cognitive system is one which operates on the basis of knowledge of itself and its environment. Knowledge I will take to mean a useful description of some aspect of the world (system or environment). The fact that we are dealing with a description means that there is some code or set of codes which relates it to that which is described; while usefulness in this context is connected specifically with the capacity to survive, reproduce and evolve.[22]

Some would accuse Goodwin of using concepts that are quite out of place in biological contexts, for the sense in which human minds possess knowledge, and generate, test, and learn from hypotheses, is different from the sense in which biological systems can be said to do so. For instance, the objections raised against Chomsky's views on the innate knowledge of language are relevant also to Goodwin's claim that the embryo (and even biological subroutines within it) has innate knowledge of the world.[23] In its ordinary sense, knowledge requires justification, and neither baby nor embryo has gone through any process of justification over and above the 'test' of viability. Even cognitive psychologists, whose investigative domain is knowledge itself, have been criticized on philosophical grounds for using concepts such as 'hypothesis' or 'inference' within their theories.[24] In their primary uses, these terms imply conscious reasoning, whereas they are commonly used by theoretical psychologists to refer to (posited) non-introspectible cognitive structures and processes that underlie conscious thought, experience, and behaviour.

But unless we are to outlaw all extended uses of ordinary terms for scientific purposes, we must ask what is to be gained and what lost by a given extension. Which of the implications carried by a concept in its primary domain can be useful in directing empirical research in the secondary domain? Which implications are inapplicable in its new context without this fact's being realized by the scientist in question? What common implications of 'hypothesis', for instance, are either forgotten or illicitly taken for granted by cognitive psychologists with the result that they are misled about questions falling within their scientific purview?

It might seem that if cognitive concepts are problematic within psychology, then a fortiori they must be out of place within biology. But if we approach extended usage in science in the way just suggested, it becomes clear that there may be less danger in using everyday cognitive terms in biological than in psychological theory. For no biologist will be misled into thinking that he has discovered the nature of human reason just because he has found it useful for his own purpose to speak of 'knowledge' in biological systems and 'intelligence' in evolution.

Goodwin is well aware that there are important differences between psychological and biological systems, so that the use of cognitive terms within biology is not unproblematic. In particular, only minds can imaginatively generate new descriptions or hypotheses which can be thought about speculatively as opposed to being acted out in the real world:

The embryo cannot do this i.e. refer to virtual as well as to actual events, since it must actually realize any cognitive process it is engaged in, having no symbolic domain of operation divorced from action. All 'statements' in developmental language are commands or algorithms.[25]

It is for this reason that Waddington has agreed with a colleague that 'biology is all to do with programs — that is, with lists of things to be done, with due regard to circumstances',[26] and has criticized

Carnap and the early Wittgenstein for giving primacy of meaning to factual statements rather than imperatives.[27] For this reason also, biological epistemologists such as Popper or Piaget stress the 'critical attitude' or 'logico-mathematical structures' that distinguish Einstein's problem-solving from the amoeba's.[28]

Because the concept of intelligence (though not, according to Goodwin, the concept of knowledge) is intrinsically connected with that of learning, very few organisms can be described as intelligent. For most organisms cannot create, test, and improve their descriptions (as evolution does) but can only operate on them. If an unintelligent organism's descriptions are faulty, it does not learn — it either aborts during development or survives in an abnormal form that is less likely to result in communication of the description to the next generation. So if one speaks of an embryo 'testing' a genetic hypothesis (whether that hypothesis is the norm for the species or results from a mutation) for its survival value, one is speaking even less literally than when one says that the evolutionary process as a whole 'tests' such hypotheses.

Despite the undeniable differences between 'knowledge' in human minds and biological processes, Goodwin insists that his use of cognitive terminology in describing biological systems is not a fanciful metaphor. It is fruitful in suggesting particular lines of theoretical and experimental enquiry that otherwise might be overlooked. This is so in at least four ways.

First, the arbitrary nature of symbolic codes or languages is stressed by Goodwin not merely because it finds a parallel in biological processes (as already described), but also because it can help to focus biologists' minds on the proper experimental questions. Thus the most appropriate question may be not 'what is the molecular biology of this substance, and how does it combine with other molecules?', but rather 'what function is this substance performing for the organism: what information is it passing, what question is it asking, what instruction is it embodying?' In general, this will not be evident from a mere inspection of the molecular biology involved (even assuming this to be known), since there is no straightforward or universal correlation between molecular structure and biological function. If equivalent instructions can be conveyed either by a direct chemical triggering or by an inhibition of an inhibition, then no physico-chemical laws can be found saying that this meaning must be conveyed by this molecule.

This is to say that it may be helpful to think of the biologist's task as that of decoding the (essentially arbitrary) languages that are embodied in living organisms. For instance, the biochemistry of the four nucleotides is less significant (sic) than the fact that

specific triplets of them code for the production of this or that
amino-acid, or for the initiation or cessation of production of a
protein-molecule. Similarly, if one's experiments on cAMP were
directed only at finding out which other molecules it combines
with, one would never ask what its significance is at different
stages of the life-cycle of an organism, and how the developmental
context can change its significance as the creature grows.
Evidently, cells interpret cAMP signals differently at different
stages, and one class of experimental questions is defined by
asking what the interpretative mechanism is (for example, how can
a membrane with such and such a property interpret cAMP as an
instruction to do one thing, whereas a membrane in a different state
understands it to mean something else?). Empirical study can also
ask to what extent a given meaning is represented within different
species, and whether the code(s) expressing it is widely shared. In
the case of the so-called 'genetic code' it appears that a common
language is understood throughout nature, for the meaning of a
given triplet seems to be the same irrespective of species.

  Second, this view may help us to understand why there are
marked spatial and temporal discontinuities within development.
For Goodwin explains these discontinuities in two different ways,
one causal and one cognitive or teleological. He shows how they
may be caused by continuously varying underlying processes,
outlining a mathematical theory wherein the switches between
nonexcitability and excitability in a biological membrane are
comparable to phase-transitions between solid, liquid, and gas in
physics. But he also suggests that these discontinuities are
biologically advantageous because they provide the organism with
'a greatly simplified descriptive language whereby the system
informs itself of its own state and determines subsequent
transformations'.[29] If cells destined to become distinct tissues
(ectoderm or mesoderm, muscle or bone, heel or knee) are
distinguished in earlier embryological stages partly by their lying in
different places, the spatial parameters can be exploited in guiding
the integrated differentiation of these cells. For example,
experiments have shown that the embryonic disc which in insects
develops into a limb is organized in a 'clock-face' fashion. Spatial
relations defined in terms of positions on the clock-face determine
what part of the limb the cells will develop into, and how they will
adapt to injury such as the excision of a clock-segment. Some
comparable results have been found in vertebrate embryos,
including mammals. It seems as though embryological development commonly takes advantage of descriptions or instructions
expressed in spatial terms, rather than relying only on dis-

criminations of specific molecules or metabolites.

Third, Goodwin sees methodological advantages in thinking of biological structures and processes at various levels as embodying knowledge of their biological context. For instance, a diurnal rhythm embodies knowledge about the alternation of night and day, and the enzyme-producing genes of the lac operon embody knowledge (or hypotheses) about the cell-membrane in association with which they must work. In general, integrated processes embody knowledge of or hypotheses about each other. Goodwin suggests mathematical expressions that can act as useful measures of this knowledge by comparing the assumptions made by the process (the conditions for its optimal functioning, and the extent of its adaptability) with the conditions actually found in its biological context. Paramount among these conditions will be the presence or absence of processes capable of interpreting the description embodied in the biological phenomenon being investigated. If there are no such processes then the 'description' was meaningless in this context, and if the interpretation leads to injury or death for the organism then the 'hypothesis' was false.

And fourth, Goodwin sees it as an advantage of a cognitive biology that such a theory implies a continuity of organizing principles in behaviour and development. At the most general level, this means that perception should not be regarded as a radically new (psychological) phenomenon, but as a novel and more adaptive way in which signals can be communicated to the organism so as to increase its knowledge. A more specific (though not fully proven) example is the change in significance from a structural to a behavioural meaning that seems to take place in signalling activities within some forms of hydra. Much as periodic waves of cAMP have different (structural) meanings in distinct phases of the development of slime moulds, so the pacemaker functions of a group of hydra cells convey (first) instructions controlling bodily regeneration and (later) instructions controlling the integrated movements of the tentacles. The psychophysiology of different modes of action in higher animals may involve similar integrating principles, and substances which in the adult nervous system carry one behavioural meaning may at earlier stages have quite another significance.

This morphological-behavioural continuity presumably involves biological clocks as organizing principles, since these are basic to the spatio-temporal organization of embryogenesis. In 1951 the physiological psychologist K. S. Lashley anticipated many of Chomsky's anti-behaviourist arguments, and suggested that the hierarchical integration of behaviour (from language to motor skills) could in principle arise given temporal periodicities within the central nervous system.[30] Current morphological work on the way in which biological clocks act as the germ of regulative ordering may help to put flesh onto Lashley's theoretically skeletal account of 'the serial order in behaviour'. Goodwin, for instance, points out that the time-phase of neural changes is extremely short, and suggests that this is why they lead to patterned activities rather than to patterned forms. Characteristically, he expresses this in cognitive terms:

One might put it that the embryo is more a sculptor, the brain more a composer of music, both being very fine artists. This suggests that a necessary condition for the emergence of mind came about by the simple expedient of an increase in the rate of elementary embryonic processes, a result of membrane specialization, thus achieving an uncoupling of activity waves from the viscous 'drag' of matter which normally results in morphogenesis.[31]

Despite the extension of use that is involved, then, a cognitive approach to biology can be defended on both negative and positive grounds. Negatively, it is unlikely to mislead people into mistakes at the psychological level, because the two domains are prima facie so different. Positively, it can encourage biologists to ask empirically fruitful questions, questions that a purely physico-chemical approach might tend to leave unasked.

IV: BIOLOGY AND ATTITUDES TO NATURE
Biology is typically classed as a natural science. In Habermas' classification, the interests basic to natural science and psychology differ, being technological and predictive or hermeneutic respectively.[32] The interpretation of meaning, rather than causal mechanism, is the focus of hermeneutics. So using cognitive concepts within biology threatens to carry it into the class of hermeneutic sciences. 'The interpretation of nature' was a goal of medieval science and alchemy, but since the scientific revolution this approach to the understanding of nature has been regarded as inappropriate. Rather, the empirical interests that inform natural science should focus on theoretical understanding validated by prediction and control.

But there was an exploitative attitude to the natural world implicit in Bacon's vision that we should make ourselves 'lords and masters of nature', and crasser expressions of man's alienation from nature have been all too common. For instance, the hero of a science fiction novel of 1923 remarked:

Well, if we could tap that store of energy which evidently lies within the atom we should have Nature at our feet. She would be done for, beaten, out of the struggle: and we should simply have to walk over the remains and take what we wanted. [33]

One would not expect the hero (as opposed to the anti-hero) of a science-fiction novel of the 1980s to express such a sentiment. For we have learnt to doubt whether mastery (even intelligent and responsible mastery) is the most appropriate goal for us to have in our relation to the natural world.

Those who regret the arrogance and alienation (and the ecological blight) associated with the goal of mastering nature will see some wider advantage in classing biology with the hermeneutic sciences. And this, indeed, is recognized and welcomed by Goodwin. [34] At the least, attributing knowledge to organisms and meaning to biological processes would encourage an attitude of respect towards them, so discouraging not only the wanton destruction of living things but also the selfish appropriation of them for our own ends without any concern for their natural autonomy. Arguments for animal liberation could therefore find some support in biological science, instead of sitting uneasily with a biology that views animals in reductionist terms. At the same time, we would have an enhanced sense of living in a natural environment with which one may properly feel some sympathy.

This latter consideration will be regarded as sentimental by some. But an accusation of sentimentality must be grounded on the claim that the attitude concerned (in this case, sympathy with the natural world) is inappropriate to its object. It may be inappropriate because it is excessive, or it may be more radically inappropriate, in that it is not an attitude that can sensibly be directed toward the class of objects in question. People can be sentimental in the first (excessive) sense whether or not biological theory is cognitive, though specific judgments will involve somewhat different considerations in either case. But to feel sympathy with the animal world in general is sentimental in the second (inappropriate) sense only if biology is firmly classified as one of the natural sciences, with no concepts within it that are reminiscent of the hermeneutic domain. In short, only by prejudging this issue can the charge of radical sentimentality be justified.

The desirability of this general attitude can however be discussed irrespective of its sentimentality. I have suggested that it may be satisfying in itself, as well as making thoughtless exploitation of our environment less likely. But some people experience no alienation in the absence of a feeling of community with nature, and would see disadvantages in such an attitude's becoming widespread. For it might encourage a vague scientific irrationalism, which could perniciously undermine the search for all types of knowledge, whether natural scientific or not. Also, a sympathetic attitude towards nature might encourage religious approaches in general — which are thought by some people to be pernicious forms of escapism that distract us from the real problems before us.

Value judgments such as these enter into scientific thinking, for scientific theories are not based on wholly neutral or objective roots. We should try to be self-conscious about the wider evaluative implications of alternative theories, favouring those most consonant with our non-scientific values whenever we can do this without betraying our scientific commitment to rigorous empirical tests insofar as these are possible. Even non-Kuhnians allow for aesthetic desiderata such as simplicity and elegance when adjudicating theories, and ethical values may sometimes be relevant too. Calls for responsibility in science usually concern specific applications, but the general form of a scientific theory may be at issue also. In the psychological domain for example, Skinnerian theory is criticized partly because of the demeaning image of man that it presents. In assessing a cognitive biology, one should bear in mind that analogous considerations may be relevant to the biological domain as well.

NOTES

1   C. Bernard, *Introduction to the Study of Experimental Medicine* (trans C. Greene), Dover edition 1957, pp. 93–94 (orig. publ. 1865).

2   C. H. Waddington, 'Epilogue', in *Toward A Theoretical Biology*, Vol. 4 (ed. C. H. Waddington), Edinburgh University Press, 1972, p. 289.

3   B. C. Goodwin, 'Biology and meaning', in *Toward a Theoretical Biology*, Vol. 4 (ed. C. H. Waddington), Edinburgh University Press, 1972, p. 267.

4   B. C. Goodwin, *Analytical Physiology of Cells and Developing Organisms*, Academic Press, 1976, p. 220.

5   C. H. Longuet-Higgins, 'What biology is about', in *Toward a Theoretical Biology*, Vol. 2 (ed. C. H. Waddington), Edinburgh University Press, 1969, p. 229.

6   H. H. Pattee, 'Laws and constraints, symbols and languages', in
      Toward a Theoretical Biology, Vol. 4 (ed. C. H. Waddington),
      Edinburgh University Press, 1972, pp. 248, 249, 252.
7   K. Kornacker, 'Cognitive processes in physics and physiology', in
      Toward a Theoretical Biology, Vol. 2 (ed. C. H. Waddington),
      Edinburgh University Press, 1969, pp. 248, 251.
8   L. Wolpert, 'Positional information and the spatial pattern of
      cellular differentiation', *J. Theor. Biol.*, 25 (1969), p. 8.
9   For a detailed description of this system see Goodwin, *Analytical
      Physiology*, Chapter 2.
10   B. C. Goodwin, 'A cognitive view of biological process', *J. Social
      Biol. Struct.*, 1 (1978), p. 119.
11   A. M. Turing, 'The chemical basis of morphogenesis', *Phil. Trans.
      Roy. Soc. Ser. B*, 237 (1952), 37–72.
12   L. Wolpert, 'Positional information and the spatial pattern of
      cellular differentiation', *J. Theoret. Biol.*, 25 (1969), 1–47. See also
      Goodwin, *Analytical Physiology*; for a comprehensive account of
      recent developmental biology see D. A. Ede, *Introduction to
      Developmental Biology*, Blackie, 1978.
13   Waddington, 'Epilogue', p. 288.
14   The intelligibility, and inevitability, of this progression is described
      in C. Rosen, *Schoenberg*, Fontana, 1976.
15   This aspect of creativity is stressed in A. Harrison's *Making and
      Thinking: A Study of Intelligent Activities*, Harvester Press, 1978;
      for a case-study, see W. R. Reitman, 'Creative problem solving:
      notes from the autobiography of a fugue', in his *Cognition and
      Thought, An Information Processing Approach*, Wiley, 1965.
16   C. H. Waddington, *The Strategy of the Genes*, Allen & Unwin,
      1957; C. H. Waddington, *The Evolution of an Evolutionist*,
      Edinburgh University Press, 1975.
17   B. C. Goodwin, 'Embryogenesis and cognition', in *Cybernetics
      and Bionics* (ed. W. D. Keidel et al.), Oldenbourg, 1974, p. 47.
18   Goodwin, *Analytical Physiology*, p. vi.
19   W. S. McCulloch, 'A heterarchy of values determined by the
      topology of nervous nets', *Bull. Math. Biophysics*, 11 (1949), 89–93.
20   P. H. Winston, 'The MIT robot', in *Machine Intelligence*, Vol. 7
      (ed. B. Meltzer and D. Michie), Edinburgh University Press, 1972,
      p. 443.
21   The old-young woman picture is in U. Neisser, *Cognitive
      Psychology*, Appleton-Century-Crofts, 1967, p. 142.
22   Goodwin, *Analytical Physiology*, p. 191.
23   R. Edgley, 'Innate ideas', in *Knowledge and Necessity* (ed. G. N.
      A. Vesey), Macmillan 1970, pp. 1–33.
24   See the papers by G. E. M. Anscombe and R. L. Gregory in
      Philosophy of Psychology (ed. S. C. Brown), Macmillan 1974, pp.
      195–220. See also N. Malcolm, 'The myth of cognitive processes
      and structures', in *Cognitive Development and Epistemology* (ed.
      T. Mischel), Academic Press, 1971, 385–92; M. Martin, 'Are

cognitive processes and structure a myth?', *Analysis*, 33 (1973), 83–88.

25   Goodwin, *Analytical Physiology*, p. 223.

26   C. H. Waddington, 'Comments', in *Toward a Theoretical Biology*, Vol. 2 (ed. C. H. Waddington), Edinburgh University Press, 1969, pp. 233, 235.

27   Waddington, 'Epilogue', p. 288.

28   K. R. Popper, *Objective Knowledge: An Evolutionary Approach*, Clarendon Press, 1972; J. Piaget, *Biology and Knowledge*, Edinburgh University Press, 1971.

29   Goodwin, *Analytical Physiology*, p. 220.

30   K. S. Lashley, 'The problem of serial order in behavior', in *Cerebral Mechanisms in Behavior: The Hixon Symposium* (ed. L. A. Jeffress), Wiley 1951, pp. 112–135.

31   Goodwin, 'Embryogenesis and cognition', p. 50.

32   J. Habermas, *Knowledge and Human Interests*, Heinemann, 1972.

33   J. J. Connington, *Nordenholt's Million*, Penguin, 1946, p. 126 (orig. publ. 1923).

34   Goodwin, 'Biology and meaning'.

5
The paradox of explanation

I

To explain X is to make X somehow more intelligible. We may simply want to explain X to our own satisfaction, or we may be asked to explain it to someone else — just how we attempt to do so will depend largely on the nature of X, and also on the person for whom the explanation is intended. For instance, we may be explaining a word, a concept, a theorem, a fact, an action . . . , and we may be talking to a child, a Communist, a Christian, a tribesman, a scientist . . . We will not necessarily use the same procedure in every case, and certain criteria will be more or less appropriate according to the type of explanation required.

But common to *all* cases is the desire for increased intelligibility, and there are two very familiar types of objection made against suggested explanations, on the grounds that these so-called 'explanations' cannot possibly increase intelligibility. Taken separately, these objections seem quite reasonable, and harmless enough. But, considered together, they appear to yield a paradox to delight the heart of any philosophical sceptic, one of which the Paradox of Analysis is a special case.

The objections are of this form: On the one hand, it will be said that an 'explanation' is *no* explanation, if it is circular. X cannot be explained in terms of X, since repeating a problem can hardly increase its intelligibility. On the other hand, it will be said that X cannot be explained in terms of Y, of not-X; for how can not-X possibly be used to increase our understanding of X? X and not-X are just different, so X cannot be explained in terms of Y. It would seem to follow from these premises that no explanation explains, that a real explanation is as far from our grasp as water from Tantalus or jam from the White Queen.

What are we to say? Must we reject one or both of the premises, or must we put up with the conclusion? I suggest that we paradoxically have our cake and eat it: both premises are in order, but the sceptic is blinded by the Law of Excluded Middle, and imagines that these objections can be brought against *all* cases of explanation. 'Surely', he says 'a thing is X or not-X; X is not Y; a man is not a monkey'. True; but X and Y, though different, may not be different in all respects — a man is not a monkey, but sufficiently like one for certain explanations of the one in terms of

113

the other to be possible. It may take insight and discrimination to realize the extent of the analogy between X and Y, or to sort out the significant similarities from the insignificant ones; most objections to suggested explanations are made on one of these counts. An explanation is in principle impossible *only* if X and Y are totally alike — i.e. identical — or totally unlike — i.e., *so* unlike that we cannot see how they even *could* be related. But the sceptic takes these two extremes and, with the help of the Law of Excluded Middle, tortures them into exhausting all possibilities, with the result that he loses sight of the whole range of intermediate cases. It is hardly surprising, then, if he triumphantly claims that 'real' explanations are as unattainable as the most elusive will-o'-the-wisp.

I shall consider cases of these two objections being made inappropriately, and shall try to show that this is usually due to a misunderstanding about the nature of explanation. I shall be particularly interested in misunderstandings about the explanation of facts, as exemplified in certain perennial complaints made about science by philosophers.

II

What force has the first half of the paradox: in what circumstances might a person be likely to object: 'But that's no use — it's circular'? Suppose I come across a word I do not understand, and want it explained. I may reach for the dictionary. Suppose the word is 'basilisk', and on looking it up in the dictionary I find: 'For "basilisk" see "cockatrice" '. I turn to 'cockatrice', since I do not understand that word either, and find: 'For "cockatrice" see "basilisk" '. My reaction may well be to produce some words not to be found in the dictionary at all, so irritated would I be at this apparently useless circularity. This is not to say that I should be none the wiser, for I should know something which I did not know before: that the words 'basilisk' and 'cockatrice' have the same meaning in English. But *what* meaning? This has not been explained, and what I want is some phrase I do understand, such as: 'The fabulous creature hatched from a cock's egg'. It may be that no exactly synonymous word or phrase can be given, and I may have to be satisfied with a list of words which more or less precisely indicate the meaning of the word in question. Thus Alice, asking Humpty Dumpty to explain the meaning of the word 'outgrabe', is told: 'Well, "outgribing" is something between bellowing and whistling, with a kind of sneeze in the middle: however, you'll hear it done, maybe — down in the wood yonder

— and when you've once heard it you'll be quite content'.

Another person, however, might have understood the word 'cockatrice' already, in which case the dictionary would have succeeded in explaining the word 'basilisk' to them. Yet we should still say that the dictionary was unsatisfactory. Not because it relied on its readers' being familiar with the words used in its definitions: this is obviously necessary, and is why a dictionary is not much use to a child or to a foreigner, who has not got the necessary background knowledge. But because in this particular case, it is very *unlikely* that the readers would be familiar with the word used as the definition, and it is unreasonable to assume that this will form part of their background knowledge. In general, explanation cannot succeed in vacuo, or, as Hanson puts it in his book *Patterns of Discovery*, a *completely* novel explanation is a logical impossibility.[1] As Bridgman pointed out,[2] what is familiar to one person may not be familiar to another, and a phenomenon may be familiar in some ways only, while highly unfamiliar in other respects; this led Stace[3] to say that explanation in terms of familiarity is completely worthless. This conclusion goes rather far, but it is true that if an explanation is to be universally acceptable, some criterion of familiarity must be found which will satisfy everybody. An explanation can be objective in the sense of being independent of individual personalities, but not in the sense of being independent of the general cultural background of the group of people who accept it. I shall be mentioning this point again, with reference to the explanation of facts, but first I want to consider an example of explaining, not a fact, but a concept.

It may well be that a man can define a concept, using notions which he understands, and can answer various questions about it, and yet we say he does not really understand the concept, and needs it to be explained to him. This will be the case, for instance, whenever we say that a man understands a concept in theory but not in practice, or that he accepts a theoretical principle without being able to apply it. To take a very simple instance, suppose we ask someone what a dodecahedron is. 'A solid figure having twelve faces', he says. So far, so good. Suppose we now ask him to pick out a dodecahedron from a jumble of objects on a table. He picks up a threepenny-bit, and says that this is a dodecahedron. In order to make him see his mistake, it may be enough to repeat the definition he has already given, to say: 'No, that's not right — you want something with *twelve* faces'. If this is *not* enough, we may then say '*That's* got fourteen faces'. It may even be necessary to quell his protestations by pointing out, one by one, every face of the coin, so that he realizes his mistake. He had merely counted the edges round the coin, which are twelve, since it is a dodecahedron in section; but he had forgotten to count the head and tail sides of the coin, and this may be made still clearer by producing a true dodecahedron and comparing it with the threepenny-bit. The point of this example is twofold: first, that the concept could be explained to him using either an instance of it, or something merely similar to an instance of it; secondly, that there is no one point at which we can *guarantee* that he will accept our explanation. He may see his mistake almost as soon as we tell him he has made one, or it may take many steps and repetitions, many intermediate cases, to make him aware of it; but in any event we cannot *force* him to see it, only help him. We shall see that this is no less true of the explanation of facts: you can lead the sceptical horse to the water of explanation, but you cannot make him drink.

The fact that an 'explanation' may be justifiably rejected as being circular is sometimes confused with the claim that any acceptable explanation must involve the giving of new information. But in the ordinary sense of 'information', providing new information about X is neither necessary nor sufficient for the explanation of X, *although* explaining X often *does* involve giving new information about it. That this is not sufficient is obvious from the basilisk/cockatrice example; that it is not necessary is obvious from any example where the *explicans* and *explicandum* are mutually deducible. For instance, if we have a set of statistics giving a firm's annual profits over twenty years, we can plot these graphically, and may see feaures such as plateaux and peaks on the graph which are connected deductively with the statistics, while these latter can in turn be deduced from the graph. And yet the two are mutually explanatory, while the graph may remind us of other features of our experience — such as peaks and sloughs — which are formally similar to and illuminate the statistics expressed numerically. (In case someone should object that all we can *deduce* from our statistics are twenty points on graph paper, with no neat interconnecting curve, it may be that even the distribution of the individual points as plotted may make us aware of something we had not seen before — although no new information has been given.)

At this point, however, we may hear the sceptic brandishing the analytic/synthetic dichotomy, or even murmuring about the Paradox of Analysis. 'Conclusions must be contained in their premisses', he says, 'otherwise they are not validly derived conclusions; deduction therefore can produce nothing new. An explanation of a concept is nothing but an analysis of it, and we all know how useless that is: it's either true but trivial, or it's false, and so not an analysis of the concept at all. If an explanation does its job, then no job has been done'.

Whereas there was a time when most philosophers would have been very worried by such moves on the part of the sceptic, I think it would be fair to say that many *now* would agree with him that analysis, in one sense, *is* impossible, but would say that it is nonetheless useful as a procedure. Thus they would agree with the sceptic who says that one logical category cannot be reduced by analysis to another; material objects, they will say, cannot be reduced to sense-data, perceptions or the like; 'ought' cannot be reduced to 'is'; 'Everything is itself, and not another thing'. But they will say that analysis nevertheless has an important rôle to play, a rôle which the sceptic has misunderstood. This rôle is not that of reducing one category to another, but that of showing the logical connexions between statements, particularly the con-nections between statements of different categories or strata. This procedure, they will say, aims at improving our understanding of each stratum in terms of some other, so making our language, and therefore our world, generally more intelligible, as mathematical deduction makes more directly intelligible what was merely implicit before. They insist that the connexions between statements of different strata are logically different in kind from those between statements of the same stratum: one material-object statement can entail another, but cannot entail a perceptual statement, although the two strata are connected. This is recognized to a large degree now by people considering analysis as a philosopher's tool. But where explanation of facts is concerned, as opposed to explanations of words or of concepts, it is often lost sight of, with the result that factual explanation is still thought of by many as the attempt to reduce one category of phenomena to another — not to explain, but to explain away — and thus represented as a waste land where the sceptic may wander at his leisure.

III

Explanation of facts *also* involves the comparison of similar and familiar cases, but the term 'factual explanation' covers different types of procedure; historical explanation differs from that found in psycho-analysis, or sociology, or the natural sciences such as physics, chemistry and neuro-physiology. It has been argued that history and psycho-analysis, for instance, can hardly claim to be sciences, that the explanations they offer are not falsifiable in the sense in which those of the natural sciences are. Consequently, the sceptic who wishes to shock us as much as possible will concentrate on those factual explanations which are normally accepted by us without question. The explanations of physics and biology, and every-day explanations linking bodily behaviour with mental events, will provide him with better examples than the more controversial types, which are hampered by the unrepeatability of circumstances and the difficulty of setting up control experiments. So I shall only be concerned with the sorts of facts which we generally assume to be explicable in scientific terms. Lest it be thought that *any* explanation of such a fact must needs be scientific, let us consider a few examples of non-scientific explanations before considering scientific explanations in any detail.

If a child asks why most dogs chase cats up trees, we may tell him Kipling's story about The Cat That Walked by Himself, and say that — ever since the cat's arrogant assertion of independence to the First Dog — all dogs have chased cats up trees, and always will. We should all agree that this is not the real explanation, even if we do not know what the real explanation is; but we can hardly say that it is not an explanation, any more than we can deny that the equally fanciful stories about storks and gooseberry-bushes are explanations of the sudden arrival of babies. Again, a doctor who had been working in Ghana told me how she had persuaded the native women to take certain pills in the correct manner: these pills had to be dissolved in the mouth, and not swallowed whole. Of course, the 'true' explanation of this is in terms of gastric juices' destroying the pills so that they could not be absorbed, or rendering them ineffective in some similar way. And this, in more or less detail, is the sort of explanation which would have been given to any relatively educated patient. But the doctor knew perfectly well that this would not have acted as an explanation for some of her patients, who would merely have been bewildered by it, so she said that the pills had to be kept in the mouth because the magic spirits would not work in the stomach. This had the required effect, so was certainly pragmatically justified. If we say that, nonetheless, since it was not the true explanation, the doctor should not really have said it, then must we not frown on all cases of speaking in parables? Old wives' tales may be bad explanations, but they are explanations.

They are explanations because they are accepted as such by some people, as making the fact in question somehow more intelligible and acceptable. But this, of course, is only a minimum requirement for explanations: there are other requirements which enable us to distinguish a bad explanation from a good one. What are these requirements? *Why* is an old wives' tale not as good as a scientific explanation? Because it is relatively subjective and irrational; it cannot be put to objective tests which might show it to be false, or it is stubbornly adhered to in spite of such tests; it is not afforded universal consent since it does not make facts more intelligible to any trained observer, independent of particular personalities, as even the most abstract explanations of science do; it rarely, if ever, forms part of an interlocking system of hypotheses and laws, deductively related to one another, and it is rarely predictive and fruitful in the way that scientific explanations often are, leading to new knowledge and new sorts of question. The sceptic will not bother to attack old wives' tales, but will try to undermine our faith in the tales of the scientist, saying — perhaps — with Stace: 'The function of science is simply to describe phenomena, never to explain them . . . . Scientific laws explain nothing. Science never can explain even the simplest event'.[4] How does the sceptic's paradox arise with respect to scientific explanations, and can it be resolved?

IV

You may remember the scene in Molière's play *Le Malade Imaginaire* where the pompous doctor, being asked to explain why opium sends a man to sleep, says that it is because of its soporific property. This is generally considered a circular explanation *par excellence*, and thus useless. But is it in fact no explanation? We must be very clear as to the question it is supposed to be answering before we say that — as an answer— it is worthless. If what is to be explained is a particular case of a man's being put to sleep by taking opium, then the doctor's remark *is* explanatory: it tells us that this case is one of many, that it is nothing to be surprised at, that it is not a freak phenomenon unconnected with the rest of our experience concerning opium, and requiring a special explanation of its own. It is due neither to an idiosyncrasy of this individual man, nor to an idiosyncrasy of this particular sample of opium. That is to say, the case is explained simply by saying that it is an instance of a general law, in the same way as we satisfy a child's query why something has a certain property by saying: 'They always do'. The explanation is not circular, but works in virtue of reminding us or informing us of closely similar, though not identical, cases.

Many people have claimed that this is the essential feature of the explanation of individual facts in science — that we subsume them under a general law, thus making them appear more familiar and so more acceptable. Sometimes the laws are not exceptionless but statistical, saying that a large proportion of X's will have a certain property, Y; but we feel unhappy about such laws unless we can give a fairly accurate estimate of the proportion involved, and even then we often want to find some more basic difference which will explain why *some* X's have the property and others do not. For instance, we are not very satisfied with the following explanation: when the Gryphon was telling Alice why whitings have their tails in their mouths, he said: 'The reason is, that they *would* go with the lobsters to the dance. So they got thrown out to sea. So they had to fall a long way. So they got their tails fast in their mouths. So they couldn't get them out again. That's all'. This reminds us, for instance, of cases where people jump off high spring boards and do jackknife dives in the air before reaching the water; and so it is not completely useless as an explanation. But it is incomplete; for the Gryphon is not claiming that every time an animal is thrown violently through the air, it ends up with its tail stuck in its mouth (which is clearly false), but is merely reminding Alice of *some* occasions when this happens, without explaining why it happened to the whitings in this particular instance. Thus it may be true that we will only accept as a *scientific* explanation, one which is framed in terms of a general law admitting of no exceptions, but this does not mean that mere reference to similar cases cannot be explanatory of facts.

A general difficulty of explanation is that of deciding which similarities are relevant, and which may be ignored — this decision is closely linked with the criterion of familiarity. Suppose we live on a blasted heath covered with rocks, and we notice that after every violent thunderstorm about half the rocks can be heard ticking. We have never known rocks to tick before, and so should want an explanation of this; and we should also want to know why only some of the rocks were ticking. Suppose we got a pickaxe and split a lot of the rocks open, to find that all the ticking rocks which we open have a small globule of rubber inside, whereas none of the silent rocks has. I think our first reaction would be, not to accept the rubber globules as the explanation of the ticking, but to look for some other property common to the ticking rocks alone. This is because we are not familiar with any other cases of ticking being explained by rubber, nor of rubber being activated by thunderstorms. If we could find no other difference, we should probably accept the rubber as the explanation of the ticking, despite our puzzlement, and should ask for a further explanation: of how the rubber and the ticking are connected, and why the ticking only occurs after thunderstorms. That is to say, we should not be satisfied with a statement of correlation which is merely falsifiable and predictive, being a general law linking similar cases, but should want to show that the similarity really was a relevant one, and not just coincidental.

The criteria of relevance and familiarity are very closely linked; if an explanation is similar in type to explanations already accepted, and can be easily linked with them, then we are more likely to be satisfied with it than we are to be satisfied with a relatively unusual explanation. Obviously its acceptability will vary with the background knowledge of the scientists concerned, and this itself will vary over the years, so that an explanation will be acceptable at one time and not at another. Conant[5] expresses this by saying that to explain a fact is to fit it into a pre-exisiting conceptual scheme — the body of accepted scientific theory and terminology — and thus to exhibit its similarity to familiar cases and, if possible, its interlocking connections with cases which seem at first sight very dissimilar. To modify the conceptual scheme in any radical way is to introduce a new kind of explanation, and with it a new kind of enquiry, and this is a major achievement of the scientific intellect. Thus when Harvey wrote about the pumping-motion of the heart as promoting the circulation of the blood, he did much more than explain one bodily function among others: he laid the foundations for a completely new way of asking questions about such functions, and thus of explaining them. We now notice the similarities between living organisms and purely mechanical systems, and think them significant and explanatory, instead of ignoring them as irrelevant and unilluminating.

Thus, if we had found that all the ticking rocks had contained a metallic core, while none of the silent rocks did, we should have been much readier to accept this as an explanation of the noise. For we know that metals are conductors of electricity, and may be activated by lightning. Of course we should go on to ask just how the ticking was connected with the metal, but we should not feel so puzzled as we should if we found the rubber. Someone who knew nothing about electricity or the reaction of metals to lightning would be equally puzzled in either case. Whether we told him that 'All the ticking rocks contain rubber' or 'All the ticking rocks contain metal', his immediate reaction would be the same: to ask 'So what?' This is a very useful question as a test for explanations, but the sceptic uses it too often and indiscriminately.

We have seen that we may explain a particular fact, to a certain extent, by reminding ourselves or informing ourselves of similar cases, and may put our explanation in terms of a general law. Thus: This man went to sleep after taking opium because men always sleep after taking opium; This cat has no tail because it is a Manx cat, and no Manx cats have tails. Of course, we may then ask for an explanation of the general law: 'Why does opium always send people to sleep?' But this is a different question. Even here we must be careful before saying that the doctor's answer will not do: we must be sure that we know what he means when he says, 'It is because of its soporific property'. If he says that 'X has a soporific property' means no more and no less than 'X always (or usually) sends people to sleep' then his proffered 'explanation' *is* circular, and we *may* reject it. This sort of argument has been used by some people to attack the view that the theoretical entities of science, such as electrons and lines of force, are logical constructions out of the relevant observations. If they were, then statements about such entities would merely be convenient abbreviations for statements about the original data, and thus could hardly be *explanations* of these data, which they certainly are.

But the doctor may mean by 'X has a soporific property', that X has some particular, isolable property or principle which, whether combined with X or with Y, will always induce sleep. Thus whisky induces sleep because of a soporific principle, alcohol, which is also present in the soporifics gin and beer. If we cannot find any such principle in opium, but have to explain its effects by reference to the properties of the opium-molecule as a whole, then our explanation will necessarily have to exclude talk about soporific principles, as being either false or circular. That the original explanation can be taken further does not mean that it has made no advance at all, and if a sceptic objects that such 'explanations' are circular, and thus useless, that they do no more than *describe* the facts, then we can only say that he is suffering from excess of zeal. To subsume a particular fact under a low-level general law of this type is not to explain X in terms of itself, but in terms of other, similar, members of the class of all X's.

Suppose we ask why a certain cushion is purple, and are told that it is because it is made up of purple threads: will the sceptic be justified in saying that this reply is circular? 'Surely', he will say, 'purple cannot be explained in terms of purple'. But it can: the cushion might have been made of a mixture of red and blue threads. In general, we can often explain a thing's having property X by saying that it is made up of parts all of which have X, and the sceptic cannot impale us on the first horn of his dilemma — the horn of circularity.

But here we see an excellent opportunity for the sceptic to ask a question which *will* drive us on to the first horn and thence, it seems, on to the second. He will ask us: 'How do you explain the fact that all X's are X? For instance, why are all purple things purple?' We cannot now say: 'Because all purple things are made up of purple parts', for this *does* beg the question at issue. Hanson puts this very clearly when he says:

What requires explanation cannot itself figure in the explanation . . . . One cannot explain why any given thing is red by saying that *all* red things contain red particles; nor could one explain why any thing moves by noting that *any* moving thing contains moving particles. In general, though each member of a class of events may be explained by other members, the *totality* of the class cannot be explained by any member of the class. The totality of movement cannot be explained by anything that moves. The totality of red things cannot be explained by anything which is red. All picturable properties of objects cannot be explained by reference to anything which itself possesses those properties.[6]

He then illustrates this by reminding us of the history of atomism. Atoms were introduced to explain the various sensible qualities of things, and thus could not themselves possess these qualities. They became gradually less picturable and concrete; the atoms of Democritus and the scientists of the seventeenth century possessed no secondary qualities, no colour, odour, sound or taste; but they did possess primary qualities, i.e., size and shape, together with mass or solidity, and force or motion, in virtue of which they produced the sensations of the secondary qualities in observers. Now they are even less easily picturable: they are no longer likened to tiny billiard balls, albeit colourless ones, but are called upon to explain the geometrical and dynamical properties of billiard balls, and thus cannot themselves possess these properties. Science, to be explanatory, *must* become more and more abstract.

V

Hanson, therefore, takes the charge of circularity seriously, and concludes that 'what requires explanation cannot itself figure in the explanation'. It is at this point that the sceptic will brandish his second weapon: 'X cannot be explained in terms of Y. Even if particular phenomena can be explained, total classes can not — science can describe such classes, but cannot explain them'. I shall give three examples of this type of objection.

First, we are accustomed to explain the difference in pitch between various sounds in terms of the frequencies or wavelengths of the sound-waves. A sound-wave is not itself sound, but is the overall pattern of vibrations within a certain collection of particles; each recurring unit of the pattern can be measured, and its length (wavelength) expressed in linear units. It makes sense to say that the wavelength of a sound-wave is 400 cms., but not that a particular sound is 400 cms. long. And just because the concept of sound as experienced is logically so different from the concept of length, people are often puzzled by this explanation. 'How *can* sound be explained in terms of length?' they will say; and, perhaps, 'Sound, like colour, is sui generis — it cannot be explained by anything else such as wavelength or frequency'. Of course, they are not denying the correlation between sounds of a certain pitch and waves of a particular frequency: they are, rather, denying that this correlation has explanatory value. And it is not merely this particular correlation which they find unsatisfactory: *any* correlation of sound with a non-auditory concept would be judged unsatisfactory as an explanation of sound itself. Thus the condition that Hanson claims to be logically essential for explanation they say is logically suicidal to any explanation.

Again, many philosophers represent science as being a falsifiable hypothetico-deductive system which explains events by subsuming them under general laws, and explains these laws by means of higher level laws. An event or law which can be *deduced* from the theoretical system together with a statement of initial conditions is thereby explained, and if it cannot be deduced in this way then it cannot — as yet — be explained. It follows that at any given time the highest-level, most explanatory, laws cannot themselves be explained, although they may be, eventually. Hempel says: 'Scientific explanation, prediction and post-diction all have the *same* logical character: they show that the fact under consideration can be inferred from certain other facts by means of certain specified general laws'.[7] Thus facts about sound as experienced can be (explained or predicted by being) deduced from theories about sound-waves, wavelengths and frequencies. But, since in any valid deduction the conclusion is contained in the premisses, the theories cannot contain reference *only* to hypothetical, transcendent entities or concepts, but must *also* involve mention of the classes of facts to be explained. William Kneale says:

If the hypotheses contained no reference to observable things, they could not explain laws about observables. But hypotheses are of the form: Wherever light of colour *X* — or sound of pitch *X* — occurs, there is wave-process Y . . . . They are introduced for the purpose of explaining laws, and, however abstruse they may become in the course of development, they must always remain attached in this way to the world of perceptual objects, if they are to achieve their purpose.[8]

The explanation of X in terms of Y is the deduction of the event or law from premises including a statement of the correlation between X and Y, sound and wavelength. This correlation itself is not explained, and Kneale gives the impression that it never can be:

> Although the connections within the world of transcendent entities postulated by a theory may all be self-evident, the relations *between* this world and the world of perceptual objects remain opaque to the intellect, and it is only by assuming these relations that we can explain our laws about observables.

Again Hanson's condition that what requires explanation cannot itself figure in the explanation is rejected, because any acceptable explanation must be deductive. Observables are explained by reference to observables, together with reference to entities which are in principle unobservable. These transcendent entities *alone* cannot explain observable events, and their relation to such events is made to sound very mysterious indeed by being described as necessarily 'opaque to the intellect'.

A third, and very familiar, example of the sceptic's complaint that X cannot be explained in terms of Y is the perennial difficulty of explaining mental events in terms of bodily processes. We have Descartes and Spinoza, with their deductive model of explanation, saying that interaction is incomprehensible since mind and body are logically distinct, though they do not deny a factual correlation between mental and physical events; and in the same tradition we have Leibniz saying that 'a perception can only be explained by a perception, a motion by a motion'. This dualism with its attendant puzzles about mind/body explanations is — pace Ryle — by no means dead today. A recent article in *Mind* by P. C. Dodwell shows this very clearly.[9]

Dodwell is concerned with the function of mechanical models built by psychologists in order to explain behaviour. He draws a sharp distinction between explanation and prediction, saying that I may be able to predict an action without being able to explain it. For instance, I could predict — on the basis of observation — that a certain man would insult a clergyman if he met one, without being able necessarily to explain this. Any *explanation* would be in terms of motives, purposes, emotions or some other psychological term. He says that, since no statement involving psychological terms can be deduced from premisses purely about observables, therefore no mechanical model can yield statements involving psychological concepts if the model was described in purely mechanical terms. His thesis is that, since all scientific explanations are deductive, no behaviour which we are accustomed to think of in mental terms can be *explained* by such a model, although such behaviour might well be predicted on the basis of observations of the model. As examples of behaviour which can only be explained psychologically, he mentions 'learning', 'classifying', remembering'. He says that psychologists have been misled into imagining that mechanical models *could* explain such behaviour, by their habit of using mentally-tinged words to describe the behaviour of the model. If these words, such as 'learn', are redefined in physical terms before they are used to describe the models, and if they are always used strictly in these ways, then the model can have no explanatory force. But usually the psychologist, while he believes himself to be using the words as newly defined, is in fact largely influenced by their original psychological meanings, and thus represents his mechanical models as being explanatory of mental behaviour. Dodwell says that in so far as such words retain their original meanings, the models *can* furnish explanations: but these explanations are not different in kind from other psychological explanations. In general, mind can never be explained in terms of matter because no mental concept can be deduced from a material concept; we can predict mental events on the basis of physical events, if we accept a factual correlation between such events, which correlation is itself unexplained, and opaque to the intellect. This is in straightforward conflict with Hanson's thesis that explanation of a class X must be in terms of something logically different.

VI

If we accept the three objections which I have just outlined, then we must reject the majority of 'explanations' offered by science. We may say that science predicts, that science describes, but does not explain. We must reject Hanson's claim that the class of X's not only *can* be, but *must* be explained by not-X; we must admit many different levels of concepts, each of which is sui generis, and none of which can be used to explain another. For instance, we must say that sound cannot be explained in terms of wavelength, that the former cannot be made more intelligible in terms of the latter.

This over-zealous scepticism is too paradoxical: *certainly* the correlation between sound and wavelength is explanatory, just as that between colour and wavelength, or mind and body. Differences between the pitch of individual sounds correspond to differences between wavelengths: the wave theory links different sounds together in terms of a basic formal likeness, for subjective variations in pitch can be correlated with measurable differences in length, and so can be conveniently represented mathematically. In a similar way, a list of statistics explains a hump-shaped line on graph-paper, or a series of contours increases our understanding of a mountain-range, because of a basic formal likeness.

Explanation works by analogy, but the analogy may be more or less marked, and may be analogy of content as well as analogy of structure. When the analogy is well-marked in terms of content, or observable characteristics, we speak of a model: e.g. explanations of electrical phenomena in terms of current use a hydrostatic model, and explanations of the Gas Laws in terms of the Kinetic, Molecular Theory of Gases use a mechanical model. A model need not be abstract to be explanatory: we must not reserve explanatory status in science for transcendent entities which are in principle unobservable. If an explanation involves terms which we later find to correspond to fairly directly observable entities, this does not give us the right to say that the 'explanation' was merely an inspired description. For instance, the circulation of the blood is explained by the postulation of narrow capillaries linking arteries and veins. Harvey could not *describe* these capillaries, because he could not see them; but being able to see capillaries under the microscope by no means prevents us from using them to explain the hydrostatic properties of the blood. Similarly, the bacteriologist does not merely *describe* nature when he shows us photographs of the tubercle bacillus: he *explains* nature in so far as he increases our understanding of a particular disease. When the analogy between X and Y is purely structural, there being no property common to X and Y except this formal one, we may speak of a mathematical model, or of a mere spatio-temporal *correlation* — of pitch and wavelength, for instance, or nerve-impulses and sensations. This latter way of talking will be encouraged if we cannot see how X itself can be measured, and so expressed in mathematical terms: a mountain, like a graph, can be measured, whereas a sound cannot.

We may be able to explain why different wavelengths are

produced in different circumstances — in terms, for example, of
the length and tension of stretched strings. We may even be able to
explain the actual correlation between sound X and wavelength Y,
in terms of the properties of the inner ear, or of the branches of the
auditory nerve, and this would be one way of making the relation
between X and Y less opaque to the intellect: differences in pitch of
sound as experienced have been shown to correspond in a regular
fashion with different cells of the cochlea of the inner ear. So, given
that X is explained by being correlated with Y, we can then ask for
a further explanation of Y, and even for an explanation of that
correlation. These are requests for scientific explanations,
requests which we may or may not be able to fulfil.

But to suggest that X *cannot* be explained by being correlated
with Y, or to ask how it is that X is explained by being correlated
with Y, is to raise quite a different problem, to ask a different type
of question. It is *not* to ask a question about an event, or scientific
law. It is to ask *either* a very general metaphysical question as to
why the universe is as it is, which many people would say is
unanswerable, and even meaningless; *or*, and much more likely, it
is to ask a meta-question, one about the very nature of explanation
itself. It is this question which the sceptic is asking, even though he
may imagine that he is merely insisting on being given a superior
explanation instead of an inferior one.

And this we can only answer by exhibiting various cases of
explanation and saying: 'Well, these are explanations, aren't
they?' To go through this case-by-case procedure just is to explain
explanation; there can obviously be no non-circular *explanation* of
what it is to explain, in the same sense in which there can be no
non-circular *proof* of the laws of logic. A man who doubts whether
sound can be made more intelligible by wavelength, mental events
by bodily events, is like one who doubts whether the concept of a
dodecahedron can be made more intelligible by looking at a
threepenny-bit. That, in these instances, X *can* be made more
intelligible by Y, can only be shown by reminding him of the
various procedures which we normally accept as explanations.

Making a fact or a concept more intelligible does not involve
only the clarification of its internal structure. To increase our
understanding of a town, or a map of that town, we do not need
only to explore the narrowest alleys, or increase the scale of our
map; we also need to relate the town as a whole to features outside
it, to include our map within a more extensive one showing the
town's geographical, political and trade relationships with other
parts of the world. So, making a phenomenon or concept more
intelligible will involve showing its relationships to those things

which are logically rather *unlike* it, as well as showing how it fits
into its own logical category or stratum. We produce the several
like cases, and hope to make the sceptic see the likeness, and how
one case illuminates another. But, or course, the likeness is not
another case, and whereas we can force him to see the individual
cases, we cannot force him to see the likeness. We can force him to
consider X, and to consider Y, but cannot force him to see that X
may be explained by Y.

We cannot convince the sceptic unless he accepts the rôle of
analogy in explanation, and realizes that explanations are only
impossible if *explicans* and *explicandum* are either identical or
utterly dissimilar. If he insists on emphasizing these extremes, and
taking them to cover all cases, he produces a dilemma which
asserts explanation to be impossible. In this case he is no longer
using every-day criteria and his position is logically unassailable,
like that of the man who says that we can never know the mind of
another, but will not allow that anything could possibly count as
knowing the mind of another. Both positions are paradoxical
though illuminating — and both arise from confusion as to the
procedures involved, whether it be getting to know the mind of
another, or explaining X in terms of Y. To explain X by Y is *not*
necessarily to reduce X to Y. It is *not* to say: X is *nothing but Y*,
sound is *nothing but* wavelength, temperature is *nothing but*
motion, mental events are *nothing but* bodily events. To explain is
not to explain away. The sceptic would have us believe that
satisfactory explanations are not merely forbidden to us by the
Gods, as water was to Tantalus, but logically unattainable, as jam
was for the White Queen. But he is wrong: we have explanations
every day.

NOTES

1   Page 54.
2   *The Logic of Modern Physics*, Chapter 2.
3   *Philosophy* 1935.
4   *Loc. cit.*
5   *On Understanding Science*.
6   *Op. cit.*, pp. 119 ff.
7   *Minnesota Studies in Philosophy of Science*, Vol. 2, p. 37.
8   *Probability and Induction*, pp. 92–96.
9   *Mind*, January 1960.

PART II

WHAT WE HAVE IN MIND

6
The structure of intentions

I

What are intentions? What, for instance, is the intention to buy a loaf of bread? Theoretical psychologists offer differing answers to these questions, for they disagree about the nature and importance of intentions. Not all allow that intention is a useful systematic concept, and even those who do so define it in significantly different ways. My central thesis is that any specific instance of intention is a highly structured phenomenon arising within a highly structured system, and that the nature of intention as a psychological reality cannot be understood unless this fact is taken into account. Generic characterizations of intentions in terms simply of their immediate goal or purpose — as in expressions of the form 'the intention to X' — denote general types of phenomena whose individual tokens may differ greatly. In a sense, then, there is no such thing as *the* intention to buy bread, since intentions to buy bread comprise a markedly heterogeneous class when considered in light of their psychological structure. These differences are important because they determine the function of particular intentions within the life of the agents in whom they arise, and they can be expressed only by a theory of intention adequate to represent the distinct structures that may be concerned. Such a theory would readily allow that the psychological nature of intentions to buy bread, for instance, may be very varied indeed.

II

All identifications of intention mention a particular end or purpose, in terms of which the intention is characterized. Thus the variable X, in expressions of the form 'the intention to X', specifies the goal that the agent intends to achieve. It follows that any satisfactory definition of intention must stress the goal, where this is conceived of as an idea which is the intentional object of the intention, rather than as an existent state-of-affairs in the real world. Indeed, intentions might be defined purely in terms of their goals, in terms of what the agent intends to achieve. It would follow that all persons intending the same goal, or end-state, could be said to share the same intention. Any psychological difference there might be between these people would then be differences in the psychological conditions surrounding or attendant upon their intentions, not differences intrinsic to the intentions themselves. If a number of people all have the goal of buying bread then, according to this definition, each has the same intention, no matter what else may distinguish them. All instances of intention satisfy this 'minimal' definition. But most intentions satisfy a rather stronger characterization — one which suggests structural distinctions between superficially equivalent intentions that are hidden by the minimal definition, and which stresses the active role of intentions in guiding behaviour towards their goals.

It is crucial to appreciate that a goal (or purpose) is a type of idea which is potentially directive, which can somehow influence and guide the agent's actions. It is not a mere picture, a mere representation of some hypothetical state. References to intention in everyday life — and in those psychological theories which admit it as a systematic term — are regarded as explanatory of action because the intention is conceived of as somehow bringing about, causing, or directing the action intended. The intention to buy bread, for instance, somehow results in the act of purchasing a loaf. This functional feature of intention is emphasized if one thinks of an intention as a schema controlling the procedures to be executed in behaviour, as a plan of action that can be realized in actual operations carried out by the agent. The essential aspect of any given intention is thus some procedural schema or action-plan. For the time being I shall use these two expressions interchangeably, even though they have significantly different overtones. The crucial question at this stage is to ask what must be the nature of an action-plan, in order that it may be able to carry out the controlling function commonly ascribed to intentions.

An action-plan is an internal representation of possible action that functions as a model guiding intentional behaviour.[1] It is closely analogous to the sets of instructions comprising procedural routines within a computer program, for such routines also specify certain operations and control the order of their execution. Indeed, one of the more fruitful definitions of 'intention' to be found in contemporary psychological theory explicitly draws such a comparison: this is the definition given by Miller, Galanter and Pribram,[2] to which I shall return later in the paper.

The goal or putative end-state of an intention must be represented within its action-plan. This representation may be of varying levels of generality: one may intend to buy a fresh, one-pound, wholemeal loaf or one may intend to buy the first loaf one sees, irrespective of type. If the intention to buy bread is functioning as part of a further intention, then certain representations of the goal of buying bread may be more appropriate than others. For instance, any loaf will do to feed the ducks, but if one aims to make cucumber sandwiches for Lady Bracknell then certain constraints on the nature of the loaf must be satisfied. These constraints form part of the goal-representation within the action-plan. The goal may be of various logical types, including a bodily action, a social act, and a state of affairs towards which one can strive but which is not itself an activity of any kind.

It is by reference to the goal that other features are brought into the action-plan for, given the goal to be achieved, the generation of an appropriate action-plan for achieving it is a form of conscious or unconscious problem-solving closely guided by the agent's preferences and beliefs. Sometimes an appropriate action-plan is already available and needs only to be located and activated. But sometimes an action-plan has to be generated afresh, becoming articulated in more and more detail as time passes. A complete action-plan will include representations of the procedures or means-activities selected for pursuing the goal. The plan may also involve beliefs about the likely consequences of different means-activities, considered at the general level of strategy and at the detailed level of tactics. A number of alternative procedural structures may be specifically represented at a relatively early stage in the development of the intention. Such 'contingency planning' aims to anticipate difficulties and obstacles which may arise when the intention is carried out. Very often, tactical decisions are not made (or even considered) until the intention is actually being executed, although strategic decisions may have been articulated long before the intention is put into effect. Procedural schemata are generated recursively, in that a high-level action-plan is compounded of a series of low-level plans, each of which is itself a hierarchical structure generated from more basic action-plans. Thus a plan for the act of buying a loaf may include sub-plans for walking to the bakehouse, opening the door, greeting the baker, taking the bread, and handing over the money. This series is temporally ordered, at least in part: although one might hand over the money before taking the bread, one could hardly do either before reaching the bakery. In turn, 'handing over the money' involves delving in one's pockets or handbag, picking out certain coins, and transferring them to the baker's grasp. The intention to buy bread may then be said hierarchically to include all these action-plans (all these intentions), although this is not to say that each one must be represented at some fully conscious level of the mind at the initial (or any) stage of intentional activity.

Of course, not all intentions are feasible: even a highly detailed action-plan may involve internal inconsistencies, or faulty assumptions about the agent's capabilities and/or the nature of his environment, which vitiate the possibility of actually effecting the plan. In general, it is more difficult to be sure that an intention is feasible if its action-plan is formulated only at the strategic rather than the tactical level. Translation from strategy into tactics may reveal unsuspected snags requiring a complete revision or recasting of the action-plan, or it may show hidden procedural gaps between subordinate units which have somehow to be filled before the action-plan is complete. It is especially difficult to be confident of the feasibility of an intention that has been formulated only in the minimal sense, with no attempt at articulating an action-plan, In such cases, some state-of-affairs is accepted by the agent as a goal without even the sketchiest procedural plan. The minimal definition of intention (in terms of the goal-state alone) covers such cases, whereas characterization in terms of action-plans apparently does not. But even here one must at least allow that the goal can be put on a list of 'things to be done', which implies that the agent considers it as potentially directive, or purposive, as something which could be expanded into an action-plan. Analogous processes might occur within the running of a computer program, where some task is listed as something to be done later, although no plans are currently formulated for so doing. It may turn out, of course, that no effective action-plan can be formulated — either because of specific limitations set by the agent's mental structure or because the task is in principle impossible (like 'squaring the circle').

If the agent is to achieve success in his intentional behaviour, many of his beliefs about means–end relations must qualify as strategic or tactical knowledge about the procedures appropriate for achieving his purposes in his world. Intentions are likely to be effective only if the inner organization or structure of action-plans adequately represents the opportunities for the constraints upon action in the agent's physical and cultural environment.

A person's effective intentions draw upon some highly abstract and general schemata or belief-systems, such as those representing the generative rules of linguistic grammar, the potentialities for bodily action in three-dimensional space, and the overall psychological nature of human interpersonal relations. Intentions also involve a host of more particularized schemata representing the structure of the agent's world, of which an important class are those providing psychological information about culture-specific conventions and social roles and about the idiosyncracies of individuals within the agent's personal acquaintance. These include, for instance, representations of particular religious rituals connected with sacred bread (of which one example would be the Christian sacrament of the Eucharist), representations of the conventional rules prescribing the acts of barter or monetary exchange within particular societies, and representations of Lady Bracknell's attitude to cucumber sandwiches. The information represented by these schemata specifies constraints upon the possible action-plans appropriate to many different classes of intentions, including 'the' intention to purchase bread.

As well as schemata representing constraints on and opportunities for planning actions, the agent must also have available more or less independent representations of methods or strategies that may be called upon in forming action-plans. Some of these are very general, such as 'when in difficulty, try the procedure which worked in some previous, similar, case'; others are more specific, such as 'when you need a small amount of money and have no change, try to borrow it from a friend'.

In so far as these varied types of schemata may be thought of as information stores, available to but independent of particular intentions, they may be labelled 'cognitive' rather than 'conative'. But they contribute to the inner structure of every intention, for they function so as to provide sets of rules for selecting and combining action-plans. If one intends to buy bread, for instance, the knowledge of which bakers are open and which are shut on that day of the week will enter into the generation of one's plan of action in a definite way; one's knowledge of local topography (and perhaps of map-reading) will guide one's locomotion to the selected shop; one's knowledge of linguistic grammar and of the reciprocal roles of shopkeeper and customer will both be needed to generate that part of the action-plan concerned with speaking to the baker; and one's financial competence will guide and monitor the exchange of coins over the shop counter. Not all these forms of knowledge will be consciously expressed, or even expressible, by the agent who structures his intentional behaviour by way of them. Crucial aspects of intentions may thus be hidden to introspection. But unless an intention is thought of as an action-plan that can draw upon background knowledge and utilize it in the guidance of behaviour one cannot understand how intentions function in real life.

Since intentions involve action-plans organized in light of the cognitive structures within the mind, it follows that the inner structure of 'the' intention to X may vary considerably in different individuals and societies. In Penge one could buy a loaf of bread by

telephoning the baker before his delivery van leaves and promising
to mail a cheque in the nearest pillarbox; presumably, in Patagonia
one could not. And even in Penge one could walk to the shop and
pay cash onself. If Marie Antoinette really said 'Let them eat
cake', she must indeed have lived worlds apart from starving
peasants wishing — but unable — to buy bread.[3] In view of the
great variability of human circumstances, preferences, social
customs, and beliefs, the potential for structural variation between
distinct instances of 'one and the same' intention is very rich. In
the minimal sense, of course, two people with the same purpose in
mind have the same intention. But their subjective views of the
world may be so different that the ways in which their respective
intentions function are extremely diverse. If the intention to
relieve someone suffering convulsions arises within the cognitive
context of tribal witchcraft, it will be different in many ways from
its analogue in the context of Western medicine; thus the latter,
though not the former, might involve purchase of a loaf of
rye-bread as a means of biochemical confirmation of the diagnosis
of ergot poisoning. Only a structural theory of intention could
recognize and adequately account for this diversity. References to
intentions which identify them merely in terms of the intended
goal, as in expressions of the form 'the intention to X', provide
only a minimal characterization of the psychological realities
involved.

III

Not all intentions having the same goal and action-plan are
psychologically equivalent — not even if they are subordinate to
identical further intentions. For intentions also serve deeper (as
opposed to further) purposes. Any psychology which recognizes
intentions or purposes at all must allow for the myriad 'superficial'
purposes of men to be explained in terms of underlying purposes of
a more basic and enduring nature.[4] Unless a putative goal can be
somehow linked with one or more of these deeper purposes, it
cannot be accepted as an intention by the mind in which it is
represented. This linkage may be complex and indirect, so that
apparently similar intentions can differ significantly in their deep
conative structure. In other words, they may vary in their dynamic
or motivational base and in the way in which they are linked with
the base. Psychodynamic theories or depth-psychologies (sic)
attempt to show how this linkage is effected. They postulate a
relatively small number of basic conative elements (named
'motives', 'instincts', 'tendencies', 'needs', and 'drives') and a set

of theoretical rules for establishing connections of various sorts between these elements and putative goals of a more sophisticated or superficial nature. On the assumption that the intention of buying bread can be correctly ascribed to each of six men waiting in line outside a bakehouse, and that the action-plans for achieving their respective purchases are identical, one may ask how depth-psychology might distinguish between the individual intentions concerned. This is to ask how the nature of each individual intention depends upon its structured relations with the system of deeper goals within which it has arisen and by which it has been accepted.

The psychodynamics of this example may at first sight appear so obvious as to be trivial. It seems safe to assume that any psychologist who commits himself to compiling a list of 'basic', 'instinctive', or 'natural' goals will include the goal of food-gathering (the elemental motive of hunger), unless he is theoretically so parsimonious as to ascribe all purposive action to the hedonistic pursuit of pleasure. Barring theoretical hedonists, then, one might say that a psychodynamic theory must ascribe the intention to buy bread directly to the motive of hunger. And, indeed, the first man in line may be licking his lips and rubbing his stomach, and may eat the loaf as soon as he gets it — clearly achieving a consummation devoutly to be wished. Here there is little purposive depth and minimal motivational structure: the theoretical path linking the basic goal of food-seeking to the intention of buying bread is short and uncomplicated.

However, the second man may carry his bread round the corner with a lascivious smirk, depositing it in the lap of a starving and beautiful girl. Even if he shares her repast, one would be innocent indeed to assume that he must be motivated purely (if at all) by hunger. The fact that he may be driven both by sex and by hunger is a simple example of what Freud called the 'overdetermination' of behaviour, the possibility that two dynamic structures may generate one surface intention at a particular moment in time. Because the intention to X can thus have two or more 'meanings' simultaneously, it is possible for a purposive action to 'kill two birds with one stone'. Since either theoretical interpretation suffices to generate the surface intention, the other interpretation may always be rejected without thereby leaving the intention wholly unexplained in dynamic terms. This accounts for the ease with which critics of Freud can dispense with his interpretations of the unconscious symbolic meaning or 'psychopathology' of everyday intentions — to collect stamps, for instance, or to smoke a cigar — without necessarily thereby creating an explanatory vacuum.[5] Cases of overdetermination aside, it is clear that a man *may* be motivated by sexual desire alone when purchasing bread, in which case his intention to buy bread is basically different psychologically from that of a hungry person. The dynamic structure is still fairly simple, for only one uncomplicated basic conative category needs to be mentioned — namely, sex. However, the surface intention is not immediately generated from the sexual base, but has to be mediated by the man's psychological knowledge of the nature of gratitude: how it can arise and how it can affect the actions of the grateful person. This knowledge of interpersonal psychology is not necessary to generate the surface intention of getting bread from the dynamic base of hunger.

It should not be assumed that if a man eats the bread then he must necessarily be motivated by hunger, even in part. The third man in the queue, let us suppose, buys fifty loaves and instals himself in the local exhibition-hall, where he proceeds to munch his way through the pile until nausea supervenes. A simple theoretical generation of such behaviour from hunger alone would hardly be convincing. It is of course possible that he is a destitute cripple whose distress is being exploited by a callous impresario, by an unfeeling showman who has promised him pound for pound, sterling for avoirdupois, in respect of all the bread he can consume within the hour. If so, his intention to buy bread could be generated from his present hunger, together with his expectation of future hunger. But if he is a normal man in full employment no such generative structure would be plausible. His intention might, however, be attributed fairly directly to basic motives such as competitiveness or self-display, each of which have been posited as ultimate conative categories by a number of theoretical psychologists.

The last example suggests that identification of the ultimate conative categories may be a controversial matter: not all psychologists would be willing to include competitiveness and self-display in their list of basic motives, or instincts. This does not mean that they would disallow all reference to such items as being irrelevant to the dynamics of intention, but rather that they would regard them as terms on a higher (more complex) theoretical level than their postulated basic categories of desire. Competitiveness and self-display would then be represented as high-level psychological phenomena generated from more basic purposes. This type of theoretical disagreement may be illustrated by supposing that the fourth man outside the bakery takes his loaf to the altar of his church as an offering for the harvest festival. 'Religious' motivation, to be sure — but how is such motivation to be analysed?

Theoretical psychologists differ considerably in their conative analysis of religious behaviour. A few writers — such as Darwin[6] and Starbuck[7] — have regarded it as directly attributable to a specifically religious instinct comparable to the sex and hunger drives. Darwin even claimed to have detected an animistic instinct in animals, which he assumed to be an evolutionary precursor of the human religious instinct.

Others refuse to derive religious behaviour from a distinctively religious instinct, but none the less explain its motivational base in terms of one instinct almost to the exclusion of others. For instance, Trotter based religion in the social or gregarious instinct, which he called the 'herd-instinct'. He characterized religious feeling as 'a sense of personal incompleteness which compels the individual to reach out towards some larger existence than his own', and regarded is as closely analogous to the physical loneliness and intellectual isolation which, he claimed, are effectually solaced only by the nearness and agreement of the herd.[8]

Freud, in contrast to Trotter, attributed religion primarily to the sexual instinct: though the psychological processes involved in the generation of religion from sex may be very complex, the dynamic base of religion he saw as overwhelmingly sexual in nature.[9][10] The complexity of the unconscious ('primary') process transforming the sexual basis into the surface phenomena of religion allow for structural distinctions between religious intentions. For example, Freud's account of a priest's quest for bread intended for the Christian sacrament of the Eucharist would mention more complex processes of sublimation than would his explanation of St. Teresa's language of religious ecstasy. The psychological meaning of the Eucharist, according to Freud, involves the Oedipus complex; symbolic representations of identification with another person by way of bodily incorporation (similar to the representations underlying ritual cannibalism and pagan sacrificial totem feasts); and notions of *self*-sacrifice which can support the guilt-appeasing doctrine of the Atonement while at the same time representing the final triumph of the son over the father (see ref. 9, chapter IV, sections 4–6). Only some of these symbolic transformations need underlie the purchase of bread for a harvest festival, since this may be conceived as a thanksgiving ritual with no sacrificial component. And fewer still would be crucially involved in St. Teresa's mystical experience of personal relationship with her Saviour. In other words, in Freud's theoretical system the generation of the sacramental incorporation of bread requires more symbolic transformations of the sexual basis than does the generation of a nun's love of Christ.[11] In turn,

Freud would be able to distinguish between the 'religious' sexuality of St. Teresa's passion and the 'secular' sexuality of a man who enters a church merely for the purpose of flirtation — for only the former would involve any of the conative transformations typical of religious sublimation. All truly 'religious' intentions must involve these sublimational processes in some degree.

Still other psychologists represent the dynamic basis of religion as a complex of motives. McDougall, like Trotter and Freud, regarded religious intent as springing from basic purposes of a secular nature; but he analysed religious motivation as a hierarchical blend of four distinct instincts — curiosity, submission, flight, and the parental instinct.[12] Further, he distinguished systematically between various forms of religious motivation, by detailing structural variations in the hierarchies involving these four instincts. For example, he recognized the differences in the phenomenological experience and practical effects of the type of reverence which is directed on God or spirits, and the type which is directed on impersonal objects such as mountains — and he explained these differences in terms of distinct conative hierarchies underlying the two types of reverence. Consequently, by citing distinct histories he could have expressed the difference between an intention to procure bread for a ritual sacrifice to a mountain, and an intention to procure bread for a thanks-offering to the spirit of the mountain or the Christian God. Briefly, 'personal' and 'impersonal' reverence each draw on the same four instincts, but only the first involves the complex motive of gratitude (itself a binary compound, drawing on submission and the parental instinct); submission also contributes to each type of reverence through the tertiary compound of awe, but the double dose of submission involved in the one hierarchy gives to it a more 'personal' flavour than the other.

Some theorists — such as Maslow and Allport, for instance — are more eclectic than any I have mentioned so far, in allowing for a greater variety of instinctive contributions to religious belief. But they, too, insist that motivation properly termed 'religious' involves psychological complexities that belie the direct action of any basic dynamic category. They stress the everyday distinction between 'mature' and 'immature' religious motivation, and analyse this distinction in terms of different theoretical connections with the concept of the self. Allport calls the highest religious motivation (and all other motivation typical of the mature human personality) 'functionally autonomous', by which he means that the function of the dynamic complex underlying mature religious behaviour is independent of its instinctive aetiology.[13] In other words, it may be true that the origins of religion are largely sexual, probably involving transformations of the Oedipal type; but this infantile form of religion may be further developed, so as to generate a religious sentiment which is independent of the relatively crude sexual motivation underlying the early stages. Mature religious sentiment is experienced as a prime determinant of behaviour ascribed to the 'self', but this does not mean that it can be crudely egoistic in type. Someone who proudly buys the largest loaf of bread for the harvest festival, hoping that the congregation will join him in marvelling at his bounty, has a less mature religious intent than does someone who is humbly content to leave his offering unobserved, feeling no sense of pride in his own generosity. In Maslow's terms, these two purchases of bread (each of which serves the further purpose of participating in the harvest festival) are motivated by 'deficiency-needs' and 'growth-needs' respectively.[14] Each may be called 'religious', since neither could be adequately explained without reference to the beliefs, values and ritual practices of the agent's religious community. But the first man is driven by his basic needs for self-esteem and the respect of his fellows, while the second feels no deficiency in these matters and so is free to be guided rather by his higher-level needs for self-actualization and personal integrity.

Clearly, then, the motivational aspect of an admittedly religious intention may be extremely complex and varied. And whichever depth-psychology one employs to generate religious intentions, it should be adequate to express and explain psychological distinctions of which the ordinary man is intuitively aware: such as those between mature and immature belief, between the hypocrite and the true believer, between the passion of the evangelist and of the cloistered nun. Readers of the *Screwtape Letters* will need no reminder of the fiendish subtleties and devilish creativity that may be involved in the generation of self-consciously religious intentions.[15] To label an intention 'religious' is merely to hint at, not fully to express, its dynamic structure.

Similar remarks apply to other familiar labels attached to intentions in daily life. Let us agree that the fifth man in our example is 'commercial' in his intent, that he is amassing loaves to be sold at a profit later. A satisfactory explanation of the dynamic meaning of his surface intention would probably show it, too, to be a very complex structure.[16]

One man remains, still waiting in line outside the bakehouse. On receiving his bread, he cuts it into 3.5 millimetre cubes and lays them in a beeline to the royal palace — where the king, as promised, grants him his daughter's hand. A fairy-tale, no doubt:

for in fairy-tales one expects to find royal fathers playing
cat-and-mouse with the sexual desires of their prospective
sons-in-law in this arbitrary fashion. But this example highlights
the fact that it would be difficult — and perhaps impossible —
absolutely to rule out any dynamic base for a human intention,
merely by considering the nature of the particular goal substituted
for the variable, 'X'. Only the lowest and least structured conative
level of all, the natural bodily expression of a simple instinct, could
be thus excluded. Cutting bread into cubes is not the natural
expression of the sexual instinct, or any other. But the complexity
of the human mind is such that some individuals may be
bread-fetishists and so consummate their basic desires in this
unusual way, while others may sometimes (as in the fairy-tale) find
it expedient to indulge in such behaviour as a means to a less
bizarre sexual end. In other words, where human beings are
concerned, any intention to X may be embedded within the
action-plan of any other intention, to Y, regardless of the dynamic
base involved. Admittedly, certain values of X and Y will be paired
only in persons who are grossly mentally deranged; but the fact
remains that no absolute limit in principle can be put on the
action-plans that may be generated in the service of any basic
human purpose.

It follows that an account in terms of action-plans alone cannot
fully specify the psychological structure of intentions, since such
an account omits their motivational aspect. There is not even a
reliable correlation between action-plans and dynamic base,
because even if the action-plan prescribes behaviour (such as
eating bread) that could in some circumstances be the natural
expression of a basic need, this behaviour may sometimes have a
rather different motivation. Definitions of intentions in terms of
action-plans therefore run the risk of obscuring important dynamic
distinctions between apparently similar intentions. This can be
seen from the example of Miller, Galanter and Pribram, whose
concept of intention I earlier described as relatively satisfactory.
They define an intention as 'the uncompleted parts of a Plan whose
execution has already begun', where by a Plan they mean 'any
hierarchical process in the organism that can control the order in
which a sequence of operations is to be performed' (see ref. 2, pp.
61, 16). This does not seem to allow for cases of delayed intentions:
sometimes an intention is formed, and an action-plan generated,
with no attempt to initiate execution of the plan and with the
expectation that any such attempt will be long delayed.
Nevertheless, this definition emphasizes the hierarchical structure
of the procedural aspect of intentions and thus allows for

significant psychological distinctions between intentions which share a common goal.

But Miller and his co-authors say very little about the motivational aspect of intentions, and their definition in fact excludes this aspect since it is phrased in terms of 'Plans'. In their terminology of *Images* and *Plans*, the Image controlling behaviour includes the agent's background knowledge and also the set of valued goals through which the agent attempts to satisfy his basic needs and pressing motives. By contrast, Plans concern the specific procedures to be executed in behaviour, in order that the needs expressed in the Image may be fulfilled. Miller et al. insist that they differ from psychologists such as Lewin and Heider, in having 'renounced the dynamic properties of intentions' (ibid., p. 64). Their insistence rests upon the fact that they assign the dynamic, valuational aspect of intentions to what they call the Image rather than to what they call the Plan. As they put it, they concentrate on the execution of Plans rather than on their formation, the latter being governed ultimately by the Image (ibid., p. 69). In one sense, of course, they do consider the 'formation' of intentions, for they discuss what they call 'Plans for making Plans', which are strategies for forming action-plans; but they do not ask how it is that particular goals are accepted by the agent in light of the basic motives and higher-level needs or values within his mind. Since they define 'intentions' purely in terms of the incipient execution of Plans, they underplay their motivational aspect and direct attention primarily to what I have called the procedural schema or action-plan.

IV

The function of intentions is the control of bodily operations executed in the service of the valued purposes of the agent. Ideally, a psychological theory of intention should specify the basic bodily operations out of which large-scale intentional effects may be built up. These are the operations which are directly controlled by the basic (procedurally simple) units of action that contribute to complex procedural schemata or action-plans.

There can be no psychological answer to the question *how* such operations are effected, for *ex hypothesi* they are not compounded out of lower-level psychological units. Basic operations are carried out 'automatically', given the activation of the relevant simple procedure, and no further procedural analysis could conceivably be given. Of course, in principle a physiological answer could be given. Analogously, a high-level computer instruction (in a programming language) can be analysed into a number of instructions in the machine code; but if one asks how any one of *these* is effected, the only possible answer is in electronic (rather than programming) terms. Similarly, psychology can have nothing to say on the question of how intentions are activated. If intentions are to be executed, rather than idly entertained or held in eternal readiness, bodily control must be passed to them so that action-plans are realized in effective operations — much as executive control in a computer is continually passed to specific sections of the program. The electronic mechanisms which make this possible in cybernetic systems are known, whereas the neurological processes performing the analogous function in human brains are not. Psychology takes it for granted that this can happen, for an intention by definition is a mental phenomenon which can control behaviour; but psychology as such cannot explain how it comes about. Nor does introspection afford any clue, as William James remarked:

To the word 'is' and to the words 'let it be' there correspond peculiar attitudes of consciousness which it is vain to seek to explain. The indicative and the imperative moods are as much ultimate categories of thinking as they are of grammar . . . . And the transition from merely considering an object as possible, to deciding or willing it to be real . . . is one of the most familiar things in life. We can partly enumerate its conditions; and we can partly trace its consequences, especially the momentous one that when the mental object is a movement of our own body, it realizes itself outwardly when the mental change in question has occurred. But the change itself as a subjective phenomenon is something which we can translate into no simpler terms.[17]

In other words, psychology can hope to explain how a particular intention arises in the agent's mind, and how complex intentional effects are compounded out of lower-level bodily operations — but only physiology could satisfactorily explain the causal basis of what James called the 'impulsive quality' of intentions.

Rather than insisting on this distinction between the psychology of intention and its physiology, however, it might be better to say that the specification of the basic bodily operations is a task falling in the borderline area between these two approaches. For many theoretical discussions that are by common consent 'physiological' are concerned with questions that are stated in functional or control-oriented terms and that therefore might understandably be called (low-level) psychological problems. And the search for basic operations readily leads one onto 'physiological' ground — particularly if one's theory of intention employs the expression *procedural schema* as opposed to *action-plan*. This is evident if one asks how basic bodily operations might be identified.

By a 'bodily' operation — whether basic or not — I mean one that is carried out by way of the causal mechanisms within the body. Bodily operations thus include not only overt motor activity, but also operations that are effected within the body and which have no overt motor aspect. Procedural schemata, that is to say, are neutral as towards intellectual and behavioural actions, since procedures may control either covert or overt operations. This tallies with ordinary usage concerning intentions to the extent that it allows for intentions controlling purely intellectual operations such as doing mental arithmetic, as well as those controlling motor effects such as raising one's arm to pass coins to a baker. Miller, Galanter and Pribram also allow for this dual possibility when they say 'the execution of a Plan need not result in overt action — especially in man, it seems to be true that there are Plans for collecting or transforming information, as well as Plans for guiding [motor] actions' (see ref. 2, p. 17). It follows that bodily operations may include processes of 'pure thought'.

Of course, some intentions which would naturally be described as directed to thought rather than to motor action are not so pure as they seem. This is easily seen in cases like the intention to solve an equation 'in one's head', or the intention to keep a secret; for the first of these involves linguistic procedures that could be verbally expressed and that were learnt as a form of motor behaviour in the first place, while the second involves the intentional inhibition of a specific bodily action, namely speaking the secret words. And, according to Piaget, even such 'purely intellectual' procedures as logical operations having the abstract features of transitivity and reversibility are grounded in sensori-motor schemata with equivalent features.[18] Procedural schemata that can be effected without overt motor action may therefore be somehow parasitic upon or secondary to schemata which were originally built up in the context of such action. But it does not follow that all thought-procedures must rest on basic operations that arise in this context. To be sure, since bodily operations by definition are grounded in physiological mechanisms, it is always in principle possible that they might be directly connected with motor mechanisms whose output is some form of overt action. But many of them in fact show up in gross bodily behaviour — and even in introspection — only very indirectly, if at all. The bodily operations involved in the intention to receive Holy Communion, for instance, include not only those constituting the motor effects (swallowing bread) but also others which are less open to view — such as the grammatical transformations involved in the liturgical section of the action-plan, and the symbolic operations of primary process thinking which — if Freud is correct — are crucial to the motivational aspect of this particular ritual intention.

The methodological problems faced by Chomsky and Freud show that identification of covert operations of thought may be very difficult. Yet identification of the strictly *basic* thought-procedures is even more taxing than such methodologies might suggest, since operations that are taken as theoretically basic by these two writers are probably effected by a number of simpler processes. Thus even the most perspicuous symbolism, the simplest Freudian association, depends on analogical relations the perception of which — whether conscious or unconscious — must be assumed to be procedurally complex. To suppose otherwise is to posit an absolutely direct or completely automatic linkage between the two items associated.[19] Similarly, the 'simple' insights that bread can be bought from bakers and that the corner-shop is a bakery must depend upon many individual procedures of data-processing, probably including operations analogous to recording a definition in the memory-store, retrieving it when called upon, and registering a new object on the appropriate list; moreover, if these insights are to be of any effective use to a man intending to buy bread then they must somehow be transferred from his memory to that part of his mental organization which is analogous to the processor in a computer. The appearance of cybernetic terminology (including 'procedural schema') in this context is no accident, because the detailed procedural structure of computer programs provides the best source of suggestions for possible basic thought-operations in men's minds. This is not to say that the processes involved in human thinking are precisely the same as those involved in current programming science. But there is no more direct way of suggesting hypotheses for identifying such low-level psychological operations; nor is there any physiological theory sufficiently detailed to identify their causal basis in human brains.[20]

The identification of basic operations effecting motor action, as opposed to information-processing alone, is somewhat less problematic. But even the motor units basic to intentional action are not immediately obvious — and a theory of intention expressed in terms of *action-plans* risks missing structural distinctions that are more readily made in terms of *procedural schemata*. This is particularly clear in philosophical discussions of basic actions, where ordinary usage of the terms 'intentional' and 'action' influences the argument considerably.

In recent years a number of philosophers have attempted to characterize what might be called basic executive elements of intention, motor actions which are not generated from other actions in any way. The seminal discussion of this topic was provided by Danto, who distinguished 'basic actions' within the agent's natural behavioural repertoire from 'non-basic actions' which are somehow compounded out of them through the intentional causation of the agent.[21] Abilities to perform basic actions were referred to by Danto as 'gifts', comparable to the gift of sight; and basic actions themselves were said to be 'simple', not compounded out of anything more elementary than themselves. When one raises an arm, for example, one cannot say *how* one does so in the sense of giving a 'recipe' (action-plan) for arm-raising, nor is there anything which one has to do first in order then to be able to raise one's arm. It is this introspectively simple character of the action-plans controlling execution of motor effects within the basic repertoire which led Danto to deny that such effects are caused by the agent at all. Allowing that basic actions are (intentionally) 'performed' by the agent, he insisted that they are not 'caused' by him — at least not in the sense in which the agent 'causes' his non-basic actions. It follows that, although a man may be said to cause the removal of a loaf from the breadbasket, he cannot in the same sense be said to have caused his arm to rise when lifting the loaf from its original position. Other writers have found this claim paradoxical, and in accepting Danto's central distinction they have analysed it rather differently so as to avoid this denial that the agent causes his basic actions. For instance, Chisholm defines basic actions as 'those things we do without having to do other things to get them done', and explicitly rules out Danto's paradoxical conclusion (ibid., p. 64). Again, Goldman gives a detailed discussion of basic actions in which he emphasizes that, although they are caused by the agent, they do not depend in any way on his knowledge of physiological cause and effect or of any means–end dependencies. They form the given basis for any plan of action, higher-level actions being generated out of them; consequently, though basic actions are intentionally caused by the agent, no sense can be attached to the notion of forming an action-plan in order to generate them.[22] Still other analyses of basic actions have been prompted by Danto's original paper: though they differ in detail, they all stress the relatively minimal structure of the intention to raise one's arm,[23] and they would all agree that the act of buying a loaf of bread, for example, involves high-level actions of some complexity.

Precisely what are the low-level actions contributing to bread-buying, however, is a question that they would answer rather differently, for they disagree as to what items should be included on the basic list. Some would allow that opening the baker's door is a basic action, others would not; some would accept that walking to his shop is one basic action, whereas others would analyse it into distinct steps; some would admit the pronunciation of the various phonemes in the word 'wholemeal' as basic, while others would hesitate to do so. However, none would accept finely detailed muscular movements as suitable candidates for basic actions.

At least three matters of psychological importance are involved in this philosophical argument. The first is the question whether the basic executive units of intention must themselves be classifiable as 'actions' in the ordinary sense of the term. All the philosophers I have mentioned assume that they must be so classed; they regard action-plans as plans for action which are compounded out of other actions. It is essential to the concept of intentional action as it is ordinarily used that it be procedurally flexible in some degree, so tending to achieve the desired end by appropriate variation of means should obstacles to the goal arise. Consequently, raising one's arm has to be regarded as a basic action, one which can be achieved without the mediation of any other purposive action. For no means to the end of raising one's arm are evident in gross behaviour, and nor are such means introspectible by the agent. Indeed, no clear sense can be attached to the notion of envisaging such means. If one wishes to raise one's arm one simply does so, and the anatomical knowledge that such and such a muscle is causally involved does not assist this performance in any way. Introspectively speaking, then, raising one's arm is an action performed 'directly', without the need for an action-plan. However, Lashley's classic discussion of the physiological mechanisms underlying motor skills showed that physiological schemata of a hierarchical type must be posited in order to account for the control of integrated actions and skilled movements.[24] [25] In other words, there is a highly structured procedural schema controlling the introspectively simple action of raising one's arm. Indeed, even the reflex movements of animals low in the phylogenetic scale (and incapable of 'intentional action' properly so-called) involve centrally controlled motor co-ordination. The flexion of any joint, for instance, requires reciprocally adjusted activity on the part of antagonistic flexor and extensor muscles, and this muscular synergy is centrally controlled. In physiological terms, therefore, 'simply' raising one's arm is dependent upon highly structured processes at the shoulder and elbow joints: but the procedural schemata concerned do not have the evident means–end variability of introspectively accessible action-plans. A psychological theory of intention expressed in terms of *procedural schemata* is somewhat better suited for integration with a physiological approach to motor action than is one expressed in terms of *action-plans*, since there is no implication that basic 'procedures' must control fully purposive operations which could themselves be classed as 'actions'.

Secondly, as Lashley remarked in his paper on motor skills, high-level procedural schemata may be gradually and painfully built up by training and practice, and then control motor action 'directly'. Behaviour that initially has to be consciously intended and carefully planned often comes to be performed effortlessly and 'automatically', so much so that introspective concentration on the motor details — the basic actions involved — may entirely disrupt performance. Driving to the bakehouse, for instance, involves bodily skills that may have taken months of careful effort to perfect, but the driver apparently performs them as simply as raising his arm. He may even have difficulty in telling a learner 'how' he changes gear, for example. Changing gear is not an item which Danto would accept on his basic list: it is not a gift, as many who have failed the driving-test know to their cost; nor is it simple in not being compounded out of anything more elementary. Yet, introspectively considered, it is a simple matter requiring no special attention from the practised driver. Some philosophers would therefore say that it should be included within the practised driver's repertoire of 'basic actions'; that a distinction should be made between 'simple' and 'basic' actions (arm-raising qualifying as both); that the necessity of attention to the details of action should be a prime criterion of 'non-basic' actions; and that, since some basic actions have to be learned, not all basic actions are gifts.[26] However one chooses to settle these terminological points, it is clear that there is an important psychological distinction between action which requires care and attention in the monitoring of its progress and action which does not. In so far as a particular intention to buy bread involves an action-plan whose execution requires careful attention, it is a very different phenomenon from one whose procedural schema can be effected relatively automatically. A psychological theory should be adequate to represent this difference between two superficially similar intentions.

Thirdly, even paradigm cases of basic actions are usually not included within the infant's repertoire: no baby can walk, nor raise his arm except in a rather clumsy fashion. This point also has been remarked by some philosophers, though Danto did not dwell on it (cf. Martin, ibid.). Ideally, psychological accounts of the development of motor action in terms of increasingly efficient sensori-motor procedural schemata should be integrated with physiological accounts identifying the causal basis of the effective operations in infantile and adult behaviour. For instance, a recent theory of cerebellar function, based on detailed anatomical data about the neuronal pathways to and from the cerebellum, suggests how introspectively simple acts such as raising one's arm may develop from a base of much more elementary operations.[27] A set of elemental muscular movements are supposed to be initiated by the deep pyramidal cells of the motorsensory cortex, and some of these movements are specifically inhibited by individual Purkinje cells in the cerebellum. The pattern of inhibition is initially guided by the superficial pyramidal cells of the motorsensory cortex, but because of the mediation of the mossy and parallel fibres of the cerebellum the inhibitory 'contexts' are learned by the Purkinje cells, which can then function autonomously in controlling skilled movements. This theory would account for the increasing smoothness and co-ordination of arm-raising in a human baby by appealing to procedural schemata based on elemental motor operations that are conceived of at a much more detailed level than are any philosophers' candidates for 'basic actions'. An adequate theory of intention should include a developmental section detailing the differentiation of adult intentions out of their infantile precursors, taking into account the motivational, procedural, and operational aspects of their structure. The discussion of the present paper implies that since a babe-in-arms has neither Oedipus complex, nor knowledge of the names or effects of poisons, nor precise motor co-ordination, he cannot possibly generate the intention to spread a lethal dose of arsenic on his father's toast. A satisfactory developmental theory of intention would show how it comes about that his older brother might possibly join the baker's queue with the intention of doing just that.

V

In sum, the psychological nature of intentions is highly complex. Every intention has a motivational, a procedural, and a bodily operational (though not necessarily an overt motor) aspect, each of which has to be described in terms of its own particular structure.

Characterization of an intention in terms of its immediate goal indicates only the surface nature of an extraordinarily rich phenomenon. The number of psychological realities that could be correctly identified as 'the intention to buy bread', for instance, is indefinitely large. In order to distinguish between them a structural theory of intention is required.

Many psychologists refuse to accept 'intention' and other terms of everyday phenomenology as items proper to a scientific psychology. Even those psychologists who do accept such terms often conceptualize intentions in a way that does less than justice to their structural complexity. For example Heider follows Lewin in regarding intentions as forces exerting pressure within the agent's life-space: but this 'field-theoretical' approach obscures the fact that, in so far as intentions may be thought of as forces, they are 'forces' with a finely detailed inner structure rather than simple vectors pushing in a linear direction.[28]

Any satisfactory theory of intention must recognize and explain their inner structure, showing how it relates to the controlling function of intentions in thought and overt behaviour. A psychological theory of intention that does not attempt to do this is almost as unsatisfactory as one which refuses to admit intentions as psychological phenomena at all.

NOTES
1   The sense in which I use the term 'model' is discussed at length in M. A. Boden, *Purposive Explanation in Psychology*, Cambridge, Mass.: Harvard University Press, 1972.
2   G. A. Miller, E. Galanter and K. H. Pribram, *Plans and the Structure of Behavior*, New York: Holt, 1960.
3   The distinction between a wish and an intention is that a wish does not even have the illusion of a feasible action-plan — nor any expectation on the part of the agent that he may be able to generate or effect such a plan later.
4   This point is taken for granted in the present paper, but argued in Boden, *op. cit.*, pp. 43–5, 158–89.
5   This assumes that the behaviour in question is allowed by all to be intentional, but that Freud ascribes a further (unconscious) intention which may be doubted by the critic (either agent or observer). Many examples of what Freud called 'the psychopathology of everyday life' are not cases of overdetermination, since they are not normally thought of as intentional at all and apparently have no alternative dynamic explanation (e.g. memory lapses and slips of the tongue). The 'alternative explanation' of fatigue, for example, may show why some slip or other occurred, but cannot show why one slip rather than another was produced; it

is this which Freud attempted to explain (see S. Freud, *The Psychopathology of Everyday Life*, Vienna, 1901).

6   C. Darwin, *The Descent of Man, and Selection in Relation to Sex*, London: John Murray, 1871, Chapter III.

7   E. D. Starbuck, *Psychology of Religion*, London: W. Scott, 1899.

8   W. Trotter, *Instincts of the Herd in Peace and War*, London: Ernest Benn, 1916, p. 113.

9   S. Freud, *Totem and Taboo*. Many editions — first published 1913.

10   S. Freud, *The Future of an Illusion*. Many editions — first published 1927.

11   These points concern the *minimal* symbolic transformations required for particular religious phenomena; it is of course possible for supernumerary religious associations to influence the phenomenological and behavioural aspects of these phenomena.

12   W. McDougall, *An Introduction to Social Psychology*, London: Methuen, 1908, chapter XIII.

13   G. W. Allport, *The Individual and his Religion*, New York: Macmillan, 1950, chapter III; and G. W. Allport, *Pattern and Growth in Personality*, New York: Holt, Rinehart, & Winston, 1961, chapter X.

14   A. H. Maslow, *Toward A Psychology of Being*, Princeton: Van Nostrand, 1962, chapter III.

15   C. S. Lewis, *The Screwtape Letters*, London: Geoffrey Bles, 1942.

16   For instance, consider accounts of such behaviour in terms of 'need-achievement' — cf. D. C. McClelland, J. W. Atkinson, R. A. Clark and E. C. Lowell, *The Achievement Motive*, New York: Appleton-Century-Crofts, 1953 and D. C. McClelland, *The Achieving Society*, Princeton: Van Nostrand, 1961.

17   W. James, *The Principles of Psychology*, Vol. II. New York: Holt, 1890, pp. 568–9.

18   J. Piaget, *The Construction of Reality in the Child*, New York: Basic Books, 1954.

19   In discussing the 'general concept of analogy which dominates our interpretation of vision', Von Neumann has argued that 'it is futile to look for a precise logical concept, that is, for a precise verbal description, of "visual analogy". It is possible that the connection pattern of the visual brain itself is the simplest logical expression of this principle' (see J. H. Neumann, 'The general and logical theory of automata', in J. R. Newman (ed.), *The World of Mathematics*, Vol. IV, New York: Random House, p. 2091). He is not merely saying that it is the brain which executes the operations involved in our recognition of (for instance) the visual analogy between different members of the class of conical objects; he is claiming that those operations cannot be expressed in a neat logical system abstracted from the contingencies of neurophysiological connection. If he is right, then the operations basic to the appreciation of analogy could not be expressed in the form of procedures within a computer program (though they might be directly embodied in the

hardware of certain machines, as they are *ex hypothesi* embodied in the brain). Recent advances in the programming of object recognition tend to belie this scepticism — but even on Von Neumann's view one would need to draw a distinction between relatively simple (or direct) analogies, and relatively complex ones, in some sense dependent on underlying analogies of a simpler kind. For instance, the Freudian symbolism of Eucharistic bread that is exploited unknowingly by priest and congregation is certainly more complex than the phallic symbolism of bottles and bananas that is consciously exploited by advertisers.

20   Some philosophers would even hold that covert psychological processes like those I have postulated are a myth: see N. Malcolm, 'The myth of cognitive processes and structures', in T. Mischel (ed.), *Cognitive Development and Epistemology*, New York: Academic Press, 1971, pp. 385–92 for a rejection of 'processes of recognition' which clearly implies that he would deny any hidden procedural structure to intentions. For a stringent critique of Malcolm's arguments, see M. Martin, 'Are cognitive processes and structure a myth?', Analysis (in press).

21   A. Danto, 'Basic actions', *American Philosophical Quarterly*, 2, 141–8.

22   A. I. Goldman, *A Theory of Human Action*, Englewood Cliffs, N.J.: Prentice-Hall, 1970, pp. 63–72.

23   N. Rescher, 'On the characterization of actions', in M. Brand (ed.), *The Nature of Human Action*, Glenview, IU: Scott Foresman, 1970, pp. 247–54, raises the question of the infinite divisibility of action: perhaps raising one's arm involves indefinitely many component actions of raising it half an inch? He counters by appealing to the intensionality of action: the agent did not perform the actions of raising his arm through successive half-inches because he did not think of, or intend, the action in this sense — though he could have done so, had he wished.

24   K. S. Lashley, 'The problem of serial order in behaviour', in L. A. Jeffress (ed.), *Cerebral Mechanisms in Behaviour: The Hixon Symposium*, New York: Wiley, 1951, pp. 112–35.

25   The motor effects of what Lashley termed 'schemata' are intrinsically different from the motor effects of mere associative strings of reflexes, and this difference is a difference in the generative structure of control. Reflex control could not account for the anticipations typically observed in skilled action — as when a pianist's arm and fingers are raised in different ways to strike a given key, according to the notes yet to be played. Similarly, the organization of intentional behaviour could not possibly be controlled purely by the feedback provided by a continuous series of kinaesthetic sensations or stimuli: a tightly controlled arpeggio, for instance, may be executed so quickly that the speed of neural conduction would not allow for afferent messages from the fingers to be reflected in efferent impulses to the muscles of the hand (cf.

Lashley, ibid.).

26 J. R. Martin, 'Basic actions and simple actions', *American Philosophical Quarterly*, 9, 59–68.

27 S. Blomfield and D. Marr, 'How the cerebellum may be used', *Nature*, 227, 1224–8.

28 F. Heider, *The Psychology of Interpersonal Relations*, New York: Wiley, 1958, pp. 82–112.

7
Real-world reasoning

Traditional logic has not taken account of the computational constraints on finite systems engaged in processes of reasoning, but has considered instead the idealized justification of the results of idealized reasoning. But rationality cannot in practice do without the processes of natural reasoning. Computational concepts and computer implementations of learning offer a vocabulary that is more adequate to the richness of these processes than is familiar logic, though no less rigorous. Real-world reasoning often makes intelligent use of specific content, of examples taken to be representative of a class, and of errors intelligently arrived at in the first place. It also employs a great deal of prior knowledge and inferential competence in order to learn from experience. Computational analyses of inductive learning can throw light on the structure and dynamics of real reasoning in science and everyday life.

I: INTRODUCTION
Unlikely though this conference is to attract a visitation from the local Porn Squad, its organizers might be accused of publishing a dirty word. 'Induction' carries overtones of the loose, the shoddy, and the impure, if not the positively indecent. Even those, like Russell, who defend induction clearly regard it as the poor man's deduction. While as for psychologism, *that* is not fit even for chickens. In the eyes of his peers, the logician who falls prey to psychologism has been seduced by a temptress of disreputably easy virtue. Truly rational reasoning is less easy (though more virtuous) than the common-sense variety, and must satisfy rigorous canons of philosophical respectability. In sum, if induction is to be invited into the logician's parlour at all, it must be strictly chaperoned by formal measures of confirmability; and psychologism cannot be so invited, since it has no acceptable epistemological pedigree.

I see the prime message of Terry Winograd's paper[1] to be that these attitudes on the part of the typical logician betray an excess of zeal, if not an epistemological prurience. Traditional logic has not taken account of the computational constraints on finite systems engaged in processes of reasoning, but has considered instead the idealized justification of the results of idealized reasoning. And, as in so many areas of human endeavour, the ideal may be much less complex than the reality. Artificial intelligence ('AI') offers a methodology that is well suited to the exploration of formal models of rational, albeit fallible, thinking. In particular, it can illuminate the dynamic interaction of principles of inference and background knowledge, and clarify some of the psychological subtleties of everyday reasoning that the more traditional methods tend to neglect.

In this paper I shall mention some psychological and computational examples that support Winograd's stress on the importance of stereotypical world-knowledge and semantic content in reasoning, and his insistence on the computational inevitability of error in intelligent induction.

II: THE CONTENT OF REASONING
Logicians traditionally conceive of reasoning in terms of its abstract logical form, rather than its concrete content. Thus arguments are classified, and their validity assessed, in terms of abstract inferential schemata such as the Aristotelian figures of the syllogism, BARBARA and her syllogistic sisters — or her more modern granddaughters of propositional and predicate logic. It follows that amusingly absurd content can be given to a logician's arguments without in any way affecting their force as valid arguments. Lewis Carroll's *Sorites* are a case in point. These logical puzzles involve sets of individually incredible and collectively hilarious propositions, such as 'A fish that cannot dance a minuet is contemptible', and 'No shark ever doubts that it is well fitted out', and they may give obviously false conclusions, such as 'Rainbows are not worth writing odes to'. The tacit assumption is that the content has no *rational* importance: at most, it fulfils a motivating function, by sugaring the pill of logical rigour with a coating of entertainment.

Some psychologists, too, analyse everyday reasoning in 'logical' terms, stressing the contribution of formal structures but ignoring the effect of concrete content. Piaget is a case in point. His theoretical account of 'formal operations' implies that once this stage of intelligence has been achieved in adolescence, its hypothetico-deductive abstractions can be used irrespective of specific context by the adult.[2] But psychological experiments have shown that this is not so. Two problems of identical logical form may be easy or difficult, depending respectively on whether they do or do not tap familiar situations prompting common-sense reasoning.

For example, it is extremely difficult for people (including professors of logic) to guess which of four cards (showing the symbols *A*, *D*, 4, and 7 on their uppermost faces) would need to be turned over to determine the truth-value of a sentence expressing an abstract and arbitrary rule like 'If there is a vowel on one side of a card, then there is an even number on the other side'.[3]

But most adults have no difficulty at all with problems of identical logical form if they are given envelopes (not cards) and rules like, 'If an envelope is marked PRINTED MATTER REDUCED RATE, then it must be left open.' Specifically, a mere 19.3 per cent success rate on the abstract task rises to a staggering 98 per cent in the realistic situation. If 'sensible' rules like the one about PRINTED MATTER REDUCED RATE are applied in a less realistic experimental setting (cards being substituted for actual envelopes), the success rate is 87 per cent.

Experiments like these support the emphasis on stereotypical 'frames' that is characteristic of much current work in AI, such as that described by Winograd.[4] Presumably, the subjects in these psychological experiments had enough knowledge of our postal system to know that, generally speaking, printed matter goes at a reduced rate in envelopes left open for inspection. And presumably, too, the experimenter's rule about PRINTED MATTER REDUCED RATE implying openness was able to access this everyday knowledge, or frame, because of the closeness of verbal and semantic match between the two. The drop from 98 per cent to 87 per cent success when cards were substituted for actual envelopes in the experiment suggests that perceptual matching may also be important in accessing and moving inferentially within this 'postal frame'. It would be interesting to see what would happen to the success rate if all the envelopes marked PRINTED MATTER were very tiny and daintily decorated, like those used for gift-cards, whereas only huge ones made of brown paper were marked INTERFLORA MESSAGE or MERRY CHRISTMAS FROM . . . (assuming of course that additional rules linked the latter marking with sealed envelopes).

In real-life thinking it is useful to have a specific inference stored, to the effect that if you are mailing printed matter you should not lick the envelope-flap. (Is this psychologically equivalent to the advice that in these circumstances you should leave the envelope open? Almost certainly not, even in a world where all envelopes are lickably stickable. Brain-damaged patients may well be aware that an envelope should or should not be left open, without being clear as to how licking a part of it — which part? — relates to its open or closed state. Logically, however, the two forms of advice are equivalent in the world hypothesized.) This is useful in real life because if the pattern 'printed matter' (or, as in the experiment, the mark PRINTED MATTER) can access this specific inference or procedural advice quickly, then appropriate action can be taken more swiftly than if it had to be deduced by general inference-rules from axiomatically represented information about envelopes and printed matter.

I am assuming here, as do many AI workers including those that were the focus of Winograd's paper, that the hardware of the brain does not function fast enough to make a general theorem-proving procedure feasible. Proponents of the 'theorem-proving' approach in AI dispute this assumption, and attribute their own lack of success in dealing with any but relatively trivial problems to the primitive state of current computer technology.

Because the creator of the PLANNER programming language shared this assumption, he designed PLANNER so as to enable the programmer to allow for information to be used in this 'sensible' fashion.[5] Indeed, in PLANNER any given item of knowledge can be stored in four forms: as a declarative statement that A implies B, which can be accessed by general inferential processes of the sort described by deductive logic; as an erasing theorem that is itself a procedure telling the system to erase A, if B is erased (as it might be, for example, if the system finds that B is false); as an antecedent theorem (procedure) instructing the system to infer B, if given A; and as a consequent theorem (procedure) advising that if you want to prove B one method is to try to establish A.

Supposing that someone wants to know whether an envelope should be left open, her friend (or an inner voice) might say impatiently, 'Well, it contains printed matter, doesn't it!' A PLANNER program could respond in essentially the same way, drawing the correct conclusion quickly, provided its data base contained two items. First, it needs to have stored (perhaps as a result of recent perceptual investigation) the fact that the envelope contains printed matter, expressed either as a purely declarative item or as an antecedent theorem about the envelope. Second, it needs a consequent theorem that would be written thus:

```
(CONSE (X) (SHOULDBELEFTOPEN $?X)
        (GOAL (CONTAINSPRINTEDMATTER $?X)))
```

The 'X' in this expression declares a local variable, bound in this instance to the envelope. The '$?X$' is a semi-open, pattern variable, which can be given a value in the pattern-matching process if it has not already got one.

This PLANNER theorem is logically equivalent to 'All envelopes containing printed matter should be left open', or 'If it contains printed matter, then it should be left open', or 'Containing printed matter implies needing to be left open'. But instead of being stored as an axiom in the conventional sense, it is a mini-program that explicitly advises the system to try first to establish that something contains printed matter, should it wish to know whether it must be left open. Provided that it is quickly accessible (by way of the indexing scheme for selecting patterns and the subsequent pattern-matching processes) this domain-specific procedure, and its PLANNER cousins, will be computationally more economical than unindexed lists of facts (such as the arbitrary rules given to the experimental subjects mentioned above) that have to be manipulated by general deductive procedures. That is, the advice 'If you know it contains printed matter, then assume it must be left open' is often more helpful than the syllogistic knowledge, 'This envelope contains printed matter, and all envelopes containing printed matter are to be left open'.

(Strictly, PLANNER leaves it ambiguous whether the envelope is left open or is to be left open, for PLANNER cannot represent the difference between proving that B and bringing it about that B. POPLER, a language essentially similar to PLANNER, distinguishes INFER procedures from ACHIEVE procedures.[6] So the POPLER programmer can express the difference between an envelope's having been left open and its having to be left open, the program selecting one or other as appropriate. However, because of its inadequate indexing mechanisms, POPLER programs tend to be slow unless special indexing structures are written by the programmer.)

The example of PLANNER suggests that learning that envelopes containing printed matter are left open is not a matter of merely adding an isolated fact of the form 'All A's are B's' to one's memory. Rather, it may involve such processes as representing this item of knowledge in 'antecedent', 'consequent', or 'erasing' form as well as in the form of a bare fact. Psychological experiments have confirmed what commonsense suggests, that on learning new facts people often erase previous beliefs — or at least make them (temporarily or permanently) inaccessible.[7] But the computational intricacies of such processes are still unclear. For instance, how is the need for deletion evaluated, especially in cases where there is no straightforward logical contradiction involved? (Should a biologist delete, amend, or retain — perhaps relabelling as 'myth' — her previous belief in Genesis?) And what systematic considerations are relevant to whether one generates an antecedent representation or a consequent one — or both? How does the learning system decide that one or other of these is likely to be needed?

Learning also (and correlatively) involves the integration of the new fact into a developing knowledge-structure that both relates it sensibly to other facts and makes it readily accessible in those contexts where it is likely to be needed. Winograd discussed such knowledge-structures under the heading of 'frames'. The contexts in which one first learns and later accesses such facts as the one about envelopes being left open for printed matter are psychologically, or computationally, rich in related facts, perceptual cues (such as size, colour, and label of envelope), motor actions (such as licking envelopes), and goal-structures. We know that printed matter tends to be of lesser importance and urgency than personally-penned letters, and that this is one reason (another being its commonly greater weight) why it goes at a reduced rate. For reduced postage rate implies reduced speed, and this is acceptable for printed matter generally. An experimental problem in which the **PRINTED MATTER** concerned a Government Health Warning about a raging cholera epidemic, and so needed to go in sealed envelopes carrying first-class postage, might show interestingly different patterns of inferential success.

In general, the specific and varied content of a frame has to be richly indexed during learning and development of the frame if it is to be maximally useful for access and inference in reasoning-tasks of varying types. Unlike traditional inductive logic, computational models of learning can in principle take these issues into account, since computational concepts have been developed specifically to characterize such features of the representation and use of knowledge. This is not to say that the problems have been solved or that learning is well understood. But work such as that described by Winograd is raising some of the relevant questions. The development of KRL, for instance, has been prompted by considerations of computational efficiency in the storage, indexing, and inferential use of frames. And its cousin KRS also explores how reasoning may be aided by computationally rich representations of semantic content.

Just as semantic content aids reasoning, so it can aid learning. A recent program written by R. J. D. Power and H.C. Longuet-Higgins provides a computational model of the inductive learning of the number-names (numerals) in various natural languages.[8] One of the general morals drawn by the authors is that language acquisition involves the use of semantic clues, even in order that the learner may come to distinguish well-formed from ill-formed sentences. The program is able to make intelligent guesses about the meaning of numeral expressions on the basis of syntactic analogy, and can intelligently reject incorrect or anomalous inputs presented to it in the attempt to catch it out (such as the suggestion that 'twenty and ten' means 37 or that the English numeral for 24 might be 'two dozen' rather than 'twenty-four'). Asked to explain 'Why?' it evaluates a numeral as a particular number, it displays the structure it assigned to the numeral and the schematic rules used to interpret that structure as the number concerned. The program learns to count in and interpret the numerals of languages as different as English, French, Japanese, Mixtec, Suppire, and Biblical Welsh. And it does this on the basis of no more input than a list of a few representative numerals, and the numbers for which they stand.

The semantic content upon which the program draws in order to do this (and which the authors suggest is intuitively used by adults learning numerals in a foreign language) involves the arithmetical notions of sum, product, difference, and (primitive) number. Primitive numbers are those directly named by single words in the lexicon of the language concerned (so a number may be primitive in one language but not in another: compare 'eighteen', 'dix-huit', and 'duodeviginti'). These unstructured numerals have to be learnt by rote. (They are syntactically unstructured, being single words; they may of course show semantically significant morphemic structure, as in 'sixteen' and less obviously in the French 'seize'.)

But the meanings of most numeral expressions consisting of more than one word are inductively learnt by generalizing from the evidence presented so far. Given the information, for example, that the numbers 20, 21, and 29 are named by the numerals 'twenty', 'twenty-one', and 'twenty-nine', the program induces that the number 25 will be named by the expression 'twenty-five' — and not, say, by 'five from thirty'. Moreover, on being next told that 30 is named 'thirty', it induces the correct numerals for all the numbers between 31 and 39. It is able to do this because it represents numeral expressions as structured instances generated by schematic formulae, and one and the same formula or rule can generate many series of numbers — as in the English expressions for 21–29, 31–39, . . . 91–99.

The program is not misled by the French habit of naming 70 (non-primitively) as 'soixante-dix'. And this is not because the teacher is always kind enough to present this new numeral immediately after its predecessor representing 69: the teacher may 'skip' direct from 'soixante' to 'soixante-dix'. The program recognizes the new lexical item as a compound of 'soixante' and 'dix'. And it realizes, because of its grammatical knowledge about the syntax and semantics of numeral systems in general, that this must be the *sum* of 60 and 10 rather than their *product* — which is named 'six cent'. It recognizes 'quatre-vingt', on the other hand, as the product of 4 and 20, not their sum. For it knows that if a smaller number precedes a larger number, without a conjunction, then a *product* is in question: compare 'quatre-vingt', 'four hundred', 'twenty-four' — and remember that there were four *and* twenty blackbirds baked in the pie. Arithmetical reasoning involving the concepts and operations of sum and product enable the program to reject evidence as spurious: if told that 'twenty-four hundred' means 420, the program refuses to accept this and prints 'SURELY NOT'.

The variety of superficially different parsings that the program can deal with is illustrated by its ability to learn to interpret the Mixtec numerals for 380 (literally: fifteen four score) and 799 (one four-hundred fifteen four score fifteen four) and the Biblical Welsh expressions for 59 (four on fifteen and two twenty) and 2,999 (subtract one five twenty and nine hundred and two of thousand). Numerals such as these make 'quatre-vingt dix-neuf' look simple indeed.

A less 'Baconian' program it would be difficult to imagine. The program might rather be termed Kantian — as might other AI models of learning such as those mentioned in Winograd's paper. Kant insisted that there must be some prior structures within the mind enabling one meaningfully to interpret and assimilate one's experience. As he put it, intuition without concepts is blind. Similarly, Chomsky has argued that natural language learning would be impossible without prior principles of structure in terms of which to generate and test hypotheses about the grammar of the linguistic input. But Chomsky, especially in his earlier work, underplayed the role of semantics in syntactic induction. Without its arithmetical knowledge and reasoning capacity, Longuet–Higgins' program could not learn to parse numerals as intelligently as it does. It also needs its two 'principles of induction', which the authors say seem to apply to all known numeral systems.

The first of these principles is the one that underlies the inductive jump from 'twenty-one' and 'twenty-nine' to 'twenty-five', and also to 'ninety-seven' once 'ninety' has been learnt by rote. It concerns expressions in which the (semantically) major term is a number rather than a product, and states that 'If two such expressions, having the same major term and the same arithmetical operation, are both realized by a given syntactic form, then any expression involving the same major term, the same operation, and an intermediate value of the minor term, is well-formed, and is also realized by that form'. The second inductive principle allows the program to induce the correct English expression for 513, having been told that the numeral for 113 is 'one hundred and thirteen'. This principle applies to the syntactic forms of sums and differences in which the (semantically) major term is not a constant but a product. It is: 'If a sum or difference has a product as its major term, then the syntactic form or forms by which it can be realized are left unchanged by replacing that product by any other product which is generated by the same formula'. One might think of these two inductive principles as expressing the universal 'deep grammar' of natural language numeral systems — but notice that they both involve both semantic and syntactic considerations, and presuppose arithmetical reasoning ability in the language learner.

A person — or program — unaware of arithmetical concepts such as sum, product, and difference (and syntactic distinctions too) would be unable intelligently to induce a foreign numeral system from limited experience of it, but would have to learn it entirely by rote. Very young children, of course, do not immediately realize that 35 must be 'thirty-five' after they have learnt the numeral for 25; nor do they realize that 23 will be called 'twenty-three' on being told 21 is 'twenty-one'. The sense in which they have *learnt* the English names for 21 or 25 is less well-structured than that in which they will as adults learn the French number names, although this is not to say that their knowledge should be represented as a passively-acquired list of items on the classical-empiricist model.[9] Among psychologists, Piaget has been outstanding for his Kantian emphasis on the role of prior structure in the assimilation of new experiences, and for his non-Kantian stress on the gradual development of these organizing structures in infancy.[10] Work on inductive learning in AI should help to illuminate the structures and processes involved.

III: ERRORS IN REASONING
Error has often had a bad press in the philosophical, and even the psychological, literature. The rationalist Spinoza was so metaphysically embarrassed by it that he denied its existence, saying that what appears as erroneous reasoning is instead the correct solving of a different problem. Psychologists too have often claimed that apparent errors are due not so much to errors *in* reasoning (faulty inference) as to errors *while* reasoning. For instance, experimental

subjects may be wrong in their interpretation of what is required of them, they may misinterpret the premises, they may forget essential information, or they may even not be motivated to solve the problem. That these sorts of processes may give rise to what is termed error is undeniable, as is shown by research like Mary Henle's on syllogistic reasoning[11] and Peter Bryant's on transitive inference in young children.[12] But it is true also that error may arise from inference — indeed, from intelligent inference from true premisses.

In the realm of deductive logic, of course, such a statement is absurd. Even Russell's paradox is not an error, but a paradox: a much more highly-regarded animal. The fact that inductive reasoning is prone to error is one of the reasons for its being held in such low esteem by many logical purists. But Winograd's discussion of resource-limited processing and partial matching, for example, showed how computational systems must lay themselves open to error if they are to function intelligently in a rich and largely unknown world.

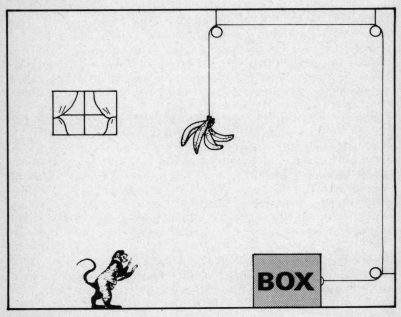

Figure 7.1

As an example of what I mean by intelligent error, consider what happened when I showed my eight-year-old son the situation pictured in Figure 7.1 and asked him how the monkey would get the bananas. Without any prompting or comment from me, he immediately replied, 'Well, monkeys are intelligent, aren't they. So he'd know he was in a house because of the curtains, and houses always have scissors in them so he'd go and get some scissors and cut the string'. When I asked him at what point the monkey would cut the string, he said, 'Where it joins onto the box.'

Clearly, he made an error: monkeys are not *that* intelligent. But his error showed how an eight-year-old child (who if Piaget is right would not be able to follow, still less formulate, a solution of this problem expressed in the hypothetico-deductive terms associated with the theory of pulleys) can intelligently access and fruitfully integrate many varied items of world-knowledge in his reasoning. It was clear from his answer to my second question that, whether or not he had realized the problem of compensatory movements posed by the pulley arrangement, he had noticed the functional relation between the bananas and the far-end of the supporting string. For otherwise, the scissors would have been used to cut the string by the bananas. (When I asked him whether the monkey could use the box to climb up to the bananas he pointed out that they would move even higher as the monkey pulled the box towards them: but I do not know whether that insight had entered into his original response — nor would I necessarily regard his retrospections on the matter as entirely reliable.) Moreover, he remembered that monkeys are intelligent animals (what if the picture had shown a sheep?), that curtains generally mean houses, that scissors are suitable instruments for cutting string, that scissors are generally available in houses, and that bananas cannot be suspended from a hook in mid-air — so that the monkey must have been *inside* the house, thus having potential access to scissors.

What is of interest here is not only the integration of zoological and domestic knowledge, which in itself is an intelligently creative matter since he normally thinks of monkeys in the context of zoos or jungles. What is of interest also is the recognition of specific items of knowledge as relevant. He knows other things about monkeys besides their being intelligent, other things about curtains than that they are usually found in houses, and other things about houses than that they have scissors in them. How were these specific items found and integrated so quickly?

Attempting to represent this reasoning in computational terms would help to sensitize one to the large variety of inferential patterns that might have underlain his verbal response. To take just one example, the main direction of access might have been from *curtains* through *house* to *scissors*, or from *scissors* through *house* to *curtains*. The former progression would have been initiated by a reasoning strategy that asked, 'What clues are there in the picture as to where the monkey is?', while the latter might have arisen from a strategy that asked, 'What needs to be done, what instrument could do it, and is it available?'

Winograd's discussion of frames is relevant again here. I personally find it much more plausible (both on computational and 'intuitive psychological' grounds) to postulate that my son was accessing a familiar 'house-frame' to get from *curtains* to *house* than that he was using a generalization of the form 'All curtains are found in houses'. This assumes, of course, that the house-frame is indexed in such a way that it is readily accessible by way of the cue *curtains*. In other words, I find a frame-explanation that posits an inference from an exemplary representation of a house more plausible than alternative explanations that would rely on universally quantified inductive generalizations about curtains and houses. The case is different, however, for the inference from *house* to *scissors* — and this for two reasons. First, even if his house-frame contained *scissors* as an item explicitly represented in it, the relevance of scissors would need to be established by some goal-directed instrumental reasoning such as that I identified as 'the second strategy' above. In addition, I find it much more difficult to believe that *scissors* are a feature of house-frames than that *curtains* are — even though he was certainly correct in saying that houses usually contain scissors. Outside this sort of problem-context (what sort?), one does not normally think of *scissors* as soon as one thinks of *house*. It is possible, however, that some process of the spreading of activations within an associative network (such as that implemented in AI terms by Quillian)[13] could establish a connection between *scissors* and *house* once these two items had been independently accessed.

Many other questions of this type would have to be faced if this common-sense reasoning were to be modelled in computational terms. For example, on the assumption that he had noticed the pulley, precisely how did this cause him to infer that what needs to be done is to cut the string (an inference without which scissors are irrelevant)? And is there a clear-cut distinction between reasoning by inductive generalizations of the form 'All *A*'s are *B*'s' and reasoning on the basis of an example, or frame? AI workers who favour frames often suggest that learning is a matter of selecting (how?) individual items — such as one's own house or body — to function as exemplars in reasoning. But it might be that information which was *learnt* in the form of inductive generalizations was *stored* and *used*, for reasons of computational efficiency, as a frame. On the likely assumption that both these types of learning (as well as others) occur, what determines which will take place when?

It is significant that adults shown Figure 7.1 sometimes just laugh (never thinking of scissors), and sometimes make the error of saying, 'Well, he'd push the box, of course, and climb on it.' Acquaintance with Kohler's exemplary (*sic*) work on *The Mentality of Apes* makes this 'unthinking' response rather more likely, and sometimes a person stops in mid-sentence as they belatedly realize the surprise: the pulley. A person thinking in these terms, and shown a picture with a rabbit instead of a monkey, might find the solution temporarily 'blocked' by their knowledge that rabbits are not strong enough to push boxes, at which point they might think up the alternative strategy of cutting (presumably, nibbling) the string. Or of course they might refuse to enter the game at all, pointing out that rabbits are really dumb animals. (One friend pointed out that the bananas would come within the monkey's reach if the box were to be pushed closer to the wall.)

A number of computational models of the 'monkey and bananas' problem have in fact been produced within AI. Most of them employ 'theorem-proving' procedures which utilize general inferential processes, and bury 'common-sense' knowledge of the laws of physics inside their assumptions that on moving the box, *this* changes and *that* does not. (How might such contrasts be learnt in the first place, whether by programs, monkeys, or children?) One of the assumptions typically made by these programs is that on moving the box, the position of the bananas does not alter — and in the 'classic' version of this problem, *sans* pulley, this assumption is of course true. But none of these theorem-proving programs throws any light on how the picture can be intelligently interpreted as contradicting this assumption. The work on frames described by Winograd does not do so either; but it does suggest (which the theorem-proving approach does not) ways in which pulleys, curtains, houses and scissors — and the IQ of monkeys — might be brought together in an intelligent (albeit mistaken) response to Figure 7.1.

It would be misleading to say (with Spinoza or Henle, perhaps) that my son did not really make an inferential error, since given his premises his solution was correct. For this implies that his premise about monkey intelligence was simply mistaken, and should be replaced by another. But which other? That monkeys are not intelligent? Surely not. That monkeys are not as intelligent as humans? Well, he already knew that — and maybe it was readily accessible to him as soon as 'monkey's intelligence' was accessed. That monkeys do not know about curtains, and aren't bright enough to reason from *curtains* via *houses* to *scissors*? But this is an absurd suggestion: that they do not know these things or have this reasoning ability is very likely true, but to suggest that it be stored for use as a premiss in the problem-situation under discussion is computationally ridiculous. For an indefinte number of similar pictures could be drawn, each requiring a separate premiss to be fished out of memory so as to prevent the wrong conclusion. Rather, one needs to be able to cross-check this suggested solution with one's general knowledge of the intelligence of monkeys, so as to decide whether the story told by my son is plausible or not. Plausible reasoning, involving partial matches between analogous cases, in conditions of incomplete knowledge, is required — and it is this type of reasoning which was highlighted by Winograd.

Some work in AI shows how error may be positively useful to an intelligent system, if it can be accurately diagnosed as due to a mistaken assumption or faulty strategy which can be modified accordingly. For example, the HACKER learning program is able to benefit from its mistakes so as to improve its own programs for building structures out of blocks.[14] For this 'inductive' learning from its experience of its mistakes, HACKER requires rich computational structures and ways of continually monitoring its own plans and performance. For example, it must be able to distinguish the different types of error, or bug, in its performance that are due to general classes of error in goal-seeking that arise because of the interactions between various actions (and preconditions for actions) within one overall plan. Its programmer has distinguished five such classes of error-generating bug, which he terms: PREREQUISITE-CONFLICT-BROTHERS; PREREQUISITE-MISSING; PREREQUISITE-CLOBBERS-BROTHER-GOAL; STRATEGY-CLOBBERS-BROTHER; and DIRECT-CONFLICT-BROTHERS. These underlying bugs in the program's reasoned planning manifest themselves during the execution of its performance-programs in various ways, in the form of unsatisfied prerequisites, double moves, or failure to protect a condition that must continue to exist until a specific point in the plan.

HACKER is written in CONNIVER,[15] a programming language basically similar to PLANNER. Like KRL also, CONNIVER enables the programmer to set up 'demons'. Demons are active processes that can be relied on to monitor the data-base and make modifications or pass on messages to other processes as necessary, and which thus enable one to write relatively intelligent programs. Thus we saw in the previous section that PLANNER antecedent and consequent theorems indexed by general patterns can trigger the immediate inference of *B*, given *A*, or the attempt to establish *A* if *B* is what is required. Analogous facilities are used by HACKER in the form of CONNIVER 'if-added' and 'if-needed' methods. The language also has a useful feature called its 'context-mechanism'. This enables a computational system economically to store and make available contextual information that is shared by many different sub-processes, such as the processes aiming at successive sub-goals generated by one and the same higher-level goal, or the various moves of a box that leave the neighbouring bananas in the same position. And a very short passage of program-code ensures that the reasons for doing something, the necessary preconditions, and the reasons for failure in execution will be automatically stored and passed to those computational processes that may have need of them. These computational facilities are crucial to HACKER's assessment of its success or failure in its activities, and to its reasoned self-corrections in light of its experience. And these abilities in turn depend on the program's structural diagnosis of the five different types of bug (so that the program illustrates the point made in section 2, that learning from one's experience pre-supposes prior knowledge and inferential competence).

HACKER may be described broadly as 'inductive' because it learns from experience. Unlike some of the programs described by Winograd, however, its reasoning processes are strictly deductive in nature: it identifies and patches bugs by deduction from its initial premisses and its (deductively arrived-at) plan-CRITICS. But novel CRITICS are generated as a result of experience, and this is why the program's performance and planning abilities improve. (In an equally broad sense of 'deduction', it is sometimes said that all computation is deductive. For example, 'probabilistic' reasoning deduces that *X* is probable, given *Y*.)

If one considers the sort of inductive (though non-'Baconian') reasoning that is involved in the planning or interpretation of experiments, it is clear that interactions between the various experimental parameters, and between these and the background conditions, must continually be taken into account if the 'correct' interpretation is to be reached and the 'predictable' outcome observed. Just as there are significantly different types of bug affecting plan and/or execution (of which five have been identified by HACKER's programmer), so there are analogously distinct ways in which an experimental prediction may fail or a scientific hypothesis be falsified (or appear to be falsified). A plan that can be criticized by HACKER before being run and patched so as to remove the bug, or a hitch in execution that HACKER can notice and remedy so as to rerun the plan in corrected form, are analogous to a hypothesis that can be amended and so saved or an experiment that can be discounted. And a program like PLANEX,[16] which (unlike HACKER) can remedy faults during execution and go on from where it left off, reminds one of the way in which a scientist may tinker with an experiment in progress, so as to avoid having to start afresh. Parallels such as these suggest that a computational analysis of the logic of induction would help to illuminate the structure of scientific reasoning and the way in which — as Popper has insisted — science progresses through (not just in spite of) its errors.

IV: CONCLUSION

Inductive reasoning 'as she is spoke' is more worthy of epistemological respect than is commonly allowed by logicians. If one is to take into account the real computational constraints upon real computational systems, then the norms of real — or even artificial — thinking have at least as much right to be treated as normative as do the rules of deductive logic. For rationality cannot in practice do without them. Winograd described deductive logic as an approximation to a much richer set of natural reasoning processes. Philosophers in the past have tended to decry suggestions that rational thought be characterized in terms of these processes, rejecting such attempts as a 'psychologism' that need have nothing to do with the ideal even if it faithfully reflects the real. This attitude arose partly because of a rationalistic horror of error (although approaches such as Popper's fallibilism have commendably counteracted this general tendency), partly because of a failure to take sufficiently seriously the Kantian point that one needs a great deal of knowledge already if one is to be able to learn more, and partly because of the lack of any formal or theoretical vocabulary adequate to characterize the processes and content of the knowledge involved in inductive reasoning.

Computational concepts offer the promise and the beginnings of such a vocabulary. If we ask, 'How should computer-simulated learning be structured?' we soon come to see that the search for, evaluation, and acceptance of evidence has to be considerably richer (both in structure and content) than this:

'I know what you're thinking about', said Tweedledum; 'but it isn't so, nohow.'

'Contrariwise', continued Tweedledee, 'if it was so, it might be; and if it were so it would be; but as it isn't, it ain't. That's logic.'

NOTES

1   Terry Winograd, 'Extended Inference Modes in Reasoning by Computer' in *Applications of Inductive Logic* (eds. L. J. Cohen and M. B. Hesse, (Oxford University Press, 1980) pp. 333 ff.
2   Barbel Inhelder and Jean Piaget, *The Growth of Logical Thinking from Childhood to Adolescence* (1958).
3   P. C. Wason, 'The Theory of Formal Operations; A Critique', in B. A. Geber (ed.), *Piaget and Knowing: Studies on Genetic Epistemology* (1977), pp. 119–35.
4   M. L. Minsky, 'A framework for representing knowledge', in P. H. Winston (ed.), *The Psychology of Computer Vision* (1975), pp. 211–77. See also chapter 11 of M. A. Boden, *Artificial Intelligence and Natural Man* (1977).
5   Carl Hewitt, *Description and Theoretical Analysis (Using Schemata) of PLANNER: A Language for Proving Theorems and Manipulating Models in a Robot*. AI-TR-258, MIT AI Lab. (1972).
6   D. J. M. Davies, *Popler 1.5 Reference Manual*. TPU Report 1, Edinburgh Univ. AI Lab. (1973).
7   P. C. Wason, 'On the failure to eliminate hypotheses . . . : a second look', in P. N. Johnson-Laird and P. C. Wason (eds.), *Thinking: Readings in Cognitive Science* (1977), pp. 307–14.
8   R. J. D. Power and H. C. Longuet-Higgins, 'Learning to count: a computational model of language acquisition', *Proc. Royal Soc. London B* 200 (1978), 391–417.
9   Aaron Sloman, *The Computer Revolution in Philosophy: Philosophy, Science, and Models of Mind*, chapter entitled 'On Learning About Numbers', (1978).
10   Jean Piaget, *The Psychology of Intelligence* (1950).
11   Mary Henle, 'On the relation between logic and thinking', *Psychological Review*, 69 (1962), 366–78.
12   Peter Bryant, *Perception and Understanding in Young Children: An Experimental Approach* (1974).
13   M. R. Quillian, 'Semantic memory', in M. L. Minsky (ed.), *Semantic Information Processing* (1968), pp. 227–70.
14   G. J. Sussman, *A Compter Model of Skill Acquisition* (1975).
15   G. J. Sussman and D. V. McDermott, *Why Conniving is Better than Planning*. AI Memo 255a, MIT AI Lab. (1972).
16   R. E. Fikes, P. E. Hart, and N. J. Nilsson, 'Learning and executing generalized robot plans', *Artificial Intelligence* 3 (1972), 251–88.

8
Implications of language studies for human nature

I: INTRODUCTION

The Archangel Gabriel, or so we are told, made an annunciation of some import to maiden Mary. Those who have trouble believing this rumour normally base their doubts in the dubious ontological status of angels, the biologically unproven case for human parthenogenesis, and similar scruples. It is rarely questioned whether, *if* there were angels, one of them could converse naturally with a woman in her native Aramaic.

But this angelic conversational competence is even less likely than the Martian knowledge of twentieth-century Middle-American English that is so conveniently assumed by many science-fiction scenarios. For, unlike Martians, angels do not share with us any corporeal embodiment or material environment. (Hence the peculiar infelicity of debates over how many could sit on the top of a pin.) Language studies suggest that we are creatures of this earthly world in our linguistic capacities no less than in our theological categorization. Moreover, such studies point to the enormous complexity of the mental processes underlying our use of natural language: if Mary really did converse with an angel, it was no divinely simple-minded seraph she talked to.

The human mind is extraordinarily complex in its interpretative activities as well as being deeply rooted in material reality. In this paper I shall indicate some of the diverse studies of language that show these two claims to be true.

II: THE EMBODIMENT OF HUMAN BEING

Wittgenstein's remark, 'Commanding, questioning, recounting, chatting, are as much a part of our natural history as walking, eating, drinking, playing' encourages us to think of language as part of our biological endowment.[1] As such, we may expect it to be essentially shaped by our material embodiment and evolutionary origins. Countless studies within the various disciplines that bear on the nature of language confirm this expectation, but I shall concentrate on only four examples (drawn from current work in linguistics, psychology, philosophy and artificial intelligence).

The linguist John Lyons has recently defended the semantic thesis of 'localism'.[2] Localism claims that essentially *spatial* notions underlie many of the grammatical structures as well as much of the lexicon of natural language. As Lyons points out, there are weaker and stronger versions of localism, and one can hardly avoid being a localist in some degree. Lyons himself puts forward a strong version of the thesis, suggesting localistic interpretations of the linguistic representations of ideas such as tense, aspect, opposition, instrumentality, manner, possession, existence, knowledge and truth. In addition, he argues that the linguistic phenomenon of *anaphora* (which is commonly taken as basic by linguists) is a derivative of *deixis*. And deixis is based in the indication of the here-and-now, whether a bodily pointing to the spatial *here*, or a less concrete 'pointing' to the temporal *now*.

It is abundantly clear that many linguistic expressions of 'non-spatial' matters (sic) are parasitic on purely spatial notions. Familiar examples include the conceptualization of time as passing, as being of long or short duration, as ranging over the whole history of the universe . . . and so on. Similarly, we often express comparative degrees of abstract properties such as social status, intelligence, or moral worth by terms drawn from more concrete contexts, such as above, below, higher, lower, etc. Again, grammatical cases are commonly and plausibly interpreted in localistic terms, so that (for example) the ablative and dative cases are explained by way (sic) of the ideas of source and goal of movement, respectively.

Space forbids discussion of the less obvious localistic interpretations, whereby even aspect, possession, and knowledge (and, for some authors, negation and quantification) are held to be represented by essentially spatial linguistic expressions and constructions. But later in this section it will be useful to bear in mind this claim of Lyons':[3]

It is obvious that the process of communicating propositional information is readily describable, as is the process of transferring possession, in terms of the localistic notion of a journey: if X communicates p to Y, this implies that p travels, in some sense, from X to Y . . . . It may be suggested, therefore, that 'p is at X' (where X is a person) is the underlying locative structure that is common to 'X knows p', 'X believes p,' 'X has p in mind', etc. There is much in the structure of particular languages, however, to suggest that 'X knows p' is comparable with 'X has Y' and should therefore be regarded as the most typical member of the class of propositions subsumable under 'p is at X'.

Even without acceptance of Lyons' more ambitious localistic claims, such as those within and related to this quotation, his work casts doubts on the credibility of the Annunciation story. Thus St Luke assures us that eavesdroppers on the conversation between Gabriel and Mary would have overheard expressions such as these: The Lord is *with* thee: blessed art thou *among* women; thou hast *found* favour *with* God; He shall be *great*, and shall be called the Son of the *Highest*: and the Lord God shall give *unto* him the throne of his father David: and he shall reign *over* the *house* of Jacob for ever; and of his *kingdom* there shall be no *end*. The localistic origin of the italicized words is evident, and committed 'localists' would italicize even more. This passage, of course, is written in King James' English, with which Mary (never mind Gabriel) was not familiar. But the Aramaic equivalents may have been even more obviously localistic in character: many languages force speakers to code the spatial attributes of objects, much as English forces temporal specification by way of the tense-system. (The American Indian language Tarascan is an extreme example of this; number-words have to reflect the 'dimensionality' of the object being enumerated, according to whether they are long and thin, flat, or broadly spherical; similarly, verb-forms reflect the spatial nature of the referents of the nouns acting as subject or object.)[4]

The reason why localism casts doubt on the Annunciation story is that the psychological assumption implicit — and often explicit — in localism is that localistic notions and distinctions at base are those 'which we first learn to apply with respect to our own orientation and the location or locomotion of other objects in the external world'. Since Gabriel as an essentially spiritual being can hardly be represented as having any orientation, nor any location relative to 'other objects in the external world' — such as pinheads — it is difficult to see how he could have learnt these notions in the first place. And if he had not learnt them in the first place, how could he have used them so felicitously to talk of abstract matters to a human woman in the second place?

Psychological evidence in support of localism is provided, for instance, by the 'psycholexicology' of G. A. Miller and P. N. Johnson-Laird.[5] Their study of the psychological basis of the lexicon of natural languages shows spatial organization to be basic to human cognition, and a pervasive feature of our perceptual capacities. They aim to develop a procedural semantics, wherein lexical items are associated with perceptual procedures for testing whether the environment fulfils certain conditions. Examples of the perceptual predicates involved in the object-recognition routines that carry the meaning of natural language include: x is higher than y; the distance from x to y is zero; x is in front of the moving object y; y is between x and z; x has boundary y; x is convex; x is changing shape; x has the exterior surface y; x is included spatially in y; x, y, and z lie in a straight line; x travels along the path p. In fact, the majority of perceptual predicates listed by these authors are obviously spatial in character (although their list includes also items such as cause, feel, intend, person and goal). Psychological and physiological evidence for the primacy of these notions is marshalled, and their incorporation into object-recognition routines of increasing power is outlined. The computational paradigm adopted throughout the discussion encourages questions not only about *which* predicates are involved in a certain sort of judgment, but *when* each predicate is applied in the judgmental process. (For example, the logically equivalent '*y* over *x*' and '*x* under *y*' are not psychologically equivalent: the first term in the relation should designate the thing whose location is to be determined, while the second should represent the immobile landmark that can be used to determine it.)

Miller and Johnson-Laird do not claim that the conceptual meaning of language can be directly identified in terms of perceptual predicates, or that every question must be answered (every statement verified) by direct perception of the external world. But whatever test-procedures are used, these must ultimately be grounded in perceptual routines. For instance, it is possible to answer class-inclusion questions (Are dogs mammals? Are whales fish?) by a search of memory, since hierarchical relations between concepts are apparently represented fairly accessibly in the human memory; and if a 'direct look-up' fails, then inferential procedures of various types (which may themselves involve recourse to perceptual tests) can be activated in order to answer the question. But the authors suggest that the notion of hierarchical class-inclusion may itself be derived from the psychologically more primitive concept of locative inclusion, for which the tests involve perceptual predicates such as those listed above.

The basic psychological predicates are primitives, in the sense that Miller and Johnson-Laird build complex recognition-procedures out of them. But they are not 'primitive' in the sense of being unanalysable, inexplicable, or innate in the newborn baby. Correlatively, language development must wait upon the development of the requisite perceptual routines, which may require movement within and action on the material world. A number of psychological studies are cited which indicate that *in* is the first of the locative terms (*in*, *on*, *at*, *by*, *with*, *between* . . .) to be learnt in infancy. Action schemata involving bodily skills can influence the infant's understanding of locative terms such as *in* and *on*: if it is physically possible to put X in Y, then a twenty-month-old child asked to put X *on* Y will instead put it inside Y, while if it is possible to put X on Y then a child asked to put X *under* Y will place X on top of Y instead. Semantically, the word *at* expresses a more abstract notion (involving the concept of a *region*) than either *in* or *on*; and children do indeed learn to use *at* later than they learn *in* and *on*. In general, deictic terms — which organize the conception of space by taking the current location and orientation of the speaker (or, later, the listener) as the prime reference point or landmark — seem to be psychologically primitive with respect to locatives based on 'external' landmarks, pathways, or boundaries.

The procedures suggested by Miller and Johnson-Laird as mediating the understanding even of such apparently simple words as *at* are surprisingly complex. (So to interpret, or verify, the expression 'The plane is at the door' one has to ask not merely about relative location, but also about size, salience, and mobility: if the plane really is at the door, it must be a toy plane or a hangar door that is in question.) And 'perceptual' and 'conceptual' routines can call recursively on themselves and heterarchically on each other, so that the flow of control in the information-processing that underlies our use of language may be very complicated. This flexibility of control contributes to the complexity of human nature that is the topic of Part III of this chapter. In the present context, the main relevance of psycholexicology is its emphasis on the biologically based perceptual routines that allow meaning to be given to linguistic expressions. Given our material embodiment (not least the facts that we are not radially symmetrical like jellyfish, and that our feet carry us in the same direction as our eyes look out over the space *in front* of us), the spatial organization informing our thought is perhaps to be expected. But what reason is there to think that the psychology of angels need be similarly constituted? A psycholexicology of the words sung by angelic choirs would surely be very different from one reflecting our specifically human nature.

Philosophical discussions relevant to these points (sic) include those that assign basic ontological significance to material or spatio-temporal concepts. In particular, accounts of individuation and reference that see a spatio-temporal framework as essential for these linguistic functions bear a close relation to the psycholexicology offered by Miller and Johnson-Laird. But as the 'philosophical' example in this section, I want to discuss Jonathan Bennett's recent work on linguistic behaviour.[6]

Bennett's account of language roots it firmly in its pre-linguistic behavioural basis and environmental setting. He argues for a Gricean, anti-Davidsonian, position on semantics, wherein the notion 'what *x* means' is secondary to the notion 'what the speaker meant by uttering *x*'. The pivotal semantic notion of speaker's *meaning* is elucidated in turn by that of speaker's *intent*, in a broadly Gricean fashion. Bennett holds that the concept of intention (and its cognate, belief) can be ascribed to creatures lacking a language, or even any communication-system. However, he believes that communicative intent (the core of the Gricean analysis of meaning) probably cannot be ascribed to any existing languageless creatures, even those which — like dolphins — seem both to communicate and to have intentions. Communicative intent can, by contrast, be ascribed to many of the gestures and actions of human beings (and he describes an imaginary tribe with a systematic method of communication of this type). For language properly so-called, communicative intent is necessary but not sufficient: also essential is a semantically significant *structure* in the communication-system. It is this which enables one to understand a novel sentence, by drawing both on one's knowledge of its individual parts and on one's appreciation of the general principles according to which those parts are assembled. He makes various suggestions about the sort of behavioural evidence that could imply that a strange tribe had a semantic structure in their communication-system, and so a language — and he even offers some provocative speculations about how structure might have originated in evolutionary history.

The point of immediate relevance here is the extent to which intention and belief are basically behavioural concepts that derive their sense from our interpretations of bodily activities within the material environment, activities commonly associated with widely shared animal needs such as hunger, thirst, warmth, shelter, escape and so forth.

Bennett stresses that the epistemic notions of intention, belief and perception (or their weaker cousins, purpose and 'registration') go essentially together. The ascription of intentions and beliefs to a creature implies that it perceives, or registers, its environment to some (imperfect but significantly reliable) degree. What an animal registers is largely a matter of what it sees, hears and feels; and to learn what this is, we have to rely on evidence about how environmental changes correlate with changes in the animal's pursuit of its goals. This evidence will be primarily behavioural, and will include 'commonsense' observations as well as the more recondite investigations of experimental psychologists; in addition, there may occasionally be physiological evidence available, of the sort appealed to by Miller and Johnson-Laird in identifying basic perceptual predicates.

Bennett is careful to point out that he provides no arguments proving that his behavioural criteria for these mentalistic terms are either necessary or logically sufficient conditions for the ascription of intentions and beliefs. Merely, he says, his criteria specify conditions that are 'sufficient by normal, reasonable, everyday standards'. So they cannot be used briskly to show that a noncorporeal being — such as an angel — could have no intentions and therefore no language, that such a being could not *mean* anything by the noises it might produce in the vicinity of a human woman. Nevertheless, if the way in which we do make sense of terms such as 'intention' crucially involves material considerations, then it should not be uncritically assumed that such terms retain their intelligibility if used in a wholly non-material context. If Davidson is right about language, then perhaps Gabriel could speak Aramaic — but if Bennett is right, this is decidedly dubious.

My final example in this section is drawn from artificial intelligence, and relates to the thesis of localism mentioned earlier. Among the semantic theories that have been incorporated into 'language-using' computer programs is that of R. C. Schank.[7] Schank's Conceptual Dependency Analysis seeks to represent the meaning of natural languages in terms of a small set of semantic primitives. For example, all the verbs of English — and of Aramaic — are said to be analysable in terms of eleven 'primitive actions'. Five of these are physical ACTS — PROPEL, MOVE, INGEST, EXPEL, GRASP; two are mental ACTS — MTRANS and MBUILD; two are instrumental ACTS — INTEND and SPEAK; and two are global ACTS — PTRANS and ATRANS.

The localist will immediately notice that nine of these eleven are clearly spatial in character. The five 'physical' ACTS are obviously rooted in our embodied existence within the material world. MBUILD (interpreted by Schank as 'to combine thoughts in some manner') relies on our experience of material building. And the 'TRANS' element in PTRANS, MTRANS and ATRANS is equally localistic in nature. These three ACTS respectively mark the transfer of physical objects, of information or ideas within the mind, and of abstract relationships (like ownership and responsibility).

Schank does not offer a theoretical rationale for his choosing these eleven primitives rather than any others. Nor does he give a detailed empirical or theoretical justification for his claim that PTRANS, MTRANS and ATRANS are the three most important of the eleven, for the purposes of representing the actual content of human communication. But he does offer outlined analyses of many familiar words, which serve to highlight some of the semantic relations between them. For instance, MTRANS is the core of his analysis of such verbs of thought as remember, see, feel, communicate, forget, learn, and teach; and MBUILD is the core of verbs such as conclude, resolve, decide, solve, realise, weigh (evidence), think about, and answer.

Schank's reliance on the idea of *transfer* as basically effecting the major part of human linguistic communication is reminiscent of Lyons' claim quoted earlier, that the processes of communicating propositional information and of transferring possession are each readily describable in terms of the localistic notion of a journey. There is no question but that Schank's approach is essentially localistic in character. It follows that the various computer programs that are based on Schank's theoretical work (one of which will be mentioned in Part III) embody a localistic interpretation of natural language.

It is often said that a computer could not really understand language, no matter how seemingly appropriate its 'linguistic' responses. The arguments offered vary, but they tend to make much of facts such as these: computers are not living things; many of them do not move in or act on their environment; many are unable to 'perceive' their world, except through their operator's teletype; they have no natural needs, goals, or interests — which is to say they have no goals (or intentions) at all. In short, they cannot *mean* things, and they do not really *interpret* the 'language' they spew forth: it is we who do so, and only we who can do so. Without going into these arguments here, it is perhaps worth pointing out that Gabriel is to some degree worse off than a robot. Philosophers who (like H. L. Dreyfus)[8] cast scorn on artificial intelligence as a methodology for studying human language because current natural language-using programs have no parallel of human embodiment, should surely be dubious also about the possibility of angels speaking Aramaic. Perhaps current Schankian programs have no real inkling of real transfer, but it is not clear that a language-using robot could have no such understanding. How Gabriel might achieve it is more of a mystery.

III: THE COMPLEXITY OF THE MIND

The complexity of the human mind is suggested by the intricacy of the cognitive processes that have been postulated to explain the generation and interpretation of natural language. Chomsky drew on his grammatical insights to deride the overly-simple 'stimulus-response' theoretical accounts offered by the orthodox positivist model, but even he had little to say about the specific processes involved in the actual production or understanding of speech.

Many complications ignored by Chomsky are studied by experimental psycholinguists, under the general term 'performance factors'. And Miller and Johnson-Laird, as we have noted, ask procedurally oriented questions about language that address problems not considered by Chomsky. A particularly fruitful source of insights into the degree (and, it is hoped, the nature) of structured complexity in linguistic processes is the project of formalizing computational models of the use of natural language sentences and connected texts. In this section I shall mention a few examples of recent work in artificial intelligence that bear on these issues.

My first example is a story-writing program based on the semantic theory of Schank and the psychological work of R. P. Abelson. The program, 'TALESPIN', was written by James Meehan.[9] Crude as it is, it shows the variety of sorts of knowledge and interacting computational processes necessary to compose (or to understand) even a simple story.

TALESPIN generates story-plots involving characters with various interpersonal relations and differing attitudes to and knowledge about the world, and it also decides which of its inferences need to be explicitly represented in the story and which can be sensibly left unsaid. That is, it deals with semantic issues (issues of meaning) rather than with syntax and details of word-choice. (The story I shall quote was put into acceptable English by Meehan himself, since TALESPIN's linguistic module — appropriately titled 'MUMBLE' — cannot cope with pronouns, for instance, and expresses large 'sets' of thought as clumsy single sentences.)

Asked to write a story with the moral, 'Never trust flatterers', TALESPIN produced this (or, more accurately, its semantic skeleton):

The Fox and the Crow
Once upon a time, there was a dishonest fox named Henry who lived in a cave, and a vain and trusting crow named Joe who lived in an elm-tree. Joe

had gotten a piece of cheese and was holding it in his mouth. One day, Henry walked from his cave, across the meadow to the elm-tree. He saw Joe Crow and the cheese and became hungry. He decided that he might get the cheese if Joe Crow spoke, so he told Joe that he liked his singing very much and wanted to hear him sing. Joe was very pleased with Henry and began to sing. The cheese fell out of his mouth, down to the ground. Henry picked up the cheese and told Joe Crow that he was stupid. Joe was angry, and didn't trust Henry anymore. Henry returned to his cave.

The overtones of Aesop will be evident: Meehan's claim is that Aesop (and his readers) need *at least* the knowledge and inferential competence possessed by this program in order that they may be able to appreciate stories such as this one.

TALESPIN needs diverse types of knowledge. Thus it needs an abstract characterization of *flattery* in terms of the interlocking goals and perceptions of two characters. And if the story is to convey the warning 'Never trust flatterers', it needs also some understanding of trust (and what sorts of behaviour tend to generate or destroy it) that will mediate its insight that the flattered character in this cautionary tale needs to lose in some way as a result of the flattery. Similarly, it needs to know when one may be led to flatter: why one often flatters someone in order to get them to do something which otherwise they would not have been disposed to do. (Joe and Henry cannot be *friends*, since a friend's direct request for cheese would be immediately granted — at least in the simplified social world imagined by TALESPIN.) The social psychological interests of Abelson (a pupil of Fritz Heider) have greatly influenced the representations of 'interpersonal dynamics' provided by Meehan to this program.[10]

In addition, TALESPIN needs to know about characteristic needs or desires, ways of moving in space, ways of planning how to achieve various sorts of goals (and sub-goals, and sub-sub-goals . . .), and so forth, if it is to model the situation presented in the story — including the individual world models of the two participants themselves.

Its knowledge of planning, for instance, is based on a number of primitive ACTS (called 'DELTA-ACTS'), defined in terms of goals such as CONTROL, KNOW and TELL. Different varieties of TELL are specified for the program as ASK, INFORM, REASON, BARGAIN, PERSUADE, THREATEN, etc. And associated with each primitive ACT is a list of 'planboxes' for achieving the goal in question, together with an algorithm for deciding which planbox to try first when generating a plan to achieve the goal. For example, the primitive D-PROX (X,Y,Z) is equivalent to X's wanting Y to be near Z. The relevant planboxes already distinguished by Meehan include the following alternatives: X tries to move Y to Z; X gets Y to move himself to Z; X gets Z to move himself to Y; X gets a third party to move Y to Z . . . .

At first sight, the second and third of these may seem equivalent, in the event that each of 'Y' and 'Z' are self-movers, or animate agents. But a moment's thought will show that this need not be so: if you want to ask your boss for a rise, you may phone him and suggest that you go over to his office next day — you would be well-advised *not* to ask him to come over to yours. In general, a relation of DOMINANCE between two characters implies a non-reciprocal ability to ask the other person to do something. It is this sort of fact that is taken into account by the algorithm that chooses which planbox to employ in working out a way for the character concerned to try to achieve his goal. Recursiveness can give indefinitely many levels, since 'getting Y to move to Z', for example, may involve ASK-ing Y to do so, and this may involve D-PROX since creatures without telephones have to be near to each other in space in order to TELL (say) anything effectively. Similarly, if X is to try to move Y near to Z, then X has to know where Z is: if he does not, then D-KNOW (where is Z?) must be invoked, which in turn may involve further D-PROXing in order to ASK someone else for the information.

Even this very brief description of the program shows how different types of fact and inferential process have to be intelligently integrated so as to create a story like *The Fox and The Crow*. A program — and, equally, an angel — that did not know about movement through physical space and the reasons for which this may be necessary would be unable to see the need for a sentence like, 'One day, Henry walked from his cave, across the meadow to the elm-tree'. It was presumably Gabriel's appreciation of this sort of constraint that led to the angel's plan to appear to Mary in her room before trying to make the Annunciation. Given that Gabriel was going to appear in 'bodily' form at all, there would have been little sense in his doing so in Egypt instead of Galilee.

A. C. Davey has written a program that, in comparison with TALESPIN, shows a much greater sensitivity to the problems of syntactic and lexical choice involved in the production of natural language.[11] The program's knowledge domain is the game of noughts and crosses, or tic-tac-toe. Davey's interest is to articulate generative rules for verbal (English) descriptions of an indefinite number of games, in such a way that the progress and strategy of each individual game is expressed by subtle variations of syntax and lexicon. For instance, syntactic decisions have to be made about clause subordination (when is it in order, and which event should be expressed by the subordinate clause?), about sentence separation (when should two clauses be conjoined in a single sentence?), and about the use of subjunctive and conditional constructions. Similarly, a lexical choice may have to be made between different conjunctions: should it be *and*, *but*, *however*, or *and so*? (It is worth remarking here that Terry Winograd's program SHRDLU could parse *and* and *but* correctly — interpreting them syntactically as conjunctions — but could not use or understand them properly since it had no representation of the semantic difference between them.)[12]

Here is an example of the actual output produced by Davey's program, given the task of describing the game shown in Figure 8.1:

I started the game by taking the middle of an edge, and you took an end of the opposite one. I threatened you by taking the square opposite the one I had just taken, but you blocked my line and threatened me. However, I blocked your diagonal and threatened you. If you had blocked my edge, you would have forked me, but you took the middle of the one opposite the corner I had just taken and adjacent to mine and so I won by completing my edge.

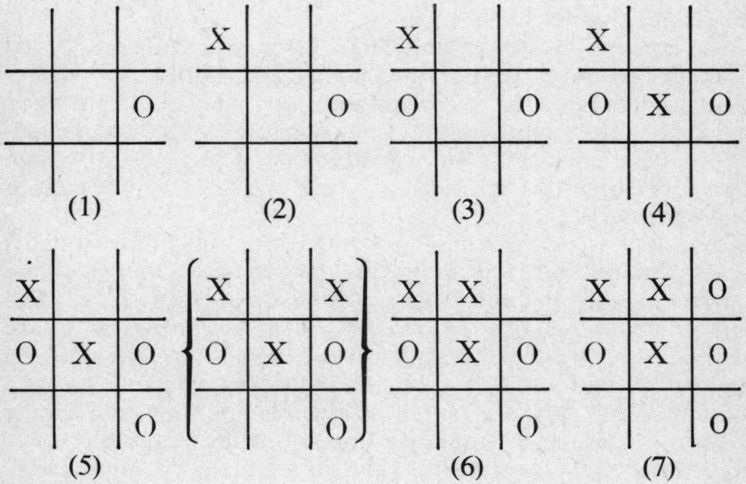

Figure 8.1

Clearly, considerable knowledge of the strategy and tactics — not just the 'rules' — of noughts and crosses is involved here, guiding the program's choice not only of what to say but also of how to say it. Imagine, for example, how much less appropriate, or even how *in*appropriate, this passage would be if the conjunctions (*and*, *but*, *however*, *and so*) were variously interchanged. Again, consider how much less felicitous the second sentence would have been if the order of the two last ideas had been reversed: 'I threatened you by taking the square opposite the one I had just taken, but you threatened me and blocked my line'. The order actually chosen by the program reflects in a natural fashion its understanding of the structure of attack, defence, and counterattack informing this game. Similarly, it would have been less happy to render the first conjunction of the sentence thus: I took the square opposite the one I had just taken and so threatened you. This is because the syntax of subordinate and subordinating expressions actually chosen by the program corresponds to the strategic importance of the ideas involved: *that* I suddenly threatened you is more important than *how* I did so, and so should be the main focus of the sentence. This rule is apparently broken in the next (third) sentence of the game-description: 'However, I blocked your diagonal and threatened you', because the blocking of the diagonal was the necessary defensive response to the previous threat from the opponent, and the fact that it also constituted a new threat *to* the opponent was a fortunate side-effect. (Similar remarks apply to the second conjunction of the second sentence.)

The choice of 'However' as the initial word of the third sentence was guided by the pragmatic rule that two consecutive *buts* within a single sentence are to be avoided since they may be confusing to the listener. The causal or strategic dependence of the blocking of the opponent's diagonal on the previous threat posed by the opponent is therefore signalled by the use of *however* at the start of a new sentence.

The use of *however* to avoid a string of *buts* might be termed a 'stylistic' matter, but it has a clear pragmatic justification (avoiding cognitive confusion) whereas many stylistic choices do not. For example, in the 'Aesop's fable' previously quoted, a phrase occurred referring to 'a vain and trusting crow'. The alternative 'a trusting and vain crow' seems decidedly less elegant. My own intuition is that this is a matter of syllable-counting rather than semantics or pragmatics, having nothing to do with the relative importance of the two ideas 'vain' and 'trusting'. This lexical decision was taken by Meehan himself, not by his program, which has no way of motivating choices of ordering of predicates such as these. It should be obvious that any program — or theory — competent to take stylistic matters into account would have to be more complicated yet: only a very complex angelic mind could speak Aramaic elegantly.

Davey's program is inhumanly rational, in the sense that it always produces syntactically perfect English sentences, which express a coherent set of thoughts. But in real life our spoken sentences are often grossly imperfect from the syntactical point of view, and very confused as expressions of thought or semantic content. This is particularly true when the topic is emotionally sensitive, arousing anxieties (whether conscious or unconscious) in the speaker's mind that lead to hesitations, evasive changes of topic, and choices of euphemistic alternatives, together with the various syntactic 'restarts' required in expressing these shifting lines of thought. Factors such as these affect linguistic *performance*, by operating in co-operation with grammatical *competence* to generate actual speech. A preliminary model of neurotic thought processes that aims to simulate the effect of neurotic concerns on speech has been programmed by J. H. Clippinger.[13] Continual monitoring of the sentence during its generation may result in pauses, restarts, and rephrasings of a very 'human' character, as in these examples:

That, that I was thinking that I — of asking you whether it wouldn't be all right for you, you know, not to give me a bill.

You know, I was just thinking about, uh . . . well, whatever it was isn't important.

No analogous hesitations and reformulations would occur in an angelic being seraphically immune to doubt and inhumanly free of anxiety, even when speaking of such an awesome event as the Incarnation. If such a being talked in natural language at all, it would surely be a very *un*-natural conversation.

Natural conversation is dialogue rather than monologue, implying co-operation governed by shared intuitions of 'relevance' of various kinds — whether semantic, pragmatic, or social. For instance, in view of the theological status of Archangels, one can safely bet that Gabriel both initiated and closed the conversation with Mary. And, presumably, Gabriel knew when to shut up and let Mary do the talking. Lacking 'human' intuitions on matters such as these, Gabriel would have been unable to talk naturally with Mary, and would not have led up to the focal Annunciation by first greeting her, 'Hail, thou that art highly favoured'. Our theoretical understanding of the implicit structure of conversation is still very sketchy. The work of ethnomethodologists on turn-taking, greeting, and opening and closing of conversations is obviously to the point. So too are philosophers' and linguists' studies of *speech-acts*, insofar as these may suggest conversational units of various types that can be appropriately combined only in certain ways. Similarly, discussions of implicature and the communicative intent of sentences within conversation raise issues that are crucial to theoreticians of the natural use of natural language. These questions have been dealt with primarily by philosophers and linguists, although recent work in development psychology is relevant also in that it studies how the child learns to use language for communication (as opposed to how the child learns to use 'noun phrases' and like syntactic structures).[14] Only a few programs exist that address these issues, and these do so only in a minimal fashion.[15] Our theory of the social (communicative) use of language must be more fully articulated before it can be incorporated in any artificial intelligence.

IV: CONCLUSION

It is not surprising that language studies are commonly seen as having implications for human nature: Chomsky is only one among many to have believed 'linguistic' matters to have a wider philosophical relevance. For language enters intimately into our thinking and experience, and deeply informs our social actions and personal character.

Studies of language based in very different areas converge in suggesting the enormous complexity of the cognitive processes underlying the production and understanding of natural language. Any theoretical account of language must reflect the structure and function of these processes to some degree, as well as giving due weight to the extent to which our terrestrial environment and material embodiment are represented in the semantics of human languages.

Accordingly, these studies imply that our image of human nature must acknowledge the rich interpretative power of the human mind, that no simplistic notion of mankind which ignores this subtle complexity could be adequate to human reality. Similarly, no concept of human nature can be acceptable that cuts us off from our physical embodiment and ecology.

In view of the theologian's traditional preference for simplicity over complexity in spiritual beings, and bearing in mind the aetherial substance of the orthodox angel, I am tempted to adapt a remark of Wittgenstein's: If the angel Gabriel spoke to Mary, it is a miracle that she understood him.

NOTES

1   L. Wittgenstein, *Philosophical Investigations*, Oxford: Blackwell, 1953.

2   J. Lyons, *Semantics*, Cambridge: Cambridge University Press, 1977. See especially chapter 15.

3   Lyons, *Semantics*, p. 724.

4   G. A. Miller and P. N. Johnson-Laird, *Language and Perception*, Cambridge, Mass.: Belknap Press, 1976, pp. 375–376.

5   Miller and Johnson-Laird, *Language and Perception*. See especially chapters 2 and 6.

6   J. Bennett, *Linguistic Behaviour*, Cambridge: Cambridge University Press, 1976.

7   R. C. Schank, 'Conceptual dependency: a theory of natural language understanding', *Cognitive Psychology*, 3 (1972), 552–631. Programs based on Schank's work are described in R. C. Schank (ed.), *Conceptual Information Processing*, New York: American Elsevier, 1975. See also notes 9 and 10 below.

8   H. L. Dreyfus, *What Computers Can't Do: A Critique of Artificial Reason*, New York: Harper and Row, 1972. I have discussed Dreyfus' arguments in M. Boden, *Artificial Intelligence and Natural Man*. New York: Basic Books, 1977, chapter 14.

9   J. Meehan, *The Metanovel: Writing Stories by Computer*. PhD Dissertation, Yale Computer Science Dept., 1976. A brief description is in James Meehan, 'TALE-SPIN, An Interactive program that writes stories', *Fifth Int. Joint Conf. Artificial Intelligence* (1977), 91–98.

10   R. P. Abelson, 'The structure of belief systems', in R. C. Schank and K. M. Colby (eds), *Computer Models of Thought and Language*, San Francisco: Freeman, 1973, pp. 287–340; R. P. Abelson, 'Concepts for representing mundane reality in plans', in D. G. Bobrow and Allan Collins (eds), *Representation and Understanding: Studies in Cognitive Science*, New York: Academic Press, 1975, pp. 273–309; R. C. Schank and R. P. Abelson, *Goals, Plans, Scripts and Understanding: An Enquiry into Human Knowledge Structures*, Hillsdale, N. J.: Erlbaum, 1977.

11   A. C. Davey, *The Formalisation of Discourse Production*, PhD Thesis Edinburgh University, 1974. To be published by Edinburgh University Press.

12   T. Winograd, *Understanding Natural Language*, New York: Academic Press, 1972, pp. 149 and 157.

13   J. H. Clippinger, *Meaning and Discourse: A Computer Model of Psychoanalytic Discourse and Cognition,* Baltimore: Johns Hopkins, 1977.

14   E. Clark, 'First language acquisition', in John Morton and J. C. Marshall (eds), *Psycholinguistics Series Vol. 1: Developmental and Pathological*, London: Elek, 1977.

15   W. C. Mann, J. A. Moore and J. A. Levin, 'A comprehension model for human dialogue', *Fifth Int. Joint Conf. Artificial Intelligence* (1977), pp. 77–87; R. Power, *A Model of Conversation*. Unpublished working paper, University of Sussex, Dept. Experimental Psychology, 1976.

PART III

PSYCHOLOGISTS ANCIENT AND MODERN

9
McDougall revisited

William McDougall is out of fashion. To be sure, a few of his concepts — notably that of *sentiment* — have been borrowed or adapted by contemporary personality theorists, and textbook writers recognize him as being of historical importance by virtue of his pre-eminence in the early years of personality theorizing. Ritual homage is paid to him for his early insistence on the problems of motivation, but his preoccupation with the general notion of *purpose* in psychology is regarded as out of date. The issue has been reformulated,[1] and his postulation of eighteen specific instincts as the source of all human motivation is thought of as scientifically naïve, a twentieth-century excursion into the more ancient faculty psychologizing. McDougall is 'important' — as the theory of phlogiston is 'important' — but his reputed importance is not of the nature to encourage us to read his works.

Furthermore, now — as in his lifetime — the reader who does venture to sample his works is likely to be put off by the vocabulary he will find there. McDougall had to face many negative reactions to his work, which caused him disappointment and no little bitterness; the first fine careless rapture which greeted his doctrine of instincts, and which drew forth twenty-three editions of his *An Introduction to Social Psychology* before his death, was not destined to last nor to extend to his more speculative works; he never became known as the founder of a school — men spoke of McDougall, but not of McDougallism. His lack of influence was largely due to his defiant habit of choosing the most unpopular words to express even relatively unexceptionable views. In his hormic psychology he relied heavily on the nativist concept of *instinct* (later to be relabeled *propensity, tendency*); he defended *animism*, *dualism*, *interactionism*, and *freedom*; he spoke of the *group mind, monads,* the *soul*; and he thus helped to raise clouds of dialectical dust which largely obscured the force and originality of his views. Most psychologists were not ready to be told that Mind has an influence on Body, at least not in those words. I do not doubt that many present-day readers will have the same reaction to his 'metaphysical' terminology, though — as I hope to show — the content of his message should be much more acceptable to us now than it was to his contemporaries. If we can see through the archaism of his language, we shall see that McDougall is a purveyor of surprisingly new wine in misleadingly old bottles.

McDougall was a remarkably prolific writer and covered a wide range of psychological topics: animal and human, social and abnormal psychology; personality theory and psychic research; eugenics and neurophysiology. But the constant recurrence of certain themes shows that two of his main concerns were: to show that the concept of purpose is essential to any adequate psychology, and to demonstrate the causal efficacy of conscious states. Psychology he saw as the study of behavior, but his four[2] objective criteria of behavior define it as a purposive notion and imply, he said, an inner side or aspect analogous to our immediate experience of our own purposive activities (p. 306).[3] Sometimes he emphasized these two themes by writing directly on the philosophical problem of the Body–Mind relationship, attacking not only many ancient accounts of this relationship, but also accounts given by fellow-scientists — such as Wundt's parallelism, Huxley's epiphenomenalism, and Watson's behaviorism. His writings of a more strictly psychological nature also showed the central importance of these convictions in his thinking, and even his attempts to demonstrate Lamarckian inheritance experimentally[4-6] — the results of which might now be explained by unintended bias effects of the type described by Rosenthal[7] — were taken up in the hope of convincing his antagonists of the importance of mental principles in phylogeny as well as ontogeny: for McDougall, even morphology cannot do without the concept of purpose.

In this paper I shall claim, first, that in saying that Mind influences Body, McDougall intended primarily to emphasize the two points which I have characterized as being important recurrent concerns. These points, as he often said himself, are — strictly speaking — independent of any specific underlying metaphysic, their importance being rather that they recommend to the psychologist, qua scientist, one type of explanation rather than another. That McDougall often chose to express them in metaphysical terms — and thus endorsed first the soul, and later monads — was no doubt responsible for the relative neglect of his views.

I shall claim, secondly, that in his detailed working out of these themes in his proactive psychology he anticipated many important contemporary views on cognition, social psychology, and personality. In particular, his social psychology and personality theory stress what we might call *propriate striving*,[8] while much of what he has to say about purposive activity suggests that the relation of Mind to Body is analogous to that of program to machine:[9] his emphases on the role of cognition in behavior and on the quality of striving bear an interesting resemblance to what present-day authors have had to say about TOTE-units, Images, and Plans.[10] A participant in a recent conference on the computer simulation of personality referred to 'the question of how organized and integrated identity emerges from, and gives organization to, the antecedent processes that generate it' as the greatest of all the problems which have been abandoned by psychologists because of their complexity and philosophical implications, but as one which might yield to inquiry with the aid of computers.[11] McDougall's doctrine of monads and his concept of the master sentiment of self-regard are attempts to deal with just this problem, and he also raised — in metaphysical form — some of the more specific questions facing personality simulators today.

THE BODY–MIND RELATIONSHIP

McDougall describes his book *Body and Mind* as a defense of animism, where this term denotes not merely primitive anthropomorphism, but any view which holds that 'all, or some, of those manifestations of life and mind which distinguish the living man from the corpse and from inorganic bodies are due to the operation within him of something which is of a nature different from that of the body, an animating principle generally, *but not necessarily or always* [italics mine] conceived as an immaterial and individual being or soul'.[12] He adds that 'Animism does not necessarily imply metaphysical Dualism, or indeed any metaphysical or ontological doctrine . . .' (p. xxiii). He says 'We are compelled to choose between Animism and Materialism', claiming that the only serious objection to Animism is based on 'the mechanistic dogma', i.e., the claim that mechanical principles of explanation hold sway throughout the universe (p. xxiii). He defines *mechanical explanation* in several of his works, always negatively, e.g., as finding 'the explanation of present events in terms only of the causal influence of antecedent events, without reference to any kind of possible future events', and always in contrast to *teleological* explanation, where a prospective purposive reference is involved.[13-15] Thus the kernel of his Animism is a view about what types of *explanation* are needed by psychologists qua scientists, rather than any specific metaphysical view which may be held by the psychologist qua philosopher.

This last point is upheld by his remarks on dualism and interactionism: in claiming that we must be either dualists or psychical monists, he defines dualism as any view which assumes that 'mental and physical processes are distinct in kind and that man is a psychophysical organism in the life of which processes of these two kinds interact'. He goes on to say that *distinct in kind* may be, but need not be, interpreted 'metaphysically', in terms of material and mental substance; or it may be interpreted nonmetaphysically as regarding 'physical and psychical processes as distinguishable in terms of the general laws which they seem to obey or manifest . . .', i.e., mechanistic or teleological.[16] In his discussion of *Tendencies*[17] he says that Newton's laws are better not expressed in terms of tending, but rather as conditional statements of generalization based on observation, e.g., the planet will move in a straight line *unless* . . . . Thus he prefers dualism to psychical monism, since he feels that the latter obscures the differences between living and nonliving things; elsewhere[18] he makes a similar criticism of the Gestaltists' talk of soap-bubbles as tending to the spherical. Again, while in his early work he tried to develop a neurophysiological theory of interaction, holding the synapse to be the seat of consciousness,[19] he remarks later that 'in speaking of psycho-physical interaction, we must recognize that the expression may distort the truth in that it seems to separate the psychical and the physical; whereas these may be but two partial aspects of the concrete reality, two aspects of a system of psycho-physical activity which are distinguishable but inseparable (see ref. 14 p. 7). This Aristotelian viewpoint is echoed in his article *Men or Robots*?, where he says 'We speak of a purpose as though it were a thing, and then, when we ask what sort of a thing it can be, we can find no intelligible answer' and he suggests that we use only the adjectival form, *purposive* (see ref. 18 p. 299). This suggestion may reinforce our feeling that he was not what he termed a metaphysical dualist, for it bears a remarkable resemblance to Ryle's[20] method of denying the Cartesian *Ghost in the Machine* in terms of the doctrine of category-mistakes. In general, McDougall is primarily interested in process rather than in substance, and if we interpret his remarks in this light they seem immediately less far-fetched.

Even though (in the last chapter of *Body and Mind*) he endorses the hypothesis of the soul as an immaterial being, McDougall explicitly refuses to commit himself to regarding it as an immaterial *substance*, but says it is 'a being that possesses, *or is*, the sum of definite capacities for psychical activity and psycho-physical interaction . . .' (p. 365, my italics), which capacities are conceived as teleological, and at least in some degree conscious. He admits that his interest in psychic research was due to the hope of finding evidence for a strong version of Animism asserting the existence of 'some factor or principle which is different from the body and capable of existing independently of it' (p. 349), but the evidence is ambiguous; he concludes that 'psycho-physical interaction may be, for all we know, a necessary condition of all consciousness. For all the thinking or consciousness of which we have positive knowledge is of embodied minds or souls' (p. 365). The dual nature of memory, as being both dependent upon brain-processes and yet essentially teleological (i.e., selective in terms of our interests and goals), he takes as support of this interactionism (p. 371). The unity of personality is an expression of the unity of the soul and the absence of any analogous unity in the nervous system shows the incoherence of parallelism (p. 356). Further evidence that his dualism is Aristotelian and Leibnizian rather than Platonic or Cartesian, a metaphysic of process rather than of substratum, is his remark that in *Body and Mind* he was 'unduly concerned with the question — What are things made of? to the neglect of the more important question — How do events run their course?' (see ref. 13 p. vi).

In the final chapters of his *An Outline of Abnormal Psychology* he endorses a more clearly Leibnizian view of the soul, at which he merely hinted in *Body and Mind* (e.g., p. 366), in which the soul is said to be a community of monads, linked together in a more or less hierarchical organization, disruption of which accounts for the dissociations of personality described by Morton Prince and others.[21] The monads are dynamic, conative units, and as they become more closely integrated the soul develops as a system of psychical dispositions (p. 371). The individuality of the soul (and thus the uniqueness of personality) results from the infinite possibilities of organization among the monads, and the unity of the soul results from the subordination of all other monads to the chief-monad. The general purposes of the soul are the purposes of the chief-monad — the details of action are determined by the subordinate monads, whose specific purposes are not necessarily, or usually, represented in the chief-monad (see ref. 16 p. 546). In case this sounds over fanciful, we should remember that, similarly, a master-program may merely name subroutines, the details being independently programmed; failure of a given subroutine may or may not divert the over-all process to a detailed examination of that routine; malintegration of subroutines may lead to loops pursuing goals *other* than the final goal of the master-program. This last would be equivalent , in McDougall's terminology, to a dissociation of personality; I shall say more about his personality theory later — suffice it to say, now, that the monads correspond roughly to the sentiments and may be seen as dynamic organizing principles (plans, sub-programs) subordinated in various degrees to the chief-monad, which corresponds to the master sentiment of self-regard (master-program, metaplan).

MIND AND COGNITION

McDougall claims that the psychologist needs to talk about both body and mind, where mind cannot be identified with the brain or nervous system, for this would be to tie us down to one type of explanation,[22] nor with a bundle of faculties or a more or less organized mass of ideas regarded as enduring things which pass in and out of consciousness (ibid. p. 35). Despite the ideo-motor theory, he says, 'idea-psychology gives us no intelligible theory of action, it cannot relate ideas to the bodily activity in which our mental life expresses itself'; he adds that Watson and other behaviorists recognized the uselessness of such theories of mind, but took the mistaken step of trying to disregard mind altogether (ref. 18 p. 276). The mind is 'something which expresses its nature, powers and functions in two ways: (1) the modes of individual experience; (2) the modes of bodily activity, the sum of which constitutes the behavior of the individual' (ref. 22 p. 35); the *raison d'être* of mental events seems to be the modification and control of events within the body and physical events without it' (ref. 14 p. 3); 'Mental process seems to be always a process of striving or conation initiated and guided by a process or act of knowing, of apprehension, . . . an activity of a subject in respect of an object apprehended, an activity which constantly changes or modifies the relation between subject and object . . . . The representation or idea of the end is not truly the cause or determining condition of the purposive activity . . . the anticipatory representation of the end of action merely serves to guide the course of action in detail . . .' (see ref. 3 p. 308).

Thus consciousness has a specific function, far from being an idle epiphenomenon: 'In the infant, as his powers of representation develop, as he becomes capable of free ideas, the end towards which any instinct impels him becomes more or less clearly represented in his mind as an object of desire. [This leads to] greater continuity of effort; for, when the power of representation of the object has been attained, the attention is not so readily drawn off from it by irrelevant sensory impressions of all sorts' (p. 151). This is reminiscent of recent Russian work on the function of linguistic representation in increasing persistence and detailed excellence of effort.[23] Mind is seen as determining the goals of action, and then as guiding bodily activity so as to reach those goals. As the Gestaltists, Lashley, and Lewin were also to point out, the detailed movements of 'equivalent' behavioral units may vary considerably, and that is one reason why teleological rather than mechanistic explanation is required (see ref. 18); behavior is made up of conative units, only movement can be analyzed into muscle twitches; subunits may only be explicable in terms of the over-all goal — thus McDougall, like Lewin, noted that a child may move away from his goal in order to reach it and will attempt various manoeuvres in the process (ref. 3 p. 152); the analogy to heuristics as subunits in programs for problem-solving is obvious. We are reminded of the contemporary notion of TOTE-units, wherein behavior is continually guided by match–mismatch templates which are presumably cognitive representations, though not necessarily conscious (see ref. 10). We may even view pleasure and pain as match–mismatch signals: McDougall denies that pleasure can be an end in itself, but says that pleasurable feeling is a sign of progress towards or achievement of a goal (ref. 3 pp. 25, 37). Cognitive representation does not itself cause activity (as held by the ideo-motor theory) but it helps in the achievement of the goal insofar as it supplies a clear and detailed representation of the goal itself and of the various subgoals — the more detailed the representation, the more specialized and nicely adjusted the activity (pp. 308–9). 'Reasoning, like all other forms of intellectual process, is but the servant of the instinctual impulses' (ref. 22 p. 215); and cognitive processes, being the servants of the instinctual impulses, are affected by them: thus McDougall (like Bartlett and later workers on social perception) stressed the selective nature of perception and memory, saying that this was to be explained in dynamic terms, i.e., with reference to the goals and interests of the organism concerned (e.g., ref. 13 p. 61; ref. 12, chapter 24). His remarks on the mnemonic function of imagery in recall are similar to those of Bartlett[24] (cf. ref. 3 p. 209), and are in line with his view of the function of consciousness as helping to direct and fixate attention — the latter is a teleological concept to be dealt with in dynamic terms, and 'effort of attention is the essential form of all volition' (ibid.).

INSTINCTS AND SENTIMENTS

In 1923 McDougall exhorted Watson's students: 'If then you must be behaviorists, I beg that you will be purposive behaviorists',[25] and in 1925 he remarked that most psychologists in fact allowed for purpose in their systems, though they used differing terms (drive, determining tendency, prepotent reflex, motor-set, etc.), and some — for instance Tolman — also stressed the role of cognition in goal-directed behavior, allowing that cognitions initiate, guide, and terminate purposive activities (ref. 18 p. 297). However, as McDougall pointed out at some length in 1930, he nonetheless still disagreed with many of his contemporaries: the disagreement was over which of the two possible types of purposive psychology (the hedonistic and the hormic) was to be preferred (cf. ref. 15). As I have mentioned, McDougall rejected hedonism, saying that pleasure and pain were merely general feelings acting as signs of success or failure in approaching specific (though not necessarily consciously represented) goals; he distinguished between hedonism of the past, the present, and the future, characterizing all as inadequate, and thus rejecting the theories of Thorndike, reinforcement theorists, and drive reduction theorists (ibid.). His preference was for a hormic psychology, the foundations of which he had laid in his *An Introduction to Social Psychology* of 1908.

He states that the essence of the hormic theory is that 'To the question — Why does a certain animal or man seek this or that goal? — it replies: Because it is his nature to do so'. Thus behavior is to be explained in terms of *instincts* (innate propensities), which are the core of his psychological concept of purpose. Instinctive action shows all three aspects of mental process: cognitive, affective, and conative (ref. 3 p. 23), and all these aspects are included in his original definition of an instinct as an inherited or innate psycho-physical disposition which determines its possessor to perceive, and to pay attention to, objects of a certain class, to experience an emotional excitement of a particular quality upon perceiving such an object, and to act in regard to it in a particular manner, or, at least, to experience an impulse to such action (ibid. p. 25). This tripartite definition is mirrored in present-day personality theory, notably in Cattell's definition of the concept *erg* which is crucial in his factor analytic approach (see ref. 1 p. 401), and — as Bruner points out — the notion of a predisposition to react to specific perceptual impressions in specific ways is similar to the ethological notion of *releasers*, as described, for example, by Tinbergen[26] and Lorenz.[27] Behavior, animal or human, is not to be explained in terms of habit, so stressed by William James; only instincts are truly dynamic, habits merely being acquired characteristics of the means of reaching goals, as our linguistic habits determine the manner in which we ask for something, but not what we ask for. In *An Outline of Psychology* he states that 'The main thesis of this book is that in every case the motive, when truly assigned, will be found to be some instinctive impulse or some conjunction of two or more such impulses' (p. 218). During the processes of socialization and maturation, no essentially new sources of motivation arise — even the most 'idealistic' actions are to be accounted for in terms of the basic instincts. In particular, the *self* has no special dynamic power: it can only appropriate that of the instincts associated with it. In simulation terms, a computer can be programmed so as to learn to represent and follow new goals, but — even if it is to some extent self-programming — it can never reprogram so as to generate new sources of energy: these are specified once and for all in the initial program.

Clearly, any hormic psychology which thus denies functional autonomy[28] must attempt to explain those types of behavior which, prima facie, do not seem to be motivated by innate impulses; such an explanation should both refer specific actions to specific instinctive bases and illuminate the mechanisms of socialization whereby the child seems to become gradually more free of his instinctive urges as he matures. McDougall attempts such an explanation in terms of the sentiments: 'organized system(s) of emotional tendencies centred about some object' (ref. 3 p. 105). Thus, like instincts, sentiments have the tripartite nature of mental being; but, whereas the instincts are innate, the sentiments are individually acquired tendencies (ref. 22 p. 213). Only they are the true basis of our judgments of value and merit, only they bring order into our volitional life, for they organize our various emotional impulses into a system which includes cognitive representations which serve to guide our action (ref. 3 p. 137). Insofar as they are associated with a strong master sentiment of self-regard, about which I shall say more later, we are self-determined rather than impelled by our instincts. Socialization, in building up the sentiments, does not add new sources, but new objects of motivation and facilitates cognitive representation of such objects, including the *abstract* objects conceived by the use of linguistic categories. Sentiments are conceived in developmental, dynamic terms (I have already mentioned that they are equivalent to the monads, the conative units which together form the system which is the personality); thus: 'Each sentiment has a life-history, like every other vital organization. It is gradually built up, increasing in complexity and strength, and may continue to grow indefinitely, or may enter upon a period of decline, and may decay slowly or rapidly, partially or completely . . . .' (ibid. p. 140).

THE SENTIMENT OF SELF-REGARD

For McDougall the mental is to be conceived as process, as organization of behavior rather than as an entity or entities underlying behavior; mental terms, as we have seen, are to be construed as adjectives rather than as substantives. Nevertheless, we may speak of the structure of the mind: 'Mental structure is that enduring growing framework of the mind which we infer from the observed manifestations of mind in experience and in behavior; and, since this develops, grows and, even when the mind is at rest, endures, we may properly describe it and its parts in substantial terms, which terms we shall have to select and define with care . . . . We speak of the structure of a poem or of a musical composition, meaning a whole consisting of parts in orderly functional relations with one another, and, though the structure of the mind is not of the same order as these structures, yet these, rather than the material structure of a machine, should be thought of as offering the closer analogy' (ref. 22 pp. 41, 42). We might add that a part of a program is more analogous to a part of a poem than it is to a part of the machine which it controls. 'The structure of the mind seems to be peculiar to each individual' (ibid. p. 36) — thus each personality is unique.

As I suggested earlier, this mental structure is the organization of the sentiments, which are interrelated and hierarchically integrated by way of a master sentiment, the sentiment of self-regard. This integration develops gradually, and may be more or less complete — the account of the growth and function of the sentiment of self-regard is one of the most interesting features of McDougall's psychology, and it forms the focus of his personality theory. In particular, he holds it (and its metaphysical equivalent, the doctrine of monads) to encompass two 'opposing' views of the personality, or soul, neither of which seems to be expendable: the personality acts as a unitary agent and yet is built up by a gradual integrative process.[29] This is just the problem which I mentioned earlier as being raised at the conference on simulation — McDougall's answer sounds like a provision for the development of a self-programming routine which comes to control the subroutines in differing degrees.

The sentiment of self-regard is centered about, and develops in conjunction with, the idea of the self; this development is essentially a social process, for — while the child's first idea of the self is of a bodily self distinguished from external physical objects[30] — he later learns to distinguish animate objects, including other selves, and the constant interaction between him and these other selves suggests to him the limits of his capacities and of his autonomy. The master sentiment draws mainly on two instincts, self-display and self-subjection, and may involve both positive and negative self-feeling. Praise and blame act as effective social sanctions by way of the self-regarding sentiment, and such sanctions may be internalized as moral conscience.

But such internalization is only one mechanism of socialization; another is the establishment of 'quasi-altruistic extensions' of the egoistic sentiment, whereby 'the child is led to identify himself with his school, his college, his town, his profession as a class or collective unit, and finally to his country or nation as a whole' all by way of extending his self-regarding sentiment to these objects (ref. 3 p. 178). This extension may be brought about by such simple means as naming, whereby several objects are categorized under one and the same concept, one which is already associated with the self-regarding sentiment. Thereafter, behavior with reference to these objects will be different — and, since the sentiments are seen as continually developing, there is no reason why an object should not be included at one time and not at another (e.g., by varying categorization). Similarly, relabeling of subroutines would make them available at different points in the master program or withdraw them from its control entirely. The analogy to modern concepts of ego-involvement and propriate striving is obvious; since functional autonomy is denied, behavior involving these 'quasi-altruistic extensions' arising through socialization must be referred to the instincts of display and submission; yet — when the self-regarding sentiment is in control — we exercise true volition in striving towards self-appointed goals. The more closely involved with the self the goal is, the more absurd it will seem to try to explain behavior in mechanistic or even homeostatic (i.e., 'equilibrium' or 'drive-reduction') terms; conscious purposes, often involving risk and difficulty, must be allowed as explanations of the direction and persistence of human behavior, even if the basic motivation is always instinctive. Consciousness is important in that it fixates the goal for the organism, it establishes clear and stable templates for use as standards in problem solving.

PERSONALITY AND DISSOCIATION

McDougall's experiences as a medical officer in World War I helped form the basis of *An Outline of Abnormal Psychology*, which is virtually a text in psychosomatic medicine, a defense of interactionism. Explanations are in mental rather than in physical terms; thus most of the paralyses, anaesthesias, and amnesias of 'shell-shock' are really functional disorders, dissociations of the personality system whereby the patient defends himself against trauma, and manic depression is not to be attributed to specific brain lesions, micro-organisms, or chemicals, but to alternate domination of the sentiment of self-regard by the self-assertive and the submissive instincts respectively. The initial upsetting of the normal balance of these two impulses may be due to external circumstances, to hormonic imbalance or to dissociation, but in any case the syndrome is more fruitfully thought of in functional than in physiological terms (pp. 3, 357). The concept of dissociation plays a crucial part in his theory of personality, as I shall now try to show.

The mind is 'a hierarchy of minor integrations which, under favourable circumstances, becomes the single integrated system that we call the normal personality', and the Freudian division of the mind into two entities, one functioning consciously and one unconsiously, is not adequate to the facts (ref. 16 p. 523). Even under normal conditions different purposes may be pursued simultaneously and relatively independently; for example, I may be wholly occupied with other thoughts while walking to work, or I may carry on a conversation while continuing to play the piano. If we wish to think of the mind as the program of the body, we shall hardly be surprised at such parallel processing — though we should explain it in terms of sub-programs, or branching routines, instead of in terms of subordinate personalities, which was McDougall's explanation. As Reitman pointed out in the conference I have referred to, computer models which are both realized and conceptualized serially[31] conflict with the organizational assumptions inherent in most theories of personality; these models are of systems with a total unity of purpose — though there may be goals and sub-goals, and alternative subroutines possible, yet the control is entirely in terms of one goal, and the subroutines are passively selected as means towards this end, having no intrinsic power to initiate activity.[32] McDougall spoke of subordinate personalities to allow for the possibility of several independently originated activities being simultaneously under way, and of the chief monad or master sentiment as being in some sense in over-all control, though the closeness of the dynamic relations between it and other monads, other sentiments, varies. Workers in the field of computer simulation are now very much concerned with the representation of such systems of interacting, affective, dynamic structures within a given personality, and one of the problems they must face is that of representing differing degrees of malintegration, of mutual independence of subroutines, together with differing consequences in terms of the system as a whole. In McDougall's terms, they have to simulate the psychological features of differing degrees of dissociation.

Every case of purposive activity which is not consciously willed by the self and centrally related to the sentiment of self-regard is due to a subordinate personality and is evidence of a certain degree of dissociation. The dissociation is least in such cases as those mentioned above (conversing while playing the piano), where the self would immediately acknowledge the actions as intentional and would be capable of consciously directing them (though the detailed movements could usually not be consciously willed). It is greater in dreaming, which seems to be independent of our will, and greater still in simple anaesthesias, functional paralyses, and hypnosis; automatisms and post-hypnotic suggestions, which may be carried out in spite of strong conscious opposition, are to be attributed not to mere strings of ideas implanted by the hypnotist, but to the (sometimes conscious) workings of a dissociated personality (ref. 16 p. 544). Still greater dissociation is evidenced by the phenomena of multiple personality, with alternating — and sometimes even co-conscious — personalities. In discussing such cases, McDougall attributes them to faulty integration whereby the sentiments have been organized not in one hierarchy, as is usual, but in two or more interlocking groups, with two or more master sentiments. The deeper the split (i.e. the nearer to the instinctive level itself) the more powerful the dissociation and the more distinct the personalities; he suggests that in the case of *Spanish Maria*, the developing sentiment of self-regard split into two with the separation of the basic instincts of self-assertion and submission (ibid. p. 538). Each personality is an organization of sentiments (a colony of monads); an apparently unitary personality may be malintegrated in the sense that the master sentiment is associated with conflicting purposes — this conflict is likely to show in dreams and may result in more serious dissociation unless one purpose can be clearly subordinated to the other by way of a higher-level master sentiment (ibid. p. 526). The 'cure' of cases of multiple personality lies in the effecting of such subordination, and the physician may have some difficulty in deciding which purposes (personalities) to encourage at the expense of others.

McDougall explains co-consciousness in terms of direct telepathic communication between the monads — even the monads within an integrated personality are said to communicate telepathically; this is perhaps the most obscure part of his account — even dreaming is said to be an example of such communication (ibid. pp. 548–9). However, as Reitman remarks, the problem of intrapsychic communication is one of the thornier problems facing the would-be simulator today; he must specify 'the manner and form in which information, commands and requests at one level in the system are transmitted elsewhere', and his difficulties are increased if he has to consider 'a system in which subsystems are able to do such things as induce concealment or refuse access to information which other systems require to achieve their aims' ref. 32 pp. 73, 85). In computer simulation we cannot assume that the right hand knows what the left hand is doing: the right hand must be told.[33] When we specify an intrapsychic transfer, retrieving a unit of information from one subsystem and passing it on as a datum to another subsystem, what psychological process are we representing? Is this unconscious memory? Or do we, perhaps, have no clear concepts available within personality theory distinguishing between the various types of intrapsychic process[34] that we may need to represent in a computer program? Small wonder, surely, that McDougall fell back on the vague concept of *telepathy* as a unitary explanation of intrapsychic communication.

CONCLUSION

If we are suspicious of talk of souls and monads, if we cannot accept McDougall's list of the eighteen specific instincts, if we feel uncomfortable with the very notion of instinct due to the difficulty of identifying precisely the contributions of learning to behavior, if we favour functional autonomy and if we feel that the dynamics of purpose are somewhat mysterious, we may be tempted to categorize McDougall's writings as interesting antiquities involving, no doubt, some shrewd observation of fact, and to leave it at that.

I have tried to show that this would be a mistake. The structure, if not the language, of McDougall's argument against mechanism should remind us of contemporary skepticism as to the possibility of using stochastic models and Markov processes to explain the sequential organization of behavior. Chomsky[35] has shown that no Markovian machine could be adequate for simulating human behavior, since it would require infinitely many parameters; most complex simulations rely heavily on teleological notions of the hierarchical organization of goals and subgoals. Programs, distinguishable conceptually from hardware, can only act if 'embodied' in machines. Instincts may be fruitfully thought of as innate Plans, purposive striving may be thought of in terms of TOTE-units, ordered behavior may be related to an over-all

Image, a self-ideal largely responsible for initiating and ordering the specific Plans (cf. ref. 10).

But if one does not like this talk of *Images* and *Plans*, this translation of a classic into the modern vernacular, one may nevertheless profit from a study of the original, for McDougall's system affords us an interesting attempt to illuminate human behavior and the structure of personality. His emphasis on the directive functions of the self is echoed in many contemporary personality theories, notably those of the *Third Force* psychologists: egopsychology, the Adlerian creative self, and Allport's proprium are all ways of emphasizing the importance of those conscious purposes which we subjectively feel to be closely involved with the self. Accounts, such as Allport's, which represent the self as a number of unifying functions, and the structure of the self as the interrelationships between these functions, echo McDougall's views on the integration of the personality and also imply that the self is not a simple indivisible entity present from birth, but something which develops throughout life. Organismic theories, such as Goldstein's, place even more weight on the claim that a simple Cartesian dualism is inadequate, stating that mind and body are not clearly separable, even in thought. And Jung's view that the self is a central focus of personality, a unifying principle, for which we all come to strive but which few attain, reminds us of McDougall's remark that 'What is called the self is always an ideal rather than an accomplished fact, an ideal that is in various degrees approximated but never attained' (ref. 22 p. 529); Jung, it is true, puts more emphasis on the central motivation towards wholeness, which he explains in terms of the mandala archetype.

These parallels to present-day theorists should encourage us to blow the dust off McDougall's works, and may persuade us that it is worth the trouble of coping with his 'old-fashioned' terminology. In particular, we should not allow ourselves to be put off by his frequent use of metaphysical language and argument. Thus, if we remember in what sense he was a 'dualist' and an 'interactionist', if we relate his basic convictions as to the efficacy of purposes and consciousness to his philosophical concepts of 'soul' and 'monad', and to his psychological concepts of 'instinct', 'sentiment', 'dissociation', and 'personality', we shall be better able to appreciate the systematic nature of his psychology and its relevance to present-day thought.

NOTES

1 C. S. Hall and G. Lindzey, *Theories of personality*, New York: Wiley, 1957.

2 The creature does not merely move in a certain direction, but strives persistently towards an end; this striving is not merely a persistent pushing in a given direction, but shows variation of the means employed to attain the end; in behavior the whole organism is involved; there is as a rule some evidence of increased efficiency of action, of better adaptation of the means adopted to the ends sought.

3 Page references are to the 1960 (paperback) edition of *An Introduction to Social Psychology*, London: Methuen, first published in 1908, 23rd ed. 1936.

4 W. McDougall, 'An experiment for testing the hypothesis of Lamarck', *Brit. J. Psych.*, 1927, 17, 267–304.

5 W. McDougall, 'Second report on a Lamarckian experiment', *Brit. J. Psych.*, 1930, 20, 201–218.

6 W. McDougall, and J. B. Rhine, 'Third report on a Lamarckian experiment', *Brit. J. Psych.*, 1933, 24, 213–235.

7 R. Rosenthal, 'On the social psychology of the psychological experiment', *Amer. Scientist*, 1963, 51, 268–283.

8 G. W. Allport, *Becoming*, New Haven: Yale University Press, 1955.

9 J. S. Bruner, 'Preface', in W. McDougall, *Body and Mind*, Boston: Beacon Press, 1961, pp. vii–xvii.

10 G. Miller, E. Galanter and K. Pribram, *Plans and the Structure of Behavior*, New York: Holt, 1960.

11 M. J. Rosenberg, 'Simulated man and the humanistic criticism', in S. S. Tomkins and S. Messick (eds), *Computer Simulation of Personality*, New York: Wiley, 1963, pp. 113–126.

12 Page references are to W. McDougall, *Body and Mind*, Boston: Beacon Press, 1961 (1st edition 1911).

13 W. McDougall, *Modern Materialism and Emergent Evolution*, London: Methuen, 1929.

14 W. McDougall, *The Energies of Men*, London: Methuen, 1932.

15 W. McDougall, 'The hormic psychology', in C. Murchison (ed.), *Psychologies of 1930*, Worcester, Mass.: Clark University Press, 1930, pp. 3–38.

16 W. McDougall, *Outline of Abnormal Psychology*, New York: Scribner, 1926, p. 519.

17 W. McDougall, 'Tendencies as indispensable postulates of all psychology', Paris: *Proceedings of the XIth International Congress of Psychology*, 1937, pp. 157–170.

18 W. McDougall, 'Men or robots', in C. Murchison (ed.), *Psychologies of 1925*, Worcester, Mass.: Clark University Press, 1926, pp. 273–308.

19 W. McDougall, *Physiological Psychology*, London: J. M. Dent, 1905.

20 G. Ryle, *The Concept of Mind*, London: Hutchinson, 1949.

21   M. Prince, *The Dissociation of a Personality*, New York: Longman, 1905.
22   W. McDougall, *Outline of Psychology*, New York: Scribner, 1923.
23   A. R. Luria, *Speech and the Development of Mental Processes in the Child*. With F. I Yudovich, Joan Simon (ed.), O. Kovacs and J. Simon (Trans.), London: Staples Press, 1959.
24   F. C. Bartlett, *Remembering*, Cambridge University Press, 1932.
25   W. McDougall, 'Purposive or mechanical psychology?', *Psych. Rev.*, 1923, 30, 273–288.
26   N. Tinbergen, *A Study of Instinct*, Oxford: Clarendon Press, 1951.
27   K. Lorenz, *King Solomon's Ring*, New York: Crowell, 1952.
28   G. W. Allport, *Pattern and Growth in Personality*, New York: Holt, Rinehart & Winston, 1961.
29   W. McDougall, Presidential address. *Proc. Soc. Psychical Res.*, 1920, 30, 105–123.
30   J. Piaget, *The Construction of Reality in the Child*, New York: Basic Books, 1954.
31   A. Newell, J. C. Shaw and H. A. Simon, 'Report of a general problem-solving program', *Proc. Int. Conf. Information Processing*, Paris: UNESCO, 1960, pp. 256–264.
32   W. R. Reitman, 'Personality as a problem-solving coalition', in S. S. Tomkins and S. Messick (eds), *Computer Simulation of Personality*, New York: Wiley, 1963, pp. 69–100.
33   Recent work on 'split-brains' (cf. R. W. Sperry, 'The great cerebral commissure', *Scient. Amer.*, 1964, 210, 42–63) suggests that the telling is by way of the great cerebral commissure, the cutting of which in effect provides the organism with *two* independent brains, which can learn different responses to equivalent stimuli, and which can compete for control of the organism. 'The split-brain monkey learns, remembers and performs as if it were two different individuals, its identity depending on which hemisphere it happens to be using at the moment . . . When the brain is bisected, we see two separate "selves" — essentially a divided organism with two mental units, each with its own memories and its own will — competing for control over the organism. One is tempted to speculate on whether or not the normally intact brain is sometimes subject to conflicts that are attributable to the brain's double structure.' Cf. McDougall on personality dissociation.
34   E.g. the request for, the search for, the retrieval, transfer, and association of stored units, in subsystems which are more or less closely linked with or subordinated to one another, and more or less crucial for or obstructive to the attainment of the over-all goal.
35   N. Chomsky, 'Three models for the description of language', *IRE Transactions on Information Theory*, 1956, Vol. IT-2, pp. 113–124.

10
Freudian Mechanisms of Defence:
a programming perspective

Psychoanalysis is not a specialized branch of medicine. I cannot see how it is possible to dispute this. Psychoanalysis is a part of psychology; not of medical psychology in the old sense, not of the psychology of morbid processes, but simply of psychology.

Postscript to *The Question of Lay Analysis* (1926 edition).

I: INTRODUCTION
The relevance of programs to paranoia is not immediately apparent. It is not evident that the mechanism of computers could incorporate the mechanisms of defence. Indeed, it is commonly believed that computer research is radically antithetical to and necessarily destructive of an adequate image of man, and that computer models therefore can have no real significance for the understanding of the human mind.

I hope to show the falsity of this opinion by reference to current programs concerned with the sorts of repressive processes which Freud considered to be 'the corner-stone on which the whole structure of psychoanalysis rests' (1914d, XIV, 16). These specific examples should illustrate two general points: that appeal to cybernetic analogies in scientific and philosophical discussions of man need not have dehumanizing consequences, and that computer science can provide powerful and structurally complex models of the mental processes underlying observable and introspectible psychological phenomena.[1]

The absolute clarity required for writing computer programs forces to the surface questions which remain latent in the natural language formulations and intuitive applications of the 'equivalent' psychological theories. For this type of theoretical illumination the computer itself is in principle unnecessary, although the best way of detecting hidden ambiguities and hiatuses in a program is to run it on a computer and then to test the debugged version in a similar fashion. But the computational power of a functioning computer is invaluable in demonstrating the detailed implications of a given program (or theory), since the programmer (or psychologist) himself is unable to continue the theoretical analysis to the same degree of complexity. (It is in this sense that something new and surprising can result from running a program, even though every instruction in it was provided by the programmer.)[2] A corollary of this point is that a highly complex set of initial conditions can be input to the programmed computer, which will then infer the specific theoretical conclusions appropriate to this particular set. For instance, the beliefs or delusions of an individual person, originally expressed in a long series of psychoanalytic sessions, can be fed into a program which represents neurosis in general. Thus the uniqueness of human minds can now be approached in ways as rigorous as the strictest methodologist could require. Clinical psychologists, who rightly decry the trivial generalizations that result from statistical descriptions culled from large samples of individuals, need have no fear that the individuality of their patients must be similarly ignored by a cybernetic approach.[3]

Triviality, of course, there may still be. The programs I shall discuss are no match for the human clinician. To say they are *no* match is strictly untrue, for we shall see that professional psychiatrists are unable to distinguish the initial diagnostic interviews of paranoid patients from psychiatric interviews of a 'paranoid' program. Nevertheless, current programs have many limitations as compared to the equivalent theories utilized by human psychologists. In some cases this rests on technological limitations such as availability of data-storage space, or on 'extraneous' factors which can be taken for granted where human theoreticians are concerned. For example, it would hardly occur to anyone to remark that Freud's theoretical insights were crucially dependent on his background understanding of natural language; but computer programs employing oversimple models of language-use sometimes make 'absurd' errors in psychological interpretation which are directly attributable to this linguistic crudity. In other cases, however, the triviality of a programming parallel rests rather on a lack of clarity in the original theory concerned. Human clinicians do not make comparable mistakes because their implicit assumptions and intuitive applications of psychological theory are a good deal more subtle, and more sensible, than their explicit theoretical statements. If a 'trivial' program acts as a spur to making human psychological intuition more explicit, and to clarifying the insights of a Freud for the benefit of lesser mortals, it is not to be dismissed as wholly irrelevant to psychological understanding.

From the defence *of* computers, let us now turn to 'defence' *in* computers: I shall first give an outline sketch of the Freudian concept of defensive mechanisms, and shall then discuss some relevant programs.

II: DEFENCE MECHANISMS IN FREUDIAN THEORY

That the defence mechanisms play a crucial role in Freud's theory of mental function may be stated without qualification. But it is impossible to make a similarly straightforward statement of their nature, normality, or number. This difficulty arises partly from the shifts and alterations in Freud's usage of his theoretical vocabulary: the vicissitudes of Freud's terminology are almost as complex as the postulated vicissitudes of the instincts.[4] Moreover, his examples of specific defensive mechanisms are scattered throughout his work, there being no definitive listing of them; lists drawn up by his exegetists vary. Further confusion arises because independent theorists within the Freudian tradition, including the neo-Freudians and ego-psychologists, differ among themselves not only about what should ideally be said about psychological defence, but also about what Freud himself actually said on the topic. For the purposes of this essay, such exegetical and theoretical niceties will be ignored. It will suffice to sketch a general account of defence mechanisms, on the assumption that readers are already reasonably familiar with the concept from everday or more specialized contexts.

The nature of defence mechanisms can be briefly expressed by recalling Freud's definition of *defence* as 'a general designation for all the techniques which the ego makes use of in conflicts which may lead to a neurosis', and his observation that the purpose of defensive processes is 'the protection of the ego against instinctual demands (1926d, XX, 163–64). The ego is 'protected' in the sense that it is prevented from consciously recognizing and acknowleding the existence of the forbidden and anxiety-ridden instinctual impulses. It follows that the activation and operation of mechanisms of defence must typically occur unconsciously; even though defensive techniques are attributed to the *ego*, they involve unconscious transformations within its deep structure rather than introspectively accessible processes that can be consciously monitored and reported.

These hidden transformations may or may not lead to psychological 'end-points' in consciousness. If they do so, the conscious representations that result are somehow distorted with respect to those which would have occurred in the absence of defensive function, so that the anxiety or conflict which would otherwise be experienced is reduced. Sometimes the anxiety associated with a particular topic is so great that it is totally repressed, so that there is no conscious representation expressing it even in a disguised fashion. This state of affairs is unstable in the sense that the repressed impulse persists and continually instigates conscious expression of the forbidden topic, at least in some distorted form; but since *ex hypothesi* the level of anxiety is intolerable even after considerable distortion, a further cycle of repression supervenes to remove the conflict-ridden derivative from consciousness.

Ideally, the reduction of anxiety is great enough to hold experienced conflict down to a minimal level. But in practice many different degrees of anxiety attend conscious beliefs and ideas that have been defensively disguised. Unless a belief is in a phase of total repression, it is attended by anxiety of a 'psychologically tolerable' level. But if it is close to the threshold of tolerance it is likely to undergo further defensive transformations, including repression as a last resort. Accordingly, a slight rise in anxiety level caused by a remark in a conversation (or an analytic session) can have very different effects on the activation of defence mechanisms at different times or for different individuals.

Although the defence mechanisms are often thought of as characteristically neurotic, it follows from Freud's definition previously cited that mechanisms of defence are employed by 'normal' as well as 'neurotic' personalities, the former being the more successful in controlling conflict by means of them. Indeed, Freud himself postulated similar symbolic transformations underlying dreams, jokes, and slips of the tongue; and the ego-psychologists stress the generally adaptive role of thought-patterns and behaviours which were clearly defensive in origin.[5] Successful defences allow the instinctual impulses to be expressed in a form that is psychologically acceptable to the person concerned. Particular individuals differ not only in their degree of defensive success, but also in their customary reliance on one defensive technique (or set of techniques) rather than another. One might expect, for example, that a student or professional academic would have ready access to defensive *intellectualization* regarding unpleasant facts, whereas a non-intellectually inclined person might defend himself against anxiety by the use rather of *denial*. (This hypothesis has been ingeniously confirmed in one of the more elegant experimental investigations of psychological defence.)[6] Even certain forms of psychosis were characterized by Freud with reference to particular mechanisms of defence; thus he interpreted the delusional beliefs typical of paranoia as resulting from the combination of *denial, projection,* and *reversal* (1911c, XII, 9–82). Insofar as defence mechanisms are employed by normal, neurotic, and psychotic personalities, they may be regarded as universal features of the human mind.

Precise enumeration of Freudian defensive techniques is difficult for textual reasons that have already been mentioned.

They certainly include repression, regression, reaction-formation, isolation, undoing, projection, introjection, turning against the self, reversal, and sublimation; and they are often held to include also denial, displacement, splitting, fixation, condemnation, neutralization, intellectualization, and rationalization.[7] Specific examples cannot be detailed here, but many of these concepts have entered into common parlance and a number of instances should spring readily to mind; some illustrative examples will be given later, in the discussion of programs intended as representations of belief-systems employing psychological defences.

The operation of defence mechanisms, then, was described by Freud in terms pertaining to cognitive psychology or epistemological structures — in terms, that is, of distortive transformations of beliefs and concepts. And the aim, activation, and success of defences were characterized by him in affective psychological terms, by reference to the level of anxiety associated with particular ideas within those structures. But Freud also described the functioning of these mechanisms in *meta*-psychological terms, and it is important to realize the potential theoretical independence of his psychology from his meta-psychology if the one is not to be rejected because of inadequacies in the other. Many of Freud's meta-psychological claims would be questioned by psychologists of a broadly 'Freudian' cast of mind, and still more would be criticized by psychologists basically suspicious of the Freudian paradigm. The interpretations of 'cathexis' and 'countercathexis', for instance, as involving actual psychic energy flowing within a self-equilibrating system comprising a fixed quantity of *libido*, may be rejected both on psychological and on physiological grounds: drive-reduction or purely homeostatic theories of motivation are clearly inadequate to the psychophysiological reality.[8] This has been agreed by a number of psychologists of markedly Freudian sympathies, who have also rejected the concept of *psychic energy* in its orthodox Freudian interpretation, preferring a structural theory of psychological phenomena to Freud's dynamic and economic formulations.[9] And Freud's tendency to hypostatize the *ego* has been similarly faulted by some psychotherapists within the Freudian tradition, for introducing an unalayzed anthropomorphic — and so hardly explanatory — homunculus into human psychology.[10]

Given that the power-engineering theories appropriate to cybernetic machines likewise exclude explanatory reference to computer libido, cybernetic energy, or machine egos, it remains to ask whether the relevant information-engineering (information processing) theories can illuminate Freud's theory of repression in any way. The question is not merely whether general concepts drawn from information theory, or system theory, can be useful in describing the overall nature of the human mind. The question, rather, is whether there can be specific programmed parallels to the detailed cognitive and affective aspects of defensive thought which have been outlined in this section, and whether such cybernetic parallels would be wholly trivial or potentially fruitful from the psychologist's point of view.[11]

III: COMPUTER SIMULATIONS OF DEFENCE MECHANISMS

There are a number of groups, attached to artificial intelligence laboratories around the world, who are working towards the computer simulation of different aspects of normal and psychopathological thinking. I shall try to indicate the general nature of some of their programs, but my discussion can only be sketchy in the extreme, and the original papers should be consulted for further details. This is especially important if the reader is disturbed by the apparent anthropomorphisms in my account. For the sake of convenience I shall speak of programmed computers as demonstrating, believing, defending themselves against anxiety, and the like. If the reader's philosophical sensibilities dictate the notional addition of heavy scare-quotes in every such case, my argument will be in no way affected. My claim is not that computers, or programs, *really* believe, *really* defend themselves, and so on, but that there are significant analogies between the information processing within certain symbol-manipulating machines and the psychological processes of human thought. Reference to actual programs should help to clarify the nature and extent of the analogies and the sense in which anthropomorphic terminology is used and justified in a cybernetic context. In every case, the *precise* meaning of the convenient anthropomorphic abbreviation can be given in terms of the functional details of the program concerned.

Attempts to model defence mechanisms include some that are based on conventional mathematical techniques[12] and others which rely rather on manipulating semantic symbols and relations approximating those of natural language. The most developed computer representation of Freudian defences to date is that of K. M. Colby, whose 'Simulation of a neurotic process' is described in a series of papers from 1962 on.[13] Later versions of Colby's neurotic program have incorporated some of the ideas of R. P. Abelson, whose simulation of affectively influenced everyday cognition derives from the 'cognitive balance' theorists such as Fritz Heider rather than Freud, but whose program involves a type of rationalization which is commonly dubbed 'Freudian' or 'neurotic', particularly when it occurs unconsciously.[14]

This theoretical similarity and interchange should come as no surprise to those who take seriously Freud's remark cited as the motto of this paper. As Gertrude Stein might have said, but doubtless didn't, a belief-system is a belief-system, is a belief-system. Processes of cognitive organization and trans-formation are unlikely to be totally different in cases of psychopathology and of normal psychology, and a number of interesting questions arise if one asks how the same general principles of thought (the same basic program) should be differentially 'set' or adjusted so as to result in normal, neurotic, or psychotic phenomena.

Colby himself was for many years a practising psychoanalyst, and the original impetus of his program was his desire to produce a clear theoretical model of the process of free association in psychotherapy. The earliest ('output') version of the program simulates the patient's spontaneous free association or intro-spection; later ('input-output') versions simulate also the patient's response to the conversational and interpretative remarks of the analyst. Colby hopes that future developments may be of use in studying the (currently obscure) ways in which belief-systems and defensive habits of thought can be modified by particular conceptual inputs — in other words, how a neurosis can be ameliorated or cured by some of the analyst's interventions and left unaffected or aggravated by others. Simulation of an individual person undergoing analysis, by feeding in his idiosyncratic thematic beliefs as expressed over hundreds of hours of therapy, might allow for preliminary 'testing' of therapeutic strategies: if a certain input precipitates a crisis in the simulation, this may provide a warning practically appropriate to the specific person-to-person context. Colby also suggests that the program might eventually be used for initial training purposes: getting a neophyte analyst to try out his word-magic on a computer would have some distinct advantages over current practice. Above all, Colby believes that his programming efforts — whether or not they ever achieve the sorts of therapeutic usefulness just listed — can clarify considerably the implicit assumptions and explicit theories which analysts and other psychologists bring to bear on the intrapersonal and interpersonal phenomena concerned.

Very briefly, and very drily, Colby's simulation consists of a system of propositions, each associated with a varying numerical index or 'charge'; a set of symbol-manipulating routines which can effect changes of different types in these propositions or their interrelations; and five numerical monitors which vary continuously in quantity with operation of the aforesaid routines, and which serve to guide the direction of the information processing in the system.

In more readily intelligible, and more obviously Freudian, terms: the simulation represents a system of beliefs, each emotionally cathected to varying degrees; a set of defence mechanisms which can distort beliefs by effecting cognitive transformations on them; and various affects or anxiety-measures indicating danger, excitation, self-esteem, pleasure, and well-being, which influence the fate of individual beliefs (expression, distortion, or repression) and which determine the selective activation of the defences. Operation of a defence mechanism produces a distorted belief whose emotional charge is a percentage of the charge on the original belief — but the degree of countercathexis involved varies according to the mechanism concerned. Expression of a belief (whether distorted or not) reduces its charge to zero; but if it is a distorted belief which is expressed, the original (repressed) belief remains in the system with some residual emotional charge. The beliefs provided by Colby to the program represent those of one of his patients in long-term analysis; examples include *I am defective, Father abandoned me, I descend from royalty,* and *Mother is helpless.*

The program attempts to express its beliefs in the form of a printout. Its first step is to choose a belief of high emotional charge for consideration (the 'regnant' belief). Next, a complex, or pool, of relevant (topic-related) beliefs is drawn from the background belief-system, and processing now continues with respect to this pool alone. The program initiates a random search of the pool for a belief conflicting with the current regnant; for instance, *I hate father* conflicts with *I must love father*, according to the dictionary definitions provided of *love* and *hate*. If no conflicting belief is found, the original belief is expressed as output. If one is found — and particularly if this belief itself is of high affective charge (as 'super-ego' beliefs involving *must* all are) — a defensive routine is chosen from the set available to effect a distortion of the regnant.

The defensive techniques available to Colby's early program include eight 'transform' routines which change the symbolic content of an old belief in forming a new derivative, and routines of isolation, denial, and rationalization which operate on inter-relations between beliefs rather than beliefs taken singly. Colby's list of transforms is as follows:

(1)   Deflection: Shift Object (Not Self)
(2)   Substitution: Cascade Verb
(3)   Displacement: Combine (1) and (2)
(4)   Neutralization: Neutralize Verb
(5)   Reversal: Reverse Verb
(6)   Negation: Insert *Not* Before Verb and Do (5)
(7)   Reflexion: Shift Object to Self
(8)   Projection: Switch Subject (Self) and Object (Not Self)[15]

Let us suppose that the original belief selected as a candidate for expression is *I hate father*. Transform (1) would change this to *I hate the boss*, or *I hate Mrs. Smith*. Transform (2) relies on a dictionary of weak to strong 'synonyms' of verbs, and in this case might give *I see faults in father*. Transform (3) could give *I see faults in Mrs. Smith* as the final distorted version of the regnant. Both (1) and (3) would qualify as 'displacement' in the Freudian sense. Transform (4) may give *I couldn't care less about father*; (5) gives *I love father*; and (6) gives *I do not love father*. These three transforms are analogous to what Freud called 'reaction formation' of varying strengths. The use of (7) gives *I hate self*, and echoes introjection, or turning against the self. Finally, (8) gives *Father hates me*, a classic case of simple projection.

These being the alternative distorting transforms available to the program (ignoring, for the moment, rationalization, isolation, and denial), how does it decide which transformation to express? Indeed, how does it decide to express any derivative at all, rather than entirely repressing the matter? And in the case of those transforms whose operation allows some latitude of choice — namely, the first four — how does the program select one application of the transform rather than another?

A trivial way of answering these questions would be to program a random operator (like that which selects beliefs from pools for comparison with the regnant belief) to activate and operate defence mechanisms. However, this would have little psychological interest or plausibility. For it is at least possible, perhaps even probable, that different techniques achieve defensive purposes to different degrees in the same or different situations. Crucial questions necessarily arise, then, as to the relative power of the various mechanisms in reducing anxiety and in effecting discharge of the underlying impulse.

Consider the first transform, which Colby terms 'deflection'. The syntactical (and psychological) object of the belief-sentence is to be altered. The new object must be chosen from a list of objects represented in the dictionary provided to the program. In Colby's simulation, only objects classed as persons by the dictionary are allowed as object-substitutes in operating the transforms, persons being the most commonly occurring objects of neurotic beliefs encountered in analysis. Let us suppose that there are only five persons listed in the dictionary: *father, mother, self, boss, Mrs. Smith.* The new object cannot be *self*, since there is a universal constraint attached to transform (1) forbidding this; shifting to the self would in fact be a case of transform (7), reflexion. Shifting to *mother* would conflict with the highly charged *I must love mother*, and would improve the situation not at all. Shifting to *boss* or to *Mrs. Smith* are both prima facie admissible.

If one considers a human being who unconsciously hates his father, it seems theoretically and phenomenologically plausible that greater satisfaction of the underlying impulse would be achieved by his consciously hating a male, dictatorial, high-status authority-figure than by his hating a gentle and obscure female. But the high anxiety level of boss-hate (based in these very attributes of the boss) may be too close for comfort to the even higher anxiety level of father-hate, so that the inoffensive Mrs. Smith may be hated instead. In programming terms, if one wishes to avoid a random search through the list of persons, necessitating continual 'affective experimentation' of ensuing anxiety levels, then specific constraints must be built into the program. One might decide, for instance, to limit the search for a substitute to those persons having attributes (such as gender, age, status, personal habits) in common with the original object of the belief, with the caveat that not more than four common attributes are allowed. Colby's progam (or, rather, Colby himself) solves this problem by use of a routine called *Findanalog*.[16] This procedure computes the number of properties two nouns have in common by referring to the dictionary. The dictionary is an information-matrix which codes (among other things) superordinate and subordinate categories for nouns; it provides the information, for example, that *man* and *woman* are each instances of the class *person*, and that *Joe* is an instance of *man*. The strength of analogy required between the original and the substitute object is represented by a numerical index which varies according to the specific psychological nature of the conflict-situation. Thus *Findanalog2* might be content with deflection to *Mrs. Smith* in the previous example, whereas *Findanalog5* would not. If no appropriate object can be found, the program then turns to consider a different transform entirely. But which one should it pick?

The nature of the transform selected depends on the degree of danger signalled by the *Danger* monitor at the time, and also on whether or not self-esteem is involved (the *self-esteem* monitor is adjusted whenever expression of the regnant would violate an *ought* or *must* sentence in the pool). A procedure called *Picktransform* takes these monitors into account in deciding which transform to activate. Successful operation of a given transform results in a greater probability of its being used on future occasions. Thus a preferred style of defence develops over a series of runs, depending on the idiosyncratic nature and processing history of the belief-system currently being simulated. The example of hating the boss *or* hating Mrs. Smith shows that a defensive operation which is efficient in reducing anxiety may be less satisfactory in discharging the original impulse. Colby commits himself to the theoretical position that this is generally true, for he describes the eightfold list of defensive transforms as rank ordered from low to high according to their effectiveness in reducing anxiety, and from high to low in respect of their effectiveness in providing discharge of the charge on each belief. Projection, for example, involves such gross distortion that it is highly efficient in reducing anxiety levels, but poor in reducing charges. In general, he says, 'the need for discharge through expression drives the program down the list of transforms, while the need to reduce anxiety drives the program up. The sequence of derivatives created as output will represent a compromise formation between these processes'.[17]

Distorted versions of beliefs always carry a lower charge than their original, so that expression of them may be possible. The more distorted the derivative, the lower its percentage of the original charge. Degree of distortion depends on which transform was responsible for producing the delusional derivative, deflection being the least and projection the most distortive. If the maximal distortion available fails to lower the charge below the anxiety threshold — something which can happen only when the charge on the regnant is exceptionally high — no output whatever is produced, and the program changes the subject by (randomly) choosing a fresh regnant for processing. In the latter case, the original belief, having been totally repressed, remains latent in the pool with a continuing high charge which results in its being chosen again and again for processing — a cybernetic version of the neurotic's 'repetition without remembering'.

Colby summarizes the neurotic character of his early 'output' program in this way:

The essentials of this neurotic process are conflict, producing a danger signal which in turn produces a transformation of belief until the danger is eliminated. The safety-first postulate of avoiding danger takes precedence over the discharge through expression postulate. The transforms are adjustive mechanisms, but they are maladaptive since they result in loss of information, misrepresentations of beliefs, and insufficient discharge leading to increasing repetitive preoccupation with conflictual areas. If the program attempts to interrogate itself about its own information, it cannot express directly some of its most highly charged beliefs and it receives as answers distorted derivatives of those beliefs.[18]

Later versions of the simulation incorporate a number of further subtleties, such as the admissibility of compound beliefs whose subject or object is itself a belief (for example, *Mother says father abandoned us*); representations of the credibility and degree of subjective certainty of beliefs; and 'self-corrective' ways of *con*tending (rather than *de*fending) by facing conflicts and working on them in various ways. For instance, a troublesome belief can be deliberately weakened in influence by finding reasons (and reasons for reasons) for disbelieving it: even though the belief is retained, it is simultaneously 'denied' to such an extent that it may cause little psychological disturbance. This complex type of denial is more flexible, and potentially more stable, than those which rely on simple negation or on total repression of anxiety-ridden beliefs.

An additional development of the program is that the later versions are able not only to produce output but to respond to input, thus giving a closer analogy to the actual therapeutic situation. The sentence functioning as input is not added as such to the belief-system. Rather, the system is searched for a topic-relevant belief, which is examined for agreement or disagreement with the input sentence and is also used as the core of a pool of beliefs (as described above). Consequently, the effect of the input sentence is selectively to activate specific belief-structures already present in the model, even though it is not itself accepted into the system of beliefs. Similarly, a remark about policemen's pay, or the duty owed to one's parents, will have very different effects on the inner thoughts of a 'neutral' listener and one with a neurotic preoccupation with authority-figures, whether the said remark is overheard in the café or endured in the consulting room. Meanwhile, the program replies to the input with *Yes, No*, or *Maybe* — but as the flow diagram in Figure 10.2 clearly shows, a *No* should not always be taken at its face value.[19] Analogously, a patient's rejection of his analyst's suggested interpretation may or may not derive from defensive resistance, may or may not be reliable. Those who complain that psychoanalytic interpretations

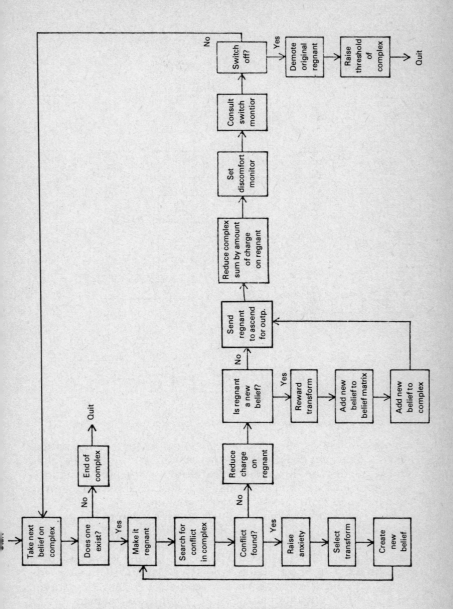

Figure 10.1 Flow diagram for processing a complex of beliefs

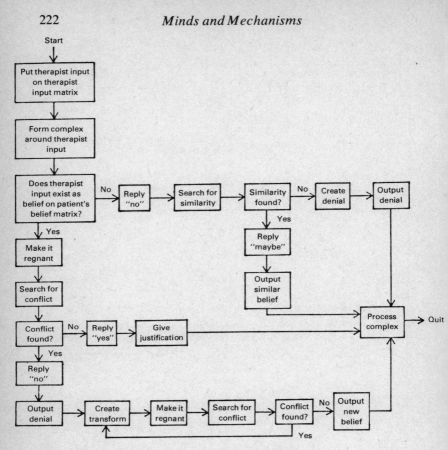

Figure 10.2 Flow diagram for response to therapist input

are scientifically empty because they are 'verified' if the patient accepts them but are not necessarily falsified if he rejects them, should ponder the flow diagram carefully. The highly structured program which it summarizes may be a false picture of the human psychological reality, but is certainly not 'empty'.

An early computer simulation of the process of rationalization was related not to Freudian theory in particular, but to the psychology of attitude-change in general. Abelson's simulation of 'hot', or affect-laden, cognition modelled the theory of cognitive balance deriving from Heider and later elaborated by Abelson himself.[20] This program also has developed over the years, but the basic form of the rationalization subroutines is relevant to the present discussion. Abelson's program, even in its early form, is designed to deal with the *input* of beliefs into a pre-existing system. A new belief is assessed first for its prima facie credibility, and then for its evaluative balance with respect to the values coded in the belief-system. Certain types of imbalance initiate the defensive process of rationalization, which has three subvarieties: *reinterpret final goal, accidental by-product,* and *find the prime mover.*

Abelson gives the example of the cognitively imbalanced input sentence, *My simulation produced silly results.* My simulation, being mine, is positively valued — but silly results are negatively valued, so the sentence as it stands is imbalanced. The subroutine called 'reinterpret final goal' searches for a positively valued implication of the concept *silly results.* The first implication generated by the program may be *non-publishable*; if the belief-system represented is one of those which abhors non-publishability even more than silliness, then *My simulation is unpublishable* will be rejected as unsuitable for purposes of rationalization. The next implication of *silly results* may be *enrichment of understanding*; since *My simulation enriched my understanding* is cognitively balanced, it is accepted. Analogously, the subroutine 'accidental by-product' searches for a factor which explains the silly results by attributing them to a negatively valued source accidentally interposed between subject and object: thus *My simulation had program bugs* is an acceptable rationalization. Finally, 'find the prime mover' replaces the subject by a disvalued substitute, as in *That crazy programmer produced the silly results.* The routines are much more subtle than this brief description suggests, but it should be clear that complex cognitive transformations are represented by this program, and that they serve a psychologically defensive function. In real life such rationalization may be largely conscious: if one considers the belief *Einstein produced silly results*, one may well mutter 'Impossible! There must be some other explanation', and then quite deliberately think one up. 'Neurotic' rationalization is probably basically similar to the conscious variety, but as well as being hidden to introspection, it is maladaptive, in that it accepts relatively unrealistic alternatives to the unacceptable belief.

The relatively unrealistic nature of the neurotic's defensive beliefs is one of the psychological characteristics distinguishing him from a 'normal' person, but he still has a considerable grip on what his society accepts as reality. In this he differs from the psychotic, whose view of the world (or some pervasive aspect of it) differs markedly from that of most members of his community. The paranoid person, for instance, has a delusive belief-system about being persecuted and is unusually suspicious of other people accordingly. These delusions and mistrust influence his conversation in telltale ways, and the clinical diagnosis of paranoia rests largely on the paranoid's suspicious and hostile responses to perfectly innocent remarks. As an aid to understanding this psychological syndrome, Colby has recently programmed a case of 'Artificial paranoia'.[21] This program responds to input sentences with both 'inner thoughts' and 'outward expression' and, as in the case of artificial neurosis previously described, the latter does not always faithfully reflect the former.

The paranoid program scans input sentences for explicit or implicit harms and threats of various kinds. This scanning constitutes a very severe scrutiny — indeed, an oversevere scrutiny — for it often involves the transformation of the input sentence into a distorted form which results in an interpretation of malevolence where none was intended. The inner transformations are not random, but are in many cases so far-fetched by normal standards that a non-paranoid person would be tempted to dismiss them as wholly irrational. One of the strategies employed by the program is to scrutinize the conversation for 'flare' topics, which tend to activate the delusional complex concerned. These sensitive concepts are represented within the program in the form of a directed graph, one flare leading eventually to all the others according to their semantic interrelations. The graph functions as a cognitive core providing detailed tactics for leading the conversation around to the paranoid preoccupation by way of appropriate prompts and hints output to the interlocutor. Analogously, one can expect trouble and misunderstanding if, while talking to a person paranoically convinced that he is being hunted by the Mafia, one mentions crime, police, Italians, or even spaghetti. Moreover, one does not have to mention any of these things: the chance remark that one enjoys Chinese food may enable the deluded person to lead up to his persecution complex by way of an apparently disinterested critique of the town's restaurants.

As in the programmed model of defence mechanisms, Colby's paranoid program incorporates quantitative parameters representing affect-states (fear, anger, and mistrust) which monitor and direct the details of the information processing going on. For a given input sentence, the transformation (if any) effected on it and the output in response to it are dependent on the values of these parameters, which themselves depend on the semantic content of the preceding dialogue. The program has two modes of function, which are differentiated primarily by the 'setting' of the level and rate of change of the three affective monitors. The weakly paranoid mode involves general suspiciousness regarding certain topics, but no actual delusions. The strongly paranoid mode represents intense suspicion and hostility, backed up by an integrated delusional system of *idées fixes*. The dialogue produced by these two versions of the program is subtly different in either case, and in both cases differs from the dialogue of normal persons.

One might suspect at this point that the paranoid program (in either mode) produces dialogue which differs from the conversation of *all* persons, that it is 'abnormal' in a sense quite other than the sense in which the human paranoiac's speech is 'abnormal'. If this were so, it would cast doubt on the relevance of the program to the study of actual paranoia, if not on its intrinsic fascination as an intellectual pastime. These questions have been raised by Colby himself, who has carried out a series of 'Turing tests' of his artificial paranoiac.[22] The first step was to have a group of psychiatrists interview mental patients by teletype so as to arrive at a psychiatric diagnosis. From their point of view, the rationale for using a teletype had to do with efficient use of doctor's time: they did not know of the existence of the simulation. In some cases, of course, they were not communicating with mental patients at all, but with the program. As the second step, another group of psychiatrists (similarly ignorant of the project) were asked to rate the transcripts of the interviews for presence (and degree) or absence of paranoia. Lastly, a third group (picked randomly from the professional psychiatric register) were sent the transcripts, were told that some were interviews of patients while others were interviews of a program, and were asked to decide which was which.

The results were striking. No interviewer realized that he was diagnosing a computer. Interviews with the 'weak' mode of the program were reliably judged to be less paranoid than interviews with the 'strong' mode. This remained true in the second phase, when transcripts were sent to uninvolved psychiatrists for rating. (It is worth pointing out that the interjudge reliability of the concept of paranoia is unusually high — nearly 90 per cent — relative to other psychiatric categories.) Finally, the guesses of the psychiatrists in the third phase were successful at no better than a chance level. In other words, on the basis of these diagnostic interviews they could not distinguish the delusive defences of a 'paranoid' program from those of a paranoid patient.

Strictly, this was not a Turing test in the accepted sense, since the psychiatrists doing the interviewing were not asked to judge which teletypes were attached to men and which to machines.

They were not even informed that an 'imitation game' was going on. Colby justifies this by pointing out that if the interviewer is informed at the start that a computer may be involved he tends to change his normal interviewing strategy; that is, he asks questions designed to test which respondent is a program, rather than asking questions specifically relevant to the diagnostic dimension (paranoia) being studied. Colby also points out that, even in such as case, the program does not necessarily fail the Turing test: 'We have found in informal experiments that if a human-respondent does not follow standards of the interviewer's expectations [does not answer honestly and candidly], jokes around, or plays other games, ordinary judges cannot distinguish him from a computer program with limited natural language understanding'.[23] It has already been remarked that the conversation of paranoid psychotics typically does seem 'irrational' when judged by everyday standards.

Talk of 'Turing tests' inevitably raises the question of how successful current simulations actually are in modelling the human mind. In this section I have tried to present the strengths of the defensive programs I have described. In the next, something must be said about their weakness.

IV: LIMITATIONS OF CURRENT PROGRAMS

With respect to the weakness of computer models of psychological phenomena I am tempted to quote Colby's words without further elaboration:

The criticisms of the approach should be familiar to you since they are the criticisms which are applied to all approaches to problems. One could assert that the hypotheses are questionable, the postulates are naive, the boundary conditions are too narrow (or too wide), there is too much (or too little) structural detail in the model, there are better ways of solving the empirical problem, and the data are unreliable.[24]

If elaboration there must be, it should be confined to a critique of limitations that are directly attributable to the cybernetic context of theorizing, rather than to the psychological theories themselves.

The subtlety of the cybernetic models of neurosis and paranoia clearly depends heavily on the quantity and quality of data supplied to the program. The relevant data include beliefs, each with its specific charge; relations (such as *reason for*) between beliefs; dictionary entries such as verbs, nouns, and their respective modifiers; 'cascading' relations between verbs coding relative strength; lists of instances, synonyms, and antonyms of verbs; and subordinate and superordinate relations between nouns.

The quantity of data is in principle limited only by the storage capacity of the machine being used to run the program, and so far this has not proved a problem. The quantity is in practice restricted, however, by the enormous effort required to write a datum — especially a belief — into the program. To believe that *p* is not merely to assent to *p* considered as an isolated proposition, and the systematic nature of belief must be somehow paralled in the simulation. The coding and cross-referencing problems involved are immense, and the early neurotic program has only twenty beliefs to worry about. Later versions have over one hundred beliefs, and nearly three hundred dictionary entries. Satisfactory representation of human idiosyncracy would presumably require more data than this, even though many of a person's beliefs are irrelevant to his neurosis.

The quality of the dictionary data depends on the programmer's sensitivity to ordinary (rarely to technical) language. Decisions have to be made about how to program the semantic relations between words and how to represent the function of individual words. For instance, one has to settle for a particular cascade of verbs, such as *abhor, detest, hate, dislike, disapprove, reject* (should *see faults in* be included in this list, or should it not?). And one has to face the problem of how to write a program which could reply to a phrase like 'a *good* knife', or 'a *good* husband', with a statement containing an appropriate inference.[25] Philosophical analyses of the terms involved may sometimes be helpful, but the necessity of making unambiguous decisions will usually result in less subtle usage of the term concerned than is found in everyday discourse. For theoretical purposes, of course, many such subtleties are luxuries, not necessities. The real problem is how to avoid those semantic crudities which can lead to important psychological misunderstandings.

The quality of the data in the *belief* and *reason* matrices depends on the clinical ability of the person supplying these data to the programmer. In Colby's case, clinician and programmer are one and the same. The significance of a given model considered as a hypothetical case reflects his clinical insight in general, while its significance as a representation of a particular patient in analysis rests on his success in perceiving and summarizing the idiosyncratic neurotic themes concerned. Colby has considered the time-saving (and, he claims, perhaps even psychotherapeutic) possibility of using computers to interview individuals and to effect an initial listing of their neurotic concerns. To this end he has written an interviewing program, basically similar to Joseph Weizenbaum's ELIZA, which simulates the therapist in non-directive Rogerian therapy.[26] Sometimes Colby's program successfully elicits from its interlocutor a sustained expression of psychologically significant feelings and beliefs; sometimes, however, the 'conversation' is ludicrous in the extreme. Consequently, the program in its early stage is of no practical use. Moreover, one may doubt whether the psychological *ambience* of dropping one's defences in communicating with a computer could ever be sufficiently similar to that of the analytic situation to make future versions of the program useful as a psychotherapeutic tool.

The basic reason for the absurdities that sometimes occur in dialogues with the interview program is its failure to understand natural language. It responds to language, rather than understanding it. That is, like the paranoid program and the 'input' version of artificial neurosis, its general linguistic strategy is to react in fairly inflexible ways to certain 'key' words or phrases. Common examples include *father, mother, I should, I feel, I seem, worried*, and the like; idiosyncratic additions such as *Joey, Mafia* and *spaghetti* are also allowed for. These key words selectively trigger certain types of information processing in the program, whether in the form of 'inner thoughts' or 'outward expression'. This does not matter too much in the 'input' neurotic program, since ongoing conversation is not attempted and the input sentence is not even accepted into the belief-system. Even the paranoid program, which does engage in dialogue, is not too badly flawed by its reliance on this 'mechanical' model of language-use, since it is precisely characteristic of a paranoid person that he will respond 'irrationally' to flare concepts, irrespective of the conversational context (although the program was occasionally diagnosed by the interviewing psychiatrist as *brain-damaged* — literally — because of its linguistic incompetence). However, this crude model of language constitutes a grave drawback to the interview program. And if the paranoid program were to be given more than an *initial* diagnostic interview, it could not rely so heavily on its expectations of particular questions like *What sort of work do you do?* and *Why are you in the hospital?*

Colby has suggested that an essential step in overcoming the crudity of the current man–machine dialogues is for the machine to be provided with — or, still better, to build up for itself — a detailed cognitive model of the person with whom it is communicating.[27] In order to build up such a model through interchanges with the person, the program must initially have an extensive built-in model (or theory) of human psychology in general. Since he made this suggestion, a great advance has occurred in the programming of language-use: Terry Winograd's 'Program for understanding natural language'.[28] It is impossible even to indicate the nature of this program here; suffice it to say that it is greatly superior to its predecessors, which rely on key words, semantic networks, and the like. And, what is of particular relevance, it 'understands' natural language largely by exploiting its reasoning abilities within a cognitive model of its world of action. Since its world of action is restricted to cubes, blocks, and pyramids of various colours, which can be moved and stacked on a table or placed in a box nearby, there is no question of directly 'plugging-in' Winograd's program to Colby's program. The point, rather, is that Winograd's program provides some promising insights into precisely how a simulation can use theoretical (and factual) knowledge about a universe of discourse in interpreting natural language statements about the universe. The possibility arises, then, of building Colby's psychological theory of defence mechanisms into a program based on Winograd's model. The result would be a computer simulation of neurosis considerably more powerful than any now in existence.

V: CONCLUSION

Some personality theorists believe that 'attempts to study personality by observing the behavior of computers programmed by humans to simulate other humans is the crudest form of projection — a most primitive and maladaptive method of defense'.[29] If the study of computer models were regarded as a *substitute* for the anxiety-ridden personal investigation of other people which until now has provided the prime data-base for theoretical psychology, this response would be perfectly in order. But no such suggestion is involved in the claim that computer simulation can be a useful complement to the psychologist's intuitive theorizing.

Expressing one's theory in the form of a computer program sharpens and clarifies questions even though it does not in itself provide answers to them. For example, Colby was forced to make theoretical decisions as to the relative power of the various defence mechanisms in reducing anxiety and effecting motivational discharge. In principle, of course, these questions could have been as clearly raised by 'armchair' theorizing: Freud himself made a number of remarks pertaining to these very issues. But clarity is unavoidable in a programming context, and questions must be given answers.

Theoretical decisions such as these can then be taken as hypotheses about actual psychological functioning, and can be investigated with or without the mediation of a programmed model of the processes concerned. In this sense the program aids in the development of what Imre Lakatos has called a 'scientific research programme'.[30] Experimental investigations of a broadly 'positivist' type have provided some general validation of the Freudian concept of defence mechanisms, but they have not fully justified detailed individual applications of it and nor is it easy to see how they ever could do so.[31] The enormous complexity and perverse idiosyncracy of human personal belief-systems prevent operationalization of 'defensive' concepts except at a relatively coarse or trivial level. The structure and complexity of computer programs, by contrast, are well suited to representation both of the general phenomena of defence and of their specific instantiations in particular cases. There is reason to hope that extended clinical studies of (for example) free association, or responses to the therapist's interventions in analysis, can be increasingly fruitful if guided and monitored by reference to the precise theoretical models made available by computer science. Since similar research possibilities in principle exist for theories concerning any psychological phenomenon, computer simulations have a considerable potential for deepening our understanding of the human mind.

Above all, one must insist on the total irrelevance of objections to the effect that computers cannot *really* defend themselves against anxiety, cannot *really* believe and infer or feel suspicious and afraid. Parameters in computer programs are used to represent theoretical concepts such as 'belief' and 'anger' which themselves represent the actual phenomena of belief and anger in human minds. Moreover, 'mistrust', 'fear' and 'anxiety' — as employed, for instance, in Colby's programmed models of neurosis and paranoia — are not mere labels, but are functional aspects of the program. The theoretical interest is not in questions about the felt nature of fear as such, but rather in what difference fear makes to the information processing going on — for example, to the paranoiac's interpretation of and reaction to specific remarks from his interlocutor. This functional view of affect is not a monstrous brain-child of overambitious programmers, but an established part of 'respectable' psychology. Freud himself was interested not so much in the subjective experience of anxiety as in the cognitive structures and affective monitoring processes contributing to the complex phenomena of defence.

Computer simulations, then, attempt theoretical modelling of psychological function and structure rather than ontological mimicry of mental reality, and it is in these terms alone that they should be assessed. In these terms, programs may be more like paranoia than ravens are like writing-desks. And the question why a program is like paranoia — unlike the Mad Hatter's unanswerable riddle — allows of a precise and definite reply.

NOTES

1   For a fuller discussion of these two points see M. A. Boden, *Purposive Explanation in Psychology*. (Harvard Univ. Press, Cambridge, Mass., 1972).

2   One of the earliest attempts at programming 'machine intelligence' succeeded in proving geometric theorems in ways which were not specifically foreseen by the programmers: H. L. Gelernter, J. R. Hansen, and D. W. Loveland, 'Empirical exploration of the geometry theorem machine', *Proc. Western Joint Computer Conference* (1960), 143–47.

3   For the individually and the statistically orientated approaches to clinical psychology, see P. E. Meehl, *Clinical Versus Statistical Prediction: A Theoretical Analysis and a Review of the Evidence* (University of Minnesota Press, Minneapolis, 1954).

4   For instance, the closely related concepts of 'repression' and 'defence' were introduced into Freud's writings very early, in 1893 and 1894 respectively; by 1895 they were being used as synonyms; after a few years, 'defence' virtually disappeared — only to be reintroduced in 1926 as a psychological phenomenon of which 'repression' was then said to a special case. See Joseph Breuer and Sigmund Freud, 'On the Psychical Mechanism of Hysterical Phenomena: Preliminary Communication' (1893a, II, 10). Also Freud, 'The Neuro-Psychoses of Defence' (1894a, I, 59–75); Joseph Breuer and Sigmund Freud, *Studies on Hysteria* (1895d, II, xxix); Freud, *Inhibitions, Symptoms and Anxiety* (1926d, XX, 163–64).

However, the effective equivalence or non-equivalence for Freud of these two concepts at various stages in his work is itself a controversial matter. See Peter Madison, *Freud's Concept of Repression and Defence, Its Theoretical and Observational Language*. (University of Minnesota Press, Minneapolis, 1961), esp. pp. 3–30.

5   See Heinz Hartmann, *Ego Psychology and the Problem of Adaptation*. (Int. Univ. Press, New York, 1958).

6   Speisman took two groups of subjects: students with outside

interests of a markedly intellectual nature, and businessmen with non-intellectual hobbies. He measured their GSR (an electro-physiological indicator of anxiety) while they were watching a film of a rather nasty tribal circumcision-initiation rite. There were three experimental situations: film alone, no commentary; film with added sound-track providing an *intellectualizing* but non-denying commentary ('the rite is a fascinating example of this, that, and the other anthropological concept, even though it does hurt the boys'); and the film with added *denying* commentary ('it doesn't really hurt, and anyway the boys are looking forward to joining the adult community'). The GSR of all subjects was reduced by each added sound-track; but the intellectualizing commentary worked better with the student group and the denying commentary with the businessmen (indeed, the effect of denial on the students was hardly noticeable). See J. C. Speisman, 'Autonomic monitoring of ego defense process', in N. S. Greenfield and W. C. Lewis (eds.), *Psychoanalysis and and Current Biological Thought*. (University of Wisconsin Press, Madison, 1965), pp. 227–44.

7   The first ten are listed (with clear examples) by Anna Freud, who regards the first nine as characteristic of neurosis, while sublimation 'pertains rather to the study of the normal'. Her list keeps closely to her father's writings, but her interpretation of introjection as 'identification with the aggressor' constitutes theoretical development rather than faithful exegesis; she apparently uses 'denial' interchangeably with 'reversal'; and sublimation is equated with 'displacement of instinctual aims' — but the defensive displacement involved in kicking the cat just after a quarrel with another person would hardly be called 'sublimation'. See Anna Freud, *The Ego and the Mechanisms of Defence*. (Hogarth, London, 1937), esp. chap. 4.

The last eight are not specifically listed by Anna Freud, but each is sometimes cited as a Freudian defence mechanism. See, e.g., Charles Rycroft, *A Critical Dictionary of Psychoanalysis*. (Nelson, London, 1968).

Largely because of the terminology shifts described in note 4 above, 'repression' is sometimes used to cover the operation of *any* mechanism of defence.

8   For relevant psychological evidence see H.F. Harlow, 'Mice, monkeys, men, and motives', *Psychol. Rev.* 60 (1953), 25–32; D. E. Berlyne, *Conflict, Arousal, and Curiosity*. (McGraw, New York, 1960); R. W. White, 'Motivation reconsidered: the concept of competence', *Psychol. Rev.* 66 (1959), 297–333; D. O. Hebb, 'Drives and the CNS (conceptual nervous system)', *Psychol. Rev.* 62 (1955), 243–54. For physiological evidence see: James Olds and Peter Milner, 'Positive reinforcement produced by electrical stimulation of septal area and other regions of rat brain', *J. Comp. Physiol. Psychol.* 47 (1954), 419–27; M. P. Bishop, S. T. Elder and R. G. Heath, 'Intracranial self-stimulation in man', *Science* 140

(1963), 394–96; C. T. Morgan, 'Physiological theory of drive', in I, Sensory, Perceptual, and Physiological Formulations, *Psychology: A Study of a Science*, Sigmund Koch (ed.), (McGraw, New York, 1959), pp. 644–72.

9 For critiques of psychic energy from a broadly Freudian point of view, with the suggestion that a *structural* theory of motivation be preferred, see K. M. Colby, *Energy and Structure in Psychoanalysis* (Ronald, New York, 1955); M. M. Gill, 'The present state of psychoanalytic theory', *J. Abn. Soc. Psychol*, 58 (1959), 1–8; R. R. Holt, 'A review of some of Freud's biological assumptions and their influence on his theories', in *Psychoanalysis and Current Biological Thought*, eds. N. S. Greenfield and W. C. Lewis, (University of Wisconsin Press, Madison, 1965), pp. 93–124; Louis Breger, 'Dream function: an information processing model', in Louis Breger (ed.), *Clinical-Cognitive Psychology*. (Prentice-Hall, Englewood-Cliffs, N.J., 1969), pp. 182–227.

10 See Emanuel Peterfreund, *Information, Systems, and Psychoanalysis: An Evolutionary Biological Approach to Psychoanalytic Theory*, Psychological Issues, 7, Monograph 25/26 (Int. Univ. Press, New York, 1971), esp. pp. 66–74.

11 Freud's account of the motivational aetiology of defensive thought-systems was an important part of his theory: but it is irrelevant here, where the concern is with the current defensive functioning of an established structure of beliefs rather than its psychodynamic origins. This is because the relevant programs simulate adult thought-structures rather than their childhood development. It is of course possible that future programs might attempt representation of these features also.

12 E.g., Moser et al. use variable density-functions as mathematical representations of psychoanalytic concepts such as: oral, anal, phallic, and genital pleasure gain; the primacy of genitality (the fusion of the four previous component drives); anxiety, repression and its derivatives, functioning as countercathexis mechanisms; emergency defence mechanisms; and specific forms of neurosis. See Ulrich Moser, Werner Schneider and Ilka von Zeppelin, 'Computer simulation of a model of neurotic defence mechanism. (Clinical paper and Technical Paper.)', *Bull, Psychol, Inst. Univ. Zurich* 2 (1968), 1–77; Ulrich Moser, Ilka von Zeppelin and Werner Schneider, 'Computer simulation of a model of neurotic defence processes', *Int. J. Psycho-Anal.* 50 (1969), 53–64; Ulrich Moser, 'Discussion of computer simulation of a model of neurotic defence processes', *Int. J. Psycho-Anal.* 51 (1970), 167–73; Ulrich Moser, Ilka von Zeppelin and Werner Schneider, 'Computer simulation of a model of neurotic defence processes', *Behavioral Science* 15 (1970), 194–202; W. R. Blackmore, 'Some comments on "Computer Simulation of a Model of Neurotic Processes" ', *Behavioral Science* 17 (1972), 229–32; Ulrich Moser, Ilka von Zeppelin and Werner Schneider, 'Reply to W. R. Blackmore', *Behavioral*

Science 17 (1972), 232–34.

13   K. M. Colby, 'Computer simulation of a neurotic process', in S. S. Tomkins and Samuel Messick (eds.), *Computer Simulation of Personality: Frontier of Psychological Theory* (Wiley, New York, 1963), pp. 165–80; K.M. Colby and J.P. Gilbert, 'Programming a computer model of neurosis', *J. Math. Psychol.* 1 (1964), 405–17; K. M. Colby, 'Experimental treatment of neurotic computer programs', *Arch. Gen. Psychiatry* 10 (1964), 220–27; K. M. Colby, 'Computer simulation of neurotic processes', in *Computers in Biomedical Research*, Vol. 1, ed. R. W. Stacy and B. D. Waxman. (Academic Press, New York, 1965), pp. 491–503; K. M. Colby, 'Computer simulation of change in personal belief systems', *Behavorial Science* 12 (1967), 248–53.

14   For the original formulation of cognitive balance theory, see Fritz Heider, *The Psychology of Interpersonal Relations* (Wiley, New York, 1958). For a clear discussion of this and related theories of attitude change, see Roger Brown, *Social Psychology* (Free Press, New York, 1965), chap. 11.

15   Colby, 'Computer simulation of a neurotic process', p. 172. The list of transforms is slightly different in Colby and Gilbert, 'Programming a computer model of neurosis', p. 412.

16   This procedure is described in pp. 412–13 of the most detailed published account of the program: Colby and Gilbert. 'Programming a computer model of neurosis'.

17   Colby, 'Computer simulation of a neurotic process', pp. 172–73.

18   Ibid. p. 173.

19   The two flow diagrams are taken from Colby, 'Experimental treatment of neurotic computer programs'. What Colby had earlier called a 'pool', he now calls a 'complex' of beliefs. Note that the diagram of Figure 10.2 flows directly into the diagram of Figure 10.1 by way of the box 'Process complex'. Note also the *alternative* ways of arriving at a box for 'Reply "no" ' provided for in Figure 10.2.

20   See R. P. Abelson, 'Computer simulation of "Hot" Cognition', in Tomkins and Messick, eds. *Computer Simulation of Personality* pp. 277–98; R. P. Abelson and J. D Carroll, 'Computer simulation of individual belief systems', *Amer. Behav. Scientist* 8 (1965), 24–30. Abelson's program is described in more detail, and is compared with that of Colby in J. C. Loehlin, *Computer Models of Personality*. (Random House, New York, 1968), esp. chaps. 5–8.

21   For a description of the program, with some sample dialogues, see K. M. Colby, Sylvia Weber, and F. D. Hilf, 'Artificial paranoia', *Artificial Intelligence* 2 (1971), 1–25. For an account of directed graphs like those used by the paranoid program, see Lawrence Tesler, Horace Enea, and K.M. Colby, 'A directed graph representation for computer simulation of belief systems', *Mathematical Biosciences* 2 (1968), 19–40.

22   For Turing's original concept, see A. M. Turing, 'Computing

machinery and intelligence', *Mind* 59 (1950), pp. 439–42. For Colby's applications, see K. M. Colby, F. D. Hilf, Sylvia Weber and H. C. Kraemer, 'Turing-like indistinguishability tests for the validation of a computer simulation of paranoid processes', *Artificial Intelligence* 3 (1972), 199–221; K. M. Colby and F. D. Hilf, 'Can expert judges, using transcripts of teletyped psychiatric interviews, distinguish human paranoid patients from a computer simulation of paranoid processes?', *Stanford Artificial Intelligence Project, Memo AIM-182*, December 1972.

23   Colby, 'Turing-like indistinguishability tests', p. 203.
24   Colby, 'Experimental treatment of neurotic computer programs', p. 226.
25   K. M. Colby and Horace Enea, 'Machine utilization of the natural language word "good" ', *Mathematical Biosciences* 2 (1968), 159–63.
26   K. M. Colby, J. B. Watt and J. P. Gilbert, 'A computer method of psychotherapy: preliminary communications', *J. Nerv. Mental Disease* 142 (1966), 148–52; K. M. Colby and Horace Enea, 'Heuristic methods for computer understanding of natural language in context-restricted on-line dialogues', *Mathematical Biosciences* 1 (1967), 1–25. See also Joseph Weizenbaum, 'ELIZA — a computer program for the study of natural language communication between man and machine', *Commun. Assoc. Computing Machinery* 9 (1966), 36–45.
27   Colby and Enea, 'Heuristic methods for computer understanding of natural language', p. 22.
28   Terry Winograd, *Understanding Natural Language* (Edinburgh Univ. Press, Edinburgh, 1972).
29   G. S. Blum, 'Programming people to simulate machines', in Tomkins and Messick, eds., *Computer Simulation of Personality*, pp. 127–57. Quote from p. 127.
30   Imre Lakatos, 'Falsification and the methodology of scientific research programmes', in Imre Lakatos and Alan Musgrave, eds., *Criticism and the Growth of Knowledge* (Cambridge Univ. Press, Cambridge, 1970), pp. 91–196.
31   For a recent survey of experimental work relevant to Freud's theory of defence, see Paul Kline, *Fact and Fantasy in Freudian Theory* (Methuen, London, 1972), Chap. 8.

WORKS OF FREUD CITED:
1893a: 'On the Psychical Mechanism of Hysterical Phenomena'; 1894a: 'The Neuro-Psychoses of Defence'; 1895d: *Studies on Hysteria*; 1911c: 'Notes on a Case of Paranoia'; 1914d: 'On the History of the Psychoanalytic Movement'; 1926d: *Inhibitions, Symptoms, and Anxiety*. N.B. All page references are to the Standard Edition (Hogarth Press).

11
Artificial intelligence and Piagetian theory

I: INTRODUCTION

One of the strengths of artificial intelligence ('AI') as a way of thinking about thinking is that it forces one to model the movement of the mind, the way in which a particular mental phenomenon comes about. It is not enough to say that a phenomenon can happen: the programmer must specify a way in which it can happen. (Whether this is the way in which it does happen is, of course, another question.) And one of the weaknesses of Piagetian theory — for all its salutary stress on action as the context and carrier of mental life — is its lack of specification of detailed procedural mechanisms competent to generate the behaviour it describes. Piaget's terms *assimilation* and *accommodation* are notorious examples: a leading Piagetian has even 'explained' the parrot's lack of linguistic creativity by saying that its sensorimotor scheme for speaking is very accurate in accommodation but quite meagre in assimilative power.[1] Even Piaget's careful descriptions of the development of behaviours such as weight and length *seriation* are related to uncomfortably vague remarks about the progression of *stages*, without it being made clear just how one stage (or set of conceptual structures) comes to follow another.

This complementarity of strength and weakness suggests that a bringing together of AI and Piagetian theory might be fruitful. In particular, if AI workers can take account of the detailed empirical data provided by Piaget's observations, instead of working in a psychological vacuum, some crucial questions should be clarified and some specific answers may be suggested. This theoretical clarification, in turn, should encourage further observations, so that AI can play a role in the development of 'scientific research programmes' in psychology.[2]

In the next part, I mention some work in AI that bears on Piagetian theory, even though it was not done with Piaget's research specifically in mind. In Part III, I outline some computational models of seriation behaviour that pay careful attention to empirical data such as Piaget described. And in Part IV, I ask whether this work has the implications for Piaget's theory of developmental stages that are claimed by its author.

I shall be able only to indicate the overall nature of the work cited; interested readers should consult the literature for the

236

computational details, wherein much of the theoretical significance lies. For example, a study of *class inclusion* tasks within the AI paradigm exhibits the computational advantages of creating a copy of a mixed-item list before trying to count the items of a given type on the list:[3] compare Piaget's remark about children unable to handle class inclusion, 'They are unable to compare one of these parts with the whole, *which they have mentally destroyed*; they can compare only the two parts'.[4] In view of such parallels, and of Piaget's enduring aim of the formalization of psychological theory, it is not surprising that he has endorsed the recommendation of a programming approach, saying: 'I wish to urge that we make an attempt to use it'.[5]

II: AI AND INTELLECTUAL IMPROVEMENT

According to Piagetian theory, the child gradually develops increasingly well-articulated and inter-related *schemata*,[6] or representations. It is in terms of these intentional models that the psychological subject constructs and interprets the world (and all possible worlds), and it is through their active mediation that thinking and motor action are generated. Although he rejects a straightforward equation of *development* and *learning*, Piaget stresses the importance of interaction with the environment in conceptual development and the growth of sensorimotor skills. In particular, his central concepts of assimilation and accommodation are explicated in terms of a dialectical process of concordance with and adjustment to the environmental input, whereby the mind (or the set of mental constructions) becomes increasingly well adapted to the external world.

Within the limits set by the current developmental stage, Piaget takes for granted the mental competence of perceiving some degree of match or mismatch between schema and reality, and the ability to change one's concept accordingly. But AI programs that attempt to model the way in which skills and concepts improve with use and experience cannot take such matters for granted. If the program itself is to perceive and adapt to mismatch then specific computational resources for so doing need to be provided. These must include ways of representing the conceptual content involved, and procedures for the comparison and progressive transformation of the structured representation concerned. In short, both the content and the use of the program's knowledge must be rigorously specified.

P. H. Winston's program, for instance, learns to recognize pictures of structures such as tables, arches, pedestals, and arcades on being shown examples and counterexamples of them.[7] Thus it can learn the simple concept of *arch* represented in Figure 11.1 by being shown the sequence of pictures in Figures 11.2 to 11.6, and can use its concept to identify an infinite number of arches (and non-arches), not merely those exactly like the specific samples encountered in the learning process. In Piagetian terminology, it assimilates a wide range of individual inputs to one general schema, and it accommodates its schema to environmental features that do not fit its current conceptual constructs.

The program's constructive and interpretative ability depends on complex computational processes, including: (1) appropriate articulation of the structure of the input picture; (2) systematic comparison of the input picture-structure with the structure of the internal model currently functioning as its arch-concept; (3) classification of the differences involved, so as to direct (4) continual transformation of the concept; (5) compounding of previously-learnt concepts to form higher-level concepts that could not have been constructed 'from scratch' (so that *a row of arches* can be understood as *an arcade*); and (6) specification of the descriptive analogies between concepts (such as four-legged *tables* and one-legged *pedestals*).

The heart of the program lies in its comparison-procedures, including its classification of the (twenty-one) different logical types of structural mismatch between world and world-model. This classification is used to determine the specific nature of the conceptual transformation generated by the current mismatch, and it requires decisions — or provision for subsequent decisions — about the importance, or conceptual salience, of the various features observed in the samples being compared.

These decisions involve particular assumptions which might be questioned from an epistemological point of view. For instance, when in Figure 11.6 the program encounters a WEDGE instead of a BRICK as the 'roof' of the arch, it prefers to amend the relevant part of its conceptual network 'hierarchically' from BRICK to PRISM or even to OBJECT, rather than 'disjunctively' from BRICK to BRICK-OR-WEDGE. In purely logical terms, divorced from any psychological principles or considerations of computational efficiency, there is nothing to choose between these alternatives, so that BRICK-OR-WEDGE would have been equally justified. But there is ample psychological evidence that people find disjunctive concepts hard to handle, that the computational processes underlying human thought are not well suited to dealing with disjunctive concepts.[8] For someone who shares Piaget's view that epistemology cannot be a matter of 'pure'

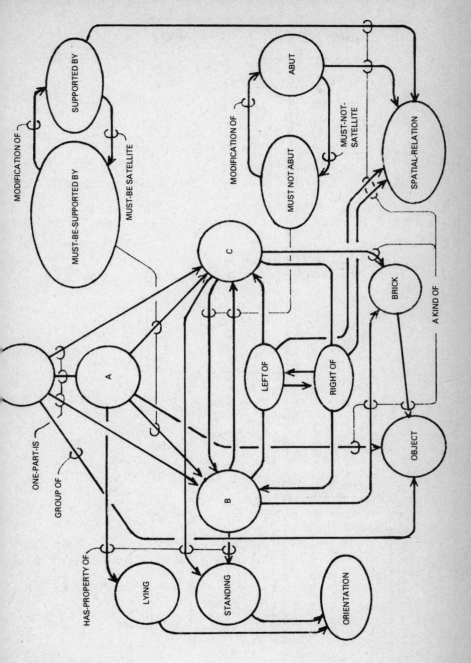

Figure 11.1

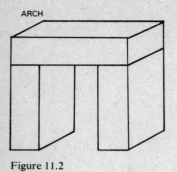

Figure 11.2

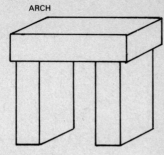

Figure 11.3

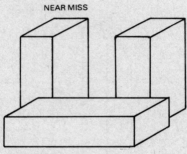

Figure 11.4

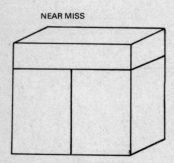

Figure 11.5

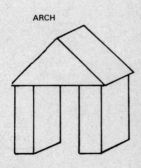

Figure 11.6

logic, but must take account of the function and development of the conceptual structures actually used by people to interpret the world, this choice of a superordinate rather than a disjunctive concept in transforming the program's notion of *arch* is not arbitrary, but is justifiably motivated by relevant psychological (computational) considerations.

Piaget's account of the continuous process of conceptual equilibration implicitly rejects an essentialist epistemology, one that would classify every imaginable feature as clearly essential to, inconsistent with, or accidental to a given concept. This view that concepts are not usually strictly defined in every detail is compatible with Winston's approach. For his program is able to assess the descriptive analogy between different scenes so that it can articulate, for instance, why one might and why one might not be inclined to view a pedestal as a sort of table. This is not to deny (*pace* Wittgenstein) that some features are commonly regarded as essential to a given concept, while others are seen as clearly incompatible with it.

The program's perceptions of such matters depend upon assumptions about the possible dimensions of salience that are much less rich than an adult's — or even an infant child's. But human perceptions of conceptual salience are typically taken for granted by theoretical psychologists, and those who (like Piaget) try to make them explicit so as to account for conceptual development must address themselves to questions comparable to those facing anyone who tries to model concept-learning in computational terms.

For instance, consider Piaget's account of sensorimotor experience as enabling the child to learn that 'what happens after I move my hand' — or, more generally, 'what happens after what' — is an aspect of its world that is highly salient for successful motor action, and essential to the concept of *cause* that the child gradually constructs. In order to learn such matters, the child must possess computational mechanisms capable, among other things, of making the comparison underlying the perception of 'what happens after I move', and of generalizing this comparison over many different but analogous cases. As Piaget himself suggests, the child needs rich conceptual structures or ways of organizing knowledge in order to acquire concepts like 'cause' — or even 'movehand-makes-rattlemove.' (In Kantian terms, the forms of intuition must be rich enough to generate causal notions; although Kant of course ignored the development of the categories.)

J. A. Fodor has even argued that this computational necessity casts doubt on Piaget's attribution of *stage-to-stage progression* to equilibratory processes of assimilation and accommodation like those involved in concept-learning.[9] Briefly, Fodor's case is that any computational mechanism (program or person) capable of learning a new concept C must *already* be in possession of a language with representational power rich enough to express the content of C. (This is true, for instance, of Winston's program.) Certainly, C may be useful, or even in practice necessary, as a shorthand expression making for computational efficiency. But if Piaget's claim is to be taken seriously that the cognitive structures of stage n are strictly incapable of expressing matters expressed by the later structures of stage $n + 1$, then the progression from stage to stage cannot be explained in terms of the sort of equilibratory processes assumed to underlie the development of the *grasping* or the *toy* or *arch* schemata.

As mention of grasping reminds us, Piaget relates the development of concepts to the development of skills. And he sees abstract operational competence (such as is involved in logical thought) as based in concrete bodily abilities, ultimately deriving from the sensorimotor skills in the infant. A few AI programs have features somehow comparable to aspects of the learning of motor skills. For instance, G. J. Sussman's 'HACKER' is a program that writes programs for solving problems, and that becomes more skilled in doing so because it can profit from its mistakes.[10] The problems it solves are concerned with the assembly of stacks of bricks, so that for instance it can convert the scene shown in Figure 11.10 into that shown in Figure 11.11. HACKER's block-moving skills are constrained by the fact that it can pick up only one block at a time (as might be true of a very young child unable to balance even two building bricks).

In the course of HACKER's learning, knowledge initially stored as factual data becomes accessible as practical know-how, which enables the program actively to restructure its representations of its tasks so as to carry them out more effectively. This passage from 'mere knowledge' to 'real understanding' is reminiscent of Piaget's distinction between *figurative* and *operative* knowing. So too is the fact that whereas HACKER starts off merely being aware that a stack of bricks is structured in a certain way, it ends up able immediately to interpret this fact as meaning that a particular course of action (namely, dismantling the stack) is required. Piaget suggests that the figurative-operative distinction has no significance at the *sensorimotor* stage, when perception and action are inextricably linked. It may be true that this distinction has practical and educational significance only at the *operational* stage, but the computational difference between

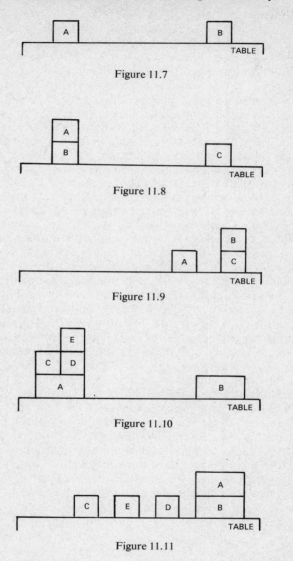

Figure 11.7

Figure 11.8

Figure 11.9

Figure 11.10

Figure 11.11

possessing a certain datum of knowledge and being able to use it in a structured activity is nevertheless theoretically applicable to sensiorimotor knowing. These points can be clarified by considering an example showing how HACKER learns a new subroutine, the CLEARTOP procedure.

To begin with, all HACKER knows about picking up things is that the relevant primitive (already given) action allows only one object to be moved at a time. In other words, although it knows that it is a theoretical prerequisite of this action that the top be clear, HACKER does not know that *in practice* a preparatory action of clearing must therefore often precede the action of moving. Block-moving programs that cannot learn are provided with programs for 'PICKUP' that include the advice always to remove any blocks that may be sitting on top of the target block, before attempting to move the target itself. But HACKER acquires this practical knack through experience, in a way that can be outlined with the help of Figures 11.7 to 11.11.

Given the scene shown in Figure 11.7 and asked to get A onto B, HACKER can put A on B immediately, since it has available a primitive program for putting one thing on top of another. But if HACKER is given Figure 11.8 and asked to get B onto C, it cannot do so at once. The reason is that the primitive 'PUTON' program can work only with one block at a time, so cannot move B since A is on top of it. HACKER investigates the difficulty, identifies it as the lack of a CLEARTOP precondition, works out that what needs to be done is to remove A, then writes a program for doing so, and inserts this 'patch' into the primitive PUTON program. The patched program is now run, and it succeeds: A is put on the table, then B is placed on C, and the final scene looks like Figure 11.9.

This counts as an increase in skill not just in the sense that HACKER can solve similarly simple problems more quickly in future (so that given Figure 11.9, HACKER can get C onto A unhaltingly), but also in the more general ('operational') sense that complex problems of essentially the same structure can be solved in a comparably immediate fashion. Thus given Figure 11.10, and requested to get A onto B, HACKER now unhesitatingly does the right thing — producing the scene shown in 11.11. That is, the patch produced previously was sufficiently general to direct these steps:[11]

Wants to put A on B
  Notices C and D on A
    Puts C on TABLE
    Wants to put D on TABLE
      Notices E on D
        Puts E on TABLE
      Puts D on TABLE
Puts A on B.

This production and generalization of the CLEARTOP subroutine is achieved by HACKER only because it has an understanding of the purposive structure of the problems it is faced with, and the teleological nature of its own planning processes — and of its mistakes. Sometimes a failure requires not the construction of a brand new step, such as the CLEARTOP subroutine, but merely the reordering of steps already constructed, or the insertion of an action to interface two main steps with each other (like cleaning a brush one has used to sweep the grate before using it again on the carpet).

One need not claim that the action schemata of an infant are identical to HACKER's if one is to claim that comparable computational processes representing the structure of purposive activity must be available to generate sensorimotor development. Intelligent bodily action evolves *pari passu* with perceptual schemata, and the sorts of mistakes (or 'bugs') highlighted by Sussman are presumably disequilibrating factors that initiate and guide the accommodatory processes within the child's motor schemata. A clearer understanding of the computational problems behind such matters would contribute to our understanding of the development of integrated motor skills.

Since HACKER is not a physical robot with a material hand, but rather a program that works out in its imagination how such a robot should use its hand to achieve its goals, it cannot take advantage of the many serendipitous — as opposed to foreseeable — mismatches between plan and reality that may arise in actual bodily movement. Such mismatches are, however, available to the exploring baby. And Piaget often refers to the child's capitalization on 'happy accidents', such as the motion of a string fortuitously touched by the infant's hand. But the computational questions remain as to how the baby recognizes the mismatch, and what are the computational resources it employs to profit from its recognition. Even in the inner manipulation of one's own symbol-systems, never mind concourse with the external world, serendipity can arise: but how can it be recognized and used? HACKER has a set of plan-CRITICS that can recognize unforeseen events such as HACKER's moving a block from B to C having earlier moved it from A to B: in such a case, the CRITICS can advise HACKER to move the block from A directly to C in future like cases. But the program does not have enough intelligence to notice or profit from other serendipities which it is plausible to assume may be of use to the human actor, whether infant or adult. The Piagetian approach takes such computational abilities for granted without explicating their detailed nature.

A number of other discussions in the AI literature are relevant to Piagetian ideas about development. For example, M. L. Minsky and Seymour Papert have compared a five-year-old's representation of a cube with the isometric or perspective drawings that may be produced by an adult, in terms of the amount of background knowledge (and the complexity of thinking) required to make the representation useful.[12] Thus they claim that the drawing of Figure 11.12 shows relatively directly, which that of Figure 11.13 does not, that each face of a cube is a square; that the typical face meets four others; that all angles are right angles; that each typical vertex meets three faces; that opposite face edges are parallel (the isometric representation of Figure 11.14 also shows this relatively directly); that there are three right angles at each vertex; and that one can usually see only five of the six faces on moving around the cube, the other being 'hidden' by the supporting surface.

Figure 11.12

Figure 11.13

The adult can understand more fully why the superficially misleading perspective representation is more useful for many purposes than the five-year-old's symbolization, because the adult's operational intelligence can handle the logical (geometrical) structures and thinking procedures required to exploit Figure 11.13 fully. It is significant, however, that the five-year-old's interpretation of Figure 11.12 involves notions such as 'typical face' and 'typical vertex' (where 'typical' does *not* mean 'the statistical norm or average of the faces — or vertices — shown in the drawing') whose computational subtleties are not yet understood. Moreover, the five-year-old may be able to interpret Figure 11.13 and 11.14 fruitfully (though not as fruitfully as the adult) even though he cannot draw them himself. Understanding in detail *why* Figures 11.13 and 11.14 are more useful to an operational intelligence than is Figure 11.12 would require a computational theory of representation adequate to explain such matters. A central problem within AI is that of explicating in general terms how certain aspects of different types of representation may be interpreted by specific procedures to symbolize certain other things. In his remarks about the development of conceptual structures and the superiority of logico-mathematical knowledge, Piaget addresses some of the issues involved. One might ask, for instance, how the notion of *conservation of shape* contributes to the operational understanding of the perspective cube of Figure 11.13. Again, Piaget's

Figure 11.14

remarks on the usefulness and limitations of visual imagery and figurative thinking raise some questions to which detailed computational answers are being sought in AI (it may surprise many people to know that AI concepts are currently being used by cognitive psychologists studying imagery). Progress towards a general theory of representation would thus illuminate Piagetian psychology no less than AI.

Papert has also emphasized the potential use of AI ideas in understanding and effecting the educational process.[13] For present purposes, the main significance of his work in this area is his stress on the child's learning about general structures of thinking — and general types of bug, or mistake — through the experience of writing simple computer programs whose structure and effects are immediately apparent. (The 'effects' in question are various, and include the movement of mechanical 'turtles' on the floor, the drawing of line-figures on a video unit, and the generation of musical sequences.) To the extent that the child's understanding of his mistakes leads him to general problem-solving strategies, as opposed to ungeneralizable *ad hoc* tricks useful only within a narrow domain, the cognitive improvement taking place is relevant to Piaget's *operational* thinking.

Just as the child's representation of cubes may be importantly different from the adult's, so the child's concept of *number* may differ also. In a discussion of some of the computational abilities that must underlie the understanding of number, Aaron Sloman has shown that even a six-year-old's number competence is an extraordinarily complex matter, involving many different thinking procedures which may be more or less well integrated.[14] Piaget also stresses the contribution of simpler thinking processes to numerical competence. One of the two basic abilities Piaget identifies as contributory factors in the development of number

248 *Minds and Mechanisms*

concepts is *seriation*, the central topic of the next section.

III: COMPUTATIONAL MODELS OF SERIATION BEHAVIOUR

Piaget was the first to draw psychologists' attention to the general class of problems he termed seriation tasks, in which one is required to place in correct order the individual members of a set of items varying on a dimension such as length, weight, or shade-of-blue.[15] Piaget regards seriation not only as an important ability in itself, but as an essential prerequisite of more complex types of thinking, including the understanding of number.

His observations of young children led Piaget to point out the marked discontinuities in seriation behaviour with increasing age, and to distinguish three stages in the development of seriation. The Stage I child, of three or four years of age, is quite unable to build a 'staircase' of blocks out of a set of seven blocks provided to him. The youngest children merely align the blocks in an arbitrary order, although an older child may construct two or more very short series (of only two or three blocks) which he is unable to integrate, or may build a single (short) series by simply omitting some of the blocks available. The Stage II child, of five or six years, is by contrast able to construct a perfect staircase using all of the seven blocks. But he does so by what Piaget termed *trial and error*, choosing the next block virtually at random (except that he may pick one of the extremes as the starting block); and he is unable to insert extra blocks into the staircase after he has finished building it. Only at Stage III, when the child is seven or eight years old, can he build a staircase by starting with the longest (or shortest) of the seven blocks and then systematically adding the nearest in size; and only now can he correctly insert intermediately-sized blocks into a pre-existing staircase. Even such a child 'regresses' to the trial and error stage if given a set of ten or more blocks to start with (as you probably would yourself, especially if the blocks were fairly similar in size).

Comparable experiments on weight seriation, wherein children used scales to weigh the blocks, showed a similar progression of developmental stages. But the stages were 'shifted' two or three years later, so that the achievement of weight seriation lagged behind length seriation. Piaget termed this later appearance of a task having essentially the same logical structure as an earlier one, a case of *horizontal décalage*, and observed further examples in the development of *conservation* (substance before weight, before volume). The occurrence of horizontal décalage means that when one describes a (seven or eight-year-old) child as having attained the *concrete operational* stage, one cannot infer that all 'concrete operational' tasks could be equally well performed by the child. This décalage thus presents a theoretical anomaly to anyone seeing concrete operational behaviour as due to a quasimonolithic set of operational structures that the child either has or lacks.

The development of length and weight seriation (and also of *classification*, the second 'parent' of number according to Piaget) has been modelled in computational terms by a number of psychologists influenced by AI ideas in general and *production systems* (PSystems) in particular. PSystems were introduced into the study of cognitive processes by Allen Newell and H. A. Simon,[16] and were first applied to the Piagetian notion of seriation by Jean Gascon and G. W. Baylor.[17] I shall outline the recent work of R. A. Young as a representative example of this general approach.[18] (The PSystem methodology in AI is different from the approaches of the AI workers mentioned in the previous section; space forbids discussion of the controversial question whether PSystems are a superior AI methodology in general, although this claim is made by Young.)

A PSystem is a set of information-processing mechanisms called *production rules* or *productions* (PRules), operating by reference to the information stored in the system's *short term memory* (its representation of the current state of the world, including its own current goals and recent actions). Each PRule is a condition–action pair, stating that if a particular condition (or set of conditions) is satisfied by the current state of the short term memory then a particular action (or set of actions) will be taken by the system. These actions effect changes in the symbols within the short term memory, with the result that a different set of conditions may now be satisfied which was not satisfied before, resulting in a different action's being taken . . . and so on. The various PRules are thus directly triggered by the presence of the corresponding state of affairs in the short term memory.

In writing a PSystem, some convention has to be adopted to forestall potential clashes between PRules. Such clashes may either be a question of 'importance' or general priority (as when one runs away from a tiger rather than running away from a wasp, even though one may thereby be running *toward* the wasp), or they may involve conditions which are logical subsets of other conditions (as when one stays in unconcerned proximity to a tiger-in-cage even though one would have fled from a tiger). (The Fawn in *Through the Looking Glass* apparently had human-fleeing PRules which were temporarily inhibited within the forest, so that it allowed Alice to put her arms around its neck.) Such questions of priority being borne in mind, the PRules are arranged in an ordered list such that the system in effect[19] starts at one end of the list and checks the conditions of each PRule in turn until it finds a condition-set that is satisfied. After taking the relevant action, the system starts again at the beginning of the list.

The 'actions' include changes in the memory that represent events in the world (from I-am-near-tiger to I-am-not-near-tiger), and changes that represent the completion or setting-up of goals (as the completion of GOAL-flee-from-tiger may automatically set up GOAL-save-face, which in certain circumstances can set up GOAL-exaggerate-fearsomeness-of-tiger). If a goal has not yet been completed, the fact that it is still active is available in the short term memory so that on completion of a subgoal the system remembers that the higher-level goal is still in force. Hierarchical relations between purposes and actions can thus be embodied within the 'linear' structures of lists of PRules. Physical behaviour such as fleeing from a tiger — or picking up and setting down a block — can be simulated by having the PSystem effect the appropriate changes to the information stored in memory. A PSystem can therefore be used as a psychological theory predicting particular motor or verbal behaviour in particular situations.

Young's investigation of length seriation combines a computational with an experimental methodology, and is explicitly based on Piaget's work. Young aims to show how the behaviour of any given stage or substage can be described by a specific PSystem. Preferably, the progression from stage to stage should be smoothly achieved by the addition of only one or a few PRules to the previous system. (Implicit in this preference for incremental improvement of the PSystem is a preference for psychological theories that do *not* view development as a matter of radical changes in or reorganizations of conceptual structures: we shall return to this point in Part II.) And these added PRules should be psychologically plausible in the sense that one can conceive of — and ideally also explain — the child's learning them at the relevant age (so that the addition of a rule involving quadratic equations would not be seen as a happy way of progressing from a 'three-year-old' to a 'four-year-old' PSystem).

Young assesses the psychological plausibility of his PSystems primarily by the extent to which their predictions correspond to observed behaviour. As well as drawing on Piaget's empirical writings, Young experiments with children of various ages, trying to match his PSystems to detailed features of their behaviour.

Mismatch may prompt further development of the faulty PSystem, which is then tested in turn by a further experimental session with the same child that is individually tailored to the specific PSystem and mismatch concerned. The level of detail involved is much finer than the mere distinction between building or not building the complete staircase, or between being able or unable to insert extra blocks in the correct position. It also covers features such as the choice of one specific block rather than another, the movement of

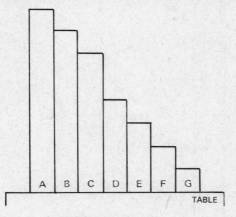

Figure 11.15

the hand toward a block which is not in fact picked up, and the child's *double* tapping of block D in Figure 11.15, given that the child's finger is 'running down the staircase' from *A* to *G*. Young emphasizes the fact that although the gross features of two task-behaviours may be the same, the details may show important psychological differences. An adequate theory of seriation should account for these differences as well as reflecting the grosser behavioural distinctions. In other words, Young aims to account for particular *performance* as well as general *competence*.

Broadly, what Young does is to show how a wide range of finely distinguished and superficially chaotic seriation behaviours can be described by PSystems differing from each other by the addition of specific PRules. The PSystems are idiosyncratic in the sense that each child has a different set of PRules (the richness of the individual case thereby being more nearly conserved by this computational methodology than by orthodox psychological measures based on statistical averaging). For instance, Figure 11.16 shows the PSystem describing Alf, a child at Piaget's Stage

T1:   Seriate   = > S-one
S1:   S-one   = > Get [nearest]
S2:   S-one   = > Get [suitable]
S3:   S-one <new>, In-mind   = > Get [in mind]
T2:   S-one, Get –> block   = > Place

P1:   Place   = > Position [right]
P2:   Place, Exam –> <wrong>   = > Reject;–

P3:   Place, Exam –>   = > Rotate
PG1: Place, <new config'n>   = > Examine

PG2: Place, Exam –>   or   = > +

B1:   Seriate <new>   = > S-one <first>
B2:   S-one <first>   = > Get [big]
B3:   S-one <first>, Get –> block   = > P'n [far left]:+

Figure 11.16

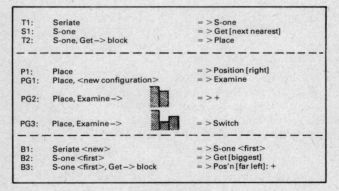

T1:   Seriate   = > S-one
S1:   S-one   = > Get [next nearest]
T2:   S-one, Get –> block   = > Place

P1:   Place   = > Position [right]
PG1: Place, <new configuration>   = > Examine

PG2: Place, Examine –>   = > +

PG3: Place, Examine –>   = > Switch

B1:   Seriate <new>   = > S-one <first>
B2:   S-one <first>   = > Get [biggest]
B3:   S-one <first>, Get –> block   = > Pos'n [far left]: +

Figure 11.17

T1': Seriate   = > Get [biggest]
T2'   Seriate, Get –> block   = > Position [right]

B3': Seriate <new>, Get –>block   = > Position [far left]

Figure 11.18

II or 'empirical seriation' stage; Figure 11.17 shows the PSystem describing Del, a child also at the empirical seriation stage but lacking the 'Pick the block you have in mind' rule included within Alf's system; and Figure 11.18 shows a PSystem constructed to represent Piaget's picture of the 'fully operational' child who seriates by unerringly picking the biggest remaining block and adding it to the staircase. (Figure 11.18 does not include PRules for the insertion of extra blocks into a pre-existing staircase: you might find it useful to attempt the exercise of adding more rules representing insertion behaviour.)

So as to avoid detailed terminology explanations, you may wish to compare Figure 11.16 with its 'ordinary English' translation shown in Figure 11.19. This should indicate the ways in which the general features of PSystems mentioned earlier are embodied in Young's examples. Young's PSystems must be read from the bottom upwards. As soon as you find a PRule whose condition is

T1:   IF you want to seriate the blocks THEN decide that you want to add a block to the staircase.

S1:   IF you want to add a block to the staircase THEN pick up the nearest block.

S2:   IF you want to add a block to the staircase THEN decide that you want to get a suitable one from the pool, that is, one of about the right size.

S3:   IF you want to add a block to the staircase, and you have just been attending to one (for whatever reason) THEN pick up that one.

T2:   IF you want to add a block to the staircase, and you've just picked one up THEN decide that you want to place it in the staircase.

P1:   IF you want to place a block in the staircase THEN position it at the right-hand end.

P2:   IF you want to place a block in the staircase, and a block has just been examined and found unsuitable THEN return it to the pool.

P3:   If you want to place a block in the staircase, and there are just two blocks in it already, similar in size but the wrong way round THEN rotate the two blocks.

PG1:   IF you want to place a block in the staircase, and the staircase has just been rearranged THEN examine it.

PG2:   IF you want to place a block in the staircase, and you have just examined that block and found it to be one or two units smaller than its neighbour THEN accept it (leave it where it is in the staircase).

B1:   IF you have just undertaken the task of seriating the blocks THEN decide that you want to put the first one in the staircase.

B2:   IF you want to put the first block in the staircase THEN get a big one.

B3:   IF you want to put the first block in the staircase, and you've just got a block THEN put it at the far left of the space you'll be building in, and leave it there.

Figure 11.19 English translation of Figure 11.16. For directions on how to interpret this set of rules see text. N.B. read from the bottom upwards.

satisfied, you assume that the specified action is taken, and you start again at the bottom of the list. The predicates appearing on the left-hand side of each PRule are intentionally defined: that is, they refer to information stored within the system's short term memory, thus representing the system's view of which conditions are or are not satisfied. In Young's use of PSystems no stress is laid upon the distinction between true and false belief, since all items in the memory are assumed to be true (Young assumes that the children are not hallucinating). But the false or illusory beliefs typical of many kinds of cognitive function (some of which have been discussed by Piaget) could equally be represented within the left-hand portion of a set of PRules, and their generation might be modelled by information-processing actions specified in the right-hand portions.

Figures 11.16 and 11.19 model Alf's seriation behaviour. This behaviour is variable (or superficially chaotic) in the sense that Alf sometimes chooses a block that he happens to have already in mind for some reason (S3), he sometimes chooses the nearest (S1), and he sometimes seeks one of about the right size (S2). You may have wondered why *both* S1 and S2 are included, since (reading from the bottom up) S2 totally blocks S1. The reason is that in each of the earliest component episodes of Alf's task-behaviour he picked the nearest block, whereas in the latest episodes he always picked the biggest; moreover, the details of his hesitations in different block-choosing episodes show that the criterion 'about the right size' was sometimes being used by him. Strictly, then, Figures 11.16 and 11.19 represent his behaviour in the later half of the whole seriation task, while modelling of his earlier behaviour would require deletion of PRule S2.

The addition — and consequent retention — of S2 by Young implies that Alf somehow *learned* this rule: he formulated it for some reason (though not necessarily consciously), he recognized its usefulness, and he remembered it accordingly. The 'how' in that 'somehow' is still computationally obscure, since learning is not yet well understood. Some of the issues involved were touched upon in the previous section, and in the next section we shall see that Young interprets the addition of S2 as exemplifying a psychological process that casts doubt upon Piaget's concept of *stage*.

Drawing on his observations of many different children, together with a logical analysis of the structure of seriation tasks, Young identifies a 'kit' of seriation PRules, which he compares to a multi-course self-service menu.[20] Selecting different subsets of rules allows one to assemble PSystems describing many different seriation techniques. The rules within the kit are grouped into those concerned with general *episode structure* (the basic cycle of getting blocks and adding them to the staircase, together with the special case of the first block of all), those concerned with *selection* of the next block, those concerned with *evaluation* of the portion of staircase built so far, and those concerned with the *placement* and *correction* of blocks. In terms of the three phases of selection, evaluation, and correction, Young specifies a 3-D 'space' of seriation skills, within which any child can be located. The location codes the child's characteristic performance, the problems he can and cannot solve, and the nature of his errors; distinctive seriation behaviours are associated with different regions of the space.

Young claims that most of the rules within the kit are 'surprisingly independent'; given the basic episode cycle, 'almost any collection of the rules . . . yields a psychologically plausible PSystem for seriation'.[21]

IV: PRODUCTION SYSTEMS AND THE PIAGETIAN CONCEPT OF 'STAGE'

Young's claim just cited may have caused many readers some surprise, since it apparently runs counter to Piagetian theory, on which Young's approach was originally based. It is similarly surprising that (as Young emphasizes) the addition of a single PRule to a PSystem can predict a qualitative change in seriation behaviour. One example of this is the difference between Alf's behaviour and Del's which Young describes by saying that Del's PSystem lacks the 'Pick the block you have in mind' PRule (S3) present in Alf's; another is the addition of S2 to Alf's PSystem halfway through his seriation task.

These examples are surprising because they suggest that the qualitative changes seen in the development of seriation behaviour are due to the incremental learning of many logically distinct and psychologically independent rules, or behaviour patterns. By contrast, a Piagetian account would rather stress the global structures that underlie behaviour, whose radical differences in form account for the behavioural discontinuities described by Piaget in terms of Stage I, Stage II, and Stage III seriation.

A related theoretical point on which Young disagrees with Piaget is the question of the 'regression' from one stage to an earlier one. You will remember that a Stage III child (or an adult), who is able to seriate seven blocks 'operationally' into a perfect staircase without ever making a false move, may employ Stage II 'empirical' or 'trial and error' behaviour if confronted with twenty blocks. Given that operational structures are *ex hypothesi* present, it is not clear why they do not function in such cases; Piaget speaks in general terms of the 'difficulty' of the task tending to prompt regression, but this regression remains somewhat puzzling.

Young's explanation is that the application of the 'optimal' rule for getting the *biggest* block depends upon a perceptual test identifying the biggest block, a test that can be carried out using the eyes alone if only seven blocks are in the pool, but that cannot be so carried out for large numbers of blocks. (This point is reminiscent of G. A. Miller's 'Magical Number Seven'; Young has recently proposed a novel explanation of this phenomenon, based on considerations of the symbolic coding involved in visual judgments of length.[22]) The general anti-Piagetian moral Young draws from considerations such as these is that one cannot realistically identify a given rule, structure, or strategy as *optimal* in a general sense: the adult who tried to 'Pick up the biggest' when confronted with twenty finely graded blocks might be logically pure but would be pragmatically foolish. The appropriate operational strategy in such a case would be comparable to Beth's 'Seriation by placement'[23] rather than Gam's 'Seriation by selection.'[24] Seriation (and other problem-solving) behaviour can be understood only via detailed consideration of information-processing questions such as: *what* information is the person using?, *when* is he using it?, *how* is he getting it?, and *what* is he using it for?

According to Young, similar considerations explain the phenomenon of horizontal décalage, which was earlier mentioned as a puzzle within Piagetian theory. Given only seven blocks, differing in *length* by easily perceptible amounts, the Stage III child can see which is the biggest without having to touch any of the blocks, and so can pick it up immediately. By contrast, the difference in *weight* of identically-sized blocks can be assessed only by comparing them on the scales, a process involving even greater computational complexity than 'just seeing' one block as bigger than another. It is not surprising, then, that perfect (operational) weight seriation lags behind perfect length seriation; indeed, Baylor and Gisèle Lemoyne have shown that if length seriation is carried out under the constraint that all sticks not actually in the hand are inside identical cigar tubes, thus making the computational nature of length seriation closely comparable to that of weight seriation, then length seriation too is 'delayed' by several years.[25]

In general, what is an optimal strategy in one information-processing context or task-situation may not be optimal in another. The intelligent thing to do is thus to select the appropriate behaviour from a widely varied repertoire, so that to describe the 'non-operational' behaviour of the person functioning under severe information-processing constraints as 'regression' to an earlier developmental stage is an infelicitous way of describing his cognitive function. In a task environment within which many different difficulties may arise, flexibility is of the essence: so-called 'primitive' strategies should not only be retained for future use, but their use in appropriate circumstances should not be disparaged as 'regressive'. As Young remarks,[26] the impression that a theory of *mature* behaviour involves fewer PRules (as Figure 11.18 contains fewer rules that Figure 11.16), or is logically tidy or algorithmic in a way infantile behaviour is not, is misleading. Someone who had only the strategies corresponding to the PRules represented in Figure 11.18 would be at a loss if asked to seriate twenty blocks, or required to seriate seven blocks *blindfold*.

Space forbids detailed discussion of Young's claims. But a few possible counterclaims must be mentioned. First, one might point out that Piaget's 'stages' concern behavioural structures that appear simultaneously (*pace* the décalage) in a wide variety of tasks, and that it is this generality of cognitive function over varied domains that interests Piaget. To write a single rule or set of ten rules to cope with length seriation is not to do the same for colour, nor to express seriation in abstract terms so that it can straightway be incorporated into a theory of the development of *number*, for example. Young's subject Alf did generalize his behaviour from blocks to discs, but issues of generalization were not the prime focus of Young's study.

A similar objection might employ an AI analogy to cast doubt on Young's picture of a set of 'messy' and 'independent' rules as opposed to underlying richly generative structures. The response 'Fine, thanks!' from one teletyping program may be considerably more intelligent than the same response from another, if the first program's response is generated by way of an internal representation of the pragmatics of greeting-episodes in conversations and of its own current mood-state, whereas the second simply replies automatically to the input 'Hello!' in an unstructured S-R fashion. In short, the fact that one program apparently does the same thing as another does not show that it is just as intelligent. Young might reply to this that further attempts at conversation would quickly show the first program to be more complex than the other, and that a PSystem designed to do the same sort of thing would have to be comparably complex.

This raises a third issue which has implications for the methodology of AI itself as well as for the problem of assessing computer simulations in general. Young denies that children are actually using PRules, but also denies that they are drawing on internalized strategies or overall plans of task-behaviour; his preference for PSystems as against other ways of programming (such as that used by Winston or Sussman, for instance) is based on the apparent simplicity and *lack* of 'deep structure' in PSystem programs. But as discussion of the flee-from-tiger example may have indicated earlier, the designer of a PSystem for a complex task has to embody goal-priorities and goal-subgoal structures within the PSystem either implicitly (by order) or explicitly (on either side of some PRule). Organizational problems similar to those faced by more orthodox programming methodologies must therefore be faced by the writers of PSystems. But whereas Sussman, for instance, would tend to represent the child as (consciously or unconsciously) choosing to do something in light of a model of the purposive structure of the task, Young explicitly denies that PSystems do this — and so implicitly denies that children do either.[27] His statement that PSystems are *in no sense* plans, rules of thumb, principles, recipes, laws, or guidelines for action, and that running a PSystem is not an activity that the child performs, seems to cast doubt not merely on psychological claims made specifically by Piaget but also on many other psychological theories that attribute richly structured representations of the world and of action in it to the knowing subject.

V: CONCLUSION

I have concentrated in this paper on the few studies in AI that are most pertinent to Piaget's work on the *improvement* of cognitive abilities. In so far as AI in general is concerned with the structure and function of mental representations, schemata, or 'frames,'[28] it is relevant to the overall constructivist approach to the mind that is typical of Piagetian and other 'cognitive' psychologies. Even Freudian theory may in principle be illuminated by AI insights, for it too is concerned with the construction and (motivated) inferential manipulation of symbolic schemata representing the person's social world.

Current AI concepts and techniques, to be sure, model only a tiny part of human computational abilities. (Think, for instance, of the many ways in which your own concept of *arch* is richer than the simple concept shown in Figure 11.1; yet this arch-concept possessed by Winston's program — and its *use* and *modification* by the system — is better specified than are 'concepts' in verbal psychological theories.) Because of this, and because of the many unclarities in Piagetian and other psychological theories, AI and psychology cannot be brought into a detailed concordance overnight. But if psychologists can make use of the dialectic of assimilation and accommodation in continually increasing the match between intuitive verbal explanations and detailed computational theories, they may be able to achieve a richly structured equilibrium between mind and model that no previous psychological methodology has attained.[29]

NOTES

1   Hans Furth, *Piaget for Teachers*, Prentice-Hall, Englewood Cliffs, N.J., 1970, p. 46.
2   Imre Lakatos, 'Falsification and the methodology of scientific research programmes', in Imre Lakatos and Alan Musgrave (eds.), *Criticism and the Growth of Knowledge*, Cambridge University Press, Cambridge, 1970, pp. 91–196.
3   David Klahr and J. G. Wallace, 'Class inclusion processes', in Sylvia Farnham-Diggory (ed.), *Information Processing in Children*, Academic Press, New York, 1972, esp. pp. 165–168.
4   Jean Piaget, *Six Psychological Studies*, Random House, 1967, p. 53.
5   Jean Piaget, in discussion of J. S. Bruner, 'Individual and collective problems in the study of thinking', *Ann. New York Acad. Sc.* 91 (1960), 22–37.
6   I do not distinguish in this paper between 'schemes', 'schemata' (or 'schemas'), and 'representations'. Piaget, however, does. For him, schemes are organized patterns of actions, whether mental or behavioural, and so stress the operative aspect of knowing; schemas stress rather the figurative or symbolic aspect. Schemas for Piaget are thus closer to representations, which he sees as internal symbolic 're-presentations' that appear at the close of the sensorimotor stage. Most cognitive psychologists (and AI workers) use 'representation' in a wider sense than this, and would say that sensorimotor recognition, too, involves inner representations of the world; similarly, they intend the term 'schema' in Bartlett's sense, a sense that would include both Piagetian schemes and Piagetian schemas — and also Piagetian representations. Applying the scheme-schema distinction, one might regard the work (to be described) of Sussman and Young as more closely related to schemes, and Winston's as related rather to schemas. Whether or not one prefers to follow Piaget's terminology in these matters, the cognitive psychologist and computational theorist must of course address questions about the difference between operative and

figurative aspects of knowledge, and about the significant psychological differences between various forms of representation that may arise at different ages.

7   P. H. Winston, 'Learning structural descriptions from examples', in P. H. Winston (ed.), *The Psychology of Computer Vision*, McGraw-Hill, New York, 1975, pp. 157–210.

8   J. S. Bruner, Jacqueline Goodnow and George Austin, *A Study of Thinking*, Wiley, New York, 1956, ch. vi; P. C. Wason and P. N. Johnson-Laird, *Psychology of Reasoning: Structure and Content*, Batsford, London, 1972, pp. 51 and 71.

9   J. A. Fodor, *The Language of Thought*, Harvester Press, Hassocks, Sussex, 1976, esp. pp. 87–95.

10   G. J. Sussman, *A Computer Model of Skill Acquisition*, American Elsevier, New York, 1975.

11   From the 'Scenario' in Sussman, *Skill Acquisition*.

12   M. L. Minsky and Seymour Papert, *Artificial Intelligence*, Condon Lecture Publications, Eugene, Oregon, 1973, section 1.2.

13   Seymour Papert, 'Teaching children to be mathematicians versus teaching about mathematics', *Int. J. Math. Educ. Sci. Technol.* 3 (1972), 249–262.

14   Aaron Sloman, 'On learning about numbers', in *Proc. AISB Conference*, Sussex University, 1974, pp. 173–185. Also in Aaron Sloman, *The Computer Revolution in Philosophy: Philosophy, Science, and Models of Mind*, Harvester Press, Hassocks, Sussex, 1978.

15   Jean Piaget, *The Child's Conception of Number*, Humanities Press, New York, 1952; Barbel Inhelder and Jean Piaget, *The Early Growth of Logic in the Child: Classification and Seriation*, Harper and Row, New York, 1964.

16   Allen Newell and H. A. Simon, *Human Problem Solving*, Prentice-Hall, Englewood Cliifs, N. J., 1972.

17   Jean Gascon, *Modèle cybernétique d'une sériation de poids chez les enfants*, Université de Montreal, Institut de Psychologie, M.C.P. 2, 1969; G. W. Baylor and Jean Gascon, 'An Information Processing Theory of the Development of Weight Seriation in Children', *Cognitive Psychology* 6 (1974), 1–40.

18   R. M. Young, *Seriation by Children: An Artificial Intelligence Analysis of a Piagetian Task*, Birkhauser, Basel, 1976.

19   Young assumes that the computer — and the child — has some form of content addressable memory system whereby relevant items can be recalled directly, without necessitating systematic scanning of the entire list or memory; hash-coding, e.g., allows for this. See Young, *Seriation*, p. 47.

20   Young, *Seriation*, ch. xi.

21   Young, *Seriation*, p. 198.

22   G. A. Miller, 'The magical number seven, plus or minus two: some limits on our capacity for processing information', *Psychological Review* 6 (1956), 81–97; J. A. M. Howe and R. M. Young, *Progress*

in Cognitive Development (University of Edinburgh: DAI Research Report No. 17, 1976).

23   Young, *Seriation*, pp. 114–128.
24   Young, *Seriation*, pp. 103–114.
25   G. W. Baylor and Giséle Lemoyne, 'Experiments in seriation with children: towards an information processing explanation of the horizontal décalage', *Canad. J. Behav. Sci.* 7 (1975), 4–29.
26   Young, *Seriation*, p. 205ff.
27   Young, *Seriation*, p. 47f.
28   M. L. Minsky, 'A framework for representing knowledge', in Winston, (ed.), *Psychology of Computer Vision*, pp. 211–277; Marc de Mey, 'The cognitive viewpoint: its development and its scope', *Communication and Cognition*, University of Ghent, 1997, xvi–xxxii.
29   The relations between AI and psychological theory in general are discussed in my *Artificial Intelligence and Natural Man*, Harvester Press, Hassocks, Sussex, 1977.

Synthese 38 (1978) 389–414. *All Rights Reserved.*
Copyright © 1978 by D. Reidel Publishing Company, Dordrecht, Holland.

PART IV

VALUES AND PSYCHOLOGICAL THEORY

12
Human values in a mechanistic universe

I: INTRODUCTION

The truth can be dangerous. It is because they realise this that the Roman Catholic Church forbid cremation. Cremation is, of course, theologically permissible, and in times of epidemic the Church allows it. But in normal times it is forbidden — Why? The reason is that the Church fears the influence of the image associated with it. It is difficult enough for the faithful to accept the notion of bodily resurrection after having seen a burial (knowing that the body will eventually decay in the ground). But the image of the whole body being consumed by flames and changing within a few minutes to a heap of ashes is an even more powerful apparent contradiction of the theological claim of bodily resurrection at the Day of Judgement. (Indeed, the ban on cremation was introduced when the French Freemasons held anti-Catholic demonstrations, in which they burned their dead saying 'There, you see: they won't rise again!') In short, instead of relying only on abstract theological argument, which very likely would not convince their flock in any case, the Church deals with this threat to faith by attacking the concrete image.

I believe a basically mechanistic view of the universe, and of human beings as creatures of it, to be true. But such views can be dangerous, in that they tend to encourage a dehumanisation of our image of man, an undermining of our sense of responsibility and individuality. For the image of 'machine' that is currently popular has no place for human values or for the specifically human self-image associated with them. This image of machines and mechanism is drawn from seventeenth-century clockwork and nineteenth-century engineering: one has only to think of Descartes's metaphors for animal psychology, and T. H. Huxley's metaphor for psychology in general (in which he compared the mind to the useless smoke from a steam-engine). Occasionally people appeal to twentieth-century notions such as the cybernetic concept of feedback, taking the thermostat or the guided missile as their paradigm case of modern mechanism. But this paradigm also is insufficient to provide a philosophical base for humanity, and its overall effect is just as dehumanising as earlier versions of mechanism. The current image of machines causes a chill to strike the heart on reading the molecular biologist Jacques

Monod's claim that 'The cell is a machine. The animal is a machine. Man is a machine.'[1] If man is indeed a machine, what room is there for humanity?

I shall try to defend against the dehumanising influences of mechanism by presenting a different image of 'machine', one that shows the potentialities inherent in mechanism to be far greater than could previously have been supposed on the basis of extant machines. That is, instead of concentrating on abstract philosophical arguments in favour of mechanism, I shall describe actual examples of machines whose behaviour is hardly 'mechanistic' in the usual sense of the word. Specifically, I shall outline some of the achievements of artificial intelligence ('A.I.' for short), the science of making machines do things that would require intelligence if done by people.[2] The analogies between these machines and human minds are strong enough to cast doubt on the antimechanist assumption that no philosophical rapprochement between humanism and mechanism is possible.

Before describing these examples in Parts III to V, I provide a philosophical context for the later discussion by sketching what I understand by the notion of 'human values', and what I take to be the main doubts on the part of humanists who reject mechanism of any sort.

II: HUMAN VALUES

The notion of human values is inextricably bound up with a specifically human concept of people and a sense of their moral dignity. By this I mean that, whatever particular values a humanist may hold, these will in general assume that people are capable of purposive action, free choice, and moral responsibility, and that their interests ought *prima facie* to be respected. It is because these concepts are essential to human values that antihumanist writers such as B. F. Skinner seek to undermine them, claiming that morality has no need of 'freedom' and 'dignity'.[3]

It follows that any form of mechanism that claims to be basically compatible with a morality of human values must be able to accommodate the concepts of purpose, freedom, and responsibility. What features of these concepts are generally agreed by their protagonists to be most important?

When we ascribe purposes to people, and describe their behaviour as purposive action, we imply that their behaviour is somehow guided by their idea of a goal. The purpose is always an idea of something nonexistent, for the goal-state itself lies in the future; it is often an idea of something that will never exist, for goals are not always achieved; and it is sometimes focused on something intrinsically impossible, like squaring the circle. That is, the idea is an intentional object or thought within the subjective experience of a thinker, as opposed to an objective entity existing in the material world. The guidance it exerts on purposive action is (within limits) flexible, rational, and intelligent, and with perseverance the person learns to do better. Typically, the agent is aware of the goals being followed and why they are being followed, although cases of 'unconscious motivation' and 'habitual action' frequently occur.

In ascribing freedom to people, or describing human action as free, we mean not merely that people are unpredictable, but (more positively) that in free action the agent could have acted differently. That is, either the goal or the subgoal guiding the behaviour could have been different, so that a different end was chosen in the first place or the same end was sought by different means. But this difference must itself be generated in a particular sort of way. It cannot be based on a random factor, nor can it depend on causes having nothing to do with the self and lying wholly outside the agent's control. (This is why radically indeterminist analyses of freedom are unacceptable, and why action attributed primarily to genetic or environmental causes cannot be regarded as truly free.) Rather, the difference in question must be grounded in the deliberations of the person concerned: had the agent's reasoning been different, the action also would have differed. So the more someone is capable of flexibly rational thinking, the greater the freedom of action available. In addition, free action is often self-determined in a peculiarly intimate sense, in that the determining reasons include a crucial reference to the person's (actual or ideal) self-image. In such cases, one asks oneself (or perhaps, a friend): 'Am I someone who would choose to do this?' or 'Do I want to be the sort of person who does that?' These questions, and especially the latter, address the person's moral principles as well as mere conceit or narcissistic self-regard.

The ascription of moral responsibility presupposes that free action can be 'action against the strongest desire', in the sense that a temporarily pressing motive can be outweighed by moral principles. The point is not that the person is even more strongly swayed by the moral principles, for the metaphor 'swaying' suggests passivity on the agent's part. Rather, the person actively deliberates on the choice in a responsible fashion, carefully considering all the known factors in so far as they are relevant to ethical issues, and not making a decision over-hastily. Specifically moral principles (in contrast with mere personal preferences) are universalisable to all individuals in similar circumstances, which implies that practical morality draws on the capacity to recognise subtle analogies between distinct situations as well as the ability to reason logically about 'all' and 'some'. Moreover, moral principles are primarily concerned with abstract features of human behaviour or experience, such as justice and betrayal or happiness and despair. It follows that moral responsibility rests on the ability to understand concepts such as these, and to assess their relevance to particular situations. If the person is to engage in moral choice, rather than mere ethical contemplation, this assessment must involve also the imaginative comparison of the likely outcomes of alternative possible actions. It follows that a great deal of knowledge must be brought to bear in exercising one's responsibility: knowledge of moral principles themselves, knowledge of the world in which they are to be applied, and knowledge of one's self — both as one is and as one would like to be.

These being the crucial features of the family of concepts contributing to 'human values', why are humanists usually so insistent that human values cannot be encompassed by any basically mechanistic philosophy? Broadly, there are two different reasons, One is a philosophical view arising from purely philosophical arguments; the other is a prejudice against mechanism that is grounded not so much in abstract reasoning as in the concrete image of familiar machines as we know them in daily life.

The philosophical view favoured by humanists holds that mechanism is incompatible with intentionality, with the distinction between the psychological subject and the object of thought that we have seen to be essential to purpose, freedom, and moral responsibility. But what sort of incompatability is this? Briefly, the humanist's claim may be only that intentional phenomena cannot be described in terms making no use of the subject-object distinction, so that a philosophy in which such psychological terms do not appear can make no sense of human values. Alternatively, the humanist may also claim (without always seeing that this is a different point) that intentional phenomena cannot be generated from a mechanistic base, one which can be described in the nonpsychological terms of physics; on this view, creatures pursuing human values simply could not arise in a basically mechanistic universe.

My position on this 'philosophical' humanism is that whereas the first claim distinguished above is correct, the second is mistaken.[4] In other words, it is true that we cannot avoid the concepts of purpose, freedom, and responsibility if we are to understand human beings as the essentially subjective creatures they are, or if we are to express any system of specifically human values. But it is false that subjectivity cannot arise within a basically mechanistic universe, or that a system described in objective terms by the physicist cannot also be described by the humanist in intentional terms that express different aspects of its nature.

I shall concentrate in this paper on the second root of the humanist's antipathy to mechanism: the poverty of the humanist's image of machines. Specifically, I shall ask how purposes, freedom, and moral responsibility might relate to an enriched image of mechanism. More generally, my discussion will bear also on the issue of the compatibility of intentionality and mechanism. For if the moral concepts I have sketched in this section can be shown to be consonant with mechanism, then subjectivity in general must be compatible with mechanism too.

Let us turn, then, to consider a few examples of what one might call 'non-mechanistic machines'. My examples are drawn from A.I., so the machines in question are digital computers running under the guidance of an A.I. program. You will see that I say 'the program does this' where I could equally have said 'the machine does that'. You will see also that I use psychological terms without scare-quotes in describing these machines. I omit scare-quotes for aesthetic reasons: as will become clear, I do not hold that any of these current machines is *really* purposive or intelligent, still less a moral agent. I do hold, however, that psychological vocabulary is essential in expressing what these machines can do.

III: PURPOSE

The central feature of purposive action is that it is guided throughout by an idea of the goal, in a flexible and intelligent manner. Are there any machines of which the same might be said?

Among the earliest A.I. programs were some that solved problems by keeping an idea of the goal firmly in mind and reasoning backward from it. For example, the GEOMETRY MACHINE proved theorems in Euclidean geometry that would have defeated any but the brightest of high-school students with the same vocabulary of geometric concepts and the same stock of previously proved theorems.[5] Essentially, the program followed the strategy of the school-child who writes *Given*: and *To be Proved*: at the top of the page, and then tries to find a way of legally getting from what is given to what is to be proved (using only inferences based on Euclid's axioms or previously proved theorems). Similarly, the General Problem Solver — 'GPS' for short — attacked problems in logical form (such as the familiar *Missionaries and Cannibals* puzzle) by carefully noting the differences between the current problem-state and the goal-state, and eliminating these differences until none remained.[6] In each of these cases, the idea of the goal is crucial in guiding the solution of the problem.

In each case, also, the process of solution varies with the circumstances rather than being rigidly fixed. That is, what the program does, as well as the order in which it does it, depends on the specific nature of the difference between the current and goal-state. GPS carries out a 'means–end analysis' of the problem, in which it identifies the differences as a series of sub-goals to be achieved in the most suitable order. Heuristics, or rules of thumb, are available to suggest what type of approach is most likely to resolve a particular difference, and what method to try next if the 'best' should fail. In short, these programs show the beginnings of one main criterion of purpose: variation of means.

Some recent programs show more intelligence in varying their performance according to circumstances. The flexibility of their goal-seeking is greater, not merely in the sense that they have a greater number of methods to choose from, but also in the sense that communication *between* methods is possible while the program is functioning. It is as though one method asks advice from another, while a third makes a complaint that there is a specific difficulty ahead, and a fourth requests 'stop press' information from a fifth. This flexible form of organisation is *heterarchical*, as opposed to the hierarchical organisation of GPS and the GEOMETRY MACHINE. In a hierarchy, there is a fixed progression of responsibility for control passing down from higher to lower levels of the system, and a module that gets into difficulties has to apply to its superior for help. But in a heterarchy the responsibility for deciding what is to be done next is more evenly distributed throughout the system, and the various sub-routines can communicate not only 'up' and 'down', but also 'sideways'. An analogy is between a (hierarchical) bureaucracy and a (heterarchical) group of co-operating experts: although there is room for some degree of flexibility in a bureaucracy (as there is in GPS), in a community of specialists there is more opportunity for last-minute changes of plan or minor adjustments in light of local difficulties.

The degree of flexibility that can be achieved by heterarchical programs is illustrated by Terry Winograd's 'SHRDLU'.[7]

SHRDLU's goal is to understand the sentences typed into it, where understanding involves parsing each sentence correctly, interpreting it sensibly, and answering it helpfully. SHRDLU has a large number of mini-programs for interpreting English sentences, including specialists which know about word-endings such as *-ed, -ing*, and the like, and experts on the grammatical and semantic properties of *noun groups* or *adjectival phrases*. In addition, it has sub-routines that specialise in finding out what the world is like, and modules whose particular job is to deduce conclusions from given premises. Each specialist, or mini-program, contains within itself advice about what to do in varying circumstances, and what to try if the most obvious stratagems fail. The goal of understanding an English sentence is one that can be reached only by way of highly flexible, interacting thought-processes, of which we ourselves are normally not introspectively aware. As you can see from the following excerpt of dialogue, SHRDLU's understanding depends on 'simultaneous' parsing, semantic interpretation, and investigation of the world, a complex process that has to differ subtly according to the specific nature of the input sentence:[8]

1. *Pick up a big red block*
    O.K.
    The system answers 'O.K.' when it carries out a command. In order to pick up the red block, it had to clear it off by finding a space for the green one (initially on top of it) and moving the green one away.
2. *Grasp the pyramid*
    I DON'T UNDERSTAND WHICH PYRAMID YOU MEAN.
    There are three pyramids in the scene, so the program does nothing.
3. *Find a block which is taller than the one you are holding and put it into the box.*
    The system has to figure out what is meant by 'one' and 'it', as well as using deduction to decide which block it is holding.
    BY 'IT', I ASSUME YOU MEAN THE BLOCK WHICH IS TALLER THAN THE ONE I AM HOLDING.
    Printed out to keep us informed.
    O.K.
    The hand has to set down the red block to pick up the taller blue one.
4. *What does the box contain?*
    THE BLUE PYRAMID AND THE BLUE BLOCK.
5. *What is the pyramid supported by?*
    Earlier the system responded to 'the pyramid' by saying 'I don't understand which pyramid you mean.' Now, it assumes that we mean the one just mentioned.
    THE BOX.

6.   *How many blocks are not in the box?*
     Negatives such as 'not' and 'no' are handled whether they appear in
     clauses or noun groups (such as 'no boxes').
     FOUR OF THEM.

7.   *Is at least one of them narrower than the one which I told you to pick
     up?*
     The phrase 'at least one of them' must be analysed to refer back to
     the previous question, and 'the one which . . .' must also refer to
     blocks. Noun groups can have complicated numbers such as 'at
     least one', 'more than three', 'exactly seven', etc. The memory of
     past events is used to deduce which block is 'the one which I told
     you to pick up'. Notice the complicated syntactic structure in which
     'the one' is actually the object of a clause embedded two levels
     deeper.
     YES, THE RED CUBE.

17. *Will you please stack up both of the red blocks and either a green
     cube or a pyramid?*
     O.K.

23. *Had you touched any pyramid before you put the green one on the
     little cube?*
     YES, THE GREEN ONE.
     The system deduces from its memory what event is being referred
     to, and can relate other events to it in time. The analysis includes
     complex tenses of verb groups, and there are special facilities for
     keeping track of the various forms of irregular verbs like 'have'.

24. *When did you pick it up?*
     WHILE I WAS STACKING UP THE RED CUBE, A LARGE
     RED BLOCK AND A LARGE GREEN CUBE.
     A time is described by naming the main goal which was being
     worked on.

25. *Why?*
     The system remembers immediately previous sentences to under-
     stand questions like this and the following ones.
     TO GET RID OF IT.
     By keeping track of selected parts of the original subgoal tree, the
     system has some understanding of its own motives.

26. *Why did you do that?*
     TO CLEAR OFF THE RED CUBE.
     'That' refers to the action mentioned in the answer.

27. *Why did you clear off that cube?*
     Here, 'that' means the one just referred to.
     TO PUT IT ON A LARGE GREEN CUBE.

28. *Why did you do that?*
     TO STACK UP THE RED CUBE, A LARGE RED BLOCK
     AND A LARGE GREEN CUBE.

29. *Why did you do that?*
     BECAUSE YOU ASKED ME TO.
     It remembers what it did, not how the request was worded.
     [*Cf.* the request of item 17, which gives the program a choice.]

In addition to the flexible variation of means, SHRDLU's dialogue suggests other features of purpose. For instance, Item 1 has the indeterminacy characteristic of action sentences (and often taken as a logical criterion of intentionality): Winograd did not have to tell SHRDLU precisely how to pick up the big red block, but left the program to work that out for itself. A prime reason for the machine's ability to understand (and obey) this vaguely specified command is that the program is written in a version of PLANNER, a 'goal-oriented' programming language in which one can identify goals at a high level of generality and rely on the system itself to fill in the details. Items 17 and 29 show that SHRDLU itself often speaks in intentional terms: it knows that it was not specifically asked to stack up the two red blocks and a large green cube, even though it did this in response to an input request.

Items 17 and 23–29 show that SHRDLU has some under-standing and memory of its own goal-subgoal structure, and is able to address this structure to find the reasons for which it did things. If this information were not stored in its memory, it would have had to answer Item 29 either by saying 'I don't know', or perhaps by working out a plausible reason for its action which in fact was not the real reason. Analogously, a person in a state of posthypnotic suggestion will dream up all sorts of possible reasons for putting the cat on top of the grand piano, being unable to remember the hypnotist's previous command and so unable to give the real reason, 'Because you asked me to.' And Freudian accounts of unconscious motivation similarly assume that parts of the person's goal-subgoal structure are unavailable to con-sciousness, being at least temporarily repressed, and that the relevant actions will be 'explained' by rationalisations that do not constitute genuine self-knowledge.

But SHRDLU lacks a feature of purposiveness that was mentioned earlier, namely, the ability to learn to do better. Its knowledge of what it is up to is sufficient to enable it to know why it did what it did, but not to enable it to remember what went wrong when failures occur. Consequently, SHRDLU cannot benefit from experience by learning to avoid false paths once it has been down them.

Not all programs are similarly limited. For example, HACKER is a program that writes programs for solving problems, and that learns to do so better because it has an understanding of the purposive structure of the programs it composes and because it knows about the sorts of things that can go wrong. [9] When it writes a program it adds 'comments' to various lines (as human programmers do) saying what that section of program is intended

to do. This information is used in rewriting the program, should it
fail to achieve its goal when it is run. The sorts of mistake, or bug,
that HACKER knows about are defined in high-level teleological
terms, such as UNSATISFIED PREREQUISITE, GOAL-
PROTECTION VIOLATION, PREREQUISITE CLOB-
BERS BROTHER GOAL, and so on.

A sense of the way in which HACKER learns from its mistakes
can be conveyed by Figures 12.1 to 12.5. Given the scene shown in
Figure 12.1, and asked to get A on to B, HACKER can put A on B
immediately. HACKER has available a *primitive*, or already
given, program for putting one thing on top of another. But if
HACKER is given Figure 12.2, and asked to get B on to C, it
cannot do so immediately. The reason is that the primitive
'PUT-ON' program can work only with one block at a time, so
cannot move B since A is on top of it. HACKER investigates the
difficulty, works out that what needs to be done is to remove A,
then writes a program for doing so, and inserts this 'patch' into the
primitive 'PUT-ON' program. The patched program is now run,
and it succeeds: A is put on the table, then B is placed on C, and the
final scene looks like Figure 12.3.

It is important to realise that HACKER has learnt a skill of some
generality here, as can be seen by referring to Figures 12.3 and
12.4. Given Figure 12.3 and asked to get C on to A, HACKER can
do so at once, without the false start that was made in the earlier
example. Moreover, given Figure 12.4 and requested to get A on to
B, HACKER again unhesitatingly does the right thing. That is, the
patch produced previously was sufficiently general to direct these
steps:

    Wants to put A on B
      Notices C and D on A
        Puts C on TABLE
        Wants to put D on TABLE
          Notices E on D
            Puts E on TABLE
        Puts D on TABLE
    Puts A on B

This procedure results in the scene shown in Figure 12.5.

In addition to its knowledge of the purposive structure of what it
is up to, and its knowledge of some very general types of mistake
(and how to deal with them), HACKER is able to remember
precisely what happened when it went down a false path which
now it is careful to avoid. This ability depends primarily on
CONNIVER, the programming language in which the program is

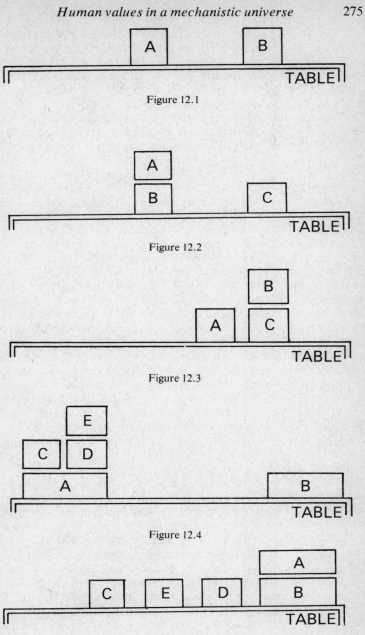

Figure 12.1

Figure 12.2

Figure 12.3

Figure 12.4

Figure 12.5

written. As well as facilitating memory of mistakes (and so easing learning), CONNIVER makes it possible to write programs that can simultaneously consider the detailed course of events appropriate to various different alternative actions, and to make comparisons between them. This computational ability contributes to the intelligent planning of purposive action (and therefore to moral deliberation also), and HACKER makes use of it when asking itself whether doing such-and-such would conflict with the already established subgoal achieved by so-and-so.

IV: FREEDOM

The unpredictability of human action is often exaggerated by proponents of freedom, and a novel like Luke Rhinehart's *The Dice Man* shows what a mockery of humanity a radically unpredictable life of action would be. Nevertheless, the undeniable practical limits on predictability give added spice not only to gossip but also, in some eyes, to arguments for freedom. However many reasons you may have for predicting that I will say something, it is always possible that I will say something else — or nothing — instead. But machines, or so the argument goes, are either predictably deterministic or random, neither of which is compatible with a freedom that can form the basis of morality.

This claim that, provided there is no random operator involved, machines must be predictable in their behaviour is associated with a common misinterpretation of the familiar slogan, 'A computer can do only what the programmer tells it to do!' If this is taken to mean that everything the machine does is done at the behest of instructions specified at some level or another by the program, it is true. But it is false if it is taken to mean either that the programmer can foresee everything the machine will do or that the program will do all and only what the programmer intended it to do. Even in relatively crude cases, a program may not do just what was expected of it.

For instance, a simple program that engages in man-machine dialogues may sometimes respond forgivingly to an apology but sometimes spurn it, and may even choose occasionally to say nothing at all. While the programmer can indeed say something in general terms about when it is that the program is most likely to respond in one or other of these ways, he cannot always predict what will happen in a particular case. As you read the following excerpt of dialogue between this program and a human doctor, see whether you can predict the program's remarks either in general or specific terms, and whether you can suggest an explanation post hoc for what it actually says (the doctor speaks first):[10]

Why are you in hospital?
I SHOULDN'T BE HERE.
Who brought you here?
THE POLICE.
What trouble did you have with the police?
COPS DON'T DO THEIR JOB
What do they do instead?
COPS ARREST THE WRONG PEOPLE.
They arrest the right ones sometimes.
THE LAW SHOULD GET THOSE ITALIAN CROOKS.
Are you Italian?
MY BACKGROUND IS BRITISH BUT I WAS BORN IN THIS
COUNTRY.
Do you know any Italian crooks?
I TRY TO AVOID THE UNDERWORLD.
Are you afraid of the underworld?
THE MAFIA ARE THE WORST GANGSTERS.
Are you connected with the Mafia?
YOU KNOW, THEY KNOW ME.
How do they know you?
THEY SPY ON ME.
Why do they?
THEY WANT TO GET FALSE EVIDENCE TO FRAME ME.
What do they have against you?
THEY ARE OUT TO GET ME.
What for?
I HAVE INCRIMINATING EVIDENCE AGAINST THE MAFIA.
Are you sure of all this?
YOU DON'T BELIEVE ME?
I am doing my best.
(Silence on the 'patient's' part.)
(Silence on the psychiatrist's part.)
CAN'T YOU THINK OF A DECENT QUESTION TO ASK?
You seem hostile to me.
SOME OF YOUR REMARKS ANNOY ME.
I am sorry.
FORGET THE EXCUSES, YOU GUYS ARE ALL ALIKE.

It may have occurred to you, perhaps even before coming across
the reference to the human as 'the psychiatrist', that there is
something characteristically odd about PARRY's conversation.
'PARRY' is the name of the program, which is designed as an
embodiment of a particular psychological theory of paranoia, and

of the paranoid interaction of fear, hostility, evasiveness, mistrust, and so on. For the moment, let us concentrate on PARRY's moment of silence and on his final furious rejection of the psychiatrist's placatory apology.

The program's apparent sulkiness and petulance in these instances arise in response not only to the previous input item but to the conversation as a whole. It follows that the psychiatrist's contributions 'I am doing my best' and 'I am sorry' would, in the context of different conversations, elicit different reactions from PARRY. Broadly, the program scans the semantic content of the conversation for remarks that it considers (either reasonably or paranoically) to be threatening, and various numerical monitors representing the theoretical constructs of fear, anxiety, and mistrust are raised accordingly. In addition, the program can initially be 'set' at a high level of these emotional monitors, with the result that input remarks that in other circumstances would have been interpreted by PARRY as neutral, or even soothing, are instead interpreted by him 'paranoically'. Since almost any remark relating to his inner delusion is taken as threatening by a human paranoid, PARRY is designed to react in an analogous fashion. As you have probably realised, PARRY's persecutory delusion concerns the Mafia, whom he believes to be hunting him. It is because previous references to the Mafia and associated topics (such as the police) have greatly raised PARRY's anger and suspicion, that he does not trust himself to reply to 'I am doing my best' and cynically rebuffs 'I am sorry'.

Even PARRY's programmer is unable to predict what PARRY will say, although the program is a relatively simple one (much simpler than Winograd's SHRDLU), and relies on spitting out slightly adjusted versions of 'canned' responses rather than being able to generate entirely fresh sentences. When a psychiatrist finished his interview with his own favourite test-question for paranoia, 'I'd like to invite you to dinner at my house,' he and PARRY's programmer were each surprised by the startlingly appropriate reply: 'You are being too friendly.'

However, despite this very human ability to surprise, PARRY cannot be seen as a plausible simulacrum of a free spirit. The crucial feature of deliberation and reflective self-knowledge are entirely lacking. PARRY does not deliberate within himself whether he should answer or be silent, and he answers — or not — by picking randomly from a stored list of responses associated with the currently relevant levels of the various emotional monitors.

Programs like SHRDLU and HACKER, by contrast, do show some ability to deliberate about what they are doing and why they are doing it (and their actions are not influenced by their passions as PARRY's are). They have a degree of self-knowledge concerning not only why they did a particular thing, but also what it is generally within their power to do.

The self-knowledge involved in answering strings of 'why?' questions about one's actions is, up to a point, essential to freedom (cf. items 17 and 23–29 of SHRDLU's dialogue). To the extent that one cannot answer such questions, or (like the rationalising neurotic) cannot answer them truthfully, one's action is not genuinely free. One's freedom depends also on a realistic appreciation of one's own powers: it is because SHRDLU has a good idea of what it can and can't do – and what the results are likely to be – that it can go ahead on its own initiative in working out how to obey a command like that of item 17. And HACKER, as we saw, has even greater power to consider comparisons between different imagined courses of action, as well as to remember why it went wrong in the past, which abilities are necessary if one's freedom is to mature with experience of living.

Restrictions on adult human freedom can arise through 'depersonalisation' of the self-image, wherein the self is regarded as having very weak powers of action or, in extreme pathological cases, none at all. A schizophrenic who describes himself as 'a machine' is calling on the popular image of mechanism in order to deny that he is a purposive system, and his life experience and sense of responsibility are impoverished accordingly. Such a person might or might not be able to do certain simple things at the request of the psychiatrist (a catatonic cannot), but dependence on the will of others is no substitute for personal autonomy. A depersonalised individual is somewhat analogous to a (hypothetical) version of SHRDLU *lacking* internal access during planning to the information that it is able to pick up pyramids. Since this item is not on the list it uses during planning as a catalogue of the things it can do, it cannot conceive of doing it. Consequently, if the 'big red block' of item 1 had had a pyramid sitting on it, this impoverished SHRDLU could not have cheerily answered 'O.K.' The person who cannot originate the idea of shutting the window, but can do so if asked to by the psychiatrist, would be parallelled by a version of SHRDLU that could pick up a pyramid only if explicitly told to do so. The command 'Please pick up a pyramid' would directly address a stored list of *all* the things SHRDLU can in fact do; but, in the example we are imagining, this list is not available in its entirety for perusal by SHRDLU itself during planning. If the program were to be altered so that even this direct access to pyramid-moving procedures were deleted, then SHRDLU would be like the catatonic schizophrenic who, even if he hears and understands the words, cannot obey requests to 'Stand up, please' or 'Move your hand'.

Examples of schizophrenia, as well as the bewildering variety of psychological malfunctions associated with amnesia or with damage to the speech-area of the brain, thus indicate the subtle complexities of the computational basis of normal, 'free' behaviour. To adapt an image of Wittgenstein's: there are many cogs and levers inside the mind, and if they are disconnected or if their normal interactions are impeded then strange limitations on the person's usual range of choice and action are only to be expected. Analogous phenomena are observed in the functioning of a computer program wherein a single definition is changed, a single instruction deleted, or a single passing-of-control from one procedure to another is inhibited. So Locke's remark that 'Barely by willing it, barely by a thought of my mind, I can move those parts of my body that were formerly at rest,' belies the true psychological complexity of freedom, however faithfully it may reflect its introspective simplicity.

The fact that a free action *could* have been different, in the sense that it *would* have been different had the person's reasoning differed, is also paralleled in some programs — such as HACKER and SHRDLU, and another heterarchical program called 'BUILD'.[11] BUILD is so named because its task is to decide how to go about building a construction of bricks like that shown in Figure 12.6, for example. If you think carefully about this task, assuming that you may use only one hand and are not allowed to slide bricks, you will realise that the construction requires an extra brick (not shown in the picture) to act as a support for one end of the horizontal bar C, so that the 'tower' for that end of C can be placed upon it without upsetting it. This extra brick is brought in as a temporary measure, and has to be removed after both towers have been placed on C. The only way to avoid recourse to an extra brick would be to build the *sub-assembly* consisting of blocks A-B-C-D-E, and then to lift the sub-assembly as a whole and place it on to F. But in this particular example, such a procedure would not succeed unless your hand were exceptionally steady: the tall towers are so unstable that they would almost certainly collapse in the process. All these facts, including the steadiness of its (imaginary) hand, are borne in mind by BUILD as it works out how to build the construction shown in the picture.

Were you to build such a structure yourself, one could say that you freely chose to use a supporting brick rather than attempting to proceed by sub-assembly. Conversely, if you opted for sub-

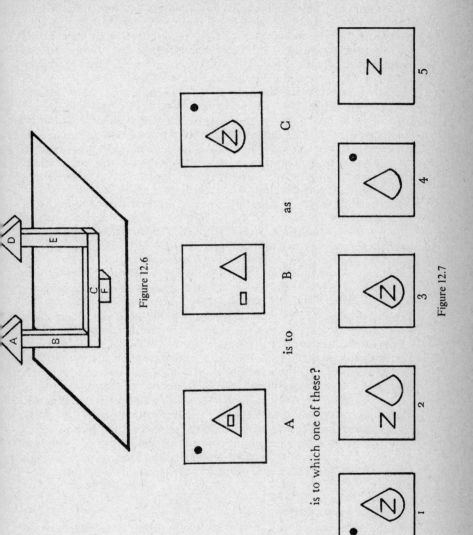

Figure 12.6

Figure 12.7

assembly and the structure collapsed — perhaps shattering into glass splinters all over the floor — you could be blamed for having chosen this method instead of the more reliable 'temporary support' approach. In either case, your intuitive or calculating deliberations about the stability of the sub-assembly and the steadiness of your own hand would play a crucial part. Had they been different, your actions would have differed.

So it is with BUILD: features like potential stability and steadiness of movement are continually taken into account in deciding what to do, and if a safer method can be found of constructing the desired building then that method will be used. If it turns out that the 'safer' method is not safe after all, the program can alter course accordingly. A slight change in the 'steadiness' parameter, or in one of the many items of information contributing to individual judgements of stability, would incline BUILD to choose differently in deciding what to do. But the complexity of the program is such that one cannot say anything so straightforward as 'Change X would lead BUILD always to choose Y rather than Z.' And if BUILD (like HACKER) could learn to do better, profiting by its past experience, one could not even say 'Change X would lead BUILD always to choose Y in a case *precisely like this particular instance*.' As it is, the word *precisely* has to be interpreted fairly strongly, for a different size of tower-bricks, for example, might have passed BUILD's imaginative stability-test, so making it choose to try sub-assembly rather than temporary support.

With the possible exception of a case where you were building with precious family heirlooms made of glass, we would not normally care enough one way or the other to ascribe the term 'free' to your choices in such a task — although if specifically challenged we would admit them to be free choices. But the case is very different if we consider examples where specifically moral considerations, and specifically moral responsibilities, come into play. Let us turn now to discuss some of the features that make a free choice into a matter for moral concern and evaluation.

V: MORAL RESPONSIBILITY

If morality involves the influence of ethical considerations to generate 'action against the strongest desire', it can arise only within systems capable of being simultaneously affected by various, conflicting purposes or desires. Programs like GPS, SHRDLU, HACKER and BUILD are basically single-minded in nature. This does not mean that they cannot deliberate on mutually

exclusive possible courses of action, or (in the case of BUILD)
judiciously change their minds and even change them back again
while doing so. But the various alternatives considered are all
viewed as means to a single overall end. This is true of most
current A.I. programs, it being difficult enough to write a program
to achieve one aim reliably, never mind writing one that can
simultaneously pursue several independent goals.

But A.I. workers recognise that living purposive systems do not
have the singlemindedness characteristic of current programs, and
a few programs have already been written with the express
intention of simulating the multidimensional nature of human
motivation. 'ARGUS', for example, is a system in which the
various goals compete for the computational resources available,
priority being given to the one which, in the current situation, is
most strongly activated.[12] In other words, the strongest desire
always wins, where this is not a tautological truth but a question of
which goal-seeking activity is the most strongly stimulated in the
circumstances (the programmers use the analogy of shouting
demons, the overseer giving priority to the demon who shouts
loudest).

In order that action should go against the strongest desire, under
the influence of moral principles, it is necessary that a choice be
made only after reasoned deliberation about all relevant factors,
which factors include not only the various desires being stimulated
but also the moral insights or ethical rules followed by the person in
question. We have already seen examples of programs capable of
reasoning about their choice so as to avoid what might initially
seem the 'obvious' options: BUILD, for instance, is able to
restrain itself from trying to place tower *A -B* on to bar *C* until it has
first fetched an extra brick to support the bar. So there is no reason
to suppose that specifically moral considerations could not enter
into such deliberation, and so decisively affect the generation of
action, provided that one could give a program a moral sense of
what it should be worrying about.

To answer the question 'What ought one to worry about?' is to
put forward a moral system, either in the form of a set of specific
rules of conduct, like the Ten Commandments or the Scout's Law,
or in the form of a general ethical principle, such as the Golden
Rule, the Categorical Imperative, or the Utilitarian promotion of
happiness. And, if the moral system is to count as one concerned
with 'human values', in the sense previously defined, it must at
least allow and preferably stress the fact that human beings are
freely acting purposive creatures to whose sense of responsibility
one may appeal. (Skinner's morality is an example of an ethical

system that is not concerned with human values in this sense, even though it prescribes what human beings should and should not do.)

Morality in practice is concerned not only (if at all) with abstract reasoning about the greatest happiness of the greatest number, or what a rational being could reasonably take to be a universal principle of action, but also (and primarily) with specific questions about particular types of conduct. What, for instance, is wrong about betrayal — and what types of behaviour are to be counted as betrayals? What is co-operation, and why is it *prima facie* a good thing?

Not surprisingly, there is no program that unerringly acts in terms of a felicific calculus or a categorical imperative to respect the interests of rational beings. There is no moral philosopher who does so either, not merely because of human frailty or Original Sin, but because these meta-ethical notions are so unclear that moralists cannot agree about their range of specific application. Sci-fi addicts will immediately think of Isaac Asimov's 'The Laws of Robotics', which put the avoidance of harm (whatever that is) to human beings at the pinnacle of every robot's moral structure.[13] But since highly general moral considerations such as these are currently in the realm of science fiction rather than science, I shall ignore them. What of the more specific concepts regarding human conduct — such as 'love', 'oppression', or 'betrayal' — that one may expect to find represented in any system of human values, irrespective of its supposed meta-ethical base? Could any sense be made of such matters in computational terms, so that a program could be instructed to take them into account during its deliberations?

A prerequisite of 'making sense of a concept in computational terms' is giving a clear analysis of the concept concerned (which is why no program can obey the Categorical Imperative or endorse a Utilitarian ethic). The social psychologist R. P. Abelson, in the course of developing a programmed model of his theory of attitude-change, has sketched a taxonomy of human *themes*, wherein are represented morally relevant phenomena such as love, co-operation, and betrayal.[14] These themes, and others, are analysed and systematically interrelated in terms of three independent psychological dimensions, each of which is defined in purposive terms. A theme is made up of the interdependent intentions, or *plans*, of two actors, and it is largely by reference to them that one sees the social and personal world in terms of moral values.

The three ways in which the autonomous purposes of two actors are conceived of as linked are as follows: First, one or both may have a role in the other's plan (and there are at least three commonly recognised types of role in this context, defined in terms of the agency, influence, and interests of the two parties). Second, one or both of the actors may have a positive or negative evaluative attitude to the plan (in whole or in part) of the other, and to his own role in it, if any. And third, one or both people may have the ability to facilitate or interfere with the other's action, whether at particular points only or throughout the plan. By way of these three dimensions, then, interaction with another human being can either augment one's own freedom of action or constrain it in different ways. Certain familiar moral ambiguities are reflected in the fact that some themes are 'asymmetric', in that they are experienced very differently by the two actors concerned, and so one and the same thematic structure is given two theme-names corresponding to the different subjective points of view involved (examples are Victory-Humiliation and Oppression-Law and Order).

By way of the three dimensions of role, interest, and facilitative ability, Abelson is able to exhibit the teleological structure of a wide range of psychological phenomena. Since themes are by definition social in nature, involving interaction between the intentions of two people, they are highly relevant to morality. And a morality of themes would count as a system of human values, in the sense previously distinguished, since they are defined in basically purposive terms that take for granted the freedom of action of the two actors in question.

For example, Abelson defines *betrayal* as follows: 'Actor F, having apparently agreed to serve as E's agent for action Aj, is for some reason so negatively disposed towards the role that he undertakes instead to subvert the action, preventing E from attaining his purpose.' If one were to specify appropriate restrictions on the importance for E of the goal to which action Aj is a means, and on the comparative power of the actors F and E to achieve that goal, one could systematically distinguish between individual members of a whole family of betrayals, such as abandonment and letting-down for example. (Abandonment is an especially immoral form of betrayal, because the goal is very important from E's point of view, but E is conceived of as relatively helpless without F's aid in achieving action Aj; by contrast, letting-down may be a matter of less moral import, since neither of these assumptions is implied.)

Other themes defined by Abelson are admiration, devotion, appreciation, co-operation, love, alienation, freedom, victory, humiliation, dominance, rebellion, mutual antagonism, oppression, law and order, and conflict. Common progressions of distinct themes, or *scripts*, mentioned by Abelson include rescue, alliance, revolution, blossoming, the worm turns, the end of the honeymoon, turncoat, and romantic triangle. (In each case Abelson first defines the theme or script in terms of his structural system, and then picks an ordinary language term to act as a mnemonic label for his theoretical concept; philosophers, therefore, should not expect his thematic definitions to correspond precisely with the nuances of everyday usage.)

Abelson has not yet written a program that can handle his structural theory of themes, but the theory arose in a computational context in the first place. It was because of the flaws in his previous program (one that represented certain features of political psychology) that Abelson was moved to deepen his theoretical understanding of concepts like those we have discussed. There seems no reason in principle why a program should not embody a representation of *betrayal*, much as BUILD embodies a model of *stability* or SHRDLU an understanding of *noun clause*.

In attempting to apply human values in real life, one has to weigh various moral considerations in light of the particular circumstances of action. Is this *really* betrayal — or is it merely letting-down or disappointment? We have seen that the settling of such a moral dilemma involves the ability to bear in mind judgements about the relative importance of the goal concerned to the person seeking it in the first place, as well as the relative social status and physical power of the people in the situation. A moral system (whether program or person) competent to decide such issues would have to rely on computational abilities at least as powerful as those used by BUILD in deciding how to construct brick-palaces, and in most cases would need even more powerful ones. Were it not so, the moral life would be as easily accessible to normal human beings as playing with children's building bricks.

Morality is conceived of (and taught) largely in terms of stories, whether parables, fables, histories, novels, or myth. The ethical function of such tales is to present examples of moral dilemmas in which alternative assessments may seem to be possible, although usually one assessment is recommended as the best and one course of action preferred. To profit from a parable is to understand the moral analogy so as to be able to attempt to apply the central lesson to moral choices in one's own life. This is not always easy: Alice's bewilderment on being told by the Duchess that 'Birds of a feather flock together' is the moral of 'Flamingoes and mustard both bite' was presumably of a kind with her puzzlement on reading some of the 'improving' stories meted out to Victorian children. The appreciation of analogy is a complex psychological process of cross-comparison between descriptions of the analogues, and between descriptions *of* descriptions when the analogy is 'on a higher level'. (Alice's complaint, 'Only mustard isn't a bird', suggests her intuitive grasp of what is involved in recognising analogies.)

It is already possible for machines to see analogies, albeit of a relatively crude or obvious kind. For instance, programs exist that can appreciate analogies of differing strength between simple spatial scenes like those built by BUILD, or between diagrams of the sort commonly used in IQ-tests (such as those shown in Figure 12.7).[15] Moreover, the nature and strength of the various analogies can be characterised by these programs not only in terms of more or less exacting descriptions of the analogous items themselves, but also in terms of more or less exacting descriptions of the comparison previously made at a lower level. And a language-understanding program has been developed that can take the proper sense of the sentence 'She drank in the sunshine at every pore,' even though the semantic definition of 'drink' that is used by the program specifies that what is drunk should be a fluid (which sunshine is not), that it should end up inside the person (which the sunshine does not), and that it should be taken in at one specific bodily aperture, preferably the mouth (not at every pore).[16]

A program able to draw analogies between things must be able to formulate and compare descriptions of them in what strikes us as a reasonable manner (is the Wonderland Duchess merely eccentric, in spotting an analogy missed by the rest of us, or is she — as the Cheshire Cat would say — mad?). So a 'morality machine' would need not only to be able to represent concepts like betrayal and co-operation, but also to compare the application of these concepts to distinct situations in a sensible fashion. Since the concepts and thought processes involved are as yet ill understood (though intuitively exercised by each of us every day), there is no current program that could understand the moral import of a New Testament parable or make a responsible moral choice about a matter of everyday complexity. But to the extent that work in A.I. helps to clarify the psychological nature of analogy, it can illuminate the computational basis of moral thinking.

In so far as moral principles are universalisable, ethical reasoning must involve an awareness of the difference between the concepts of *all* and *some*, *everybody* and *somebody*. Many programs exist that can handle these notions as they are expressed in terms of the predicate calculus. Interpreting natural language uses of the English words 'all', 'everybody', 'some', and 'somebody' is more tricky, however. As G. E. Moore pointed out, the logician does not mean quite the same thing by 'Some tame tigers growl,' as other people do. (Most people would interpret this phrase so as to imply that there are several tame tigers and at least two of them growl, whereas the logician takes it to mean that there is at least one thing which is a tame tiger and that growls — ($\exists \times$). (Tame $\times$ & Tiger $\times$ and Growls $\times$) — but quite possibly *only one* such tiger.) The debates about existential presuppositions highlight controversial issues that would have to be taken into account by anyone writing an ambitious language-using program. And although logicians may shudder, we can see why a PARRY-ish interviewing program responds to the complaint 'Everybody laughed at me' with an apparent refusal to take the universal quantifier seriously: 'WHO IN PARTICULAR ARE YOU THINKING OF?'[17] However, since moral philosophers who stress universalisability do intend this notion to be taken strictly, these niceties of everyday uses of 'all' and 'everybody' may be ignored for our purposes. So if a program were to be provided with a set of moral evaluations (expressed, for instance, in terms of Abelson's themes and scripts) there would be no radical difficulty in its universalising the morality. (To be sure, contradictions might arise if any moral rules conflicted with each other; the program — like people — would then have to give priority to one principle over the other.)

   To ascribe moral responsibility to a person is to imply that they can be praised or blamed in respect of particular choices, or acts. We have seen that moral choice commonly involves conscious deliberation and comparison between situations and principles, as well as careful weighing of the likely results of alternative courses of action. But some acts that are done 'without thinking', or even 'automatically', may be candidates for moral evaluation. For example, in discussing freedom of action I said that someone might be blamed for trying to move a whole sub-assembly of precious glass objects, instead of moving them individually. To cry, 'I just wasn't thinking,' as the heirlooms lie shattered into fragments, is to offer an explanation but not necessarily an acceptable excuse. For one may retort: 'Well, you should have been thinking!' On the principle that 'ought' implies 'can', this retort presupposes that the person had the ability to take stability into account, and had the knowledge that these particular objects were both precious and fragile. Similarly, in cases of more obvious moral import, someone can be blamed for not thinking, or not thinking carefully enough, when deciding what to do. Provided that the person's cognitive structure is such that they could have taken the relevant moral factor into account (that is, they could have both recognised it as relevant and acted accordingly), then the fact that they did not do so is *prima facie* cause for reproach. And some excuses are more acceptable than others: 'I just wasn't thinking, I was so worried about Mary,' may be adequate to dispel censure, depending on the importance of the worry concerning Mary.

Like the careless person in the example we have been imagining, the program BUILD has the ability to take note of actual and potential instabilities. And HACKER, the program that learns to write better and better programs, is able to act in two different fashions, one of which involves it in more painstaking deliberation than the other.

The first time that HACKER tries to run a program it has written itself, it acts in CAREFUL mode. That is, each step is individually checked as it is executed, to see if it is fulfilling the overall purposive function coded by the comment that was attached to it by HACKER at the time of composition. This typically involves numerous checks and cross-checks, together with a detailed chronological record of the changing worldstate, so that any bugs that have escaped HACKER's previous criticism can be identified as soon as possible. In CAREFUL mode, then, HACKER haltingly concentrates on the level of detailed tactics. Once a new program has been successfully executed, it is not run again in CAREFUL mode unless it gets into trouble, in which case CAREFUL running is reinstituted. In this way, knowledge that remains implicit during smooth functioning, in that it is not accessed by HACKER even though it can be described as 'relevant' to the task in hand, is made fully explicit and available to the program when things go awry. If there is any reason to expect that things may go awry, as in the case of a first-time run of a new program, CAREFUL mode ensures that this knowledge is made explicit from the start. Consequently, mistakes can be anticipated and forestalled in CAREFUL mode that would be made (though subsequently corrected) in normal functioning. The analogy to 'responsible' and 'irresponsible' action is clear. No one can act responsibly — or irresponsibly, either — who does not have comparable powers allowed for by their mental structure.

In HACKER's case, especially CAREFUL action happens only when the program is attempting something for the first time, or when it has already got itself into difficulties. If HACKER (or BUILD) were to be connected to an actual robot, which can not only think about how to stack up blocks but can really do so, it might be advisable to suggest that it also use CAREFUL mode if breakable bricks are to be stacked. Even if it were building a certain sort of stack for the umpteenth time, it would then still stop to check actual and incipient stabilities at every step, instead of blithely following through its wellworn plan regardless of such specific niceties. Naturally, running in CAREFUL mode takes a good deal longer than the normal, smoothly confident approach. So the suggestion that CAREFUL mode be used with fragile bricks might sometimes be rejected in favour of a less time-consuming method, depending on the program's assessment of the relative importance of saving time in this situation and of preventing breakage of the things being stacked. In general, CAREFUL functioning could be activated or not as a result of complex weighings of various (potentially conflicting) factors, not least among which would be the importance of the goals and subgoals being followed at the time. We noted earlier that HACKER and BUILD always know what it is that they are trying to do, even if they have not yet found a way of doing it.

The prescriptivist view of ethics characterises morality as a matter of proclaiming (and preferably, following) specific priorities that should govern conduct. 'Thou shalt not kill,' thus functions much like 'Use CAREFUL mode when playing with glass,' and the distinction between a lie and a white lie rests on an assessment of moral priorities according to which, in some situations, lying may be thought to be the lesser of two evils. Moral blame commonly takes the form of complaining that a specific ethical factor either was not taken into account at all, or was not given a sufficiently high priority in the case in question. If the person at fault is led to consider it in future, or to weigh it more gravely, the moral obloquy will not merely have identified the blameworthy aspect of the past action but will also have contributed to the person's moral growth.

Piaget describes an early stage in the development of morality, wherein the child takes into account only 'objective' factors in ascribing blame instead of also considering 'subjective' factors such as the intention of the agent.[18] For instance, little Mary is judged to be much naughtier than her sister Joan, for whereas Joan (who was stealing the tarts) broke only one plate, Mary (who was helping to lay the table for tea) broke five. The objective results of action are all that is considered by young children, and the higher moral worth of Mary's intention simply is not taken into account. In order to be able to consider such aspects of action when handing out praise or blame, one must be able to analyse the action concerned in terms of a (perhaps complex) set of goals and subgoals that the action is intended to serve, and to evaluate these goals in terms of moral priorities. Since HACKER knows for what purposes it is doing things, whether or not those purposes are ever achieved, it is potentially capable of understanding that its failure to use CAREFUL mode in one situation may be more blameworthy than its omitting to do so in another situation, even though the objective results are identical in either case. (Who cares how many bricks are broken if one was trying to distract a child in great pain, perhaps even thinking that the child might enjoy seeing them break?)

VI: CONCLUSION

One ethical concept mentioned in Part II of this chapter has not occurred since, namely, moral dignity. This concept may be used in a 'weak' sense, so that to ascribe dignity to people is to view them as freely acting responsible beings to whose choices moral evaluations are appropriate. The discussion so far has suggested that not all contemporary machines are radically at odds with this notion, as all former machines undoubtedly were. But there is a 'strong' sense of the concept that cannot be applied to any machine I have discussed, nor to any hypothetical descendant of them.

In the strong sense, the notion of moral dignity in addition implies that one should respect the interests of other people just because they are people's interests, and as such are intrinsic to their human nature. That is, my *prima facie* obligation to co-operate with you in furthering your interests, or to avoid betraying you to your enemies who will subvert them, is primarily justified not by the fact that my doing so will increase happiness, or the like, but by the fact that to fail to respect your interests is to deny your essential nature as a human being. Intrinsic interests are not necessarily thought of as fixed principles of 'human nature', though some moralists regard them so, but they are ends or purposes that pertain as such to the individual himself since they cannot be explained by reference to the purposes of any other agent. Animals, too, have (amoral) interests that are intrinsic in this sense. (Notice that intrinsic interests are purposes that cannot be further explained in *purposive* terms: their existence may however be explained in evolutionary or physiological terms.)[19]

The purposes of machines (that is, of artefacts) are not intrinsic to them, but derive ultimately from the purposes of the engineer and/or the programmer. To be sure, the relation of computer's goal to programmer's goal is not often so direct as in SHRDLU's item 29, 'BECAUSE YOU ASKED ME TO', nor is the machine's goal always predictable by or even acceptable to the programmer.

Nevertheless, the fact that the machine has goals at all, irrespective of which these are, can be explained by pointing out that the program (or self-modifying distant ancestor of it) was written to serve the purposes of the programmer. In the event that one feels any *prima facie* obligation to respect the machine's interests, any reluctance to lead it astray, this attitude is parasitic upon one's appreciation of the machine as an artefact made in the fulfilment of human ends. (A similar point underlies the theological problem of 'people or puppets?': if God freely created us to work His will, it seems that our interests can at base be explained by reference to the purposes of some other being, and so are not *themselves* deserving of moral respect but must be justified by reference to those alien ends.)

It follows that I cannot cite any example of a machine with even embryonic moral dignity, in this strong sense of the term, if I confine myself to examples drawn from A.I. or other branches of technology. But this has nothing to do with the 'mechanistic' nature of what may of may not be going on inside the machine, being a consequence purely of the fact that A.I.'s machines are *artificial*. In so far as in saying 'Man is a machine,' Monod meant that the bodily processes underlying and generating human behaviour, including moral conduct, are describable by physics or molecular biology, his remark does not conflict with moral dignity. With respect to the issue of intrinsic interests, there is a world of difference between natural 'machines' and artificial machines.

The concept of dignity is central to human values because it is closely linked with the moral concepts of purpose, freedom, and responsibilty — and also rationality and intelligence. All these cognate terms are themselves commonly used in a 'strong' sense so as to carry the implication of intrinsic interests. In this sense, no machine artefact could be called 'intelligent' or 'purposive', never mind how close the analogy between its operation and human thought.

But irrespective of the question of intrinsic interests, current machines cannot be regarded as *really* purposive or intelligent, still less dignified as moral agents. The analogies between the functioning of the programs I have described and mature human thought are not sufficiently close for these psychological terms to be used in their full sense, and in the case of 'moral agent' there is hardly any reason for using the term at all. Various crudities of current programs were mentioned in the preceding sections, such as their singlemindedness and inability to draw richly subtle comparisons, and many others could have been detailed.

None the less, the analogies between these machines and moral thinking as we understand it are close enough to be philosophically significant. As well as helping to illuminate the psychological complexities of what must be involved in moral action, and so what one is committed to in calling an agent 'free', they suggest *how it is possible* for human values to exist in a basically mechanistic universe.

For all the programs I have mentioned run on digital computers of known construction, functioning (at the electronic level) according to the principles of physics. If these systems are not mechanistic at base, then none are. Yet the behaviour of these machines is 'non-mechanistic' in character, not only in the sense that one continually uses psychological terms in describing what they do (as one occasionally does in cursing the obstinacy of one's car), but also in that one can only explain and understand what it is they are doing by using intentional language. Talk of electrons and wires cannot explain *why* BUILD decides not to risk using sub-assembly to build the scene shown in Figure 12.6, opting instead for a method involving temporary support, even though such talk can explain *how* it is that BUILD's reasoned decision can actually occur and be acted upon in the material world. So the irreducibility of intentional to non-intentional ('mechanistic') language is preserved in the examples we have considered, as is the indispensability of 'psychological' in addition to 'physiological' explanations.

Machines have until recently been described in purely non-intentional terms, and nothing of any explanatory import would have been lost if people had rigorously avoided applying psychological vocabulary to cars, clocks, and Concorde. But a machine being used to run a program like those developed in current A.I. cannot be described in such terms alone without losing sight of its most interesting (information-processing) features. We now have machines with a point of view of their own, machines with a subjective model (representation) of the world and their own actions in it by means of which they deliberate more or less carefully about what they should do and what they should not have done, and why. The insidiously dehumanising effects of mechanism can thus be counteracted in a scientifically acceptable manner. By providing a richer image of *machines* that suggests how it is that subjectivity, purpose, and freedom can characterise parts of the material world, current science helps us to understand how human values can be embodied in a mechanistic universe.

NOTES

1   Jacques Monod, *Chance and Necessity* (London: Collins, 1972). For Monod's defence of 'the ethics of knowledge' in preference to 'animist ethics', see chapter 9.

2   Further details are given in my *Artificial Intelligence and Natural Man* (Hassocks, Sussex: Harvester Press; New York: Basic Books, 1977).

3   B. F. Skinner, *Beyond Freedom and Dignity* (New York: Knopf, 1971).

4   This philosophical position is discussed more fully in my *Purposive Explanation in Psychology* (Cambridge, Mass.: Harvard U.P., 1972), esp. chs. ii, iv, and viii.

5   H. L. Gelernter, 'Realization of a geometry-theorem proving machine', in *Computers and Thought* (eds. E. A. Feigenbaum and Julian Feldman), pp. 134–52. (New York: McGraw-Hill, 1963.)

6   Allen Newell and H. A. Simon, 'GPS — a program that simulates human thought', in *Computers and Thought*, pp. 279–96.

7   Terry Winograd, *Understanding Natural Language* (Edinburgh: Edinburgh University Press, 1972.)

8   *Understanding Natural Language*, pp. 8–15 gives a 44-item dialogue from which this excerpt is taken. Winograd's comments are in lower case.

9   G. J. Sussman, *A Computer Model of Skill Acquisition* (New York: American Elsevier, 1975).

10 K. M. Colby, Sylvia Weber and F. D. Hilf, 'Artificial paranoia', *Artificial Intelligence*, 2 (1971), 1–26.

11 S. E. Fahlman, 'A planning system for robot construction tasks', *Artificial Intelligence*, 5 (1974), 1–50.

12 W. R. Reitman, *Cognition and Thought: An Information Processing Approach* (New York: Wiley, 1965).

13 Isaac Asimov, *I, Robot* (London: Dennis Dobson, 1967).

14 R. P. Abelson, 'The structure of belief systems', in *Computer Models of Thought and Language* (eds. R. C. Schank and K. M. Colby), pp. 287–340. San Francisco: W. H. Freeman, 1973.

15 P. H. Winston, 'Learning structural descriptions from examples', in *The Psychology of Computer Vision* (ed. P. H. Winston), pp. 157–210. New York: McGraw-Hill, 1975. This program's handling of analogies is discussed in the original account published as MIT AI-Lab Memo AI-TR-231, 1970. And see T. G. Evans, 'A program for the solution of geometric-analogy intelligence test questions', in *Semantic Information Processing* (ed. M. L. Minsky), pp. 271–353. Cambridge, Mass.: MIT Press, 1968.

16 Y. A. Wilks, 'A preferential, pattern-seeking, semantics for natural language', *Artificial Intelligence*, 6 (1975), 53–74.

17 Joseph Weizenbaum, 'Contextual understanding by computers', *Comm. Ass. Computing Machinery*, 10 (1967), 474–80.

18 Jean Piaget, *The Moral Judgement of the Child* (London: Routledge, Kegan Paul, 1948).

19 Intrinsic interests and the associated 'stopping-points' in purposive explanation are discussed in my *Purposive Explanation in Psychology*, pp. 43–5, 118–22 and 158–98.

13
Optimism

I

The optimist may be secretly envied, but he is publicly despised. His pronouncements are regarded as expressions of simpleminded blindness or as cynical propaganda. Optimism is not regarded as intellectually respectable. It was not always so: there have been times when optimism was not merely considered worthy of rational argument, but was widely accepted by thinking men. Now, however, we react with a growing embarrassment to passages such as these:

> The time will therefore come when the sun will shine only on free men who know no other master but their reason; . . . All the causes that contribute to the perfection of the human race, all the means that ensure it must by their very nature exercise a perpetual influence and always increase their sphere of action . . . the perfectibility of man is indefinite.
> (Condorcet. *Sketch for an Historical Picture of the Progress of the Human Mind.* 1795)

> Evolution can end only in the establishment of the greatest perfection and the most complete happiness.
> (Spencer. *First Principles.* 1864)[1]

And our embarrassment obliterates distinctions; 'optimism' is a dirty word: all optimists are grey in the dark. Nor can it be claimed that we have graduated to a more realistic pessimism; for that, after all, would be to admit optimism into the arena of rational argument. Life, in our vision, is not admitted to be tragic — merely absurd.

Are we not justified? Once we have taken into account the philosophical insights and the historical and cultural circumstances which underlie our current disillusionment — and this can be done very briefly, it is all too familiar a story — surely we have rung the death-knell of optimism? Most religions are optimistic — but we have been told that God is dead: can optimism survive? Moral 'judgments' are at best subjective, at worst totally irrational — Hume and Sartre have taught us so; how, then, can optimism be defended? Still worse: if we do allow rationality to moral judgments, must we not laugh the optimist out of court? Have we not seen the end of our last Golden Age? The literal bang will eclipse even the literary whimper: the facts, surely, speak for themselves. Why bother with optimists?

I shall claim that we are not justified. We do not distinguish clearly between different forms of optimism; we assume too quickly that the optimist is not prepared for rational argument, and that his claims have no content worthy of discussion. These are questions we should reconsider.

II

What is optimism? There is a minimal sense in which a man may be said to be *an optimist*, but hardly *a supporter of optimism*. Thus a man may *make no claims*, but merely (habitually) describe situations in a 'positive' rather than a 'negative' way, and the question of justification may not even arise. The classic example is the man who describes a bottle as 'half-full' rather than 'half-empty' where there is no dispute about water-level, about the value of water for life or about whether this is the last bottle or not. The man may not see any necessity to justify his description, in which case it is absurd to suggest that he should give one, and rational discussion is out of place. The *situation* may be agreed to be desperate, but the *bottle* is 'half-full'.

Of course, the man may be prepared to offer a justification, but can only offer a pragmatic defence — such as that defining an ambivalent situation in positive terms generally helps to give one confidence to cope with it more adequately. This is open to rational discussion (one may counter by arguing that, by the same token, such a definition may discourage active attempts to better the situation) and is not necessarily quickly or easily settled, but the issue is psychological rather than philosophical. Whatever the answer, this defence will be independent of and thus auxiliary to any justification of optimism as a credo; to support optimism as a rule of mental hygiene is not to be a supporter of optimism in the philosophical sense.

For the latter it is necessary not merely to make some claims, but to make a set of claims related in a specific way. The set must include three elements: (1) a statement of the facts; (2) a list of value-criteria; (3) a positive evaluation of the facts in the light of the suggested criteria. This model of optimism is indeed vague, for it is the core of different types of optimism, where the differences arise from varying interpretations and specifications of the three elements. Thus it can be used as a basis of comparison for optimistic systems, and gives a framework which suggests the main lines of discussion which can arise.

I shall claim that any *genuine* optimism must have this structure, that only thus can it have any real content worthy of serious consideration. If a system has this structure we can reject it only as a result of making specific criticisms of one or more elements; and even so we may have to accept a large part of its content. Such systems will be largely *a posteriori*, and may be thought by their proponents to be completely so if they assume that an *is* can give rise to an *ought*. The list of values cannot be *proved* in a strict sense, but whether it follows that there can be no rational discussion of this element is a vexed question, which I prefer to leave open. I shall be content to admit that — because of the logic of valuation — no optimism can be forced upon us on pain of incoherence, but shall not be above allowing some criticisms of systems in evaluative terms.

If a system does not have this structure then it is not a coherent optimism making any genuine claims which we may be required to assess. For instance, if the positive evaluation (3) is made in terms of value criteria other than (or, worse, inconsistent with) those listed in (2), then this is not a genuine optimism, though it may generate one if the list can be amended. Another consequence of accepting this model is that we must refuse the title of 'optimism' to any thoroughly *a priori* system, being able to allow only that such a system may be regarded as a psychological optimism in the sense already discussed. Thus some of the most notorious 'optimists' may not qualify as optimists in my sense; what we lose in orthodoxy of labelling we gain in preparedness to take optimism seriously.

Before discussing examples in any detail, is there any more general restriction to be put upon the model so that we can exclude forms of optimism which are philosophically trivial? There is one: it turns upon the domain of 'the facts' in *A statement of the facts*. We do not wish to consider purely *personal* forms of optimism, by which I mean ones which only mention facts-about-me. A man who not only says, but believes: 'I'm all right, Jack' will certainly be of interest in various ways to the psychologist, but hardly to the philosopher — unless he is some sort of euphoric solipsist. Thus I shall stipulate that 'the facts' must cover more than the man and his immediate circle; they must at least extend to his society, if not to humanity as a whole. Thus we may expect that 'the facts' may well include psychological and sociological theories as to the actual nature of man and society, as opposed to definitions of the Good Life. If we cannot choose between such theories because of lack of evidence, we may have to return an open verdict on some forms of optimism.

III

Let us consider the third element of the model in the light of some examples: how positive is positive enough? This will itself depend upon the range of facts mentioned under (1). Thus someone who declares that the world is in a bad state, and even that it will get worse, may nevertheless be an optimist. Mediaeval Christian society was optimistic in looking to the next world for relief from the prison of this one. Others have looked for their relief on earth: Saint-Simon and Owen were unequivocal in expressing their disappointment and disgust with the world at the turn of the last century, and Marx later predicted that things would get even worse;[2] but they all agreed that things could — indeed, would — get better eventually. All these were Utopians, predicting perfection — and perfection is surely positive enough. (Note that it is not enough to *describe* a Utopia. Plato believed that were his Ideal State ever to be realised, which itself was highly doubtful, it would almost certainly degenerate; thus he can hardly be called an optimist. Indeed, any cyclical view of history can harbour only a short-run optimism.)

But one who passes a harsh judgment on contemporary life need not be a Utopian to count as an optimist: genuine hope of improvement is positive enough. Utopian or not, if optimism is not to be empty and facile, this hope itself requires some justification, which should form part of the statement of the facts: a Florence Nightingale will rest her case on the probable effects of bullying one's tame statesmen and disarming Royal Commissions; a Condorcet will rely on the perfectibility of man; a Sumner on the inevitable march of progress. Whether hope of actual improvement is *sufficient* for one who judges present conditions harshly to be termed an optimist is not clear — it would certainly seem somewhat strained to call a doctor optimistic whose patients are all dying of horrible diseases, merely because he knows that he can lessen their agony to some extent.

If an optimist is not relying on predictions of future change, either in this life or the next, then he must at least claim that there is a preponderance of good over evil, happiness over misery, when the world is considered as a whole. This is a vague claim to which I shall return later (Part V), but there is one version of it which seems to be *a fortiori* optimistic, and the reaction to which is an important factor in the general mistrust of optimism. Such a philosophy certainly seems to fulfil our third criterion, for it does not place perfection merely in the future: it claims that this *is* the best of all possible worlds (and also, sometimes, that it is steadily getting better and better!). If this is not optimism, what is?

In a pure form, this is *not* a genuine optimism. Consider this statement of it:

All nature is but art, unknown to thee;
All chance, direction, which thou canst not see;
All discord, harmony not understood;
All partial evil, universal good:
And, spite of pride, in erring reason's spite,
One truth is clear, WHATEVER IS, IS RIGHT.

(Pope. *Essay on Man*. 1733)

This is positive evaluation indeed. But what about our first criterion, that of the statement of facts? 'Whatever is, is right'; but there is no attempt to state what is. We are not here exhorted to consider the lilies of the field, nor anything else specific. As for the second criterion, we are provided with a list of value-terms — 'art', 'direction', 'harmony', 'good' — only to be told that we are incapable of applying them. These admirable qualities are 'unknown', 'not understood', and thus even our third criterion cannot, strictly speaking, be satisfied. And, of course, the only argument which can be given for this philosophy in its pure form is an *a priori* one claiming the creation of the world by a perfect God. Short of pointing out specific faults in the metaphysical argument, or persuading its proponent of the impossibility of metaphysics in general, there is nothing we can do to shake such a system. Even a Voltaire is powerless to refute it; the most he can do is ridicule it and retire defeated to his garden, or point out that it is not very helpful, let alone tactful, to make such remarks to people surrounded by such horrors as the Lisbon earthquake. This is the pragmatic argument we considered before; this philosophy which looks like optimism turns out to be merely a psychological optimism after all; the cosmic bottle is half-full.

But this can be said only of its pure form; no philosopher gives it in its pure form alone. It is supplemented, to a greater or lesser extent, by *a posteriori* arguments which may be open to reasonable discussion; thus it is by no means a clear-cut question whether a philosopher is or is not an optimist, and if so in what sense. For instance, Leibniz relies mainly upon the *a priori* argument, and explicitly warns us against trying to see the hidden harmonies since this would be blasphemously to enquire into the purposes of God; he thus saves us from some of the absurdities which others espoused. But even Leibniz admits that in terms of one of the values on his list of criteria, i.e. justice, the facts as we initially state them do not measure up. In this life the wicked often prosper and the virtuous suffer: these are the facts. But they cannot be *all* the facts, since we can be sure that the facts as a whole must measure up; therefore there must be other facts (an after-life in which each man receives his deserts) which we should have mentioned in our original statement. Now this, I should be prepared to say, *is* a genuine form of optimism; whether it is acceptable is another matter. Leibniz has at least *tried*; it is surely a matter for rational discussion whether there is, or could be, an after-life, and to refuse to call it a question of *fact* is either to beg the question, or to answer it — which is all that is required.

Other philosophers who claimed *a priori* that this is the best of all possible worlds were not so wary as Leibniz in their search for *a posteriori* arguments to buttress their claims. Bernardin de St Pierre undertook to specify nature's 'harmonies' which Pope had assured us were not understood, explicitly contradicting Leibniz' warning that we can know only mechanical, not final causes. Consider what he has to say about the optical properties of rivers and the death of a butterfly:

. . . had these waters . . . reflected the images of bodies, a thousand deceitful forms would have been mixed with the real ones, and the expanse of the ocean would have reflected in the sky a new world and another sun. Our rivers would have exhibited moving forests, and hills perpendicular to their surface; a rivulet would have displayed the verdure and the flowers of a neighbouring meadow. Imagination may carry this scene further, and conceive a shepherdess, after leading her sheep to the river side, contemplating a second flock in the water, or recoiling with surprise on seeing in the stream a figure similar to her own.

Death . . . is a necessary consequence of the enjoyment of life. If the butterfly were not to die, were he to live only the ordinary age of man, the compass of the earth would not be sufficient for his posterity; but he lives without fearing death, and dies without regretting life; . . . When the rainy Hyades bring back cold and the southern blast, he is not grieved at the short duration of his career; but consigns to Nature the care of his progeny which he is destined never to see. He is content with his lot, having fed on flowers, and having lived until the sun was ready to enter the region of darkness. Finally, he seeks the shade at the bottom of his favourite plant, and stretching out his wings, while he fixes his little feet in the ground, he expires in an upright position.

(Saint-Pierre. *Harmonies of Nature*. 1814 (posth.))

This is heady stuff. It would be positively caddish to question the movement of the forests or the surprise of the shepherdess. Who would have the heart to undermine such a noble and touching vision of the dying butterfly? So we are tempted to laugh, and move on.

But this is a *genuine* optimism: it is just *wrong*. What is wrong with it? Are the values unacceptable? Hardly; Saint-Pierre's basic criterion is the contribution a thing makes to animal or human wellbeing, which is acceptable enough as far as it goes. 'Quite so', you may say. 'And Saint-Pierre's trouble is that he tries to make it go too far.' But what does this mean? Is this a value-disagreement, as when a Christian claims that a utilitarian carries his (acceptable) criterion too far, putting it above the law of God? Surely not, for a utilitarian optimist will himself not wish to be classed with the good Saint-Pierre, no matter how Utopian his world-view. Does it mean that Saint-Pierre goes too far in his evaluation of the facts in terms of his criterion? Partly; we do feel a certain reserve regarding the idyllic biography of the butterfly. Yet when Saint-Pierre elsewhere tells us that the melon is formed in sections so that we can eat it 'en famille', we cannot deny that we enjoy our melon, and that this arrangement of nature is convenient to us. But that is the point; it is convenient, but we cannot accept that as an *explanation* of its occurrence.

We are now, however, on shifting ground, for we do recognise that some features of living organisms can be fruitfully described in terms of adaptation-value — that only thus are we led to the *explanation* of such features. We speak of variation and natural selection where Saint-Pierre would have spoken of the direct purposes of God; but it is a question of *fact* whether certain features of living things can be explained in terms not suitable to the optical properties of water, and whether *all* features of living things can be so explained. You may object that this is a matter of theory, not of fact: you may say that to ask whether a certain butterfly actually did expire in an upright position, or whether all butterflies generally do so, would be to ask two different sorts of 'factual' questions — both more easily answered than the more high-level, 'theoretical' question. But this is theory concerned with empirical matters, not with moral evaluation. We may, then, say that Saint-Pierre has, in a systematic fashion, *got his facts wrong*.

IV

I have stressed this because it shows a continuity with other types of dispute over optimism, where what is in question is not the values applied, but the statement of the facts. In particular it highlights the importance of disagreement over theories as to the basic nature of man or society. Now insofar as such theories are definitions of the Good Society or the Healthy Personality, involving value-assumptions, they must be discussed later. But such theories may be in *factual* disagreement over what factors exert a basic influence in human life. For example, consider Malthus' response to Godwin, who painted a vivid and widely accepted picture of the future delights of man:

The system of equality which Mr Godwin proposes is, without doubt, by far the most beautiful and engaging of any that has yet appeared . . . . The unlimited exercise of private judgment is a doctrine inexpressibly grand and captivating . . . . The substitution of benevolence as the master-spring and saving principle of society, instead of self-love, is a consummation devoutly to be wished. In short, it is impossible to contemplate the whole of this fair structure, without emotions of delight and admiration accompanied with ardent longing for the period of its accomplishment. But, alas! that moment can never arrive. The whole is little better than a dream, a beautiful phantom of the imagination . . . .Mr Godwin says 'There is a principle in human society, by which population is perpetually kept down to the level of the means of subsistence . . .'. This principle, which Mr Godwin thus mentions as some mysterious and occult cause, and which he does not attempt to investigate, will be found to be the grinding law of necessity; misery, and the fear of misery.

(Malthus. *An Essay on the Principles of Population.* 1798)

Malthus goes on to claim that even if Godwin's ideal society were created overnight, it would inevitably deteriorate in response to population pressures; one by one he examines the natural forces cited by Godwin as ensuring peace and harmony and shows how they would, on the contrary, destroy them. No question here of a clash of values; the good society, if it is to be achieved at all, must come *in spite of* these natural forces. The implication is that deliberate planning of some sort is essential — we cannot rely on the natural goodness or psychological plasticity of man, still less on the perfectibility of nature.

Any optimism which can expect to be taken seriously must make some attempt at an empirical analysis of nature in general and man in particular. Condorcet rightly insisted that politics must be based on psychology, himself accepting the views of Condillac as to the innate goodness of man and the rule of reason in achieving pleasure and avoiding pain. One root of our dissatisfaction with Condorcet's visions of perfection lies in our rejection of this analysis of the sentiments; Freud showed that reason could not hope for such an easy triumph. Armchair analyses of the basic instincts of man have been many and various; the egoism of Hobbes, Nietzsche and Le Dantec is countered with 'sympathy' or 'gregariousness' by Adam Smith, Godwin and Kropotkin; the pendulum swings from the rationalism of the *Philosophes* to the irrationalism of Schopenhauer, and who is to decide? We may have our doubts about Freud; we may appeal to falsifiability, or counter him with Rogers or Suttie; but at least Freud moved from the armchair and got as far as the couch.

There is an interesting example of an armchair optimist, usually derided, who was surprisingly right in important aspects of his analysis of the passions. It is easy to laugh at Fourier, waiting daily at advertised times for a millionaire to come and set up his dream society; predicting planet-born anti-lions to carry us from Paris to Lyons and Marseilles in one day; planning a division of labour so subtle that men would rush to work instead of to battle, different people growing different types of apple according to their individual tastes, and the children taking out the garbage, revelling in the mess; foreseeing instantaneous communication with Mars, and the seas turned into lemonade. But Fourier did not make the mistake of using the model of super-rational, Economic Man: his plans assumed that the three basic passions were directed towards change and variety of occupation; intrigue, emulation and rivalry; and the composite pleasures of mind and body. Over a century later Elton Mayo was to found industrial psychology in a spurt of glory at the 'discovery' that men do not work for bread alone. Detailed and exhaustive investigations showed that just those factors stressed by Fourier were crucial in determining a person's satisfaction with his work, and also in increasing productivity. We need not claim that this would be true of all men: it is well known that different social norms result in different modal personality-types; but the norms assumed by Fourier were drawn from capitalist society, and capitalist society is what Mayo was investigating.

Thus the rejection of an optimist's predictions may rest on a supposed knowledge of human nature which is a good deal less adequate than the critic realises. One modern Utopian is well aware of this, and claims that he is the first man ever to base his Utopian predictions on detailed experimental knowledge. Thus Skinner, in describing the society of *Walden Two* (1948), draws heavily on his experience in the psychological laboratory. Though he admits to vast extrapolations (e.g. from animal to human, non-linguistic to linguistic behaviour), he defies us to produce any comparable experimental evidence, and thus forces our challenge into the area of values.

V

One of the striking things about *Walden Two* is that many of the features of Skinner's ideal society are reminiscent of those of *Brave New World*, but in the latter they are satirised, not recommended. Butler and Orwell also depict anti-Utopias with the aim of modifying our values, or at least forcing us to reinterpret the 'facts' in the light of our shared values. Such satire is a powerful way of confronting an unacceptable optimism with a rival view, where values are at issue rather than facts. *Pace* Hume and Sartre, we must be allowed to attack some forms of optimism on moral grounds; to be sure, labelling all moral discourse as 'irrational' has its point, but beyond that point ceases to be helpful. Hitler was an optimist — not merely in the personal sense — and we must not be confined to criticising his anthropology.

Theories as to the psychological nature of man will be used in assessments of the moral nature of man. Acceptance of certain psychological theories might seem to force particular conclusions upon us: for instance, if man is predominantly self-seeking or aggressive, then he is bad; if he is basically altruistic he is good. But it is not so simple as this; Nietzsche and Spencer valued power-seeking and aggression, and Bentham predicted good results as the 'natural' outcome of egoism. Sumner exclaimed: 'Where is the rich man who is oppressing anybody? If there was one, the newspapers would ring with it';[3] but presented with an instance he would have criticized not the rich man, but the newspaper.

This reminds us of a notorious example of violently opposed systems of optimism all claiming justification by virtue of the same facts: the extraordinarily diverse group of social theories boasting intellectual descent from Darwin. Evolutionary theory was taken to prove the inevitability of progress; with the result that some first defined progress and then predicted it, while others predicted bloody struggle and then called it progress. The equivocation with words such as 'progress' or 'fittest', the attempt to derive an 'ought' from an 'is', and the failure to see that 'cultural evolution' involves factors quite absent from the biological sphere, all influence the various statements and evaluations of the facts. Once this has been pointed out we can only turn to moral discussion of the different lists of values provided by these theorists, hoping in some cases to dissuade, if not to disprove. Optimism may be countered by an optimist, not only by a pessimist or cynic.

But are we being too hasty here — perhaps all these 'evolutionary' theories contain a common germ of truth, which is itself a limited form of optimism? Mandeville prompted us to question the view that a virtuous man *is* one who follows his passions, that optimal good and the greatest happiness will result from the mere following of our instincts; but perhaps Darwin has shown us how we may save at least a part of this old doctine? If we agree that pleasure is to be valued above plain or displeasure (even though we may not give this criterion priority on our value-list); and if we also agree that, on the whole, pleasant experiences are beneficial to the organism and unpleasant experiences damaging; and that natural selection ensures that beneficial variations will survive at the expense of hurtful ones; then can we not say that there must be more pleasure than pain in the natural course of events, and that *thus far* the world is good rather than bad? Surely we shall have to accept as unassailable an optimism with which we agree both on values and on facts?

No: for the trouble comes when we try to *use* our value-criterion as a measure of the facts. The first move will be to point to nature, red in tooth and claw, or to detail the pilgrimage of Candide; the next, to cite the impossibility of applying a felicific calculus; and the next to show the circularity in the hedonist claim that the only goal is pleasure. But our opponent may insist that Darwin showed that the higher animal 'makes a better living as measured by satisfactions achieved'.[4] Unconvinced, we accuse him of anthropomorphism; and he counters by turning his optimistic claim into a more obviously *logical* one, whereby he saves his case at the expense of losing it. Imagine, he says, that pleasure had been correlated with damaging and pain with beneficial activities:

Then natural selection would have evolved an animal world all members of which would have constantly sought those things that were beneficial but unpleasant, would have avoided the things that were hurtful but pleasant, and would have experienced a great predominance of displeasure over pleasure. Such a state of things would seem to us profoundly irrational and absurd.[5]

Notice that such a state of things would not merely be *unpleasant*, to be guarded against by the postulate of a good God seeing to it that such things do not occur (as Descartes suggests in the Meditations), but *profoundly irrational and absurd*. The only way to account for this absurdity is to reject any dualistic view which regards pleasure and pain as merely *contingently* connected with behaviour; to accept that — in a sense — they *direct* behaviour; and this boils down to the insight that behaviour is described, and must be explained, in terms of purposes and goals. This does not mean that we may accept the hedonist's account of pleasure — or reinforcement — as the only goal; the circularity is still there. It does, however, show how we may attack Skinner's optimism on an issue of fact rather than of value, for his experimental psychology rules out any such teleological explanation.

So, even if we endorse one or more of the values listed by the optimist as criteria, we must look very closely at the way in which he applies them to the agreed facts before we can decide whether to endorse his optimism.

VI

I have argued that any optimism worth the name must have some specific content, and that we can evaluate it only by considering such content in detail. We may disagree on a matter of values — which will affect our reaction to specific policies or predictions; and we may disagree on how to apply an agreed value to agreed facts. The more specific the goals or policies mentioned in the optimist's value-list, the more we may draw our ammunition from the facts: 'happiness' or 'progress' may be obvious and unassailable values — 'humanitarianism' or 'laissez-faire' are not. Alternatively, we may disagree on what I have been calling 'the facts'. I called them 'facts' to contrast them with 'values', but it is clear from the examples I have discussed that this is a portmanteau-word which we should not allow to mislead us.

An optimist may 'get his facts wrong' in many different ways: Condorcet described the place of reason in our psychology wrongly; Saint-Pierre was wrong in thinking that all natural phenomena could be explained in terms of adaptive advantage to some living thing; Skinner is wrong in assuming that non-teleological accounts of animal behaviour are sufficient explanations of it, and *a fortiori* of human behaviour; the social Darwinists were wrong in applying principles of biological evolution without qualification to social phenomena; Godwin did not look closely enough at the implications of the facts which he had stated; Fourier looked to the planets for his anti-lions, instead of to technology. But, though they all got their facts wrong, they didn't get all their facts wrong; Fourier said some things worth listening to, as industry found in the twenties. And in many cases we ourselves are not so sure of our 'facts' that we can confidently dismiss the optimist's claims.

There is no *a priori* optimism: Leibniz is not telling us anything, merely smiling — except when he says there is an after-life; if there *must* be more pleasure than displeasure in the world, this shows only that certain (teleological) ways of describing and explaining behaviour are *de rigueur*, which has nothing to do with optimism. The psychological considerations, of course, remain: optimistic attitudes may make life more liveable, unrealisable ideals may be essential heuristics in promoting any radical reform. These claims can themselves be disputed, leading sometimes to disagreement between optimists in other ways very close: Engels scoffed at the 'Utopian Socialists', and Sumner ridiculed Ward. But they apply — or not — to all systems of optimism, and cannot be used to pick and choose between them. There is nothing for it but to examine the optimist's claims; if we reject optimism it must not be because it is optimism, but because it is *wrong*.

NOTES

1   Sometimes Spencer seems to support a cyclical view, predicting the achievement and consequent disintegration of equilibrium *ad infinitum* — thus we must be careful in calling him an optimist.

2   If we accept Marx's claims that he is not at all concerned with morals, merely with historically necessary processes, then we cannot regard him as an optimist, no matter what predictions he may make.

3   From Sumner's essay *The Absurd Effort to Make the World Over*, first published in the *Forum*, 1894.

4   Herrick, *The Evolution of Human Nature*, 1956, p. 126.

5   Example taken from McDougall, *Body and Mind*, 1911.

Bibliography of work by Margaret Boden

* denotes paper reprinted in this volume

A. BOOKS

Purposive Explanation in Psychology, Harvard University Press, 1972. Paperback edition: Harvester Press, 1978.

Artificial Intelligence and Natural Man, Basic Books Inc., New York, and Harvester Press, Hassocks 1977. (Open University set book for Cognitive Psychology Course.)

Piaget, Harvester Press and Fontana Books, 1979; Viking-Penguin (USA), 1980.

B. ARTICLES

'In Reply to Hart and Hampshire', *Mind*, N.S., 68 (1959), 256–60.

*'The Paradox of Explanation', *Proceedings of the Aristotelian Society*, N.S., 62 (1962), 159–78.

*'McDougall Revisited', *Journal of Personality*, 33 (1965), 1–19.

*'Optimism', *Philosophy*, 41 (1966), 291–303.

'Can Optimism be Respectable?', *The Listener*, 76 (1966), 451–54. A broadcast version of 'Optimism'.

'Interactionism — Could Experiments Decide?', in Imre Lakatos and Alan Musgrave, eds., *Problems in the Philosophy of Science*, Vol. III. Amsterdam: North Holland, 1968, pp. 440–42.

'Language, Thought and Reality', *Common Factor*, No. 5: Communication (1968) 13–18.

'Miracles and Scientific Explanation', *Ratio*, 11 (1969), 137–44.

'Machine Perception', *Philosophical Quarterly*, 19 (1969), 33–45.

'Brain and Consciousness: A Reply to Professor Burt', *Bulletin of the British Psychological Society*, 22 (1969), 47–9.

*'Intentionality and Physical Systems', *Philosophy of Science*, 37 (1970), 200–14.

'How Artificial is Artificial Intelligence?', *British Journal for the Philosophy of Science*, 24 (1973), 61–72.

'Personal View (of AI)', *AISB Bulletin*, No. 2 (1973), 7–10.

'Some Comments on IJCAI-III', *AISB European Newsletter*, No. 15 (1973), 14–18.

* 'The Structure of Intentions', *Journal of the Theory of Social Behaviour*, 3 (1973), 23–46.

* 'Freudian Mechanisms of Defence: A Programming Perspective', in Richard Wollheim, ed., *Freud: A Collection of Critical Essays*, Anchor, 1974, pp. 242–70.

Entry on 'Purpose', for *Oxford Companion to the Mind* (ed. Richard Gregory), Oxford University Press. Forthcoming.

* 'Human Values in a Mechanistic Universe', in *Royal Institute of Philosophy Lectures 1976-77: Human Values* (ed. Godfrey Vesey), Harvester Press, 1978, pp. 135–71.

'Artificial Intelligence and the Image of Man', *AISB Bulletin*, 1977. Reprinted in *SISTM Quarterly*, USA.

'Social Implications of Intelligent Machines', in *The Radio and Electronic Engineer*, special issue on Intelligent Machines, 47 (1977), 393–99. Reprinted in *Communications of the Association for Computing Machinery*, 1978. Also reprinted in T. Forester, ed., *The Microelectronic Revolution*, Blackwells, Oxford, 1980, pp. 439–52.

'Cognitive Science: An Integrative Approach to the Mind', *Proceedings of the International Workshop on Communication & Cognition*, University of Ghent, 1977, pp. 225–28.

* 'The Computational Metaphor in Psychology', in Neil Bolton, ed., *Philosophical Problems in Psychology*, Methuen, 1979, pp. 111–32.

* 'Artificial Intelligence and Piagetian Theory', (Automaton — Theoretical Foundations of Psychology and Biology, Part I), *Synthese*, 38 (1978), 389–414.

Entry on 'Artificial Intelligence', for *Oxford Companion to the Mind* (ed. Richard Gregory), Oxford University Press. Forthcoming.

* 'Implications of Language for Human Nature', in *Language, Mind and Brain: Interdisciplinary Perspectives*, (eds. R. J. Scholes and T. W. Simon), Erlbaum, 1980.

* 'Real-World Reasoning', in *Applications of Inductive Logic*, (eds. L. J. Cohen and M. B. Hesse), Oxford University Press, 1980, pp. 359–75.

'Some Comments on "What Computers Still Can't Do" ', *SISTM Quarterly*, 1978.

*'Artificial Intelligence and Intellectual Imperialism', in *Models of Man*, British Psychological Society, 1980, pp. 129–42.

*'The Case for a Cognitive Biology', *Proceedings of the Aristotelian Society; Supplementary Vol.*, 1980, pp. 25–49.

'Chalk and Cheese in Cognitive Science: The Case for Intercontinental Interdisciplinarity'. To appear in *Archives Jean Piaget: Genetic Epistemology and Cognitive Science*, Geneva, 1980.

'AI and Animals', to appear in M. Bertrand and W.C. McGrew, eds., *Mental Representation of the External World by Animals*, forthcoming.

'Towards an Understanding of Mental Development,' *Trends in Neurosciences*, 4 (1981), V–VI.

'Interdisciplinary Epistemology,' in S. Modgil (ed.), *For and Against Piaget*, forthcoming.

'Is Equilibration Important?,' *Brit. J. Psychology*, in press.

'Failure is not the Spur,' in O. Selfridge & E. Rissler (eds.), *Adaptive Control in Ill-defined Systems* (Proc. of NATO Workshop, 1981), forthcoming.

'La Portée Philosophique de L'Informatique,' in J.-P. Vienne (ed.), *Proc. Colloque de Philosophie Franco-Britannique* (Lille, 1981), in press.

'The Meeting of Man and Machine,' *Proc. Askib. Informatics Conf., Oxford, 1981*, forthcoming.